Bernese Oberland *Selected Climbs*

SELECTED CLIMBS
by Les Swindin

General Editor: Les Swindin

ALPINE CLUB . LONDON
1993

Bernese Oberland *Selected Climbs*

First Published in Britain by the
Alpine Club 55/56 Charlotte Road London EC2A 3QT

First Edition (Collomb) 1968
Second Edition (Collomb) 1979 in two volumes

Produced by the Alpine Club

Topo and photo diagrams drawn by Rod Powis

Cover photographs
Front Dave Wilkinson on SE ridge of the Bietschhorn (Stephen Venables)
Back Mark Hutchinson on Motörhead at Eldorado (Roger Payne)

Typeset in Plantin from the author's word processor by
EMS Phototypesetting, Berwick on Tweed
Printed by The Ernest Press, Glasgow

British Library Cataloguing in Publication Data. A catalogue record for this book is available from the British Library

ISBN 0-900523-59-X

Contents

List of topo diagrams and photographs

Topo diagrams

Photographs

Rock Climbing Areas

All unaccredited photographs are by the author.

General editor and author's preface

This is the fourth in the new series of guide books to the major Alpine regions being prepared for the Alpine Club and it replaces the previous two volume edition, Bernese Alps East and West, published in 1979. It extends the area covered in the 1979 volumes and in addition it features the description of an appreciable number of rock climbs. The layout of the book follows the pattern established in the Ecrins Massif, Dolomites and Mont Blanc Massif volumes published in the last five years.

The Bernese Oberland has plenty to offer every alpinist from the novice to the most experienced, and the selection of climbs included should offer something challenging for the whole spectrum of abilities. Naturally all the big mountains are included, but there are also descriptions of routes on far less well known peaks that are sadly neglected, by British alpinists at least. Some descriptions are quite detailed, especially where route finding is not reasonably obvious, whilst others are quite brief and intended for the experienced climbers who are prepared to make their own decisions as to the ideal line.

For those with an adventurous spirit, there are in the Oberland some fine long ridges to be traversed in what could be multi-day outings. Some of these are hinted at in the text but it is left to the reader to piece together the various sections and to make up their own itineraries.

There is no doubt that the Oberland will never attract the numbers of climbers and tourists who visit the Mont Blanc Massif or the Valais mountains south of the Rhône valley since, by the geography of the region, only the determined person will reach its heart. There are plenty of peaks that have easy access but there are many, and some quite major, peaks which don't. Therein lies some of the attraction of climbing in these parts; remote high mountains, few other people, spectacular scenery and an area steeped in the history of mountaineering. One only has to look at the first ascent details to appreciate that you are following in the footsteps of some of the great names of the past and also the present.

The development of modern routes in the high mountains has been much less than in the Mont Blanc range – here what developments there have been have taken place on the cliffs on the fringes of the region. These developments are taken into account in the relevant section of the book.

The north faces of the Oberland are renowned, and descriptions of routes on many of them have been included. The climber should however be conscious of the fact that these descriptions assume what might be called normal snow and ice cover. This is something that has been greatly lacking in recent years, and whilst this trend has not stopped a regular stream of climbers ascending the Eigerwand, some of the other faces are seeing very few, if any, ascents, at least in summer at the present time.

The change in name from Bernese Alps used in the 1979 edition to Bernese Oberland is not for any esoteric reason, it is simply that I have always known the region by this name and prefer it so. Readers will realise that the name is not entirely suitable since quite a lot of what is described does not actually lie within the geographical area of this name, which in itself is almost a misnomer since a large part of the massif is situated in the Canton of Valais (Wallis).

The Alpine Club welcomes any helpful comments about the route descriptions used, and details of any worthwhile ones that have been omitted which might be worth including in future editions. We also welcome offers of good quality photographs that might be used in the preparation of photo-diagrams. All the comments and offers should be addressed to the general editor at the Alpine Club.

I would like to thank everyone who has helped me in the preparation of this guide book especially Andy Reid, Lindsay Griffin, Dave Wilkinson, John Cleare, Jeremy Whitehead, Rod Powis, Rick Graham, Stephen Venables, Dave McKeown and members of the Swiss Alpine Club. A special word of thanks also to my wife, Barbara, for the understanding way that she has put up with me disappearing into my office for hours on end, month after month, and also for accompanying me on the many outings we have made in this wonderful mountain range.

Les Swindin, Gloucester 1992

RECENT DEVELOPMENTS

In the same way that rock climbing has been the main activity that has seen great development during the 80s in the Mont Blanc range, so too in the Bernese Oberland. The difference here however is that in the Oberland most of the development has been on relatively low altitude crags, as opposed to the high mountains of the Mont Blanc massif. These developments have taken place on both granite and limestone and in both cases it has become the practice to used fixed protection although not quite to the same degree as say in the Verdon gorge.

The succession of winters with relatively little snowfall followed by hot summers has led to many of the ice routes for which the Oberland was once renowned almost disappearing, and the only time of year that some of these routes now see an ascent is in the winter. On the ever popular Eiger N face the icefields have almost gone, but even so it is still possible to find a new line to climb, although this tends to be accomplished only in winter conditions.

On the other high mountains in the region there has been little new route development, certainly in the summer months, in recent years and this will probably continue to be the case until there is a climatic change.

MAPS

The guide is designed to be used in conjunction with the Carte nationale de la Suisse (CN) / Landeskarte der Schweiz (LK) 1:50000 series of maps, although quite a large number of these are required to cover the whole of the area described. All the heights and nomenclature used in the guide are those used on the maps, and often different from those used in previous editions of AC Bernese Alps guidebooks. Approaches to huts are often by well waymarked paths which are clearly shown on the maps, and in these cases only outline details are given in the way of route description.

In each section of the book the appropriate maps for the area being described are noted in the introduction.

USING HUTS

The Swiss have some of the best-appointed huts in the Alps and almost all the climbs described can be started from one of these high mountain bases. Practically all the huts have a resident guardian in summer except in sustained bad weather, and all the SAC huts have a winter room which is always open when the guardian is absent. When the guardian is present (approximate dates are given in the hut details) meals are usually available or the guardian will cook food that you have carried to the hut. There are no self-catering facilities. If you do take food try to make it simple to prepare and tell the guardian when you arrive that you want your own food prepared. In this way you will make his/her task easier and probably your own stay more comfortable. Reduced fees are available in SAC and affiliated huts on the production of an alpine club card (but not AC) or a UIAA reciprocal rights card. In addition to the overnight fee and the cost of any meals and drinks that you purchase you can expect to pay for hot water, especially if you have it during the daytime (it may be free at breakfast and at dinner). The charge for this is rather variable and is determined by the individual section of the SAC that owns the hut. In addition to all other charges there is likely to be a supplement towards the cost of the hut improvement programme that is being undertaken by the SAC throughout the Swiss Alps. This was 3SFr for members in 1991.

Bivouac huts are usually spacious and comfortable with blankets provided. Stoves in these huts are only (usually) for emergency use and so one should always be carried if you intend to stay at such a place. It is also worth carrying cooking and eating implements.

The SAC ask that all hut users treat the huts and their furnishings carefully and that the huts are left clean. Hut users are considered friends of the mountains and as such they should conserve the natural environment and carry their litter etc. back to the valley.

USING THIS GUIDE

MOUNTAIN ROUTE DESCRIPTIONS vary considerably in detail from a few lines to quite lengthy descriptions. For the rock climbs descriptions have been omitted in most cases, and a topo diagram and photograph have been used to show the line of ascent. In all cases every effort has been made to ensure accuracy but absolute accuracy cannot be guaranteed. This might be because the route in question has had few ascents, or because of changing conditions on the mountain, or even that the author has got it wrong. Whatever the case the climber should always be prepared to use his or her own judgement as to the best line of attack.

Common British usage in naming routes and features has been maintained e.g. ridge is used rather than arête although the terms dièdre and couloir are used throughout. The names of modern rock routes have not been translated.

The terms L and R, Lwards and Rwards and L and R side are always used with reference to the direction of movement of the climber. For mountain features such as glaciers, couloirs etc. the orographical reference to L and R is applied when viewed in the direction of flow or looking downwards.

Where routes are shown on photographs or topo diagrams, this is indicated in the margin by a solid or open rectangle respectively with the appropriate reference number shown within the rectangle.

FIRST ASCENT details have been included to supplement information on the climbs. In some cases, where this is appropriate, the date of the first winter ascent is given. This normally would fall within the period designated winter by the UIAA which is 21 Dec to 20 March inclusive.

GRADING OF CLIMBS as indicated in the margin is determined not only by the general level of technical difficulty but also by the seriousness of the enterprise reflected in the associated objective danger, length, altitude and commitment. An attempt has been made to grade hut walks, and one or two passes, for the benefit of the walker as opposed to the alpinist. In order of difficulty these are: P, which refers to routes on good footpaths with little or no objective danger and on which steep sections are made safe. Such a designation suggests that the route is suitable for any reasonably fit person. PE, which refers to routes that are suitable for the experienced mountain walker, who does not mind a degree of exposure and who can find the way when paths become indistinct or none existent. Use of hands may be necessary to maintain balance and snow and/or dry glacier may have to be traversed. RE, which refers to routes suitable for the experienced scrambler. Rock moves of grade I or II may be encountered, possibly needing a rope. Steep snow fields may have to be crossed, requiring the use of an ice-axe to maintain stability.

In the rock-climbing section traditional routes have mostly been given adjectival gradings, as is the normal practice in Switzerland, but the modern routes have only been given a numerical grading which usually refers to the hardest section encountered on the climb. A glance at the topo will indicate whether or not the climb is sustained at the grade.

On all mountain routes, whether on rock, snow or ice, an adjectival grade is given which should not be confused with the British rock climbing grades.

In order of increasing difficulty: F Facile (easy) PD Peu Difficile (not very hard) AD Assez Difficile (fairly hard) D Difficile (hard) TD Très Difficile (very hard) ED Extrêmement Difficile (extremely hard).

Further refinement of grades is possible by adding plus or minus signs to the grades up to TD, whilst the ED grade is made more open-ended to cater for rising standards and better grading of existing routes of this standard eg ED1, ED2 etc. On the climbs where the main difficulties are on rock, unless otherwise stated, the overall grading reflects a free ascent even though there may be an abundance of in situ protection (aid?) on various pitches. Some climbs, graded AD to TD, although not technically demanding are extremely serious for their grade and this has been noted in the introduction to these routes.

UIAA numerical gradings have been used for all rock sections. A table of international grading comparisons has been included but should only be used as a general indication, especially at the higher levels. Artificial climbing is graded from A1 to A3. On A2 and A3 slings or, better, étriers will generally be necessary but short sections of A1 with in situ aid points can be overcome by most strong climbers wearing rock boots simply by pulling on the gear. Some pitches have been graded A0; this implies that the pitch is climbed almost entirely free with just the odd move requiring a pull on in situ (usually) gear.

SNOW AND ICE. With climbs involving technical difficulty on snow and/or ice, grading is less precise due to the variable conditions throughout the season and from one year to the next. Some areas of glacier can, at times, become almost impossible to cross. Routes involving hanging glaciers and ice slopes with sérac formations are undergoing constant change. As a consequence difficulty and objective dangers on these climbs will vary enormously and it would be wise to seek up-to-date information before making an attempt (probably hut guardians and local guides are as good as anyone to ask). No attempt has been made to compare the difficulty of alpine snow and ice with Scottish grades, as it is more likely that the two will only really be comparable on mixed terrain. When difficulty exists on ice this is generally indicated by the steepness of the slope but even this must be considered in relation to the prevailing conditions of snow cover and temperature.

PHOTOGRAPH NUMBERS are shown in the solid rectangles below the route grade although this pattern has been varied in the rock-climbing section. On the photographs the route numbers are marked and the line of ascent indicated. Some routes or parts of routes may be visible on more than one photograph and, when this occurs, these additional photograph numbers appear at the end of the introduction to the route. A dotted line signifies that this section of the route is not visible. In a few cases routes which are visible have been omitted to avoid overcrowding, but in these cases the starts are usually shown. There are also, on some photographs, lines shown with no number but with a technical grade. These are climbs which may have been referred to in the text but not described or they may be lines which are known to have been climbed but are not described or mentioned in the text.

HEIGHTS, when quoted, for the whole route refer to the vertical interval from the base of the route to its top and not to the amount of climbing involved which may be much longer.

ROUTE TIMES give a good indication for a rope of two fit climbers, competent at the standard and experiencing no delays due to other parties, weather etc. They may also aid the decision as to whether or not to carry bivouac equipment on the route.

ABBREVIATIONS are used for points of the compass and for left and right. Others frequently used are: Pt (point where this refers to a spot height), Kl (Klein), Gr (Gross) and SAC (Swiss Alpine Club).

EQUIPMENT

With so many manuals now available on the craft of alpinism, there is little point in dwelling on the subject here. When it comes to equipment, most parties tend to use an 11mm rope on middle-grade climbs where long abseils are not involved. They will carry a few hexentrics, wired wedges, slings for spikes and plenty of karabiners for in situ protection. On modern rock routes a minimum of 45m double rope is normal and a selection of wedges, wires and camming devices should be carried. Information about in situ protection is given in the rock-climbing section. Where there is doubt a full rack should be carried. Where pitons are required on rock routes this is usually indicated in the text. On more difficult mountain routes which involve some technical rock pitches a selection of pitons should be carried.

OTHER GUIDE BOOKS TO THE REGION

The Swiss Alpine Club produce the definitive guide books to all the areas described except the Engelhörner which is responsibility of the University of Bern Alpine Club. There are also some selected climbs books in both large and pocket-sized format, the former being one of the 100 Best series and Schweitz-Extrem the most useful for the serious rock climber. Below is a list of those believed to be currently available with the date of publication and ISBN number.

Alpes et Préalpes Vaudoises (SAC) 1985 M Brandt 3-85902-046-3
Berner Voralpen (SAC) 1981 M Brandt 3-85902-028-5
Berner Alpen 1 Sanetsch bis Gemmi (SAC) 1991 3-85902-103-6
Berner Alpen 2 Gemmi bis Petersgrat (SAC) 1982 J Müller 3-85902-034-X
Berner Alpen 3 Bietschhorn–, Lötschentaler Breithorn–, Nesthorn– und Aletschhorngruppen (SAC) 1976 (new edition expected soon)
Berner Alpen 4 Tschingelhorn-Finsteraarjoch-Obers Studerjoch (SAC) 1989 K Hausmann 3-85902-100-1
Berner Alpen 5 Grindelwald-Meiringen-Grimsel-Fiesch (SAC) 1982 U Mosimann 3-85902-038-2
Guide des Alpes Bernoises Sélection d'itinéraires (SAC) 1982 M Brandt 3-85902-021-8
Schweitz-Extrem (Filidor) 1989 J von Känel
Engelhörner and Salbitschijen (West Col) 1968 J Talbot
Sanetsch et Miroir d'Argentine (Private) C and Y Remy 1991
Clubhütten (Cabanes/Cappane/Huts) (SAC) 1987 3-85902-061-7

VALLEY BASES

There is no single valley base from which the whole of the area described in this book can be easily reached, but the whole of the area is highly developed to support the tourist trade. There are large and small resorts, all of which provide hotel accommodation and many of which have camp sites, although these appear to be progressively being taken over by caravans at the expense of the tent dweller. Pre-booking of places on camp sites looks as if it will soon be the only way of ensuring a pitch; even now it is not uncommon to find camp sites with full signs.

The Swiss National Tourist Office, The Swiss Centre, New Coventry St, London W1V 8EE (Tel 071 734 1921) is the best source of information about accommodation. Ask for details about specific valleys to get the most comprehensive information. This office is also able to supply maps.

Some centres do post weather forecasts (usually at the local tourist office) but these might be several days out of date. The most reliable method of obtaining information about the weather is from telephone recorded messages. Simply dial 162 to hear the message in the language of the region. An alternative is to read the local newspapers which can be consulted free in most places where you can buy a drink. These forecasts usually give the outlook for the next five days with a weather map.

Weather forecasts can be obtained from Zurich Airport – a report is given by English-speaking personnel. Telephone (after 2 pm) 01252 7644 or 01 256 9270.

GRADING COMPARISONS

UIAA	UK	France	USA	DDR	Australia
III		III	5.4	III	
IV–	V Diff M Severe	IV–			
IV		IV	5.5	IV	12
IV+	4a	IV+			
V–		V–	5.6	V	13
V	4b	V		VI	14
V+		5a	5.7	VIIa	15
VI–	4c	V+ 5b	5.8	VIIb	
VI	5a	5c			16
VI+	5b	6a	5.9	VIIc	17 18 19
VII–			5.10a 5.10b 5.10c 5.10d	VIIIa	20
VII	5c	6b		VIIIb VIIIc	21 22
VII+	6a	6c		IXa	23
VIII–			5.11a 5.11b 5.11c 5.11d	IXb	24
VIII	6b	7a		IXc	25
VIII+		7b	5.12a 5.12b 5.12c 5.12d	Xa	26
IX–				Xb	
IX	6c	7c		Xc	27
IX+			5.13a 5.13b		28 29

H1 P **Salbit hut** 2105m 685.18/170.08 tel 044 654 31 SAC, 60 beds, 15 June – 15 Oct. Signposted from Pt 1195m in the Göschener Tal (car park). Goods lift from Ulmi to Regliberg. 2½hr

H2 PD **Salbit bivouac hut** 2402m 683.03/170.03 SAC, 17 places. Approach from Wiggen in the Göschener Tal. Take path to the Voralp hut almost to Horefelli then climb a couloir Nwards to the hut. There are fixed ropes in places. 3½hr. Alternatively approach from the Salbit hut by a path engineered by the guardian. 1½hr

H3 P **Bächlital hut** 2328m 664.68/159.87 tel 036 73 11 14 SAC, 50 beds, weekends. Approach from the Räterichbodensee below the Grimselpass on the N side (car park below the dam). 2hr

H4 PE **Grueben hut** 2512m 662.85/161.95 no tel SAC, 28 beds, occasional guardian. Approach from Handegg. 3hr

H5 PE **Lauteraar hut** 2392.5m 660.08/157.94 tel 036 73 11 10 SAC, 50 beds, 15 June – Sept. Start at the Grimsel Hospiz. Descend steps on the N side and cross the dam. A tunnel leads to a path above the Grimselsee on its N side. Follow the path, passing the slabs of Eldorado at the W end of the reservoir, to the moraine on the N side of the Lauteraar glacier. Descend onto the rubble-strewn glacier and follow way-marks (cairns, sticks etc) on the R side of the glacier before leaving it on the R (signpost) to join a path which climbs quite steeply up a coombe before contouring round to the hut. 4hr

H6 **Lauteraar hut – Oberaarjoch hut connection.** See Route 7.

H7 P **Gauli hut** 2205m 659.58/163.91 tel 036 71 31 66 SAC, 55 beds, Aug – Oct at week-ends and other times for large parties. Approach from the road head in the Urbachtal (drive from Innertkirchen). 5hr

H8 F **Oberaarjoch hut** 3258m 656.35/153.01 tel 036 73 13 82 SAC, 55 beds, most of the spring and summer. Approach from the Grimselpass, see Route 4.

H9 F **Oberaarjoch hut – Finsteraarhorn hut connection.** See Routes 70 and 71. An alternative to crossing the Gemschlicke is to descend the Studerfirn Swards onto the Galmi glacier and follow this SW (crevasses) to S of Pt 2843.3m where the Fiescher glacier is joined.

Climb its E bank to the glacier bay inlet just NW of the Finsteraarhorn hut. Climb this to the hut. 2-2½hr

H10 P **Engelhorn hut** 1901m 656.17/170.48 tel 036 71 47 26 AAC Bern (SAC rec. rights), 60 beds, June – Oct at week-ends. Approach from Rosenlaui by taking the path to the Rosenlauischlucht then the L fork (signpost). 1½hr

H11 PE **Dossen hut** 2663m 655.95/167.36 tel 036 71 44 94 SAC, 65 beds, Aug and Sept, order meals in advance. Approach from Rosenlaui by taking the path to the Rosenlauischlucht then the R fork heading S. Pass the Rosenlaui bivouac hut (SAC, closed in summer, enquiries to Kaltenbrunnen restaurant) before finally reaching the ridge on which the hut stands. 4½hr

H12 F **Aar bivouac hut** 2731m 654.72/156.27 tel 035 2 41 07 SAC, 17 beds, no resident guardian, take cooking equipment (emergency gas stove). Water supply can be a problem. If the trickle close to the hut has dried up the glacier below the hut is the only scource.

Approach from the Grimsel Hospiz as for the Lauteraar hut. Instead of turning off the glacier continue up it on the R side of the central moraine (cairns) to where the glacier becomes flatter and the going eases. Keep on the flat part for some distance until roughly level with the Lauteraar hut. A large cairn marks the place where a descent can be made L onto bare ice in the middle of the glacier. Continue in a sort of valley to where this glacier joins the Finsteraar glacier. Keep up the R side of this to some large boulders and way-marks which indicate the way onto the rubble strewn Strahlegg glacier. Climb this for a little way, still way-marked, working up to the R of the central moraine before turning R to reach the hut. 6-7hr

Aar bivouac hut – Schreckhorn hut connection. See Routes 49 and 50.

H13 F **Finsteraarhorn hut** 3048m 651.86/152.52 tel 036 55 29 55 SAC, 115 beds, Mid April – mid June and July – mid Sept.

Approach from Fieschertal via the Fiescher glacier. Follow the road for about 2km beyond the village and park at a fork in the road. Follow signs in either direction to the Fiescher glacier and reach this in about 1½hr, after following a water pipeline above the glacier. Go up the L side of the glacier (rubble) to Pt 2028.6m (bivouac site) and then, a little above this and after a crevassed zone, get onto a grassy terrace on the L (way-marked). Follow this before descending again to the glacier. Continue up the L side of the glacier, between rock and ice with some traverses on rock (way-marked), as far as Pt 2572m. Just above this point cross the glacier NNE to reach its R side below Rotloch. Follow Route H9 from here to the hut. 8-10hr

Approach from the Jungfraujoch, descending the Jungfraufirn by Route 150 as far as the rocks below Pt 3411.1m. Continue down the R side of the glacier but cross to the L side near the bottom to Grünegg. This way avoids the swamp that can develop on the Konkordiaplatz. Now get onto the Grüneggfirn and follow Routes 90 and 91 to the hut. 4-5hr

Approach from Grimsel and Oberaarjoch hut, see Route 4.

H14 P **Burg hut** c 1900m on the ridge on the E side of Glingulwasser N of Fieschertal village 653.52/144.63 property of Fiesch guides. Make bookings via Volken Sport in Fiesch (tel 028 71 13 18). Approach from Fieschertal by driving through the village and continue for about 2km. Park at a fork in the road. Follow signs in either direction to the Fiescher glacier. The hut is on the ridge where a path joins the ridge from W, at the top of a gully due W of the Fiescher glacier snout. 1½hr

Kühboden hotels 2212m sited at the top of the first stage of the lift to the Eggishorn from Fiesch. A Youth hostel with 96 beds tel 028 71 17 46 and the Jungfrau Hotel with 130 dormitory beds tel 028 71 19 88

H15 P **Gletscherstubba hut** c 2375m just W of the reservoir at Märjela 651.00/143.45 property of Fiesch guides. Make bookings via Volken Sport in Fiesch (tel 028 71 13 18). Approach from Fiesch either by driving to Fieschertal village and following signs to Märjela (road for 2km), 4-5hr, or use the lift to Kühboden and follow a good path from there to Märjela. 1½hr

H16 RE **Schreckhorn hut** 2530m 650.60/159.15 tel 036 55 10 25 SAC, 90 beds, July – Sept. Approach from Grindelwald by lift to Pfingstegg then take the path via Stieregg above the E side of the Und Grindelwald glacier and the Und Ischmeer before climbing the rocks of Rots Grufer (ladders and cables). The going eases but there is some danger of avalanche in the gullies which must be crossed. 4½hr

Grosse Scheidegg hotel 1962m sited at the col of the same name tel 036 53 12 09. Dormitory accomodation available. Note that the road to the pass is private and closed to cars other than those of the local inhabitants. There is a bus service.

H17 PE **Gleckstein hut** 2317m 650.40/163.97 tel 036 53 11 40 SAC, 100 beds, June – Sept. Approach from Grindelwald by car or post-bus to the Wetterhorn Hotel. Walk from here or take the post-bus towards Grosse Scheidegg as far as Loichbiel. Either way reach Pt 1590m then take the rising track SW, which climbs above the Oberer Grindelwald glacier to the hut. There is a waterfall to negotiate on the way. 3½hr or 2½hr

H18 F **Konkordia hut** 2850m 647.18/150.09 tel 036 55 13 94 SAC, 129 beds (some in the old hut), April – Sept.

Approach from Fiesch by lift to Kuhboden then path to Märjela. Pass on the N side of the Märjelesee to Platta and follow traces of rough track down to the Aletsch glacier. Climb the glacier close to its central moraine and then before it makes a final rise to the Konkordiaplatz, move over to the E side and follow the lateral moraine to the rocks upon which the hut stands. Follow these round to where a metal staircase leads up to the hut from the N side of the rocks. The last part of the glacier is quite crevassed. 5hr

From the Jungfraujoch follow Route H13 to the Grüneggfirn and cross this to the metal staircase. 2hr

From the Hollandia hut by reversing Route 205 (1½hr) and from the Finsteraarhorn hut by Routes 91 and 90. 2½hr

H19 AD– 62 **Mittellegi hut** 3355m 644.76/159.30 property of Grindelwald Guides, 14 beds, no resident guardian, often crowded. There is a second hut reserved exclusively for guides but there is space for a few people in the wood shed if overcrowding is desperate in the old hut. Obtain the key from the Guides bureau in Grindelwald or from the Mönchjoch hut.

From the Eismeer station on the Jungfraujoch railway go out onto the glacier via a tunnel. Turn L and climb N through a short sérac zone onto the Challifirn. Follow the snow slopes round to the rocks at the second, narrow tongue of snow cutting into the rocks below the big tower on the Mittellegi ridge. Climb the rocks on the E side of the tongue of snow (III–) then move up over easier, ledged rocks diagonally Rwards to the hut on the ridge. There is danger of stonefall all the way. 2-2½hr

An approach can be made from the N side of the ridge. This is D. It is also possible to approach from Grindelwald on foot. See approach to the Bergli hut.

H20 F 62 **Bergli hut** 3299m 644.62/157.44 SAC, 20 beds, no resident guardian.

From the Jungfraujoch station follow the route to the Mönchjoch hut then follow Routes 122 and 123 to the hut. 2-2½hr

From Grindelwald an approach can be made on foot although this is long and tedious. Impossible crevasses may be encountered below the hut. From Grindelwald follow the approach route to the Fiescherwand. Once on the Unt. Grindelwald glacier cross it Wwards and climb a track on the opposite side up the area called Challi to reach the N edge of the Fiescher glacier. Climb this under the Obers Challiband before finally turning S to reach the hut up severely crevassed slopes. 8-9hr

H21 F **Mittelaletsch bivouac hut** 3013m 644.95/146.12 SAC, emergency tel, 13 beds, no resident guardian.

From Kühboden follow Route H18 onto the Gross Aletsch glacier. Climb up into the middle of the glacier then descend to its junction with the Mittelaletsch glacier. Climb this moraine covered glacier on the R side to about hut height then slant R to the hut. 6hr

An hour can be saved by starting at Bettmeralp and taking the lift towards the Bettmerhorn. A track leads down to Roti Chumma where the Gross Aletsch glacier can be joined. Cross it to the junction with the Mittelaletsch glacier, then as above. 5hr

H22 F 67 **Mönchjoch hut** 3650m 643.50/156.11 tel 036 71 34 72 private, 120 beds, no reduction for reciprocal card holders. Spring and July to mid-Sept.

From the Jungfraujoch station follow Route 120 to the Ober Mönchjoch. The hut is a few m above the col on the N side. 45min

H23 PE **Oberaletsch hut** 2640m 641.14/141.65 tel 028 27 17 67 SAC, 60 beds mid June – mid Sept.

From Blatten take the lift to Belalp and follow a path past the

Belalp Hotel, where it descends steeply, to reach the S edge of the Oberaletsch glacier. Descend the moraine onto the glacier then follow a way-marked track up the glacier. This gradually works its way into the centre of the glacier then goes up (the centre) until at about the level of the hut. Now cut up Rwards, keeping well L of the rock walls below the hut before finally turning SE and crossing a jumble of rock and ice to the ladders and track leading to the hut. 3hr

Eigergletscher hotel 2320m sited close to the entrance of the Jungfraujoch railway tunnel through the Eiger tel 036 55 22 21 private. Dormitory accomodation available.

Kleine Scheidegg Bahnhof buffet 2061m. Dormitory accommodation available.

H24 PE 69 **Guggi hut** 2791m 641.08/156.97 SAC, 24 beds, week-ends June – Sept, no meals.

From Kl Scheidegg follow the track towards the Eigergletscher station as far as the zig-zags. Take the R turn leading to the moraines of the Eiger glacier. Descend these a little, before turning S and crossing a torrent (difficult after rain) to gain the grass and stone covered slopes on the W side of the Eiger glacier. Follow traces of track then climb short steps up stone-strewn ground heading SE until level with the hut. Traverse R to the hut. There is no real advantage in taking the train to the Eigergletscher station. 3½hr.

H25 F 80 **Hollandia hut** 3235m also called Lötschen hut 640.06/147.24 tel 028 49 11 35 SAC, 106 beds, April – May and mid July – mid Aug. One of the coldest huts in the Alps. Recently completed renovation should have improved this condition.

From Fafleralp follow Route 204 to the Lötschenlücke. The hut is on the N side of the pass. Reach it by circling round on snow to a point on the ridge a little above the hut (crevasses). 6-8hr

From the Jungfraujoch or Konkordia follow Route 205.

H26 PE 70 **Rottal hut** 2755m 638.83/152.88 tel 036 56 24 45 SAC, 46 beds, week-ends July – Aug, no meals.

From Stechelberg the route is signposted past Stuefestein. There is slight danger from ice avalanches. Not recommended in winter as it is avalanche prone. 5-6hr

H27 RE 71 **Silberhorn hut** 2663m 637.96/156.42 SAC, 12 beds, no resident guardian.

The hut can be approached from Wengen but this particular way is quite dangerous. It is much safer to start at the Schilthorn lift station N of Stechelberg. From the S entrance to the parking area walk S on the road to Stechelberg for about 300m to a stream. Walk up the N side of the stream for 150m to the start of the climb. The route is marked from here. Zig-zag up fields and undergrowth to a steep rocky section. Climb this by a couloir to the N, then cross another couloir before climbing straight up through more undergrowth and stony slopes with short rock steps until 50m below a rock wall. Move 600m S, at first through woods then climbing gradually up little gullies and through bushes, to reach a big open couloir. Cross a slab (cable) then climb straight up for about 200m (cables near the top). There is a bivouac cave under the rocks here. Traverse S, with little ascent, through undergrowth and across pastures with a few pines to a flat area and fine view point.

Follow a rocky ramp SE to its end then go up steep grass and stone slopes for about 250m, at first straight up then towards the S to a broad and flat grassy area at about 2080m. Turn NE and climb rocky steps and grassy slopes then up the edge of a gully to reach the area called Strälblatti. Climb a rock band by a metal ladder and reach the hut in a few mins. 6hr

H28 PE **Schmadri hut** 2262m 634.83/149.86 AAC Bern (SAC rec. rights), 12 beds, no resident guardian. A marked path from Stechelberg. 3½hr

H29 P **Baltschiederklause hut** 2783m 634.70/138.28 tel 028 52 23 65 SAC, 40 beds, July – mid Sept.

From Ausserberg (signposted from Visp via Baltschieder and from Pt 636.2m on the Visp to Turtmann road) drive through the village (road to Ranft) as far as the first hairpin bend. Just above this a short sliproad L leads to a tunnel entrance (parking). Either walk through the tunnel (20min) and then follow a near horizontal path into the Baltschiedertal to join a water course, or from the hairpin bend descend a few m E and follow a spectacular path alongside another water course that the tunnel route joins. In descent follow the signpost "Zum Stollen" for the tunnel route.

Leave the water course at a chalet just N of Pt 1284m and climb steadily up a path to Pt 1483m, where a bridge crosses the river near a cluster of chalets. On the other side of the river continue

N and then steeply NE up meadows to Martischipfa where another bridge is crossed. There is a bivouac near here (1960m, white marker) with straw and blankets). Continue, past the tiny chapel at Hohbitzu, on a winding track to a painted sign on rocks directing the way to the Stockhorn bivouac hut. For the Baltschiederklause hut keep to the path and cross a third bridge. Follow a flat and rather indistinct path on the E side of the river to a signpost at the start of the final climb. This is up boulder strewn slopes at first then crosses Lwards, over numerous streams issuing from the Innre Baltschieder glacier, to the lateral moraine which leads, via a short rock scramble, to the hut. 5-7hr

H30 PE **Stockhorn bivouac hut** 2598m 634.04/136.32 emergency tel SAC, 12 beds, often crowded.

From Ausserberg follow the route to the Baltschiederklause hut to just beyond the chapel at Hohbitzu. From the painted sign follow traces of track NW to the foot of the N-most gully cutting through the rock wall. Climb this using the 200m of chains as necessary, to reach grass and stone slopes leading W to the hut. 5-6hr

H31 P **Lobhorn hut** 1955m 632.97/163.11 private property of the Lauterbrunnen section of the SAC, 24 beds, week-ends end June – early Sept. Reservation necessary and to obtain key telephone 036 56 12 07.

From Lauterbrunnen take the rack railway to Grütschalp then the path to Sous-läger. From there another path leads via Chüebodmi to the hut. 2½hr

Tschingelhorn hotel c1685m sited on the path from Stechelberg to the Mutthorn hut tel 036 55 13 43 private. Dormitory accommodation available June – Oct.

Obersteinberg hotel 1778m sited on the path from Stechelberg to the Mutthorn hut, W of the Tschingelhorn Hotel tel 036 55 20 33 private. Dormitory accommodation available June – Oct.

H32 F **Mutthorn hut** 2898m 630.07/148.40 tel 036 53 13 44 SAC, 100 beds, July – early Sept.

From the Gasteretal follow Route 203 but instead of climbing to the Petersgrat continue easily up the Kanderfirn to the hut. 4-5hr

Note: the road into the Gasteretal is a toll road. Pay at the café alongside the Stockbahn lift station. There is a bus service.

From Stechelberg follow signposted paths to Obersteinberg and from the hotel there continue on a path to the Oberhornsee at 2065m. Get onto the moraine of the Tschingel glacier and climb this to the N foot of Chanzel. Continue SW up the Tschingelfirn to the hut. 6-8hr

From the Kiental climb to the Gspaltenhorn hut then follow Routes 284 and 283 to the hut. 6hr from Griesalp

From the Lötschental follow Route 191 to the Wetterlücke then walk under the S face of the Tschingelhorn. Contour W to the Petersgrat and descend to the hut from the saddle at Pt 3122m. 5hr

H33 P 86 **Bietschhorn hut** 2565m 629.10/138.26 AAC Bern (SAC rec. rights), 40 beds, week-ends July – Sept. Approach from Wiler or Blatten in the Lötschental. 3hr

H34 P 96 **Gspaltenhorn hut** 2458m 630.07/151.34 tel 033 76 16 29 SAC, 75 beds, July – Aug and week-ends in June and Sept. Approach from Griesalp in the Kiental. Rather wet in one section. 3hr

Note: the road to Griesalp is a toll road. Pay toll at the bakery (Bäckerei Aellig) in Kiental village or at a caravan further along the road. There is a bus service.

H35 P **Blüemlisalp hut** 2834m 625.56/151.03 tel 033 76 14 37 SAC, 100 beds, June – mid Sept. Approach from Kandersteg: walk to Oeschinensee then via Underbägli and Oberbägli (sign-posts to Hohtürli). 5-6hr. If the lift is used from Kandersteg to Läger take the upper path to Oeschinensee at the fork then take the next turn L (sign-posted Hohtürli and Oberbägli). 4hr

An approach can be made from Griesalp in the Kiental by way of Bundalp. 4hr

H36 P 91 **Fründen hut** 2562m 623.28/148.08 tel 033 75 14 33 SAC, 90 beds, July – Aug. Approach from Kandersteg on foot or by lift (to Läger) to Oeschinensee. Follow the path on the S side of the lake to the steep path leading to the hut. 3-5hr. See also photo 92

Berghaus Lauchernalp c1960m sited in the Lötschental N of Wiler tel 028 49 12 50 private, 39 beds. Open summer and winter.

Lötschenpass hut 2690m sited at the pass private, 35 beds. See Routes 290 and 291.

Gfelalp hotel 1847m sited in the Gasteretal on the path to the Lötschenpass tel 033 75 11 61 private. Dormitory accommodation available June – Oct.

Berggasthaus Heimritz 1635m sited at the end of the road in the Gasteretal tel 033 74 14 34 private. Dormitory accommodation available June – Oct.

H37 **Doldenhorn hut** 1915m 619.87/148.43 tel 033 75 16 60 SAC,
P 45 beds, July – Aug and week-ends in May, June and Sept. Approach from Filfalle S of Kandersteg. 2½hr

H38 **Balmhorn hut** 1955m 619.29/144.45 SAC, 28 beds, week-ends
PE July – Sept.
89

Approach from Kandersteg by the road into the Gasteretal (see Route H32). At the bridge at 1352m take the path to Waldhus, continue to Pt 1367m and take the R fork before climbing steeply to the hut. 2-2½hr from the bridge

H39 **Schwarenbach hotel** 2060m 614.30/142.30 tel 033 75 12 72 private, 140 beds. Approach from Kandersteg on foot or by lift to Sunnbüel then follow an easy path towards the Gemmipass. 1hr from Sunnbüel. From the Gemmipass take the path on the E side of the Daubensee. 30min

Wildstrubel hotel 2314m sited 5min below the lift station at the Gemmipass. A large private establishment with dormitory accommodation.

H40 **Lämmeren hut** 2507m 610.48/138.85 tel 027 61 25 15 SAC,
P 78 beds, March – May and July – Sept. The hut was damaged by avalanche in 1989 but has been rebuilt. Approach from the Gemmipass. 2hr

Engstligenalp hotel 1954.4m sited a few min from the lift station at Engstligenalp S of Adelboden tel 033 73 22 91 or 73 34 51. Dormitory accommodation available.

H41 **Wildstrubel hut** 2793m 602.27/136.80 tel 030 4 33 39 SAC,
P 74 beds, July – Aug. Approach from Lenk. Bus to Iffigenalp (2hr on foot) then a way marked path. 3½hr

H42 **Wildhorn hut** 2303m 596.10/136.43 tel 030 3 23 82 SAC,
P 125 beds, week-ends in winter and July – mid Sept. Approach

from Lenk. Bus to Iffigenalp (2hr on foot) then an easy path to the hut. 2½hr

H43 P **Gelten hut** 2002m 592.34/135.36 tel 030 5 32 20 SAC, 87 beds, July – mid Sept. Approach from Lauenen (SE of Gstaad). A toll road leads to Büel near the Lauenensee then on foot. 2hr

H44 **Diablerets hut** 2485m 582.81/131.94 tel 025 53 21 02 SAC, 80 beds, July – mid Sept. Approach from the Col du Pillon by lift to Tête au Chamois then 5 min walk. On foot from the Col du Pillon is PE. There are cables on part of the route. 2½hr

H45 P **Rambert hut** 2580m 576.52/119.91 tel 027 27 11 22 SAC, 44 beds, July – mid Sept. Approach from Ovronnaz (above Riddes in the Rhône valley). Drive up the road towards Odonne to the bend at 1482m and just after this take a road R and follow it to a parking place a little higher. A signposted path leads to the hut. 3½hr

Note: The dates of opening of huts given above are only a rough guide. Actual opening and closing dates depend on the prevailing conditions of weather and mountains.

Grimsel Pass to Lauteraarsattel and Unders Studerjoch

The mountains described in this section are of relatively modest altitude and can provide good climbing when their more illustrious neighbours are ruled out by climatic conditions. The most important and best known peak is the Wetterhorn whose ascent by Alfred Wills in 1854 was a major milestone in the history of mountaineering.

Most of the peaks have fine rocky ridges with steep faces between. In a few cases the faces provide good snow and ice routes. Long glaciers traverse the area and provide the approach to many of the routes described. It is a good place for the alpine novice and is usually far from crowded.

In and around the Grimsel Pass there is to be found some superb rock-climbing on perfect granite. Not far away in the Engelhörner the same can be said, except that here the rock is limestone. The climbing in both areas is comparable in quality with just about anything found elsewhere in Europe. A good selection of these climbs is described in this guidebook in the rock-climbing section.

Maps covering this section are: Nufenenpass (265), Sustenpass (255) and Interlaken (254)

Wasenhorn 3446.8m

B and Frau Tauscher with A Pinggera and J Reinstadler, 14 Aug 1885

The mountain has three ridges one of which, the W, bifurcates in its lower part. In years of normal snow cover the NW face makes an interesting climb.

1 **WEST RIDGE BY SOUTH BRANCH**

PD

42

From the Finsteraarhorn hut follow the L side of the Fiescher glacier to the foot of the rocky promontary called Rotloch (2843.3m). Cross the Galmi glacier Swards and climb up mixed grass and rock into the coombe between the two branches of the W ridge. Get onto the S branch via an easy rock couloir and follow the ridge to the summit. 5hr

The climb can be made from the Oberaarjoch hut by

following Route H9 (alternative) to the junction between the Galmi and Fiescher glaciers. The time is the same.

The route can be reversed, or the descent can be made by following the NE ridge (first ascent party) to the col at 3141m. F+

2 **NORTH-WEST FACE**

D

42

M Brandt, A and R Voillat, 21 July 1958

The face is about 550m high and mostly glacier. In recent years this has shrunk, but should normal snow cover return, the face will provide a good climb.

From the Oberaarjoch hut climb down to the col then descend SSW across the Studer and Galmi glaciers to the bergschrund at about 2900m. Climb up to the R side of the sérac zone via a steep and icy couloir (100m), then cross the easier slopes to a second bergschrund below and L of some rocks which protrude from the steeper summit slopes. Climb the icy slope (53°) to a rock rib which leads to the top, a little to the NE of the summit. 5-6hr

It is almost as easy but a little longer to start at the Finsteraarhorn hut and follow Route H9 (alternative) until below the face.

Vorder and Hinter Galmihorn 3517m and 3486m

A Barbey, L Kurz with Albrecht and Seiler, 12 July 1884

These are two peaks with an attractive glaciated northern flank.

3 **TRAVERSE**

F First ascent party

42 *A pleasant, undemanding outing. It can be taken in either direction.*

From the Oberaarjoch hut climb down to the col and descend the Studer glacier, at first WSW then S. Pass below Pt 3060m and cross the Galmi glacier to the foot of the Vorder Galmihorn. Either climb the glacier slope direct to the summit or follow the easy bounding rock ridge, over the W summit, to the top. 2½hr

Descend the snowy N ridge to the Bächilicke and ascend the easy SW ridge of the Hinter Galmihorn over scree, snow and easy rock. 1hr

Another easy rock ridge leads down to the Galmilicke from where straightforward glacier work leads back to the approach route (1hr). 5-6hr in all

Oberaarjoch 3223m

A high pass giving the only easy access to the higher, central peaks of the Oberland from the W. Although the pass itself is high the starting point is also quite high and so the height gain is not excessive. It makes a fine start to a traverse of the Oberland from the E. The W side is a straightforward snow slope leading onto the Studer glacier.

4 **FROM THE EAST**

F

From the Grimsel Pass drive up a rough track as far as the Oberaarsee dam, just beyond the Oberaar Berghaus (large car park). The traffic on this roadway is controlled by traffic lights. Ascent can be made, from 8 am onwards, on the hour and for the next 10min and the drive should be completed in 20min (it takes much less). You can descend on the half hour similarly. The road is closed at night from 8pm.

From the dam cross the dam wall and follow the track along the N shore of the Oberaarsee. Keep up R of the Oberaar glacier snout and, where the angle eases, walk onto the glacier and up the middle of it, usually on bare ice. The angle eventually steepens and the glacier becomes snow covered. Continue up the glacier, more or less in the middle or just R of it, avoiding several crevasses, to the col. 5hr from the car park

Oberaarhorn 3637m

L Stephen and M Anderegg, 23 Aug 1860

A fine rocky pyramid with an easy angled snow slope on its SW flank. It is very frequently climbed and has magnificent views all round from its summit.

5 **SOUTH FLANK**

F+

52

First ascent party

The route can be combined with (an ascent/descent of) the W ridge to make a traverse of the mountain. The W ridge is PD and is reached at the col between Altmann and the Oberaarhorn. The rock tower can be climbed or avoided on the S side.

Behind the Oberaarjoch hut toilet a way-marked path leads steeply Nwards to the snowfield which forms the upper part of the route. Climb this, sometimes icy, to the summit. 1-1½hr

Altmann 3468m

T von Hahn with F Amatter and F Kaufmann, 8 Aug 1907

An unimportant summit best climbed in combination with a traverse of the Studerhorn. See Route 66.

Grunerhorn 3438m and Scheuchzerhorn 3462m

E J Häberlin with A and J Weissfluh, 30 July 1872

6 **TRAVERSE**

D/PD *The two peaks can be combined in a traverse starting from the Aar bivouac or the Oberaarjoch hut. From the former it is more difficult on the excellent NW ridge of the Grunerhorn.*

From the Aar bivouac cross the Finsteraar glacier to the foot of the ridge (2714m). Get onto the ridge crest by slanting up Rwards over snow and rock slopes. Easy climbing leads to a sharp snow arête which is followed to the SW ridge. Continue on this to the summit of the Grunerhorn. 3-4hr

From the Oberaarjoch hut climb down to the col and then cross the upper slopes of the Oberaar glacier Nwards. Pass below the two projecting ridges descending from Pts 3500m and 3437m and climb the fairly steep snow slope SE of the summit of the Grunerhorn to join the SW ridge. 2½hr

From the summit descend the NE ridge and skirt round Pt 3377.9m on its S side (can traverse it but an unpleasant steep ridge has to be descended) to a col at the foot of the W ridge of the Scheuchzerhorn. Climb this on mixed rock and snow to the summit. 1hr

Follow the NE ridge which curves E to the Scheuchzerjoch. There is one short, but steep, S facing snow slope to avoid the rock of Pt 3352m. 30min

Descend to the Oberaarjoch hut or the Lauteraar hut by Route 7. Allow 6hr for the round trip from the Oberaarjoch hut and 8-9hr from the Aar bivouac.

Scheuchzerjoch 3072m

First traverse by E von Fellenberg with J Tännler and B Marti, 6 Sept 1877

The pass provides a means of connecting the Lauteraarhorn and Oberaarjoch huts. Fairly popular in spring with ski-tourers. The Tierberg glacier is quite steep low down and usually bare ice in summer.

7 PD **TRAVERSE NORTH TO SOUTH**

From the Lauteraar hut descend to the Unteraar glacier and cross it to the the foot of the Tierberg glacier. Keep to the L or the R on entering the coombe and continue to a steepening in the glacier. Follow the coombe round to the L, to avoid the steepest part on its E side, and get onto the flatter part of the glacier at about 2800m. Head SW (crevasses) to the bergschrund below the col. Cross it, usually on the R, and climb a steep snow slope to the col. If the bergschrund is too difficult or the slope above it too icy, it is better to climb the rocks to the E of the slope to the col. 3½hr

From the col climb about 100m up the ridge running W then traverse horizontally SW across the snow coombe. Near the foot of the SE ridge of the Scheuchzerhorn cross the ridge onto the snow slopes on its W flank. Contour round the next coombe, passing below the ridges emanating from Pts 3437m and 3500m, and follow the glacier below the E flank of the Oberaarhorn to the Oberaarjoch and hut. 2hr, about 6hr in total

Brandlammhorn (East summit) 3089m

Miss S Koenig, R Koenig and C Montandon, 3 July 1892

The Brandlammhorn has two summits with a distinctive gendarme separating them. The E summit is the lower. Descending S from the twin cols between the summits is a steep snow couloir, although rock becomes exposed at the end of the season and in years of low winter snow fall.

8 PD **SOUTH FLANK COULOIR**
First ascent party

The route should only be attempted when the couloir is snow-filled.

From the Lauteraar hut follow Route 11 to just below the snow-patch under the Fellenberglicken. Traverse E again to the snow/scree slope W of the Brandlammhorn and gain the couloir. Climb it and its R branch to the col between the E summit and the gendarme. Continue up the W ridge to the summit. 4-5hr

9 **SOUTH-SOUTH-WEST RIDGE**

AD

H Lieberherr and H Stahel with F von Bergen, July 1946

Good rock climbing with the added attraction of excellent views over the Grimsel lake.

From the Lauteraar hut follow Route 8 to the snow/scree slopes W of the Brandlammhorn. Descend SE to the foot of an obvious couloir in the W flank of the ridge (2½hr). Climb the rocks on the S edge of the couloir, keeping as close as possible to it (bits of IV–), to reach the col just N of Pt 2906m (45min). Follow the ridge crest as closely as possible (mainly II with bits of III) until about 100m from the summit, where there is a steep step 15m high (piton belay). Climb direct for 4m to a small ledge, then make a big step R to a narrow ledge from which good holds lead back to the crest and a large block (IV+). Easier climbing leads to the summit. 5-6hr from the hut

Fellenberglicken 2996m

E von Fellenberg with B Marti and J Tännler, 4 Sept 1877

A useful pass between the Bächlital and Lauteraarhorn huts, which gives access to the Bächlistock. Not named on the map.

10 **FROM THE NORTH**

PD

43

From the Bächlital hut follow Route 14 as far as the flat glacier basin. Climb more or less direct to the col (Pt 2996m) which is reached after crossing a bergschrund, usually easy, followed by a short rocky section. 2½-3hr

11 **FROM THE SOUTH**

PD

From the Lauteraar hut follow the path coming from Grimsel for 300m then work Nwards in a shallow valley to Pt 2532m. Now traverse Ewards round the ridge, descending from Pt 3118m, to the scree slopes around Pt 2787m. At this level contour round the rocks of the Bächlistock to a large scree terrace. From here the pass can be seen as the lowest point between the Bächlistock and the Brandlammhorn. Climb up to below a small snow-patch below the gap and climb a rock step to get onto it. Climb the snow to its upper L edge then easily onto the bounding ridge, which is followed for

80m W before an easy descent can be made over blocks to the col. 3-3½hr

Bächlistock 3247m

H and A Baumgartner and E von Rütte with P Baumann (father and son) and M Michel, 26 July 1892

The mountain has twin summits, NW and SE, the former being the higher. The SE summit was climbed four years earlier by P H Baumgartner and M Brémond with J von Bergen and J Tännler, 27 Sept 1888. The ridge connecting the two summits is almost horizontal.

12 **TRAVERSE**
AD+
43

A worthwhile climb along the ridge between the Fellenberglicken and the Obri Bächli Licken. The Fellenberglicken is not named on the map but is marked as Pt 2996m.

From the Bächlital hut follow Route 10 to the Fellenberglicken. 2½-3hr

Climb the first step of the SE ridge direct (III). Easy climbing, at first on the L then R side of the ridge but all the time close to it, leads to a gendarme on the level part of the ridge. Abseil 15m on the N side to easy terrain. Contour round the other gendarmes on either side (although the last one is best past on the L side) and reach a gap below the summit. Climb as direct as possible from the gap to the summit. 3½-4hr

Descend easily to a gap on the ridge connecting the two summits, then follow the more-or-less level ridge to a final section which has a number of small gendarmes. These are best traversed (III) to reach the NW summit. 1hr

Turn NNE along the crest of the ridge, which is mostly shattered rock, with a few deviations onto the SW flank, to the Obri Bächli Licken. (1hr). From the col abseil about 20m, depending on the level of snow on the slope below, then reverse Route 14 to the hut. About 10hr in all

Obri Bächli Licken 3074m

E Farner, F Monnard and C Montandon, 5 Oct 1890

A high pass providing a means of passage between the Bächlital and Gauli huts and access to the Bächlistock and Gr Diamantstock.

13 **FROM THE WEST**

PD From the Gauli hut take the path past Chammliegg to a 80m couloir leading down to the Gauli glacier. Descend the couloir on easy but polished rock and then cross the glacier to the stream issuing from Hiendertellti. Climb up the W side on moraine to the lower, stone covered glacier. Climb the glacier in a SE direction and reach the coombe below the Hindertelltihorn. Turn S up the glacier and continue to where it begins to steepen at about 2800m. Climb directly up to the col to the SE, crossing a bergschrund and climbing some easy rocks just below the col itself. 4hr

14 **FROM THE EAST**

PD

43 From the Bächlital hut follow a path W to the Bächli glacier. Climb the glacier and pass to the R of the sérac barrier to reach a flat glacier basin. Climb a steep rocky slope NE to below the Undri Bächli Licken (W gap). Traverse onto the N part of the Bächli glacier and follow it under the rocks of the SW ridge of the Gr Diamantstock to below the col. Climb to the col up slabby rocks (III, pitons). 3hr

Gross Diamantstock 3162m

G Hasler with C Jossi and U Fuhrer, 25 Sept 1902

A fine rocky peak with some good climbing along its granite ridges. Any pair of the 3 ridges can be combined into a worthwhile traverse of the peak but without doubt it is desirable to include an ascent of the E ridge in the itinerary. The NW ridge (AD–) is rarely climbed.

15 **SOUTH-WEST RIDGE**

PD First ascent party

43 *The easiest route on the mountain. Pleasant, easy climbing.*

From the Bächlital hut follow Route 14 to the Obri Bächli Licken. From the col keep on the W side of the ridge and climb the steep part on good holds (III–). Easier climbing on the crest leads to the summit. 1½hr from the col.

It is possible to get onto the ridge from the Bächli glacier without going to the Obri Bächli Licken. Climb easily up the E flank of the ridge from a small snow basin situated directly below the summit. This has the advantage of shortening the route and gives the quickest descent, but it does miss the best of the climbing. About 3½hr from the hut

16 **EAST RIDGE**

D– H Anderegg, H Baer, W Preiswerk and H Zürcher, 4 July 1911

43 *A really good climb with the greatest difficulty at the start, although this can be avoided.*

From the Bächlital or Grueben huts follow Routes 18 or 17 to the Undri Bächli Licken. Climb the first step on its SE side (an excellent pitch, IV-V) or traverse round its base on the N side. Keep to the ridge, which is more or less horizontal at first and then inclined gently, going over or around the numerous gendarmes. One fairly tall gendarme is climbed on its S side before descending into a gap before a pronounced step. Climb this by a crack, close to the edge on the N side (IV), then keep to the crest over several short steps (III and IV–). On the upper part of the ridge difficulties can be avoided on the S side but it is more elegant to keep to the crest and reach a platform below the summit. Climb a crack on the S side (III+) or easy large blocks on the N side. 4-5hr in all

Undri Bächli Licken c2720m

Probable first traverse by climbers: L Liechti, F Monnerat and C Montandon, 24 Aug 1886

An unimportant pass, although it provides a means of connecting the Grueben and Bächlital huts and gives access to the E ridge of the Gr Diamantstock. It has 2 gaps separated by a few small pinnacles. The W gap is close to the foot of the E ridge of the Gr Diamantstock.

17 **FROM THE NORTH**

PD The 1886 party

From the Grueben hut descend SW onto the Grueben glacier and cross it SSW. When below the gaps climb straight up and, after crossing the bergschrund, get onto the unpleasant broken rock.

Climb this diagonally L to the E gap. Climb easily along the ridge on its N flank for 50m to the W gap. 1½hr

18 **FROM THE SOUTH**

F Follow Route 14 as far as the W gap. 1½hr

Alplistock 2877.4m

F Gardiner with R and P Almer, 4 July 1905

Situated immediately N of the Bächlital hut this has a double summit, the E one being lower (2818m) and some 400m from the W summit.

19 **TRAVERSE WEST TO EAST**

AD+ Probably E Liechti and H Vögeli, Sept 1930

An excellent climb.

From the Bächlital hut follow the path W for about 100m then turn N and climb up into the stony coombe below the S face, at first up a gully system and then over slabs. Slant up L to a couloir which leads to the W ridge of the W summit. Climb the couloir and the ridge, over large granite blocks, to the W summit. 2-2½hr

Pass under a block very close to the S ridge and reach the first gap in the ridge joining the 2 summits. Cross a slab to a 10m high tower, which is climbed direct, then continue along the crest over gendarmes to a steep drop. Abseil 15m on the N side to another gap. Follow the crest to the last gendarme, which overhangs on the N side. Pass it by abseiling 20m on the N side or climb up its S rib to reach an abseil point and then descend 15m. Continue on the ridge to the E summit. Most of this is III with some IV. 3hr

Descend SE down couloirs and short walls until it is possible to work back under the SE ridge of the E summit. Descend to Pt 2319m and then to the hut in a few more minutes. 1hr, about 7hr in all

Hiendertelltihorn 3179.4m

C Montandon and H Kümmerli, 24 Sept 1888

An impressive peak with very well defined ridges, the most

accessible and probably best being the E ridge. The NW ridge can be climbed from the Gauli hut (AD–) in about 5hr, whilst the others are approached from the Grueben hut. The S ridge is PD+ and the N ridge is AD–; both require about 4hr.

20 **EAST RIDGE**
D H Anderegg, F Lodwiz, W Preiswerk and H Zürcher, Aug 1937
44 *A good climb on sound granite.*

From the Grueben hut climb the Grueben glacier to the foot of the ridge, or go more directly from the flat part of the glacier over the rock band which projects into the glacier from the N. Move round the NE side and find, at about 2800m, an easy line leading L onto the ridge just above its blunt nose. This position can be gained by climbing the blunt nose of the ridge starting in a dièdre 30m L of its foot. Climb this dièdre to its top and then gain the crest of the ridge via 2 small overhangs (V).

Climb the first step (piton) then an easy ramp to its end. On the R climb a steep 10m crack then move L (piton) to a belay (IV+). Move straight up the ridge for 40m (IV+ then IV) then avoid the next step on the E side and regain the crest. Follow it to a steep tower about 50m from the fore-summit. Turn this on the R about 10m below the crest (delicate, IV, pitons) or on its L side into a couloir (III). Continue up a couloir on the N flank to a gap, before climbing some small gendarmes to the summit. About 5hr

Descend the route, abseiling where necessary, or go down the S ridge to a col and from there get onto the Grueben glacier to rejoin the approach route.

Ritzlihorn 3263.1m

J Frey, between 1811 and 1818

A big mountain for these parts, with long and rather tedious approaches. It is rarely climbed but no worse for that. There is one worthwhile route.

21 **EAST RIDGE (ÄRLENGRÄTLI)**
TD– **O Gerecht, H Hüss, E Meir and G Strässle, 21 Aug 1949**

A good climb away from the frenzy of the Handegg 'klettergarten'. The ridge is about 1.5km long and leads to Pt 3193m on the S ridge of the

mountain. The start of the climb is at the deepest gap in the ridge between Pt 3193m and the Stampfhoren.

From Handegg take the path to the Grueben hut as far as Ärlen Alp (1780m). Turn NW up the Rindertal. A steep stony slope on the W of the river leads to some slabs. Cross these (sheep track) to reach a point above the torrent near Pt 2150m. Climb up to the Wyssenbachlimelti below Pt 2479m. 3hr

It is also possible to approach from the Grueben hut by an almost horizontal traverse, after passing N of Pt 2623m. 3hr

From the col climb along the ridge (II-III) as far as the first major step (Pt 2814m) at about halfway. Traverse on the S side of the step until slabs and short walls can be ascended back to the top of the step. From the next gap keep to the crest (III-IV) as far as a steep slab on the R with a crack. Climb the crack (20m, V, pitons) and reach a belay a bit higher. Climb another step (grey rock) by keeping a bit to the R for 20m (V, pitons), on some rocks which overlap at the bottom. Continue on the ridge to a gap below a 50m high tower.

Traverse horizontally R to a dièdre which is climbed Lwards for 5m to a narrow ledge leading back to the crest (40m, V). Reach the summit of the tower by a slab (IV). Easy climbing with one 10m abseil leads to the top of Pt 3193m. 6-7hr

The summit of the Ritzlihorn is reached fairly easily by the S ridge. 1½-2hr

Descent is from Pt 3193m. Climb down the S ridge for 80m (II-III) to a small gap. From the gap head down E towards 2 ledges 60m below the ridge at the side of the gully running down to the Ärlen glacier. Abseil the last 20m onto the S-most of the ledges. Descend 15m between the ledges then make 2 more abseils (40m in all) before climbing down slabs for another 60m (III). Finally abseil another 40m to the glacier. Regain the approach route via the glacier. 1½hr

Hienderstock 3307m

W Coolidge and F Gardiner with R Almer and C Almer jnr, 15 Sept 1886

The mountain has twin summits, the NE being just one metre higher than the SW which was climbed in 1889 by

H and A Baumgartner and party. It is frequently climbed from the Lauteraar Hut.

22 **TRAVERSE**

AD V Fynn and W Murphy, 14 Aug 1891

This is an excellent climb on good rock, being a little easier in the direction described but equally good in the opposite direction.

From the Lauteraar hut ascend Nwards up a steep slope cut by steps and ledges, to the SW, stony foot of Rothorn (3003m). Follow the base of the SSE ridge of the Hienderstock onto the E side of the Hinter Trift glacier, which is then climbed to the obvious col at the foot of the W ridge. The col is gained by by climbing a short rocky couloir. 3hr

Now climb the easy angled ridge, on good granite up slabs and short steps, to the SW summit (1-1½hr). The ridge connecting the two summits is followed on the crest or close to it, the numerous short but sharp teeth being traversed or avoided. The highest, shovel-shaped tooth is turned by a 10m long ledge on the N side (1hr). Do not be tempted to try the traverse using the NE flank of the ridge as the rock is very shattered and unstable.

Descend easily down the E ridge, over short steps to a distinct shoulder. A dièdre leads down (III+) to a 20m traverse R on good rock back to a debris covered ledge on the crest (or abseil to this point). Two pitches along the sharp ridge lead down to the Hiendertelltijoch. 1½hr

Climb down about 10m of yellowish rock on the S side of the col then go down snow slopes on the Vorder Trift glacier, in a SSE direction, to the top of a rocky barrier orientated N-S. A wide couloir of snow or loose rock leads through the barrier. Follow the stream-bed down to the level of Pt 2532m. Descend the shallow valley SW of this point, working down to join the path from Grimsel about 300m from the hut. About 9hr in all

Gaulipass c3200m

E Desor with J Leuthold, 1841

The pass is probably the easiest passage between the Lauteraar and Gauli huts, but not the shortest. The pass itself is not the lowest point on the ridge between the Trifthorn and Ewigschneehorn but the wide depression between the latter and Pt 3217m.

23 **FROM THE SOUTH**

F From the Lauteraar hut follow Route 47 to about 2500m on the Lauteraar glacier and then cross to the R side by Pt 2561.7m. From here a track leads up to the Gaulipass (c3200m), which is reached by climbing a rocky couloir. 4-5hr

24 **FROM THE EAST**

PD From the Gauli hut follow Route 13 onto the Gauli glacier and cross this SW to the Grienbärgli glacier. Climb this glacier, heading for the upper part of the SE ridge of the Ewigschneehorn, and reach the col by a short but steep rock section. 4hr

Ewigschneehorn 3329.4m

E Desor with J Leuthold, 1841

This peak provides an interesting excursion between the Lauteraar and Gauli huts.

25 **TRAVERSE**

PD *The traverse can be made with equal ease in either direction but is described from S to N.*

From the Lauteraar Hut follow Route 23 to the Gaulipass. 4-5hr

Follow the ridge, comprised of large blocks of gneiss, easily to the summit (20min). Now descend the NE ridge (Grienbärgligrat) which is reached from the summit by a steep snow slope. Go down the narrow crest of the ridge until close to Pt 2686.3m, where a short steep couloir allows the slopes of Grienbärgli to be reached. Descend to the E foot of Grienbärgli and cross the Gauli glacier NE to the foot of an 80m high couloir, which is climbed easily on polished rock – some stonefall danger. Walk along a scree covered terrace and join the path leading down to the Gauli hut. 3-4hr, 7½-9½hr in all

Bärglistock 3655.6m

C Aebi with P Egger and P Inäbnit 26 Sept 1864

This is a fairly remote summit and quite a long way from any hut base, and consequently it is infrequently climbed. Maybe a good reason to do it!

26 **NORTH RIDGE**
AD W Graham with P Baumann father and son, 30 Sept 1886

Can be climbed starting from either the Dossen or Gauli huts. Both approaches are described.

From the Dossen hut follow Route 31 over the summit of the Dossen to the Ränfenjoch. Easy snow slopes lead SSW past Pt 3250m to Rosenegg. 4-5hr

From the Gauli hut take the path towards Chammliegg but where the path turns SE, keep to a ravine going roughly SW. Pass under Pt 2610m on a terrace which leads, with a short descent, to the Gauli glacier near Pt 2589m. Follow the edge of the glacier NW to the snow slope below Wätterlimi. Gradually swing round to the W and pass to the L of Pt 3250m from where Rosenegg is easily reached. 4-5hr

Now go S, keeping on the snow to the E side of the N ridge, as far as the Bärglijoch. Some good climbing over a couple of gendarmes, then mixed snow and rock and finally snow, leads to the summit. 2½hr, 6½-7½hr in all

27 **SOUTH RIDGE**
D Either J Earle and M Brodley with M Kohler, 4 Aug 1905 or F Pollock with P Baumann and P Rubi, 26 Aug 1868

This is climbed from the Lauteraarsattel which is approached from either the Gleckstein or Lauteraar huts.

Reach the Lauteraarsattel by Route 46 or 47 (4-5hr). From here keep to the W of Pt 3250m then, by a subsidiary ridge with a short sharp section, get onto the SSW ridge. Coming from the Lauteraar side this point can be reached by a snow couloir. Cross a narrow snow couloir and climb rocks on its R bank, which transform into a distinct ridge, as far as a tower barring the way ahead. Get into the narrow couloir on the L, climb it for a little way then leave it on the L side, where easy climbing leads to the S ridge at a gap by the S summit. From the gap exposed climbing (III with bits of IV–) on some gendarmes leads to the main summit. 4hr, 8-9hr in all

Hangendgletscherhorn 3291.9m

C Aebi and R Gerwer with P Michel and P Inäbnit, 15 Aug 1863

The peak is frequently climbed from the Gauli hut. It has a massive but uninteresting N face. The best climbs are the SE and NW ridges.

28 **SOUTH-EAST (CHAMMLI) RIDGE**

AD– From the Gauli hut follow the Chammliegg path to where it first turns sharp L. Now follow the line of a ravine to its upper end and get onto the ridge. Mostly easy climbing leads to a rocky plateau on the ridge. Pass a gendarme on its R and descend 2-3m to reach the top edge of a snow slope. Cross the snow Nwards and then, back on the ridge, climb gneiss slabs and scree to a big gendarme. Pass this on the L and climb a couloir (20m) onto the E ridge. Easier climbing leads to the summit. 4-5hr

29 **NORTH-WEST RIDGE**

AD A Baumgartner and P Koenig, 19 July 1900

From the Gauli hut follow Route 26 up the glacier, passing below Pt 2795m, until directly S of Pt 3209m. Now climb the slopes between a rock buttress on the L and the ridge, descending from the summit, on the R to gain the col between the Ränfenhorn and Hangendgletscherhorn (c3050m). 3½hr

Climb the ridge to a gap (can be reached direct from below by a couloir) and then continue more easily over or round (S) Pt 3209m to another gap on its E side. Climb the following step on its N side (crux) then the easy ridge to the summit. 2-2½hr, 6hr in all

Ränfenhorn 3259m

A Girdlestone and J Matthews, 1867 (they found a cairn on the top!)

Only worth climbing for the view and exercise.

30 **SOUTH FLANK**

F First ascent party

From the Gauli hut follow the previous route to the slope between the rock buttress and ridge. Once above the buttress climb the slopes direct to the summit. 3-4hr

31 **NORTH-WEST FLANK**

PD From the Dossen hut follow Route 32 to the summit of the Dossen. Descend easily down the S ridge to the Ränfenjoch, from where easy snow slopes lead to the summit. 3½-4hr

Dossen 3138.2m

J Hugi, 13 Aug 1828

Another fine viewpoint.

32 **NORTH RIDGE**
PD First ascent party

From the Dossen hut follow traces of track SW, on the E side of the ridge, to the col S of Pt 3032m (Dossensattel). If the glacier is very icy it is better to climb the ridge running SW from the hut, climbing a step at half-height direct (III) or turning it on the L more easily, before descending to the col from Pt 3032m.

From the col climb a 5m step a bit to the L of the ridge-foot and get into a slabby dièdre a few m L. Climb the dièdre and then keep on the ridge to the summit (one step of III–). 2-3hr

Rosenhorn 3689.3m and Mittelhorn 3704m

Rosenhorn: E Desor, Dupasquier, Dollfus and Stengel with J Währen, M Bannholzer, J Jaun and three other guides, 28 Aug 1844. Mittelhorn: M Speer with K Abplanalp, J Jaun and J Michel, 8 July 1845

These two summits, along with the Wetterhorn, form the group known as the Wetterhörner. They are attractive looking peaks seen from N or E and well worth the attention of alpinists.

33 **TRAVERSE**
AD+ E Panchard and J Martin, 18 Aug 1901
46

The two peaks are best combined in a traverse which can also include an ascent of the Wetterhorn. It is a lengthy undertaking involving varied rock and snow and is best done in the direction described. It is possible to start and finish at either the Gleckstein or Dossen huts. See also photo 45

From the Gleckstein hut follow Route 34 or from the Dossen hut follow Route 37, to the Wettersattel (3508m). About 4hr

From the saddle climb the Wetterhorn in 45min by Route 34 or ignore this summit and turn S to climb the Mittelhorn, at first up a broad and steepening snow slope and then along the narrow W ridge. Below the summit take the R fork in the ridge to the final steep slope. If this is icy it is better to climb a dièdre lower down to a shoulder L of the summit. 1hr

Descend the SE ridge easily to a secondary summit. The continuation of the ridge is very steep so it is better to descend the shoulder S of this summit, turning L to reach the Mitteljoch (3502m). 45min

The traverse can be abandoned at this point, descending to the Gleckstein hut via Hick, or to the Dossen hut via the Rosenlaui glacier to the Wellhornsattel and Route 37. If continuing, get onto the W ridge of the Rosenhorn and follow it to the first step, which is turned on the W close to the crest. Other obstacles are climbed direct or past on the R. 1½hr

Descend the rocky SSE ridge to a slight depression, cross it and descend a snow slope to Rosenegg. 45min

To return to the Gleckstein hut descend the Oberer Grindelwald glacier SW then WNW to the coombe below the Mitteljoch. Cross the coombe passing above Pt 3339m and go between two rock islands to Hick. Reverse Route 34 (alternative) to the hut. 3hr, 11-12hr in all

To return to the Dossen hut reverse Route 26. 2½hr, 11-12hr in all.

Wetterhorn 3701m

M Bannholzer and J Jaun, 31 Aug 1844

The most important and best known mountain in this section of the guide-book. Although not quite the highest, it dominates the view from Grindelwald. Seen from this aspect it appears to be primarily a rock peak having an extremely steep and impressive NW face. Seen from the E it is much less daunting and there is much more snow cover; it is no suprise that the mountain was first climbed from this side. The first confirmed ascent from the Grindelwald side in 1854 is considered to have marked the start of the 'Golden Age' of alpinism. To climb the mountain is a 'must' for any alpinist visiting Grindelwald for the first time.

34 **SOUTH-WEST FLANK**
AD– A Wills with A Balmat, A Simmond, U Lauener and P Bohren,
45 17 Sept 1854

This is the normal summer route up the mountain. The route climbs the Willsgrätli to the Wettersattel where it joins with the route from the E

(Dossen hut). There is some danger of rock fall and some quite awkward slabby rock on the approach to the Willsgrätli, but the ridge itself is good rock and provides some very good scrambling. It is not easy when snow covered or verglassed but there is an alternative approach to the Wettersattel by way of the gap called Hick, which links the Chrinnen glacier to a bay on the N part of the Oberer Grindelwald glacier. In good snow conditions this is quite straightforward and only PD (in less favourable conditions it becomes AD and can be quite dangerous). See also photo 45

From the Gleckstein hut follow a cairned track NNE to the Chrinnen glacier. Go NE up the glacier, avoiding crevasses on the L, to a snowy bay (which can be very crevassed) on the L (NW) of a rock spur which almost divides the glacier into two parts. From the top of the bay get onto this spur (bergschrund to cross) and continue up the crest, which is gneiss, to where it gives way to slabby limestone (2½hr). Climb up unpleasantly for another 200m before crossing a wide, shallow couloir on the R to get onto the Willsgrätli.

Keep to the crest of the ridge (II and III–) to where it peters out just below the Wettersattel. Traverse R and climb snow and rock to the col at about 3500m (1½-2hr).

Turn N and follow the snow crest which narrows towards the top and merges with the steep upper slopes of the mountain. Reach the summit rocks and either climb the steep snow slope Rwards to the easiest point through the cornice, or climb rocks further R, or climb a dièdre trending L to a shoulder just below the summit (45min, 5-6hr in all).

To climb the alternative route to the Wettersattel reach the Chrinnen glacier as above, but then go up the E part of the glacier to the obvious narrow couloir in the ridge running S from the Wettersattel. Climb the couloir (some stonefall danger), which is about 200m high, and then the steep glacier bay on the other side of the ridge. Finally reach a saddle a little to the E of the Wettersattel by climbing smooth gneiss slopes (or snow). Follow the route described above to the summit (5-6hr).

Descend by either route.

35 **SOUTH-WEST RIDGE**
D+ S Uramatsu with S Brawand and F Steuri, 24 Aug 1928
46

The ridge is about 1km long and when viewed from the Chrinnen glacier appears as a giant staircase with 5 steep steps. It provides an excellent climb, the difficulties being mainly on rock with one steep descent on snow or ice. At one time there were fixed ropes on the ridge but these have long gone. Pitons should be in place. See also photo 47

From the Gleckstein hut follow Route 34 to the Chrinnen glacier. On the glacier turn N and head for a rock couloir leading to the crest of the near horizontal part of the ridge between two high points. About 20m L of the couloir climb good rock, trending first L (some IV+) then back R on debris-covered but easier ground, to the crest. Follow this easily to the col E of Pt 3053m. This is called Chrinne and is close to the foot of the ridge. It is usual from here to make a short descent on rock and then a steep snow/ice slope to the Gutz glacier. Turn R and cross the bergschrund where possible. Get into a dièdre leading to the gap between the first and second gendarmes on the ridge. This can be very trying when verglassed. This point can be reached from Chrinne by climbing one pitch R onto the S face then directly up to the ridge, which is followed for a short way before moving L onto the NW flank. This leads to the gap.

From the gap move round to the R of the ridge and climb Lwards for a pitch (III and IV) to a belay in the middle of the tower. Climb a further 8m, then move R to an exposed dièdre which is followed to the ridge where it becomes less steep (40m, IV and V). Follow the ridge with one short steep step, to the base of the third gendarme. Climb this direct (40m, IV). From its top a steep descent on snow/ice leads to another gap (the Sichel). Mixed ground now leads more easily to the summit. Allow 6-9hr from the hut

36 AD+ 47

NORTH-WEST RIDGE AND NORTH-WEST FACE

Ridge: J Farrer with D Maquignaz and J Köberbacher, 11 Aug 1897
Face: R and A Voillat with H Anäbnit, 8 July 1945

The ridge is a shorter and easier climb than the SW ridge route and although not often climbed, it is quite worthy of attention. It can, however, be quite tricky if wet or verglassed. The face is quite straightforward in good snow conditions and makes a good training climb. The angle is 45°-50°. See also photos 45 and 46

From the Gleckstein hut follow Route 35 to the Gutz glacier. Cross it NEwards to reach snow slopes on the NW face leading directly to the summit, or continue to the W side of the NW ridge. Climb to the large gap alongside Pt 3455m (bits of III) and then follow the ridge directly, via short dièdres (III), to the snowy upper part and the summit. 6-7hr for either route

37 **EAST FLANK**
PD M Bannholzer and J Jaun, 31 Aug 1844

The route is basically a long glacier plod, the only difficulty, apart from climbing the final ridge, is avoiding crevasses.

From the Dossen hut follow Route 32 to the Dossensattel. Descend a steep snowy couloir on the W side of the col (possibly ice or scree) for 100m to the upper basin of the Rosenlaui glacier. Go SW up the glacier before curving round to the W to reach the Wellhornsattel. 2½hr

Make a gradual descent W to the long glacier slope leading directly to the Wettersattel. Climb to this (1½hr) and then follow Route 34 to the summit. About 5hr from the hut.

Scheideggwetterhorn 3361m

G Hasler with P Bernet and C Jossi, 13 May 1901

It cannot be truly considered to be a separate mountain, (and the spot height 3361m is not quite the highest point) being more a shoulder of the Wetterhorn; nevertheless it presents a most imposing spectacle when seen from Grosse Scheidegg. The N side of the peak is a massive rock wall cut by large ledges and running with melt water. It is this face which provides interest for mountaineers. All the climbs on this side are long and serious undertakings and have been compared to routes in the Dolomites such as the Civetta N wall. On all the routes pitons are in place but a selection should be carried.

The climbs described are reached from Grosse Scheidegg – reached by Post bus from Grindelwald or Rosenlaui. There is no access for private cars.

38 **WEST PILLAR DIRECT**
ED1 P Von Känel and H Trachel, 4/5 Aug 1970. The upper part of the
47 ridge had been climbed in June 1945

The pillar forms the R (W) edge of the N face and provides about 1000m of free climbing. It is considered to be one of the best rock climbs in Switzerland and has a number of unforgettable pitches. At the foot of the ridge there is some danger of sérac fall from the Gutz glacier but there is shelter to be had in the dièdres and overhangs. Ice axes are essential for the descent. See also photo 46

From Grosse Scheidegg take the ridge abutting the face and climb the first rock wall by a couloir to a large terrace (about 150m, III+). Traverse 300m R, descending about 50m, to below 2 massive yellow dièdres. Climb to the foot of the R-hand of these to a ledge (invisible from below), which leads in turn to the foot of the pillar where the climb begins. 2hr

From the end of the ledge go round the spur (20m, IV) to belay on the pillar itself. Climb direct for 10m (VI) then traverse R for 25m (IV). It is this pitch which is exposed to sérac fall. Straight up a superb crack (35m, V) for another pitch and continue in the crack (V) to below an enormous overhang which is climbed free (VI–). Now climb up to another roof and overcome it taking a line leading Rwards, then continue upwards bearing slightly R (35m, V). A 35m dièdre (V) leads to a crack on the R which finishes as a chimney (35m). Now straight up for 10m to a mossy overhang before traversing 8m L (V) and then straight up a slab and wall (VI–) to a belay. On the R easier climbing (25m, II and III) leads to an 80m crack. Climb this with increasing difficulty to an overhang (V) which is climbed (V+, delicate) to another crack. Easier climbing (20m, III) leads to a big terrace (bivouac site). 5-7hr

Climb the R side of the yellow/red wall then a short terrace and grey slab to a belay on the edge of the pillar (40m, IV+). Continue to the L over tile-like rock across a rib, then regain the crest and climb straight up it (30m, V+). 50m of easier climbing on the L of the pillar leads to a prominent wall 40m high. Climb the R side of the wall by a steep slab. Where it becomes vertical make a delicate step L and after 6m follow a dièdre to a platform (30m, V+ and VI). 35m of splendid climbing up walls follows (IV) and then after a few more metres (III) reach a wide ledge and a gap in the ridge . 3-4hr (It was from this point that the upper part of the ridge was first climbed by Pargätzi's party in 1945, the approach being made by the NW face. There are good bivouac sites here).

The next step in the ridge is about 200m high and is climbed on the SW face. From the gap abseil 8m and climb the first crack to a small niche (30m, V). Another crack on the R leads to a dièdre (35m, V+) which is climbed to a cave (35m, V). Pass a narrow chimney towards a gorge then climb Rwards in a dièdre (40m, V+). A crack now leads to a belay below an overhang (V+, delicate). Traverse R on a slab to pass the overhang then climb back L to regain the crest 50m higher (60m, III and IV). Several pitches of II-IV on the pillar lead to a prominent crack at the start of a grey, tile-like slab. Climb direct up the slab and then L to the gap (35m, V–). Above this is a 60m high buttress. Traverse R from the gap to a vertical dièdre which is climbed to the crest (30m, V). Follow the crest for 10m then climb on the R by slabs to a ledge below an overhang (30m, V+). On the R of the crest pass a yellow overhang (V+) and climb a short dièdre (IV) to a belay in 30m. This is the end of the difficulties. Continue on the R of the crest for about 100m before the final 2 pitches (III-IV) lead to the summit. 6-8hr, 16-21hr in all

39 **NORTH FACE DIRECT**

ED2 S Abderhalden and M Niedermann, 12/13Aug 1954.

47 Winter: A Hermann and members of GHM les Aiglons, 21 Dec 1971-2 Jan 1972

This is a most impressive climb. Many pitons are in place and are used for aid although much of the route can be free climbed. It is extremely long (about 1300m) and is among the most difficult big Swiss climbs on limestone. The upper part of the face needs to be dry otherwise verglas can be a problem. A good selection of pitons should be taken as well as nuts and ice-screws. See also photo 46

From Grosse Scheidegg follow Route 38 to the first terrace. Traverse R towards 2 pillars and climb between them to a belay (IV-V). Follow a chimney on the L to the top of the pillar (bolt belay). Climb the face on the L by a 10m vertical crack (bridging) then another crack on the R to a niche and bolt belay (VI–, A1-A2).

Climb the chimney going up Rwards (IV-V) then from the first terrace, continue further R to below the next step. Climb this at its lowest point going straight up at first then by a crack going L to a belay at the top (VI, A1). Keeping to the L on slabs reach the next step. Traverse 100m L to a chimney which is below the most westerly pillar in the centre of the face. Climb the chimney in 2 pitches (VI, A1) and the following step to the foot of the pillar.

Now climb a chimney (1 pitch) to a belay on the L edge of the pillar (V+, VI). From the belay keep to the edge for 10m (V) then via the chimney reach the next belay. The last few metres are quite trying (VI). Continue in the back of the chimney (2 pitches) to the top of the pillar (VI, V+). Traverse a long way R on a ledge (about 200m) to an overhang (bivouac site). Climb straight up over the overhang to a belay in a chimney (A3, A2, V+ and VI). Continue further up the chimney (VI) to the next belay (bolt). Traverse 10m R then over ledges to another belay (III, IV). Now a vertical pitch finishes with a crack (V+, A1).

Keep to the crest for 1 pitch, vertical at first then up L to easy ground (IV, III). Climb a further 3 pitches Lwards towards the large pinnacle 40m L of the final chimney (II/III with bits of IV). Descend 10m and traverse horizontally L to the foot of a chimney. Climb this on the L edge then in the back to a belay (VI, A2). Keep in the chimney to a niche (VI) – again a trying few metres. The chimney becomes less steep and wider and leads to a bifurcation (IV, V). Keep in the L branch to the next belay on the NE ridge of the mountain (V, VI–). Gain the summit in 4-5 pitches more or less on the ridge all the way (IV, V). About 25hr

40 **NORTH FACE AND NORTH-EAST FLANK**
TD N Finzi, J Biner and J Knubel, 10 Sept 1929
47

The first climb on the face but still a serious undertaking, having all the characteristics of a N face route. Route finding is not particularly easy.

From Grosse Scheidegg follow Route 38 to the large terrace at the top of the first step and then traverse L to a scree cone and snow patch. Move up R, passing a short step, to the edge of the first terrace (III). Follow the terrace a long way R over inclined slabs. Climb over 2 steps (III) to reach a long, horizontal gorge. Follow this easily to its W end and surmount a step by a chimney on the L or on the R to reach the second terrace at about 2700m.

Follow this terrace back L (E), descending a little, before climbing up to a higher terrace below some impressive yellow pillars which form the boundary between the N and NE faces. Keep going L, crossing a gorge, to the almost vertical NE ridge (all this is easy). Climb Lwards in a stepped chimney (III) then up a steep wall on poor holds to a ledge belay (crux of the climb, IV with 2 bits of IV+, very exposed). Another pitch in a dièdre (IV) leads to easier ground. Follow a ramp of broken rock L to a ledge leading R into a large amphitheatre. Move up this and get onto a shoulder abutting the NE ridge (some III). Continue by short steps and couloirs on the NE face to the summit (III). This last section may have some snow or ice cover. About 12 hr

41 **NORTH-EAST PILLAR**
TD+ M Epp and J Talbot, Aug 1963
41

The pillar forms the E edge of the N and NE faces of the mountain and rises in 5 steps to a snowy fore-summit. The rock on the steep steps is generally good but loose rock is to be found on the sloping interconnecting

terrain. In places the limestone forms characteristic, tile-like slabs inclined to the N. These can be very difficult when wet or verglassed, and the climb should not be attempted in these conditions. The terrain through which the route passes gives the climb a certain grandeur, and a feeling of commitment to the alpinist, although it is possible to escape from the route below the fourth step. See also photo 47

From Grosse Scheidegg descend E to a snowfield below the ravine of the Hengstera torrent. Climb easily up the L side of the ravine and then cross R towards a massive area of slabs. Now climb about 40m and then, by delicate slabs and small steps (V), move up Lwards to the foot of an 8m wall. Climb this by the edge above the ravine (V). Move up L easily to the start of a line of weakness in the yellowish rock. Climb this line for 20m then traverse R 6m to a belay on a slab. Next climb up L (V, piton) to reach easier ground. Climb straight up to a chimney and climb this (IV) and some short rock steps (III) to the crest of the pillar.

The second step is started just R of the crest. Climb a crack up a stepped wall (60m, V) to a big dièdre in the tower. Fine climbing up the dièdre for 25m (V) then reach a line of weakness 20m to the L. On the L edge of this line of weakness climb straight up (V) to the top of the step. The next tower, 40m high, is avoided on the L or R to a gap from where a vertical crack (V+) is climbed to the top of the step. Water can be obtained here from the glacier, and an escape can be made across the Hengsteren glacier to the Wellhornsattel.

The imposing fourth step is climbed mainly by its crest. Start a few metres L at a niche below the ridge. Climb a crack for 45m to an obvious notch in the crest (V). Keep to the crest for 15m (V+) and then climb up to a small roof (V–, V+) before moving R (3 bolts, A1). Follow slabs trending L (V+) then a crack to get back onto the crest. Climb to a niche, then over an overhang on the crest (V) and finally the L side of the crest to the top of the step.

The next step is also climbed on the crest which is reached by slabs and cracks on the L (IV-V). This is the fore-summit and the end of the difficulties. Follow the ridge (II-III) and the snow/ice slope to the pinnacled ridge joining the Wetterhorn to the Scheideggwetterhorn. 10-13hr

42 **DESCENT TO THE GLECKSTEIN HUT**
46 First ascent party
AD

From the summit traverse the towers of the SE ridge to reach the lowest point in the ridge (3370m) (II-III with one bit of IV and some abseiling). From the gap descend the couloir leading to the Gutz glacier and reverse Route 36 to the hut. 2½-3hr

Wellhorn 3191.6m

E Von Fellenberg with C Almer and P Egger, 31 July 1866

This mountain along with the Klein Wellhorn forms an impressive rock wall overlooking the Rosenlaui glacier. It is frequently climbed from the Dossen hut by the E ridge (PD+)

43 **TRAVERSE VIA THE NORTH-EAST RIDGE**
AD+ G Bell with U and H Fuhrer, 12 July 1902
45

A magnificent climb with a remote feel to it. Normally climbed in conjunction with the Kl Wellhorn whose S summit is turned on the S face.

From the N summit of the Kl Wellhorn climb about 100m down the S face to a grassy terrace. The last 10m is III+ (or abseil). From the terrace climb diagonally across the S face of the S summit towards the gap to the S, this being reached by a rocky step.

Follow the interconnecting ridge to the first step of the NE ridge where a grey slabby pitch is climbed on the L. The next pitch follows a curving crack and leads to a gendarmed section of ridge. Climb these direct with one abseil (or IV–). Keep on over slabs to the next step which is climbed by a slab on the E side (or more sportingly to the R of the edge). Continue over a level section of the ridge, a snow or scree slope and a few humps to a gap below the third step.

Climb short vertical steps on good holds, at first by a crack, then a chimney (piton, III+), to the summit slopes of rock and snow (possible cornice). 4-5hr

Descend the E ridge until above the lower of 2 terraces on the SE face. Climb down to the terrace via limestone slabs and traverse onto the glacier. On the glacier head S, then in a wide arc to the L reach the col below Pt 3032, N of Dossen. Keep on the E side of the ridge to the Dossen hut. About 2½hr

Klein Wellhorn North Summit 2685.5m

C Freeman and H Bowen with H and S Zurflüh, 7 Aug 1893

The peak lies to the NE of the Wellhorn and has a fine SE wall overlooking the Rosenlaui glacier. The rock on this face is good, and it supports some fine modern routes as well as one worthwhile one in the '50s style. Just N and below the Läsisattel are some fine looking pillars of rock that can be clearly seen from the valley road. These may well be worth a visit on an off day.

44 **NORTH FLANK AND NORTH-EAST RIDGE**
PD+ First ascent party
45

The easiest route on the mountain. Used for descent and in combination with Route 43 for a traverse of the two peaks. Despite many traces of track and cairns the route is not easy to follow in poor visibility, especially in descent.

From Rosenlaui or Schwarzwaldalp take a path to Scheenenbielalp (1673m). Keep to a track on the R side of the stream, going WSW to the W end of a rock outcrop at the top of a grassy slope. By traces of track climb L across a steep, slaty slope and then continue in the same general direction past an avalanche couloir (path is exposed in places but is more obvious) to a saddle on the N ridge (the Läsisattel). The last part of this is almost horizontal. 1hr

Grassy slopes lead in about 20min to a rock step which is avoided on the L. Continue on the NE flank towards the first steep rise in the terrain (45min). Keep to the R of this and, when above it, move up L, crossing a distinct gully, before climbing a system of gullies and couloirs to an obvious horizontal break leading L. From the extreme L edge of this climb straight up to a small gap. On the S side of the gap climb up to the NE ridge via ribs and couloirs (some III–) and then follow the ridge to some grassy steps leading across the SE flank (traces of track). Climb for about 150m parallel to the ridge before regaining it a little way below the summit. 2-3hr, 4-5hr in all

45 **SOUTH-EAST FACE**
TD– E Reiss and D Reist, 15 July 1950
45

A fine climb in impressive surroundings. Although the difficulties are never severe the line is not particularly easy to follow and should not be undertaken lightly. About 600m of climbing.

From Rosenlaui take the route to the Dossen hut (Route H11) as far as the bridge crossing the Rosenlaui gorge. Keep on a good path on the W side to reach the foot of the lateral moraine N of the Rosenlaui glacier. Climb to the top of the moraine and traverse L for about 200m (debris-covered rock) to a rock niche. 1½hr

Move up L for 50m to the start of a steep couloir cutting through the lower wall of the face from R to L (III). Climb the couloir for 2 pitches to a stony niche (IV, IV+) and then, via a crack, reach a grassy terrace on the L (III, IV). Climb another 20m and then traverse L for 1 pitch to a grass ledge (exposed, III, IV). Now climb straight up at first, then Rwards to the start of some slabs that lead Lwards to the foot of a pillar. Climb 1 pitch up the R edge of the slabs (IV) to a belay on turf ledges.

Traverse L along the bottom edge of the pillar and make a 20m abseil from a flake into a grassy niche. Next climb Lwards to a large terrace at the foot of a deep gorge. Climb the gorge easily for several pitches until it steepens and narrows. As soon as possible get onto the crest of the pillar on the R by a system of vague cracks (III) then follow the ridge directly for several more pitches to a large platform (III, IV).

On mixed rock and grass climb first L then R (III) to a cave (route book). 2 more pitches trending R (III) lead to a system of cracks. Climb straight up to some large blocks (IV then III) then up an obvious dièdre which leads R to a grass ramp below the summit rocks. Climb these direct to the top. 4-7hr from the foot of the face

See the rock climbing section of the guide-book for other routes on this face.

Lauteraarsattel 3125m

J Berger and M Girard, July or Aug 1842

A magnificent glacier pass between the Nässihorn and the Bärglistock, linking the Lauteraar glacier to the SE with the Oberer Grindelwald glacier to the NW. The approach route from the Gleckstein hut has been made safer and easier to follow by the construction of a new path. There is a good bivouac site at the pass.

46 **FROM THE NORTH-WEST**
PD M Bannholzer and J Jaun, 31 Aug 1844

From the Gleckstein hut descend a little to the path heading towards Beesibärgli and take the R fork (red and white waymarking). The path descends gradually to reach the edge of a big gully. Go down into the gully (cable and man made steps). This is the lowest point and there follows an ascent of moraine, scree and grass to a band of rock which has a fixed cable to aid its crossing. At this point the old route is joined at about 1hr from the hut. Continue climbing steadily before finally reaching a track descending gradually R to a terrace close to the glacier just below Pt 2662m. 2hr

Climb the the easy angled but very crevassed glacier to the flat upper part below the col. Climb up to the col passing between or to the L of 2 rocky areas (steep). 2hr, 4-5hr in all

47 **FROM THE SOUTH-EAST**

F First ascent party

From the Lauteraar hut descend (fixed cables etc) SW to the Unteraar glacier and climb this WNW keeping close to the central moraine. Continue up the Lauteraar glacier and the steep and crevassed upper slopes to the bergschrund. This can be very wide and the crossing point varies from year to year. If it can't be crossed directly below the col it may be possible further R (E). Snow or ice lead to the col. 4-5hr

Lauteraarsattel and Unders Studerjoch to the Aletsch Glacier and Jungfraujoch

In this section are found some of the major peaks of the Oberland, amongst them several exceeding the 'magic' 4000m mark. Not only are the mountains high but they are also relatively remote. It is not such an easy task here to 'tick off' peaks in the way that one might do in the Valais. Even to get close to some of the peaks involves considerable effort. The highest peak in the Oberland, but not the best known – the Finsteraarhorn – is in this section as is the Lauteraarhorn. Amongst the 4000m peaks in the Alps they must rank with peaks like the Dent d'Herens and the Aiguille Blanche de Peuterey in terms of difficulty of access although not in terms of difficulty in climbing.

Not only are the mountains high but the glacier system is massive, the Aletsch glacier being the longest in the Alps. Most climbs in the section require a good deal of commitment and good luck with the weather for a successful outcome. Given good conditions several days at a time can be profitably spent high in the mountains, traversing peaks and moving from hut to hut; or if you simply wish to enjoy the mountain environment and not climb, hut to hut tours via the glacier system and interconnecting cols can be very satisfying.

Maps covering this section are: Jungfrau (264) and Interlaken (254)

Strahlegghorn 3461.2m

Blanckley, F Schuster with P Baumann, C Bernet and 2 other guides, 14 Aug 1888

An unimportant summit but an excellent view point, probably worthwhile climbing if higher peaks are out of condition.

48 **TRAVERSE VIA SOUTH FLANK, SOUTH-WEST RIDGE**
PD **AND NORTH RIDGE**

S flank and SW ridge: K Struve with P Ogi, 20 Aug 1907

From the Schreckhorn hut follow Route 64 almost to Pt 2922m. Before reaching this point turn more or less N and climb the snow slopes to gain the SW ridge near Pt 3174m. Keep on the ridge to the summit. 4-5hr

Descend the N ridge easily to the Strahlegg Pass and reverse Route 49 to the hut.

Strahlegg Pass c3340m

R Meyer with A Abbühl and K Huber, 3 Sept 1812

A high pass providing the easiest high level crossing between Grindelwald and the Grimsel Pass and access to the Schreckhorn from the Aar bivouac. It is steep on the E side and descent of this side should be avoided in the afternoon.

49 **FROM THE WEST**

F From the Schreckhorn hut follow the track to the site of the old Strahlegg hut across moraine and snow patches (1hr). A good track leads steeply up into the coombe to the E and is followed to an easy angled rock ridge. Climb it to a snowy shoulder at about 3200m. Head up now to the foot of a rock ridge descending SW from Pt 3428m and, keeping to the R (S) of this ridge, reach the col by less steep slopes. 2hr, 3hr in all.

50 **FROM THE EAST**

PD From the Aar bivouac descend to the Strahlegg glacier and climb up to the top of the central moraine. Follow this for about 500m before descending onto the clean glacier on the L. Keep more or less in the centre of the glacier, and where it begins to steepen turn NW to reach the bergschrund at the foot of the snow couloir leading to the col. Cross it where practicable (often on the R) then climb the couloir, crossing some loose rock/scree on the R near the top. 3hr

Lauteraarhorn 4042m

E Desor, A Escher and C Girard with M Bannholzer, D Brigger, Fahner, J Leuthold and J Madutz, 8 Aug 1842

Along with its twin, the Schreckhorn, this forms a most impressive sight from just about every aspect. It is one of the more difficult 4000ers to climb on account of its remoteness, the approach to its base from any direction being a lengthy undertaking. The building of the Aar bivouac hut has increased its popularity and it is frequently ascended from here. The mountain has three ridges on which much of the rock is bad except for the top 100m or thereabouts. Consequently good rock is found on the NW ridge (Lauteraargrat) linking it with the Schreckhorn.

51 **SOUTH FACE COULOIR AND SOUTH-EAST RIDGE**

AD– First ascent party

48 *This is the ordinary route on the mountain and the means of a fairly quick*

ascent if conditions are favourable, but there is little to recommend it apart from the last 100m or so of climbing on the SE ridge. Since the route is S facing the snow quickly softens and this can make descent a problem. There is also avalanche danger after fresh snow (it was the scene of a major accident in the mid 1980s). Wet snow-slides down the face are frequent and the runnels made by these should be avoided if the snow is at all soft. In such circumstances it is better to avoid the face and keep to the shattered rock crest on its W side either in ascent or descent.

From the Aar bivouac descend to the glacier and climb to the crest of the central moraine. Walk up this for about 500m then descend to the L onto bare ice. Continue up the glacier, over a crevassed zone, to the foot of a triangular snow slope below the couloir (1½hr). Climb the slope and the rock band above it to another snow slope, then another rock band above that to reach the foot of a broad snowfield. Climb this trending L towards a narrow couloir. Climb this (steeper) and the snow slopes above, now keeping to the L, to finish on the ridge on the L just below a large gendarme on the SE ridge. Climb snow on the L of the gendarme to get onto the SE ridge at a gap beside the gendarme (it is also possible to gain the SE ridge on the R of the gendarme and traverse it to reach the same point). 2½-3hr

Superb rock scrambling leads to the summit in about 30min. About 4½-5hr in all

In descent it is possible to follow the ridge on the W side of the face to the foot of the narrow couloir mentioned in the ascent. Below this point the snow is easier angled and less dangerous when soft than on the higher slopes.

52

TD–

48

SOUTH-WEST RIDGE

A Rubi and Miss M O'Brien, ca 1930

The ridge rises in 3 distinct sections from the Strahlegg Pass. The first of these is fairly straightforward and fairly level. The next is rather loose and is steeper but still quite easy. The last section of about 300m is the 'raison d'être' of the climb. Here the rock is good and steep although the difficulties are not excessive. Not often climbed.

From the Schreckhorn hut or Aar bivouac follow Routes 49 or 50 to the Strahlegg Pass (3hr). From the pass climb towards Pt 3428m and reach the start of the ridge. Follow it without any real difficulty, mainly on its W flank until the ridge loses itself in the W flank of the first big step. Now climb gradually Rwards for 3 pitches up steep but fairly loose ground to regain the ridge. Now keep to the ridge as far as the foot of the steep third section where the difficult climbing begins.

A few metres L of the ridge climb a chimney/crack system for 1 pitch (IV, V). Get back onto the ridge and continue to a shoulder below the final steep section and directly below the summit. Traverse L for 10m, then up to reach a crack on the L. Climb this and join another crack on the R which leads back to the ridge. Climb the last step direct to the summit (V). 5hr from the Strahlegg Pass.

53
AD+
48

SOUTH-WEST RIDGE, SOUTH FACE AND SOUTH-EAST RIDGE

G Lammer solo, 3 Aug 1885

The most direct route from the Schreckhorn hut, it avoids the difficulties of the SW ridge and enjoys the best part of the S face couloir route. Not particularly pleasant.

From the Schreckhorn hut follow Rt 52 to the foot of the third section of the SW ridge. From here traverse across the S face below the steep summit wall, at first descending a short couloir and then crossing ribs and couloirs as far as an easy but loose couloir which leads up to the SE ridge. Follow this as for Route 51 to the summit. About 7hr

In descent the point at which the S face traverse is started is not easy to find if you have not already climbed this way. It is worth descending the ridge to the E of the loose couloir until you can see the shoulder on the SW ridge. The traverse across the face is at the height of the shoulder. In this way you should avoid a tempting higher traverse line which disappears into difficult terrain.

54
D+
50

NORTH-WEST (LAUTERAAR) RIDGE

H Kuntze with P and R Bernet, 24 July 1902 and on the same day G Bell with H and U Fuhrer

The climb is described from the Schrecksattel but is probably best combined with an ascent of the SW ridge and a descent of the SE ridge of the Schreckhorn (Routes 57 and 56) to make a magnificent, but lengthy traverse of the twin peaks. The ridge itself is saw-toothed with many small gendarmes. Since both flanks of the ridge are loose it is advisable to keep the crest over all the obstacles.

From the Schrecksattel (3914m) follow the crest as closely as possible all the way. The most difficult step is a 4-5m high tower which lies between the first and second steeper parts of the ridge. This is climbed either on the L or the R side (III+). 4-5hr

55 D+ 50

BY THE EAST-NORTH-EAST RIDGE OF POINT 4011m

W Baumgartner and H Schneider, 2 Aug 1907

This is a fine remote climb on good gneiss which is rather delicate if it is not free from snow. From Pt 4011m the summit is easily reached.

From the Lauteraar hut climb the Lauteraar glacier by Route 47 to the level of the foot of the ridge. Get onto Pt 2995.2m by rock or snow from the L. Now continue easily on snow to about 3450m. Get onto the rock ridge ahead from the L and follow it, making short deviations to the L to the top of a rock triangle. Keep to the crest from here to Pt 4011m. Keep to the crest of the NW ridge to reach the summit of the mountain. 10-12hr

Schreckhorn 4078m

L Stephen, C and P Michel and U Almer, 4 Aug 1861

A splendid mountain whose summit is much sought after. Unlike most of the Lauteraarhorn, its close neighbour, the rock is of excellent quality. It also supports a very fine snow/ice route on its N face.

56 AD+ 49

VIA THE SCHRECKSATTEL AND EAST-SOUTH-EAST RIDGE

E Von Fellenberg with P Michel, P Inäbnit and P Egger, 4 Aug 1864

This was at one time the normal route but it is rarely climbed these days, partly on account of lack of snow in the couloirs below the sattel, partly because of the difficulty in crossing the bergschrund and also the difficulty of climbing the Elliottswengli on the SE ridge. Below the sattel the route is exposed to stonefall and snow-slides (especially in descent). It is described here as a means (when conditions allow) of reaching the Schrecksattel in order to climb the NW ridge of the Lauteraarhorn. The ESE ridge is described in descent for the combined Schreckhorn – Lauteraarhorn traverse. See also photos 48 and 50

From the Schreckhorn hut follow Rt 57 to the foot of the couloir leading to the Schrecksattel (3½-4hr). Cross the bergschrund and climb the snow slope into the couloir. Climb Rwards on a rock buttress, which is easy, as far as the bend in the couloir. Now follow the couloir back L to the sattel. 1½-2hr

To descend from the Schreckhorn summit by the ESE ridge follow the ridge to a fore-summit to the SE then follow the ridge crest on good rock to a small gap at the start of a steeper section that has a number of small gendarmes along it. These are passed on the L (N) side on steep snow or ice (Elliottswengli – named after J Elliott who fell from here in July 1869). There are several pitons in place. The ridge then leads easily down to the Schrecksattel. 1½-2hr

57 **SOUTH-WEST RIDGE**

D– J Wicks, E Bradby and C Wilson, 26 July 1902

49 *This climb has become established as the normal way up and down the mountain. It is probably one of the best ordinary routes on a 4000m peak. It can equally well be climbed from the Schreckhorn hut or the Aar bivouac. See also photo 48*

From the Schreckhorn hut follow Route 49 towards the Strahlegg Pass. A little way before the pass a long rib of rock, originating at Pt 3428m, terminates at a snow slope at about 3200m. Pass to the L (N) of this rib and traverse horizontally NE on a snow or ice slope (care) to reach the N foot of Pt 3428m. Move up into the glacier bay of the Schreckfirn and keeping to the R to avoid crevasses gain height before curving round to the foot of the big couloir in the S face. 3½-4hr

From the Aar bivouac follow Route 50 to the Strahlegg Pass. From the pass descend a little way to the W and as soon as possible cross the rocky rib on the R. This gets you onto the snow/ice traverse leading to the N foot of Pt 3428m mentioned above. Same time

The route continues up the long ramp leading to the obvious shoulder on the SW ridge. Cross the bergschrund at the foot of the couloir (the position varies from year to year) and contour round rock ribs to the snowy foot of the ramp. In very snowy conditions it is possible to climb the snow slope to the shoulder but usually it is better to climb the rock to the L of this. This is all solid gneiss with short pitches of II. 1½-2hr

From the shoulder keep more or less to the crest of the ridge (with only occasional deviations from it) on good rock (bit of III), with just one short section of scree, to the fore-summit. Descend to a gap, sometimes delicate snow, before climbing easily to the main summit. 1½-2hr, about 7hr in all

In descent a lot of the ridge can be abseiled (slings in place) but beware of snagging ropes. In good conditions (rare) below the shoulder descend the snow slope, otherwise keep to the rock on its R. Take care crossing the (traverse) slope below Pt 3428m. 4-6hr

It is inadvisable to descend to the Aar bivouac late in the day as the descent from the Strahlegg Pass can be very unpleasant and dangerous if the snow is soft.

58 **SOUTH PILLAR**

D+ H Kocher, P Luzuy, R Perrenoud and P Girardin, 24 July 1955

49 *This is a brilliant high mountain rock climb, certainly the best route on the mountain and one of the best in the Alps. It clears quickly after bad weather and is objectively safe. It is mainly III and IV with short crux sections of V. Most of the pitches have in situ pitons. It follows the pillar immediately L (W) of the long couloir descending the entire length of the face. About 600m of climbing. See also photo 48*

From the Schreckhorn hut or the Aar bivouac follow Route 57 to the bergschrund. Cross it and head for the rocks on the L (true R bank) of the snow couloir. Climb the rocks and sometimes snow patches easily (II) to the foot of a striking pillar with an overhang at the start.

Avoid the overhang by a couloir on the R and climb this to a slabby buttress. Climb the buttress for about 100m to where it becomes vertical. Traverse R on a narrow ledge to reach a parallel buttress which is climbed by a dièdre as far as an overhang. Go under the overhang into a couloir and climb this to a terrace below a steep wall (all this is III and IV).

Move L for 20m and climb directly up to the start of a steep dièdre/crack. Climb this for 30m to a niche below a roof (V). Move up R on a steep, smooth wall (V) and reach the crest of the pillar on the R. Climb a smooth 5m slab with 2 thin cracks (V), and then straight up for 2 pitches to a horizontal ledge at the foot of a smooth rib (III). Avoid this by a steep chimney on the R which leads back to the ridge. Climb the last step direct (IV) and descend into a gap from which easy rock leads to the fore-summit. 5-6hr from the bergschrund

59 **NORTH-WEST (ANDERSON) RIDGE**

AD+ J Anderson and G Baker with U Almer and A Pollinger, 7 Aug 1883

50 *Yet another good climb, quite different in character to the SW ridge. It is narrow and rises in short steps for more than half its length and then,*

after a short steep section, leans back at a gentle angle. The situations are superb and the rock is good, the only drawback is the long approach. It can be climbed from the Gleckstein hut, the Lauteraarhorn hut or the Schreckhorn hut. The latter provides the shortest approach, but the couloir that has to be climbed has become progressively less pleasant in recent years as the snow cover has decreased. It is as well to check locally on conditions before attempting this approach.

From the Lauteraarsattel (possible bivouac), reached by Route 46 or 47, follow the ridge SW over rotten rock steps to Pt 3311m. Continue on the ridge and then by steep snow slopes to the Nässijoch (3733m). 2½hr

From the Schreckhorn hut go E along the base of the rocks of Schwarzegg, on a vague track in the moraine, to a scree/avalanche cone at the foot of the couloir leading up towards the Schreckhorn. Climb the couloir (stone and icefall danger) and where it curves L, follow it round onto the small glacier on the W side of the Nässijoch (3hr). Now climb the glacier Nwards to its upper edge and then either by snow or a steep rock buttress climb direct to the Nässijoch (some danger of falling stone and ice). 2hr, about 5hr in all

From the col follow the fine snow crest to the N foot of the ridge proper. Climb the first step direct, or turn it on the L, to reach a gap. Keep to the crest now (less steep) over short steps and gendarmes to an almost horizontal section of the ridge which becomes a snow crest towards the foot of the last rise. Climb this steeply but easily over large blocks and short steps until an easing of the angle. Keep to the crest now to the summit. 2-3hr from the Nässijoch

60 NORTH FACE DIRECT

TD+ H and A Schelbert, 1980

50 *The route climbs onto the snow/ice terrace at the foot of the face up the ice wall. The first ascent party encountered 80° ice although this is very variable from year to year as is its height (c100m).*

From the Gleckstein or Lauteraar huts reach the foot of the face as for Route 61. Climb direct to the terrace and continue more straightforwardly up the slopes beyond to the summit. 5-10hr from the foot of the face

61 NORTH FACE CLASSIC ROUTE

TD+ I and J Taguchi with S Brawand and C Kaufmann, 25 Aug 1928

50 *The face is 600m high and averages 50°. It is one of the great mixed*

routes in the Bernese Oberland, the lower part being on snow/ice and the upper third on difficult, broken rock. Because of its easterly aspect it catches the sun early, and so requires a much harder frost than most N face routes to make it safe. The climb has a feeling of isolation about it.

Reach the foot of the face from the Gleckstein or Lauteraar huts by Route 59 towards the Nässijoch (from the latter hut it may not be necessary to climb up to the Lauteraarsattel before turning L to reach the face). Get onto the snow/ice terrace above the lower ice wall by climbing the NE rib, and then take a line slanting gently R towards the summit. According to conditions, either climb direct to the summit or exit onto the interconnecting ridge between the SE fore-summit and the summit. 10-12 hr from either hut

62 **NORTH-EAST RIB**
D+ W and P Pendlebury with P Baumann and P Kaufmann,
50 11 July 1873

A fine but neglected route. A splendid achievement by the first ascent party considering the date it was done.

From the Gleckstein or Lauteraar huts follow Route 61 to the snow/ice terrace but instead of setting foot on the terrace continue up the ridge to the SE fore-summit. 10-12hr from either hut

Klein Schreckhorn 3494m

E Anderson with C Almer and P Bohren, 7 Aug 1857

A good view point but otherwise a modest summit.

63 **NÄSSI GLACIER AND SOUTH-EAST RIDGE**
PD Miss Brevoort and W Coolidge with C and U Almer, 4 June 1875 but descended earlier

From the Schreckhorn hut descend the path towards Grindelwald for a few minutes, then climb grass and scree slopes, with traces of path, under the W flank of the Schwarzegg ridge to reach the Nässi glacier. Slant L up the glacier and get onto a lower tier further N which slopes up towards the summit of the Kl Schreckhorn (both parts of the glacier can be quite crevassed). Avoid some séracs on the L and above these get into and climb a short couloir (rock or snow) leading to the foot of the SE ridge. The rock ridge leads easily to the summit. 4-4½hr

Finsteraarjoch 3293m

H George with C Almer, 28 July 1862

A high pass between the Obers Ischmeer and the Finsteraar glacier. It offers an alternative route between Grindelwald and the Grimsel Pass to the crossing of the Strahlegg Pass. It also provides, with the Agassizjoch, a means of connecting the Schreckhorn and Finsteraarhorn huts. It compares in grandeur with the Lauteraarsattel.

64 PD **FROM THE NORTH-WEST**

From the Schreckhorn hut follow Route 49 to the site of the old Strahlegg hut. From the rocks to the SSE of here get onto snow slopes leading towards Pt 2922m and follow them passing just below this point. According to conditions pass below or above the next rock island and then, by steep slopes, reach more level ground to the W of Pt 3454m (Alte Strahlegg). Turn S and cross the glacier below Pt 3468.7m to the pass. 3½hr

65 PD/D **FROM THE SOUTH-EAST**

The difficulty on this side depends on the state of the crevasses.

From the Aar bivouac head S across the Finsteraar glacier to the foot of the NE ridge of the Studerhorn. Climb up under its N face, avoiding the first sérac zone to the S, before turning NW and reaching the upper glacier to the L of the second sérac zone. Pass below the Agassizjoch and reach the pass with no further difficulty. 3-4hr

Studerhorn 3638m

R Lindt and G Studer with J and K Blatter and P Sulzer, 5 Aug 1864

An unremarkable mountain from the S but possessing an attractive N face which is frequently climbed. From the summit there are fine views of the Finsteraarhorn, Lauteraarhorn and Schreckhorn.

66 F 53 **TRAVERSE VIA ALTMANN**

A pleasant and undemanding outing from the Oberaarjoch hut. See also photo 52

From the hut descend to the col and walk down the Studer glacier until level with the foot of the rocks on the R. Turn N and climb easily up to the col between the Oberaarhorn and Altmann.

Traverse the E ridge of the latter to the summit, avoiding the first step on the S flank. Easy snow slopes lead to a col. Continue, still on snow, to a second col (Unders Studerjoch) before climbing to the summit of the Studerhorn up easy snow slopes with the odd steeper step. 3hr

From the summit walk down the NW ridge and descend onto the Studer glacier a little way before reaching the Obers Studerjoch. Descend the easy angled glacier to join Route 71 and return to the hut. 2hr, about 5hr in all

67 **SOUTH RIDGE**
PD+ C and M Blum, 9 Sept 1980
53

A short climb direct to the summit from the Studer glacier. More sporting than the traverse.

From the Oberaarjoch hut follow the Studer glacier to the foot of the ridge. Start at a little snowy bay just on the R then keep to the ridge (III) which is a bit loose in places. 3hr

68 **NORTH FACE**
TD– P Bonnant and Miss L Boulaz, 1 Aug 1940. Winter: H Lussy,
51 W Manz and W Stoll, 2/3 Jan 1970

The face is 600m high and reaches 58° at its steepest. Often climbed.

From the Aar bivouac follow Route 65 to the foot of the face. Start up the face on the R of the lower sérac band and work back L towards the middle of the face. The exact line of ascent will then depend on the state of the séracs in the upper part of the face. It is usual to pass these on the R and avoid the summit cornice on the R also. 5-8hr

69 **NORTH-EAST RIDGE**
PD+ A Moore and H Walker with M and J Anderegg, 24 June 1872
51

Not often climbed but the easiest way of reaching the Oberaarjoch hut from the Aar bivouac,

From the Aar bivouac cross the Finsteraar glacier and climb up into the glacier bay round the E foot of the ridge. Traverse R onto the ridge where it levels out above the steep lower part. Continue on the ridge to the summit. 4-5hr

Gemschlicke 3335m

R Meyer with a shepherd, 25 July 1812

A pass at the foot of the SE ridge of the Finsteraarhorn, much favoured in summer as a route between the Oberaarjoch and Finsteraarhorn huts. It is not very pleasant on the W side, especially in ascent.

It is possible to climb the Finsteraarrothorn by its NW ridge from the col. PD, bits of II, 1hr

70 **FROM THE WEST**

F

From the Finsteraarhorn hut descend the L bank of the Fiescher glacier to the foot of a coombe below and SW of the col. Climb up loose slopes to the foot of a steep couloir, about 150m high, which leads to the col. Climb the couloir direct or the rock rib to the S of it. 1½hr

71 **FROM THE EAST**

F

From the Oberaarjoch hut traverse the Studer glacier and climb easy snow slopes to the col. 1hr

Finsteraarhorn 4273.9m

Possibly: R Meyer with A Volker, J Bortis, and A Abbühl, 16 Aug 1812 although they may only have reached a fore-summit. Most likely: J Leuthold and J Währen, 10 Aug 1829.

The highest point in the Bernese Oberland. A remote and magnificent peak from any angle, easily picked out in distant views from other parts of the Alps. It has an impressive, high and rocky E flank and a fine, long SE ridge. The ordinary route is popular in both spring (ski touring parties) and summer.

72 **SOUTH-WEST RIDGE**

AD V Fynn and W Murphy, 15 Aug 1892

54

The ridge can be climbed from its foot but it is more usual to start it at the point where it is crossed by Route 73.

From the Finsteraarhorn hut follow Route 73 to the col in the SW ridge at 3616m. Now follow the ridge to the foot of the last 100m high step which is climbed direct. 5hr

73 **SOUTH-WEST FLANK AND NORTH-WEST RIDGE**

PD J Leuthold and J Währen, 10 Aug 1829. Winter: E Boss and

54 U Almer, 8 March 1887

The ordinary route, rather exposed above the Hugisattel. See also photo 55

From the Finsteraarhorn hut climb a steep track (rather loose) to just above Pt 3231.3m. Climb the glacier Nwards (crevasses) towards the middle part of the SW ridge. Get onto this at a rocky projection into the glacier and so reach the col at Pt 3616m via rubble slopes. Traverse more or less horizontally from the col onto the slopes beyond, which are climbed to the Hugisattel.

The route now follows the NW ridge to the summit but at the start it is normal to keep on the SW flank over mixed rock and snow (II). Once on the ridge avoid obstacles on their W side. 4-5hr, 2hr in descent

74 **NORTH-WEST RIDGE**

PD/D G Foster with H Baumann and P Bernet, 28 July 1868

55

The NW ridge can be climbed in its entirety from the Agassizjoch. It is quite difficult when verglassed. See also photo 54

From the Agassizjoch climb the first rock step on the crest or on the SW side with no particular difficulty. The next step is generally snow and leads to the Hugisattel where Route 73 is joined. 3-4 hr to the summit

75 **NORTH-EAST RIB**

ED1 A and F Rubi with Miss M O'Brien, 3 Sept 1930. Winter: P Etter,

55 U Gantenbein, A and E Scherrer, 21/22 Dec 1970

The whole of the E flank of the mountain is interspersed with ribs and couloirs. This climb takes the most northerly and longest of the ribs, starting from the Finsteraar glacier. It is 1000m high, becoming steeper towards the top where it merges into the face, and is mostly rock with two important sections, the Red and the Grey Tower. There is a good deal of route choice on much of the climb and the Grey Tower can be avoided on the L (G Hasler and F Ammatter, 16 July 1904). It should only be attempted after a long spell of fine weather. Some of the rock is loose and stonefall is always a problem. The final slopes are often icy and difficult. Mostly III with several pitches of IV and V.

From the Aar bivouac reach the foot of the rib by Route 65. Turn the first rocks on the R and get onto the rib. Climb good rock to the L side of a triangular wall. From the top of this the rib becomes much more distinct. Climb it by a series of steps and gendarmes (the lowest of which is called the Red Tower) to about 3400m where it eases.

At 3950m reach the Grey Tower, 25m high, which bars progress. Avoid it on the R by a broken ramp followed by a slightly overhanging dièdre leading back to the crest at a pronounced gap. Climb the next, 20m high, smooth step on its L flank then a dièdre, at first slightly overhanging then vertical, to easier ground. Keep on the rib over blocks and short steps to another narrow and smooth rib. Traverse horizontally 40m to the R (delicate) to a couloir which is followed on good rock to an overhang. Climb a secondary rib on the R to where it becomes impassable and get into the couloir on its L. Climb the system of couloirs and grooves to the ridge 60m from the summit. 10-12hr from the foot of the rib

From the start of the 40m traverse the rib has been climbed direct at V+ and VI– (K Glazek and K Zdzitwieckt, 19 Aug 1967).

76 **EAST RIB**

TD O Brügger and H Winterberger with H Kohler, 29 Sept 1929

55

A shorter and much safer route than the NE rib, having excellent rock on all the steep sections, the lower and very unstable part being avoided altogether by starting at the Obers Studerjoch. The rib falls from the summit and bifurcates at about 4000m. The route takes the R-hand rib to this point. Pitches of IV, fairly serious.

From the Oberaarjoch hut climb the Studer glacier to the foot of the rib at a deep couloir which originates at a saddle to the L of the first gendarme on the rib. 2hr

Climb the couloir but leave it as soon as possible on the R (better rock but more difficult) or on the L (loose but easy) and reach the saddle (stonefall danger to here). Climb the rib over a series of gendarmes, all taken direct, to an unclimbable one (shiny gneiss). Avoid it on the L by a dièdre/crack. Above, the rib peters out at a level section into the face above. Climb for one more pitch and then reach another rib on the L, at a gap R of a pointed gendarme, by making a rising traverse on mixed ground to below the gap. Climb direct to the gap via rock, snow and an icy scoop. From the gap climb another series of gendarmes, which can be avoided on the L when too difficult to climb direct, to a few metres from the summit. 8-9hr, 10-11hr from the hut

77 **SOUTH-EAST RIDGE INTEGRAL**

D Meyer's party in 1812 but probably to a fore-summit. First to the

56 summit: H Cordier's party with J Anderegg, 1876. Integral: H Pfändler, F Suter and G Bohren, 9 Aug 1923

The ridge is 2½km long, starting at the Gemschlicke, but can be joined at various points along its length from the W or E sides. Undoubtedly one of the finest ridge climbs in the Oberland if not in the whole of the Alps. The difficulties, where they occur, are on rock which is interspersed with sections of snow. The main problem with the climb is its length, in case of a change in the weather. However, just as it can be joined at various points, so it can be abandoned.

It can be divided into three distinct sections: the first is from the Gemschlicke to a snow col NE of Pt 3604m which is at the top of a hanging glacier on the E side; the next has 3 evenly separated towers and ends on snow N of the last tower above another hanging glacier on the E side; the last climbs steeply to the fore-summit and is then almost horizontal, but jagged, before a last short step to the summit. See also photos 54 and 55.

From the Gemschlicke reach the foot of a 40m high wall by scree slopes on the L or snow slopes on the R. The wall is split from top to bottom by a crack. Start 6m L of this at a parallel but shorter crack which is climbed for 10m before a narrow sloping line L allows the L edge of the wall to be gained. Follow the edge Rwards to a small stony shoulder (mainly II-III). Easier climbing on the ridge with a few, more difficult, gendarmes leads to Pt 3604m. 2½hr

Descend to the snow col beyond. The first tower follows and is climbed on the crest (III, exposed). Make a short descent before traversing a smaller gendarme and reaching the foot of the second tower. Climb this on the R keeping close to the crest (II). 1½hr

Continue along a fine snow crest, with a few rocks protruding, to the top of the third tower. More snow and rocks follow to a distinct steepening from where good rock leads to the fore-summit (4167m). 1½hr

Keep on the crest now (exposed but almost horizontal) over a number of small gendarmes to a snowy gap before the final step. Traverse L onto the W flank and cross a 5m slab on poor holds (III) to reach a steep chimney. Climb this for 12m (III) before moving L onto a snow and rock crest and the summit. 2hr, about 8hr for the ridge.

Alternative approaches to the ridge on the E side are:
1 By the hanging glacier to the col N of Pt 3604m. AD, 2hr
2 By the rib leading to the summit of the second tower. AD, 3½-4½hr
3 By the NE snow slopes of the second tower. AD, 4-4½hr
4 By the rib S of the upper hanging glacier. AD, 4-4½hr

All times are from the Oberaarjoch hut to the ridge

Alternative approaches to the ridge on the W side are:

1 To the col N of Pt 3604m. AD
2 To the gap between the second and third towers. AD
3 The 'Südroute' which joins the ridge between the third tower and the fore-summit:

From the Finsteraarhorn hut follow Route 73 to Pt 3231.3m then climb NE up the glacier to the foot of the SW ridge of the fore-summit. Descending from the SE ridge in the bay on the R of this ridge, are two snow couloirs. Climb the rib between the couloirs to the ridge N of the third tower. AD, 5hr

Agassizjoch 3749m

First recorded crossing NE-SW, J Hornby, T Philpott and F Morshead with C Almer, C Lauener and J Anderegg, 7 July 1866

A high pass connecting the Walliser Fiescherfirn and the Finsteraar glacier. Useful as a means of crossing between the Schreckhorn and Finsteraarhorn huts in conjunction with the Finsteraarjoch, or linking the latter hut with the Aar bivouac.

78 **FROM THE SOUTH-WEST**

F

From the Finsteraarhorn hut climb, after a short descent to the glacier, the L bank of the Walliser Fiescherfirn until below a rock buttress beneath Pt 3406m. Just beyond this climb NE up snow slopes to the col (usually quite crevassed) taking care to keep to the L in the middle part of the climb to avoid possible icefall from the R. 2-2½hr

79 **FROM THE EAST**

AD

This is a straightforward but fairly steep snow/ice slope. There is avalanche danger after fresh snow.

From the Finsteraarjoch (Route 64 to 65) traverse horizontally S to the foot of the snow/ice couloir leading to the col. Coming from the Aar bivouac it is not necessary to go to the Finsteraarjoch. Climb up the middle of the couloir, cross the bergschrund and at about 3500m climb onto rocks on the R side which leads out onto the face of the Agassizhorn. Climb the rocks until about 100m below the ridge then traverse L across snow couloir and climb the rocks on its S side to just above the col. If snow conditions are favourable it is possible to climb the couloir all the way. 2hr

In descent take the second rocky rib to the N of the col; the first one is short and merges with the couloir after a short distance.

Agassizhorn 3953m

W. Coolidge with U Almer and C Inäbnit, 7 Sept 1872

A nice peak but rather overshadowed by its mighty neighbour.

80 **SOUTH-EAST RIDGE**

F First ascent party

From the Finsteraarhorn hut follow Route 78 towards the Agassizjoch. Before reaching the col climb the S flank onto the ridge which leads easily to the summit. 3½hr

81 **NORTH-EAST RIDGE**

TD F Egger and B Lauterberg, 23 July 1913

About 650m of climbing in a remote situation, the first half being quite easy.

From the foot of the ridge, situated between the E foot of the Agassizjoch and the Finsteraarjoch, ascend easily to about mid-height, sometimes on one flank and sometimes the other. Climb over a gendarme and by-pass another on the L to reach a high step. Avoid this by climbing on the NW flank to a level slab. Get back onto the ridge above the step (exposed) and climb it, passing a slim tower on the L. From the gap below the summit rocks, climb direct for 20m (exposed) then slant up L on broken rock.
7-8hr from the start

Strahlhorn 30265.5m

A rocky peak at the S end of the Walliser Fiescherhörner which is gaining some popularity with the opening of hut accommodation at Märjela.

82 **STRAHLGRAT**

PD M. Bruce and A Sloman with J Elsig, 6 Aug 1912

This is the long ridge running due S from Pt 3186.9m and terminating at the Strahlhorn summit. There are several tops on the ridge, all higher than the Strahlhorn itself, and once on the ridge it is actually descended to the Strahlhorn. There are difficulties of II to III on sound rock.

From the Gletscherstuba hut (or Kühboden) follow a track to Märjelewang then head N over meadows and scree slopes to reach the small glacier at the S end of the Walliser Fiescherhörner. Climb the glacier NW to reach a snow saddle on the ridge. Turn SW and follow the crest of the ridge with no particular difficulties over all the summits of the Strahlgrat. It is best to stay on the crest and to avoid the flanks. 4hr

To descend, follow the ridge SSW and then later head SE over grassy slopes to Märjela.

Wannenzwillinge 3481m and 3432m

These are twin peaks on the ridge running S from the Kl Wannenhorn, only the higher one being given a spot height on the map. The E ridges provide some good rock climbing, on granite, in a remote high mountain setting. There is a convenient bivouac by Flesch (Pt 2028.6m) on the W side of the Fiescher glacier. It is also possible to bivouac at about 2550m in the Sulzbach basin reached from Fieschertal; alternatively start at the Burg hut.

83 EAST RIDGE OF POINT 3481M

TD– C Blum and H Grossen, 3 Aug 1975

A good free climb on sound granite. About 600m of climbing.

From the bivouac at Flesch climb the crest of the R hand moraine and then the small glacier below the Kl Wannenhorn to the couloir between the two ridges. Cross the bergschrund (difficult) and about 30m higher leave the couloir and cross grassy ledges to the ridge at a shoulder. Climb the first step on the N side by a couloir/chimney system and slabs (one pitch of IV) back to the ridge. Continue up the ridge (sometimes snow) and climb a gendarme (IV) to attain the foot of a big step.

Climb the first 70m of the step by starting up a dièdre, then climbing a cracked slab just on the N side of the rounded crest. Next make a rising traverse across a 20m steep slab (V) then climb 35m Rwards in a crack (V+, several pitons). More slabs (easier) lead to a diagonal chimney/crack which is climbed (V). At the top traverse to a window. Get back onto the crest by a short crack on the L. Climb an overlap with aid, then straight up (V+) to where a 25m crack (IV+) leads to an easing of the angle. Four more pitches lead to the top (III, IV). 7hr from the foot of the ridge

Descend by the N ridge and the Wannenhorn glacier on the

W side to the Aletsch glacier or, to return to the bivouac, descend the couloir between the ridges (stonefall) and abseil over the bergschrund.

84 EAST RIDGE OF POINT 3432m

D+ P Fähndrick and P Nigg, 18 July 1979

Somewhat easier than the previous route. Most difficulties are about IV with the odd bit of IV+ and V– and long, easier sections.

From the bivouac at Flesch climb up the R hand moraine by its crest and then the small glacier towards the ridge close to Pt 2681m. Get onto the terrace above the rounded base by a series of cracks and dièdres on the L at the weakest point. Cross the grassy terrace Rwards (c100m) to a dièdre about 30m L of the base of the ridge.

Climb the dièdre for 3 pitches then continue easily up the ridge (possibly snow) to a slabby, 40m high shoulder. Climb this by flakes then move up easy ground to the next step which is climbed by a widening chimney (back and foot). Broken rock leads to a gendarme whose top is the shape of a hare's ear. A crack and short traverse lead to the gap 20m below the top of the gendarme. Traverse L and then climb up to belay in the 'ear'. Follow the edge for a few metres, descend 4m on the N side to a horizontal ledge then move R to the gap behind the gendarme.

The sometimes snowy ridge continues to the next spiral-like tower. Climb this, at first on the L over rocks interspersed with grass, then slant up L for 40m on flakes (the corrugated wall). From a short earthy terrace descend 15m to a small ledge and climb a dièdre to a belay a bit higher than the earthy terrace. Next climb slabs under a grey overhang and traverse L into a couloir. Climb the rib on its L before following the ridge to the next tower (possibly on snow).

Climb first on the L of the edge for 80m to a platform. Under a jagged edge follow cracks and slabs to a stance on the W side of the tower. Abseil 15m to a horizontal section of ridge. The next tower has a deep chimney, 60m high, in its SE flank. Descend L to its foot and climb it, passing outside several jammed blocks at 50m. Next climb a shallow dièdre Rwards followed by a small roof to get back to the crest. Keep on the crest to a short wall on the L of a big slab. Climb the wall and then the crest to the top of this tower before abseiling down a vertical wall to the next gap.

Avoid another gendarme on the N side before the next step. Climb this on loose rock on the N side for two pitches (delicate) and then traverse 15m into a grey dièdre which leads R to a niche. Climb the detached slab to the L to a dièdre with an embedded block (the Blade). Climb the block and reach a fist-sized crack on the L and climb to the crest. 50m of loose rock/snow lead to the summit rocks. Climb slabs on the R to a wide ledge which merges into the rock wall on the L. Climb the wall, where there is a lot of quartz, to a V-shaped gap (piton protection). The last pitch is up the crest on superb rock. 6-9hr from the foot of the ridge.

Descend the W side for a few metres, abseil 20m down a dièdre then climb down easily on the R to snow and down to the Aletsch glacier. Or, as for Route 82, descend the couloir between the ridges.

Klein Wannenhorn 3706.7m

S Taylor, W Gladstone and C Parker with F Schwick and J Tännler, 23 Aug 1866

This is the high point at the S end of the group of mountains known as the Walliser Fiescherhörner, well seen from the Eggishorn and Bellwald. The whole group is infrequently climbed in summer. This is not because of any poor quality of climbing but more likely the fact that there are so many peaks close by which surpass the 4000m contour.

85 **SOUTH-EAST PILLAR**

TD G Harr, M Niedermann, E Näf and H Zurfluh, 20 July 1975

This is a 750m high granite pillar terminating on the S ridge close to the summit. A fine climb especially in its upper part. Pitons are in place. The climb can be abandoned at about 3500m by a 20m abseil onto the tiny glacier to the S. A steep snow/ice slope leads to a small col between Pt 3481m and the Kl Wannenhorn.

From the bivouac referred to in Route 83 climb the moraine and either the E or W bank (according to the state of crevasses) of the small glacier. Reach the start of the climb at a snow/scree couloir (depending on the season) which starts at an enormous tower detached from the SE wall. Climb the couloir or cracks 15m S of it (3m of IV+) and reach the tongue of the hanging glacier. Ascend diagonally R and get back onto rock 60m above the start.

Climb up R and traverse into a rocky couloir which cuts

through the lower wall. Climb it for 200m (II, III, 20m of IV) to easier and less steep ground. Climb the couloir which comes from another big tower. 80m below the tower leave the couloir on the R and traverse for 1 pitch to the R across a slabby step (III). Move up L into a couloir, which narrows to chimney proportions in places before it eventually merges with the slopes near the crest. Climb it for 2 pitches to a ledge (bits of V+). Another 2 pitches lead to the crest (V, some V+, A0). Follow the crest to its junction with the S ridge (III, IV). Climb this ridge to the summit (IV). 9hr from the foot of the ridge

Descend the ridge NW towards the Gr Wannenhorn (F) and from the saddle descend the S branch of the Wannenhorn glacier to the Aletsch glacier.

Fiescher Gabelhorn 3875.8m

P and C Montandon, 8 Aug 1889

The mountain has an airy, rocky, double summit. These are separated by an impressive gap which proves quite difficult to cross.

86 **NORTH-EAST RIDGE**
AD O Hug and A Simmen, 12 Aug 1922
57

A pleasant outing from the Finsteraarhorn hut.

From the hut cross the glacier almost S and pass S of the rock buttress below Pt 3291.3m. Climb the easy snow slopes to the col at 3532m. From the col more easy snow slopes lead to the ridge which is followed more or less on the crest all the way (bits of III, some difficulties can be avoided on the L). 4hr

87 **TRAVERSE OF THE WALLISER FIESCHERHÖRNER**
AD
57

The ridge, starting at the Wyssnollen and ending at the Kl Wannenhorn, provides a long but easy high level traverse over mixed terrain and with little company. If the Fiescher Gabelhorn is missed out the route is a little easier. It can be started from the Konkordia or Finsteraarhorn huts and can be left at various points.

From either hut reach the Grünhornlücke by Route 90 or 91 and climb scree and snow slopes to the summit of the Wyssnollen (3595m) in 1hr. Descend to the col at Pt 3532m and climb the NE ridge of the Fiescher Gabelhorn as for Route 86 (2hr). Descend the

SE ridge, avoiding a step at half-height on the E flank, to the col before the Schönbühlhorn. This same point can be reached from the Wyssnollen by turning the foot of the E ridge of the Fiescher Gabelhorn and climbing the snow slope beyond it to the col.

From the col climb the snow ridge to the W summit of the Schönbühlhorn and then cross the near horizontal crest, via 4 gendarmes, to the E summit (3845m, interesting). 1½hr from the Fiescher Gabelhorn. Descend easily to the next col and pass 2 towers on the W side to another, slightly higher col at the start of the NW ridge of the Gr Wannenhorn. Climb the first step easily, partly on the crest and partly on snow on the L. The second step is quite airy but with good holds on the crest (II-III). The final step is steep and exposed at the top with a few difficult but well protected moves. A few gendarmes are then traversed to the summit (3905.9m). 1½hr

Cross snow to the S summit and descend SE on snow slopes as far as a gendarme on the SE ridge. Turn this on the E side and climb onto the ridge via a slab. Go down the ridge passing another gendarme on the W side then climb the spiky ridge to a snow dome. Reach the col beyond by easy rocks and snow (1-1½hr). The N ridge of the Kl Wannenhorn can be climbed easily in 20min.

Descend the S branch of the Wannenhorn glacier to the Aletsch glacier and Märjelessee (2½hr) from where a path leads easily to the Kühboden cable station. Allow 12-15hr in all

Fülbärg 3242.6m

This is a high point towards the W end of the long ridge running W from the Fiescher Gabelhorn and has some good rock climbing. The traverse of this summit and the continuation to Chamm is considered one of the best climbs in the Oberland.

88 **WEST RIDGE**

AD E Birk and P Borcher, 30 July 1914

From the Konkordia hut reach the foot of the W flank via scree and large blocks. The flank is cut diagonally from R to L by a steep crack, of chimney dimensions at the bottom. At the bottom of the chimney is a chockstone. Climb past the chockstone then slant L quite steeply with few holds for a few metres before climbing straight up overlapping slabs (crux). Easier climbing leads to a shoulder on the W ridge. Keep on the crest, airy and sustained, to an easing just before the summit (III, 15m of IV). 1½-2hr

Descend the E ridge, passing some towers on the R, before taking the last step on the N flank (PD, 15min) to a col (Fülbärgpass, 3170m). A couloir on the S side now leads down into the stony cirque of Fülbärgchumme. Pass the S foot of the Fülbärg to reach the hut. 1hr, about 3½hr in all

Chamm 3866m

A rocky peak on the long W ridge of the Fiescher Gabelhorn. It has a distinctive summit block that can be picked out from some distance away.

A very fine view point.

89 **WEST RIDGE**

AD J du Bois with C Rubi, 2 July 1919

The ridge is 1300m long and has some good and bad rock. Key sections are on sound granite.

From the Konkordia hut either traverse the Fülbärg (Route 88) or reverse the descent of that route to the Fülbärgpass. From the pass keep on the ridge, steep at first, to a steep step about 300m high (1hr). Climb this step directly on the crest to reach point 3605m. The angle eases before steepening again to give some exposed climbing to the summit. 8-9hr in all

Descent is by the SW couloir. From the summit get down onto the small hanging glacier on the S side and descend it to the SW rib. Descend this on the crest (nice climbing) then slant R into a gully below the hanging glacier which in turn is decended to the snow couloir (some danger of falling ice). Either descend the couloir or the rock rib on the L side. Below the couloir traverse the slope to the W and pass round the foot of the SW ridge of Pt 3605m before more traversing across Fülbärgchumme leads to the hut.

Grünhornlücke 3286m

R Meyer with A Abbühl, K Huber, A Volker and J Bortis, 11 Aug 1812

The pass provides a route between the Aletsch and Fiescher glaciers and is one of the most frequented in the Oberland, especially by ski-touring parties in the spring. It provides probably the easiest approach to the Finsteraarhorn hut.

90 **FROM THE WEST**

F From the Konkordia hut descend to the Grüneggfirn and climb easy snow slopes (possibly some bare ice low down) to the broad col. 2hr

91 **FROM THE EAST**

F From the Finsteraarhorn hut descend to the Fiescher glacier and cross it (crevasses) before climbing easy snow slopes to the broad col. 1½hr

Grünegghorn 3860m

F and G Gardiner with R and P Almer, 8 Aug 1901
An unimportant summit usually climbed in combination with the Gr Grünhorn.

92 **SOUTH-WEST RIDGE**

PD From the Konkordia hut climb the Grüneggfirn to about 3000m. Follow steep and crevassed snow slopes Nwards (the slopes can get very soft in the afternoon and great care should be taken in descent) to a snow couloir descending from a depression on the ridge NE of Pt 3475m. Climb the couloir then follow more snow slopes fairly steeply to the fore-summit (3787m). An easy rock ridge leads to the main summit. 4-5hr

93 **SOUTH-EAST RIDGE**

PD T von Hahn with F Amatter and F Kaufmann, 5 Aug 1907

A fine climb of no great difficulty on good rock.

From the Konkordia or Finsteraarhorn huts reach the Grünhornlücke by Route 89 or 90. Now climb unpleasant slopes (scree) to get onto and climb the S ridge of Grünhörnli (3494.5m). From this summit a spiky rock ridge leads to a reddish granite step which is turned on the E side (slight descent). Gendarmes and short rock or snow sections on the ridge lead to the summit. About 5hr from the pass

Gross Grünhorn 4043.5m

E von Fellenberg with P Egger, P Michel and P Inäbnit, 7 Aug 1865

A splendid mountain well worthy of its 4000er status. It has good rock and a distinct difference in character between its W and E sides; the former, being principally snow, provides the ordinary route whilst the latter is mostly rock on which there are 2 excellent climbs.

94 **SOUTH-WEST RIDGE**
PD First ascent party
58

The ridge itself is quite short, starting at the col between this mountain and the Grünegghorn. It is mostly climbed from the Konkordia by traversing the Grünegghorn, but since the opening of the Mönchjoch hut an ascent to the col from the Ewigschneefäld is gaining popularity (this is the normal route on skis).

From the Konkordia hut follow Route 92 to the summit of the Grünegghorn. Descend easily to the snowy col. Now climb the ridge, on the crest at first then on the W flank, to the summit. 5-6hr from the hut

From the Mönchjoch hut (or the Bergli hut) descend the Ewigschneefäld until directly W of the summit and climb the crevassed slopes as directly as possible to the col at the foot of the SW ridge. On the last steep section it may be necessary to move R onto the NE slopes of the Grünegghorn to reach the col. Then as for the other approach. 4-5hr

95 **NORTH RIDGE**
D J Farrer and H Reade, 4 Aug 1907

A first rate climb which when combined with the SW ridge makes a fine traverse of the peak. There is no great technical difficulty but it is quite committing (III with bits of IV, exposed). It is most commonly climbed these days from the Mönchjoch hut but can also be climbed from Konkordia (longer but more convenient for descent)

From the Mönchjoch hut (or Bergli hut) descend the Ewigschneefäld to about 3300m then slant up the slopes S of Pt 3415m to cross the SW ridge of the Lk Grünhorn. Continue up snow slopes to the lowest point in the ridge between the Kl and Gr Grünhorn. 3hr

From Konkordia get onto the Ewigschneefäld and climb the R side in a snowy hollow until level with Pt 3175m. Now head NE up crevassed snow slopes to the same point on the ridge, or a slightly higher one further S. 4hr

Follow the ridge fairly easily to where it steepens. The first wall is climbed on the L then the ridge is followed to a steepening. Now cross a couloir on the R and climb a short wall to gain a rib on the W side of the ridge. Climb this back to the ridge and then keep to the crest, except for one detour on the W side, to the summit. 3-4hr, about 8hr in all

96
D+
58

EAST PILLAR

C Blum and U Frei, 27 July 1967: Winter, P Etter, U Gantenbain, R Käser and A Scherrer, 10 Jan 1973

A magnificent climb on sound rock and in very fine surroundings. Mostly III with several bits of IV and one of V–. Snow and ice gear is needed. The pillar, not very pronounced in the lower part, separates the SE flank of the mountain from the NE face.

From the Finsteraarhorn hut cross the Fiescherfirn NW to the foot of the pillar. Here a narrow ice couloir, which turns to rock at the bottom and can be seen from the hut, comes down to the glacier. Cross the bergschrund and climb slabs on the L (S) of the couloir, then the crest of the rib on its L side to where it faces into slabs (III, IV). Make a difficult traverse R to a shoulder then descend slabs to a ledge on the edge of the icy couloir. Cross the couloir and climb rocks on the other side to the top of the first steep section of the face (IV).

The next step is climbed on its NE side. Some detached blocks lead to a 10m wall on the R of a couloir emanating from a tiny notch in the pillar. Climb the wall (V–, crux) and continue straight up in an exposed position to the notch (IV+). Above the notch climb on the R side and then traverse pleasantly round the crest into a couloir. Climb this to its upper part where it steepens. Now climb on the L side to get onto the SE face a few minutes from the summit. 8-11hr from the hut

97
D
58

SOUTH-EAST FACE

F von Bethmann-Hollweg with O and O Supersaxo, 26 May 1913

A classic route with some pleasant rock climbing (II and III). There is some stonefall danger.

From the Finsteraarhorn hut cross the Fiescherfirn and climb the snow coombe on the SE side of the mountain (starting from Konkordia, cross the Grünhornlücke to reach the same coombe) as far as a steep snow couloir about 100m NW of Pt 3585m on the SE ridge. Climb the couloir and then the tongue of snow (steep) to reach the rocks as high as possible. Now climb directly up the face (no particular line) to finish a little R of the summit. 5-6hr from the Finsteraarhorn hut

Klein Grünhorn 3738m

G. Lammer and A Lorria, 13 Aug 1885

Lies on the continuation of the N ridge of the Gr Grünhorn and probably best climbed in combination with that route. Of necessity it is included in the traverse from the Gr Fiescherhorn to the Gr Grünhorn.

98 **SOUTH-EAST RIDGE**
PD T von Hahn with F Amatter and F Kaufmann, 5 Aug 1907
58

From the Mönchjoch, Bergli or Konkordia huts follow Route 95 to the low point on the N ridge of the Gr Grünhorn. Easy climbing leads to the summit. Gendarmes are passed on the W side. 4-5hr

99 **SOUTH-WEST RIDGE**
PD First ascent party

From the Mönchjoch or Bergli huts follow Route 95 to where it crosses the ridge. From Konkordia follow Route 95, but instead of slanting up to the N ridge get onto the SW ridge at about 3500m. Follow the ridge on snow and then excellent rock to the summit. 3½-4½hr

100 **NORTH RIDGE**
PD H Kintze with her guide, 28 July 1903

Probably the best way of climbing the N ridge of the Gr Grünhorn from the Mönchjoch hut and a means of climbing that route from the Finsteraarhorn hut.

From the Mönchjoch or Bergli huts descend the Ewigschneefäld until W of Pt 3415m, then climb easy snow slopes (crevasses) to the col at 3739m (Kl Grünhornlücke). 2½-3hr

From the Finsteraarhorn hut climb the Fiescherfirn NW until below the col at Pt 3739m. Climb directly to the col (D). 3hr

From the col climb the crest of the ridge or its W side (easier)

to the steep summit rocks. Climb on the W side to the summit. 1½hr, about 5hr in all

101 **EAST RIB**
D C Blum and U Frei, 24 July 1967
58

A good rock climb but not much frequented. Mostly II and III with bits of IV.

From the Finsteraarhorn hut climb the Fiescherfirn to below the rib. A short but steep snow slope is climbed to reach its foot a bit R of the mouth of the couloir bordering the rib on its S side. Climb the rib until just below the final rise to the summit. In the wall (facing E) is a couloir, narrowing to a chimney in places, leading to a small ledge on the rib on the R. Climb the couloir to the ledge then traverse a few metres R before moving straight up to regain the crest of the rib a few minutes from the summit. 5-6hr

Hinter Fiescherhorn 4025m

G. Lammer and A Lorria, 28 July 1885

A popular mountain among ski-tourers, which although surpassing the 4000m mark can hardly be classed as a separate mountain. It is more akin to a 'Munro top'.

102 **SOUTH-EAST RIDGE**
F J Liniger, R Winterhalter and J Bulli, 7 Sept 1899
59

Descended on the traverse from the Gr Fiescherhorn to the Gr Grünhorn.

From the Kl Grünhornlücke (see Route 100) climb the ridge on good rock to a distinctive tower. Traverse this or turn it on its W side to a gap to its N. The easy ridge leads to the summit. 1½-2hr

103 **SOUTH-WEST RIB**
PD L Purtscheller and C Blodig, 3 Aug 1898

A little shorter and more sporting than the SE ridge, which it joins at a conspicuous tower.

From the Mönchjoch hut follow Route 100 until W of Pt 3415m. Climb directly up the glacier slope, passing just S of this point, and continue close to the rib until finally getting on to it a little way below a level section. Above this climb directly to the top of the tower on the SE ridge or traverse, on the NW side, to the gap beyond the tower. The easy ridge beyond leads to the summit. 5hr

104 **NORTH-WEST RIDGE**
F First ascent party
59

From the Fieschersattel (see Route 105) follow the ridge, passing the first gendarme on its E side, to the summit. 30min

Gross Fiescherhorn 4048.8m

H George and A Moore with C Almer and U Kaufmann, 23 July 1862

An important mountain whose main feature is the Fiescherwand, the N face extending from the summit of the Walcherhorn in the W to the Ochs in the E. This face and its climbs are described separately below. The mountain itself is principally snow covered, with poor rock except on the crest of its ridges.

105 **SOUTH-EAST RIDGE**
PD F Bischoff with P Bohren and P Egger, 10 Aug 1871
59

The ridge can be approached from the Mönchjoch, Bergli, Finsteraarhorn and Konkordia huts (not frequently from the latter). Combined with the ridge it provides a very gooa traverse of the mountain. The route is slightly more difficult when approached from the Mönchjoch, Bergli or Konkordia huts. See also photo 61.

From the Mönchjoch or Bergli huts descend the Ewigschneefäld to below the glacier bay leading up to the col (3923m) between the Gr and Hinter Fiescherhorn – this is the Fieschersattel. Climb the R-hand side of the bay until above a crevassed zone then move L to avoid more crevasses. The slope steepens somewhat (50°) below the col. Climb this snow slope and cross the bergschrund about 100m below the col, then climb ice, snow or rock, according to conditions, to the col. 4hr

From the Konkordia hut follow Route 95 onto the Ewigschneefäld and climb the same glacier bay to the col. 5hr

From the Finsteraarhorn hut climb the Fiescherfirn NW to the sérac zone near its head. The route through the zone is quite variable. If conditions are suitable climb through its middle but more commonly the only way is by the L (E) bank (exposed to the danger of falling ice). Either way, once above the séracs get onto the high snowy plateau to the E of the Fieschersattel. 4-5hr

From the Fieschersattel climb the crest of the ridge on good rock (one tricky descent at about half-height) to the summit. 45min, 5-6hr in all

106 **NORTH-WEST RIDGE**
AD H. Wolly with C Jossi and H Kaufmann, 31 July 1887
59

This constitutes the ordinary route from the Mönchjoch or Bergli huts. It achieves the grade given because of the exposed climbing (usually on ice) close to the summit. See also photos 60 and 61.

From the Mönchjoch or Bergli huts get onto the upper slopes of the Ewigschneefäld. Pass just below the foot of the S ridge of the Walcherhorn then slant up snow slopes to a col at the foot of the SE ridge of this mountain (3613m, not marked). Continue along the ridge or just on its S side with one or two steep (and sometimes icy) steps, to the final section. A rock rib sits on the crest of the ridge and can be climbed (II, III) or it can be turned on the L (E) side where an exposed and frequently icy slope is climbed back to the crest. Follow the crest easily to the summit, turning the last few rocks on the R. 4-5hr

Ochs 3900m

E von Fellenberg with P Inäbnit, U and P Kaufmann, 28 July 1864

Also known as the Klein Fiescherhorn, the mountain has an impressive 1300m high, glaciated E flank and its N face forms the L part of the Fiescherwand. Quite frequently climbed by its short SW ridge in combination with the Gr and Hinter Fiescherhorn.

107 **SOUTH-WEST RIDGE**
PD W Coolidge with C Almer jun and R Almer, 22 July 1888
60

From the snow saddle between the Gr Fiescherhorn and Ochs, reached easily from the Fieschersattel described in Route 105, climb the snow ridge to the summit. The ridge may be difficult because of ice or cornices. 30min

108 **NORTH RIDGE**
D E Whitwell with C Lauener and P Schlegel, 2 Aug 1878
61

A worthwhile snow/ice climb in a fine setting. The ridge is reached 100m S of Pfaffestecki (3054m). See also photo 60

From the Schreckhorn hut cross the Obers Ischmeer SW then climb diagonally up the glacier slopes above to the col S of Pfaffestecki. If the state of the glacier allows, before reaching the col turn up the slope to reach a higher col S of Pt 3343.4m. From the lower col this one is reached by climbing the snow and rock crest over Pt 3343.5m. Continue up the ridge without any great difficulty over snow and rock to Pt 3578m and the N edge of a snow terrace below and E of the summit. This point can be reached from Route 109 by crossing the terrace (or the climb can be abandoned here by crossing the terrace to join Route 109). The final steep ridge (55°) is the crux and requires good technique on ice. The ridge finishes on the SE ridge (usually corniced) about 20m from the summit. About 7hr

109 **NORTH-EAST FLANK**
AD+ De Villiers-Schwab, 5 Aug 1920
61

This face of the mountain has a number of rock ribs interspersed with glacier slopes. Several routes have been recorded but most are impractical at present due to the crevassed state of the glaciers. The route described is the one most likely to be in condition. The route can be used in descent by parties climbing on the NW face or the N ridge. The slope below the séracs provides a rapid means of descent for parties willing to run the risk.

From the Schreckhorn hut cross the Obers Ischmeer SW towards the rock buttress below Pt 2975m. Climb the steep slope to the R of the buttress (fairly active séracs above) then traverse L on the obvious snow tongue. (It is possible to climb on the rock buttress via a couloir from about half-height; the second pitch is steep but on good holds. The way is difficult to locate in descent.) From the end of the snow tongue climb a broken rock ridge easily to snow slopes above. Climb these to a snow terrace rising Rwards below 2 rock ribs in the face above. Follow the terrace (some danger of sérac fall from above) Rwards to the S side of the snow terrace below the summit of Ochs. From here climb the narrow, often icy, E ridge which steepens towards the fore-summit on the SE ridge. Continue along the SE ridge which curves round to the main summit (often very difficult because of cornices). 8-9hr

P von Schumacher and W Amstutz, 3 Aug 1926

One of the great N faces of the Bernese Oberland and of the Alps, it is about 4km wide (extending from the Walcherhorn to Ochs) and some 1200m high, and is seamed with rock and ice. The climbing here has a great feeling of isolation and seriousness. Several of the routes have a major risk of sérac fall and much of the rock is poor (but not all). The objective dangers account for the lack of popularity of these climbs; however a fast party, in the right conditions, can minimise the risk to no more than one would find on some of the more crowded Chamonix routes. In previous guides the position of routes has been identified by numbering the rock ribs. This has been abandoned as confusing, since the various ribs are not clearly defined.

110 APPROACH
F

The approach to the face is from Grindelwald or from Eismeer station. The latter is most convenient in winter but is expensive.

From Grindelwald: Follow the route to the Schreckhorn hut and then, between Stieregg and Bänisegg go down a grassy moraine crest slanting R into trees, from where a path leads to the glacier. Go SE up the glacier, crossing it to reach a small promontory at the NW corner of Zäsenberg. Climb a shallow stream bed just L of the promontory and get onto a path leading E. Follow this to an old hut at 1948m. Follow a faint path over rocks and grass, traversing up and Lwards (E) to a ridge bounding a rocky bay. The path turns SW and rises slowly before turning back E to arrive at the ridge again above the steep walls of the bay. Follow the ridge on a discontinuous path to the edge of the upper part of the Fiescher glacier at about 2350m. There are good bivouac sites with running water near a commemorative wooden cross. 4hr from the top of the Pfingstegg lift.

The foot of the face is reached from here in 1½-2hr.

111 NORTH SPUR OF GROSS FIESCHERHORN FORE-SUMMIT
TD–/TD
60

D Wilkinson and R Brevitt, Aug 1988

The most obvious feature on the R-hand side of the face is the NE spur of the NW fore-summit of the Gr Fiescherhorn. To its R the face is characterised by a Y-shaped couloir. The route climbs the L bounding rib of this couloir. There is some stonefall danger in the first few pitches, otherwise objective dangers are not great. Since the rock is not good the climb is best attempted in cold snowy conditions.

From the foot of the Y-shaped couloir get onto the rib on the L and climb this to join the N rib route near its top. 8-10hr from the foot of the face.

112 NORTH RIB OF GROSS FIESCHERHORN FORE-SUMMIT

TD/TD+ First ascent party

60

The most obvious and one of the easiest lines on the face. It is a long mixed climb, which Welzenbach found more difficult than expected during the second ascent. Most of the climbing is on the rib (poor rock) and is quite safe but it has definite N face feeling about it. Average angle is 65°, the difficulties depending on conditions. With dry rock there are pitches of III and IV.

Start on the R of the rib at 2780m. Get onto and climb the rib to where it merges into the face. Traverse L and then climb slabby rocks for about 150m before moving L again to get onto a continuation rib. Continue up this to where it fades into a snow ridge. Climb this to the summit crags which are climbed by a couloir. 8-10hr from the foot of the face

113 REISS ROUTE

TD+ E Reiss, D Reist and H Sollberger, 28/29 June 1947

60

This route appears to be fairly safe and seems to be the most frequently climbed one on the face. It is a bit more direct than the Friele-Sprang route and probably better than this route in snow free conditions. The main difficulties are at mid-height where mixed ground reaches 65°. The top ice slope averages 55°.

Start at the foot of the rib just R of the fall-line from the summit. Climb the rib to where it steepens not far below the upper icefield (II-III with some steps of IV-V according to conditions). 2 steep pitches on mixed ground are climbed, then slant L to the upper icefield where a choice of line leads to the summit. 10-14hr from the foot of the face

114 FRIELE-SPRANG ROUTE

TD+ G Friele and G van Sprang, 29 July 1980

60

This route climbs a couloir L of the rib of the Reiss route to where it joins a ramp line leading Rwards to join or cross the Reiss route below the upper icefield. It is somewhat easier than the Reiss route. It was climbed

by D Wilkinson and W Barker at Easter 1982.

115 **WELZENBACH ROUTE**
ED2 W Welzenbach and H Tillmann, 5 Sept 1930.
60 Winter: M Dörflinger, U Kämpfer and P Jungen, 10 March 1969

This is probably the most direct route to the summit of the Gr Fiescherhorn. It climbs a complex line up the face and is seriously threatened by the sérac band L of the mountain's summit. The rock is generally poor with pitches up to IV.

Start just L of the Freile-Sprang route and climb the next gully line on the L. Get onto the rib on the L and climb this (mixed) to where it merges into almost vertical slabs. Move L up icefields to the next prominent rib and climb this to a very steep icefield. Move up Rwards and over a rock band to the upper icefield. A snow ramp leads Rwards in the upper part to an ice bulge at the top of the face. This is the line of the route to the summit. 14hr from the foot of the face

116 **STEURI-HEDIGER AND PARTY ROUTE**
ED2 B Hediger with H Steuri, P Maurice and a Dutch guest, c 1948
60

This climb is exposed to sérac fall like the Welzenbach route and cannot be recommended. See the photograph for the line of the route.

117 **WILKINSON-McCARTNEY ROUTE**
ED2 D Wilkinson and S McCartney, July 1977
60

The route climbs the face between the Steuri-Hediger and the Lüthi-Steuri routes to the col between the Gr Fiescherhorn and Ochs. The rock is quite good, but the route is exposed to sérac fall like the other routes on this sector of the face.

Start just L of the Hediger-Steuri route and make a zig-zag ascent of the face trending L to exit at the col.

118 **LÜTHI-STEURI ROUTE**
TD/ED1 Frl M Lüthi and H Steuri, 9 Aug 1935. Winter: M Boos and
60 P Hilber 29/30 Jan 1981

This climb can be recommended. There is no sérac danger and the stonefall risk is not serious. The rock is not good but it is a lot better than further E on the wall. It is at its best on the harder part of the climb (the upper wall) but even here there is debris on the ledges and some loose holds. The ideal line on the upper wall (if there is one) is not easy to follow.

From the bivouac site go S to reach the flat part of the glacier. Continue in the same direction, then go up snow and glacier ice to the snowfields below the wall rising to the N ridge of Ochs. Traverse these to the R to reach the glacier bay below the face.

Cross the bergschrund on the L and reach the foot of a rocky spur splitting the lower part of the face. Climb this on good rock at first (III) then progressively worse rock to an easing of the angle. Climb easy mixed ground to an obvious snow/ice couloir splitting a short rock wall. Enter this from the L and either climb the ice direct or move 5m R and climb a short rock wall and then icy steps to the wide couloir above. Climb this trending L to rocks, then climb the icefield above to the bottom L hand corner of an ice bay at the foot of the summit walls.

Climb a groove for 40m (III-IV) to reach a ledge which crosses the face (there is an obvious large crack system about 40m R). Move 10m L and climb a groove for 10m (III) to reach a ledge on the L below an overhang. Traverse L, horizontally at first and then rising slightly for a further 50m before climbing cracks on the L to a small bay below some extensive wet slabs. Take an overhanging crack on the L to a ledge (V) then step L and climb a short rib (IV+) to reach smooth slabs. Move up 5m (V) then traverse R to a small niche (IV+). Move R to a rib, climb the overhang (IV+) and continue up slabs to easier mixed ground. After a further 40m reach a ledge system that crosses the face. Direct finishes are possible from here but are very loose. Instead, traverse L along the ledge (bivouac sites) to reach the N ridge of Ochs a few pitches from the summit. 13-15hr

Trugberg 3932.9m

E Burckhardt with P Egger and P Schlgel, 31 July 1871

The Trugberg separates the Jungfraufirn from the Ewigschneefäld, rising like an island in a sea of ice. Its N limit is marked by the Obers Mönchjoch. The best feature of the mountain is its long rocky crest running roughly N-S with three separate tops.

119 TRAVERSE NORTH-SOUTH

AD *An interesting climb with a very short approach. Mixed, with rock of grade II but when snowed up or verglassed it becomes quite difficult.*

From the Mönchjoch hut climb a snow/ice slope to the first rocks which are climbed on the L. Avoid a steep wall on the R then climb a couloir to the N summit. The next rocks are taken on the L. Now follow the snow crest which becomes quite narrow. Mixed rock and snow follows to a large gendarme. Climb an icy slope to the gendarme and then the rocks on its L side. Descend into a gap before the fore-summit. At first climb direct and then Lwards to get onto the crest just beyond this summit. Reach the main summit by a steep crack or by the crest. 3½hr

Descend Swards, turning a gendarme towards a snow crest, before a series of rock teeth lead to the S summit. Snow slopes lead down to the Ewigschneefäld for a return to the Mönchjoch, or continue down the ridge past Pt 3542.6m to Konkordiaplatz. 6-7hr in all

Obers Mönchjoch 3629m

K Rohrdorf and his guide, 27 Aug 1828

The col, just below the Mönchjoch hut, links the Jungfraufirn with the Ewigschneefäld

120 **WEST SIDE**

F From the Jungfraujoch station entrance (if you can find it from the railway!) walk out onto the Jungfraufirn (usually a bulldozed track in the snow to start) and follow the gently inclined snow slopes ENE to the col. There is some danger of ice falling from the S face of the Mönch and there are a few crevasses close to the col. 1hr

121 **EAST SIDE**

F From the Unders Mönchjoch reverse Route 122. 45min

Unders Mönchjoch 3529m

K Rohrdorf and his guide, 27 Aug 1828

The col is the lowest point on the ridge between the Mönch and the Gross Fiescherhorn. It provides a means of access to the Bergli hut.

122 **SOUTH SIDE**

F From the Obers Mönchjoch descend into the snowy coombe at the head of the Ewigschneefäld and follow the slopes NW to the col. 30min

123 **NORTH SIDE**
F
From the Bergli hut climb the rock ridge, turning to snow, that is behind the hut and then by a steep snow slope reach the col (there are often wide crevasses in this section and there can be soft snow on ice. There have been several accidents involving parties descending in the afternoon). 45min

Eigerjochs 3759.3m and 3614m

L Steven, W and G Matthews with U Lauener, J Croz and M Charlet, 7 Aug 1859 (S Eigerjoch)

The name is given to the two cols on the ridge linking the Mönch and Eiger. Since the building of the Mönchjoch hut the climbing of the S ridge of the Eiger has become quite popular and involves a traverse of the ridge between the two cols.

124 **TRAVERSE OF THE RIDGE BETWEEN THE NORTH AND**
AD **SOUTH EIGERJOCH**
62
The interconnecting ridge is mainly gneiss, turning to limestone just before the N Eigerjoch. It is stepped with short snow crests and gives some enjoyable climbing even though the rock is a bit loose.

From the Mönchjoch hut descend a little way into the snow coombe at the head of the Ewigschneefäld before turning N to cross the ridge below point 3687m. Easy snow slopes lead NW to the S Eigerjoch (3759.3m). 1hr

An approach can be made from the Bergli hut by following Route 123 to the Unders Mönchjoch and climbing the ridge from there to Pt 3687m and then as above. 2½hr

From the S Eigerjoch climb to the highest point (3770m) keeping to the crest. The rocks below this point are cut on the W side by a chimney. Descend this to its base (often verglassed) and from the gap beyond climb back to the crest. It is also possible to traverse out of the chimney at about half-height using some hidden holds. Continue along the ridge to the N Eigerjoch. Bits of III–. 1½hr, 2½-3hr in all

Eiger 3970m

C Barrington with C Almer and P Bohren, 11 Aug 1858

A mountain known by name to the general public probably better than any other peak in the Alps on account of its famous N wall. In recent years many more routes have been added to this face and some will be described here. However the Eiger is not all about the N wall; there are other good climbs but the ordinary route on the SW flank is not one of these.

125 SOUTH RIDGE

AD G Foster with H Baumann and U Rubi, 31 July 1876

62

Since the installation of the Mönchjoch hut this route has become increasingly popular and rightly so. It is an interesting climb and better value than the Mittellegi ridge. In poor conditions it is probably safer to descend this route than to descend the SW flank route.

Reach the N Eigerjoch from the Mönchjoch hut or the Bergli hut by Route 124. From here keep to the L of the crest and climb as high as possible to a rock outcrop. Traverse L for some way to a couloir which is climbed back Rwards to the crest (abseil the outcrop in descent). Keep to the ridge to its junction with the SW ridge (few belays). The rocky towers just below this point are turned on the L side. An easy rock ridge leads to the summit. 2½-3½hr, allow 7-9hr from the Mönchjoch hut

126 SOUTH-WEST FLANK AND WEST RIDGE

AD First ascent party

63

Most of the SW flank is like a tiled roof covered in debris. There are cairns and in many places the route is a quite well worn track, but the best line can be difficult to follow especially in descent, in fog or in the dark. The tracks zig-zag about and in places there are quite long traverses. It is advisable to look very carefully for the cairns. Parties involved in the 'Climb for the World' event in the autumn of 1991 placed many stakes and pitons over the whole length of the flank and left them in place as useful belays. With other parties on the route there is considerable danger from stonefall. Another disadvantage of this route is that there is no suitable hut base from which to make the climb, although there is hotel accommodation at the Eigergletscher station (with dormitory). If approaching the latter on foot from Kl Scheidegg it is better to follow the path system than to walk up the railway track. The climb is described in ascent and in descent.

From the Eigergletscher station turn the S foot of the Rotstock (2663.2m) on a vague track over debris-covered slabs or snow to reach the vicinity of the col between the Rotstock and the SW flank of the mountain. Climb Rwards on slabs and snow to the foot of the rocks. Climb the first step via a steep, often snow-filled, couloir or on the rocks L of the couloir. When the angle eases make a rising traverse L to the ridge and follow this, keeping on its R flank, to the next steepening. This is just below a rock obelisk projecting from the N face (Kanzeli or Pilz). Make a rising traverse R under the steep rocks (snow, rock, debris) before returning to the W ridge at a saddle. Follow the ridge and and reach the summit up a final snow/ice slope or the rocks on the L. 6-8hr

In descent there are a number of places where there are fixed abseil anchors, but it is probably just as quick to climb down and so reduce the risk of dislodging stones on other parties.

Start by descending a snow/ice slope Wwards to a levelling. Abseil anchors (marked in red) indicate the start of a couloir in the S flank of the W ridge. Go down this, then straight down for about 100m. Descend slightly Lwards for another 100m before turning R round a rocky projection (more cemented abseil anchors). Descend over small steps, snow/ice and debris, directly to the rib bordering a couloir on the L (cairn). Get into the couloir (abseil points) and descend obliquely R to the level of the rock obelisk projecting from the N face. A zigzagging track with several cairns leads down to the top of a steep step. Move Lwards to a couloir (often snow-filled) and descend this or the rocks on its R (abseil anchors). Descend more easily now on snow and/or slabs until close to the col between the Rotstock and the SW flank. A track lead round the S side of the Rotstock to the Eigergletscher station. 4-5hr

Eiger North Face

H Harrer, A Heckmair, F Kasparek and l Vörg, 21-24 July 1938.

After the much publicised exploits of the 1930s this face has become the best known of all the Alpine N faces. Usually referred to as the Eigerwand, it now has about 20 routes if the NE face is included. All the routes are serious.

It is still possible to find new lines to climb on the face although they are only ever likely to be attempted in winter conditions. One of the most outstanding of these was climbed (solo) in March 1991 by Jeff Lowe. He took a very direct line on the R of the Harlin route requiring seven days to complete and was given the name, Metanoia. It is mostly free but contains one pitch graded A5.

127 **GENEVA PILLAR**
ED2 G Hopfgartner and M Piola, 13-16 Aug 1979. Winter: N Joss and K Ochsner, 12-16 Feb 1981
64
1

The climb has good rock in its upper part but is sometimes loose elsewhere. There is some rockfall danger. The climb starts at a large scree slope at the bottom of the face.

128 **THE SANCTION**
ED3 D Anker and M Piola, 5-7 May 1988
2

1000m of ascent from the foot of the face. All equipment left in place by the first ascent party. It is an impressive and exposed climb which is difficult to retreat from after the 7th pitch. Variable rock quality, good stances. Carry water.

129 **NORTH CORNER**
ED3 C and H Howald and M Rüedi, 26-27 Aug 1981
64
3

1200m of ascent from the foot of the face. It has some very demanding free climbing with only a few pitches requiring aid. It has loose rock in places and at times poor protection.

130 **GHILINI-PIOLA ROUTE**
ED3/4 R Ghilini and M Piola, 26-30 July 1983
64
4

Another very demanding route directly up the overhanging pillar of the Rotefluh (graded by Piola ABO inf, ABO = abominable). There is 1400m of climbing on which protection is often difficult to place. Retreat is very difficult after the 2nd bivouac. The rock is mostly compact so there is little danger of stonefall. The 2nd, 3rd and 5th bivouacs are 1 person sized, the 2nd and 4th have water. The start is up easy but loose ground directly below the impressive yellow wall of the Rotefluh. The most obvious landmark is the railway entrance sited on the R-hand edge of one of the last snowfields below the Rotefluh. It is important to identify this in case of retreat.

131 **JOHN HARLIN ROUTE**
ED3/4 D Haston, S Hupfauer, J Lehne, G Strobel and R Votteler with help from J Harlin, C Bonington, L Kor, D Whillans, K Golikow, P Haag, R Rosenzopf and G Schnaidt, 23 Feb-25 March 1966
64

The route takes a very direct and fairly obvious line up the N face and was the scene of a great deal of media attention during the first ascent when John Harlin was so tragically killed. There is good rock to the Spider but it is bad above this. In summer the stonefall danger makes the

climb unjustifiable (although it has been climbed in this season) and so it is usually only attempted in winter, or in cold autumn weather, when the rock is covered with a few cm of ice. Belays in the rock sections are in place but otherwise there is no fixed gear. The first ascent was achieved by "expedition style" climbing but the route has had "alpine style" ascents and done in this fashion a party starting at night (recommended) should be able to reach the Death Bivouac in one day. Descent in the event of bad weather is by abseil straight down the line of ascent.
See also photo 65

Start directly below the gallery windows. Climb 70° ice for about 30m and then move L for 10m before climbing more steep ice (70°-80°) for 25m. A snowfield (50°) leads up for about 250m to a narrow ice couloir (75°) on the L of the rock buttress. Climb this and then traverse R over poorly iced slabs (III+) to a stance on a snow slope. More steep ice (75°-85°), at first slightly Lwards and then straight up leads in about 35m to a bolt belay. Move L on steep ice to an iced-up corner and climb this (vertical) to the next ice slope (15m in all). Now climb 60-70m up 50° ice which then steepens (60° but with some steeper steps) for about another 130m to below the gallery windows and the First Rock Band.

Climb up R of the gallery for 25m (A3) to belay in slings at a bolt stance. Continue straight up using aid for about 10m, then traverse R (6-7m) into a dièdre which is climbed for 10m before moving R again (6-7m) to below a smooth bulge which is climbed to another belay in slings (A3). Now climb a strenuous overhang above the stance, and then more easily to another stance in slings at the top of the First Band (30m, A3). Climb steep ice (70°) with a few bulges for 20m; then more ice with the odd bulge leads to a stance on a slab in another 35m. Difficult mixed ground straight up for about 12m exits onto a snowfield which is climbed for one pitch to the second bivouac (ice cave).

(If the climb is being done 'alpine style' it is more logical to climb the First Rock Band by moving 50m R of the gallery windows just round a bulge. Two aid pitches are followed by a pitch of steep mixed climbing to an easy traverse back L to the First Icefield.)

Climb the First Icefield for about 90m and then traverse R at its top before moving back Lwards into a poor crack which leads into a prominent gully system in the Second Band (45m). Climb a crack (about 12m) then traverse R on snow for 30m before climbing a gully above on poor snow with some ice steps. On the L of the stance is a 15m chimney: climb this (crux of the Second Band, V+,

IV) and then traverse L on steep ice (30m) to gain the top of the Second Band and the third bivouac (ice cave).

The next pitch is on steep ice above the arête at the top of the Second Band and leads to below the L side of the Flatiron (45m). Traverse R under the base of the Flatiron for about 60m and then climb the Second Icefield, mainly on snow, for about 160m. Now traverse R on snow for 60m before climbing a vertical crack (common with 1938 Route) to an ice pitch and belay (30m in all). Continue on poor ice to the top of the Flatiron (about 50m) then traverse L (about 90m) to its crest and the Death Bivouac.

Go round the corner from the bivouac and straight up the Third Icefield (hard water-ice) to its top (75m). Mixed ground leads onto the crest of the rib which leads to the Central Pillar (V+, 35m). Go up the crest to a stance on the R side of the Central Pillar. Traverse L on aid to a bolt and sling stance at the L end of the Central Pillar (sustained A3, 35m). This section is the Kor Traverse which can be negotiated with just one point of aid in snowless conditions. A line of holds leads across and slightly down the wall until it is possible to tension diagonally L (6m) to reach a flake and another line of holds leading to the end of the traverse. Sustained climbing on thin ice up a groove (35m) and then an ice trough (25m) leads to the top of the pillar.

A narrow neck connects the pillar to the main face. Go along this for 10m and then climb a crack system starting in a roof to a bolt and sling stance (sustained A2, 45m). Continue straight up using mixed aid and free climbing for 30m (A2 and V). Traverse R into some icy grooves and climb these to the foot of the rib at the bottom of the Spider (35m). Go up the Spider to the start of a traverse line leading out of its R side (65m). Traverse R for three pitches on mixed ground to the Fly. Climb this to its top L corner.

Three more pitches on mixed, loose ground lead to the foot of a prominent chimney system (sustained IV and V). Climb the chimney in two pitches to an awkward stance (V, V+, steps of A1). Go up to the overhang behind the stance and traverse R to the foot of a chimney (V, V+, steps of A1, 40m). Climb the chimney (12m) then move diagonally L on icy slabs to a poor stance at the foot of a Lward sloping diagonal fault (V+, 40m). Climb the fault on mixed ground to its end (V, 40m). Move back R and up for 30m on icy slabs (V+) and then climb the summit icefield for 90m on water-ice. Pass to the L of a rock bulge and go straight up to the summit (45m). Allow about 3 days

132 **1938 ROUTE**
ED2 First ascent party. Winter: W Almberger, T Hiebeler, A Kinshofer
64 and A Mannhardt, 6-12 March 1961

There can be few alpinists who have not day-dreamed of climbing the N wall of the Eiger by this famous route. For most it will always remain a dream. Those who do climb it often wait for years (20 or more in at least one case) for the right conditions to make an attempt. The climbing is easiest when the rock is dry, but in such conditions the danger of rockfall is higher. If there is a lot of snow on the face, warm conditions lead to some very wet climbing. Very cold conditions are safest but then the rock is verglassed and more difficult. Even in a 'dry year', if it is cold, the rock above the Death Bivouac is likely to be ice-covered where it is anything less than vertical (Scottish winter IV rather than rock grade IV). In these condition the harder pitches are likely to be either verglassed or pouring with very cold water, depending on the time of day (all Scottish winter V in crampons). In 1991 the first icefield had virtually disappeared and the second and third were much reduced in size. In all there is about 1700m of climbing, ice pitches of 55°-60° and rock up to V. Most parties will make at least one bivouac although the route has been climbed in under 5hr. To minimise objective dangers it is probably advisable to make a bivouac at the Swallows Nest then have a long day to the Traverse of the Gods before climbing to the summit on the third day. Retreat from the face can be very difficult in the event of bad weather. Autumn appears to be a favoured time to do the climb. Winter ascents are fairly common and it has now been soloed in winter by a woman in a single day. Nevertheless it remains a serious undertaking at all times.

The description given below is for dry conditions. There are many minor variations, especially below the Wet Cave Bivouac and between the end of the Second Icefield and Death Bivouac. See also photo 65

Start 200m R of the First Pillar (Pt 2561m) by an inverted and elongated rock triangle almost surrounded by bands of old snow and avalanche debris. Climb up an obvious gully/snow slope cutting through these rocks. Cross the snowband above Lwards to the Entry Chimney. This is a 5m high, L facing corner with a small white plaque above. Climb the corner exiting R (IV) then traverse easily R for 100m. Trend L back to a triangular snowslope and climb this to its top L before trending further L over easy ledges with occasional awkward moves (small cairns) to the foot of the Shattered Pillar. Move up R towards the Roteflue aiming for a small metal box which is 15m up and R of the Stollenloch (tunnel window). The last 20m to the tunnel is IV. There are other variations to most of this section.

Traverse L for 100m to a short chimney which leads to the Wet Cave Bivouac below a vertical wall. Move L up ledges and traverse Rwards (IV) to the Difficult Crack. Climb this (IV+). A fixed rope normally hangs down this section. Continue up a little groove above (20m, IV) and then make a rising traverse L below the Roteflue for 150m to reach the Hinterstoisser Traverse. Follow the fixed rope L for 30m, then climb a chimney for 10m and exit L to the Swallows Nest (small bivouac site). Traverse L to the First Icefield and climb it for 90m to the rockband separating it from the Second Icefield. On the R is the Ice Hose. Climb it direct or by rocks 15m L for 12m (IV) before making a diagonal traverse onto it. The latter is usually the easier option. Another option is to climb up diagonally Lwards (40m, IV) then traverse R (40m, V). In the lean conditions that are becoming common the Ice Hose may be merely a wet/verglassed runnel in which case two further pitches may be necessary, zig-zagging up the wall about 30m L of the Ice Hose (VI, V+, regular but spaced pitons).

Climb the Second Icefield direct (3-6 pitches depending on conditions) to its top edge. Now traverse L along the edge to the top L corner which is about 50m R of the crest of the Flatiron. Climb a vertical crack (10m, IV, pitons) then traverse L on a ledge for 10m to a chimney which is climbed (IV) before exiting R. An easier pitch diagonally L leads to the Death Bivouac at the top of the Flatiron and below a vertical wall. Now make a rising traverse L across the Third Icefield to its top edge with a short descent at the far end to reach the foot of the Ramp.

Climb the Ramp for 150m (IV) to the foot of an icy chimney or waterfall. Climb this (25m, IV+) or avoid it on the R (VI, Terray Variation). Continue for 25m to the Ice Bulge. Climb this direct (10m) or avoid it on the L (IV+, pitons, waterwashed) to reach a snow/icefield overlooking the Ramp below. Climb the snow/icefield trending R to reach a platform at the start of the Brittle Ledges. These are the key to the upper part of the face and must be taken. Traverse R for 20m (II) to a crack. Climb this (30m, IV), turning an overhang on the R, to reach a good bivouac site at the start of the Traverse of the Gods. Traverse 150m R (III) to the Spider.

Go up the middle of the Spider on its blunt crest to its upper R edge (130m) to enter the R-hand of two obvious gullies which slants diagonally L. Climb the gully (IV) for 150m (may be all ice) to the Quartz Crack. Climb this (IV+), swinging out L at the top (tension useful), then climb easily for 10m to a traverse line. Follow this L for 15m to a small terrace (Corti Bivouac, 50m in all from the foot of the Quartz Crack). Go down L for 6m (fixed rope) to reach the Exit Chimneys. This shallow wet or icy gully is the L-most and easiest of several vertical fissures. Climb this for 3 pitches (IV, III if not ice covered). Turn a rock knoll on its R then climb up rocky gullies for four pitches (II) to the top of the rib separating the NW and NE faces.

Two pitches up the summit icefield lead to the crest of the Mittellegi ridge about 200m from the summit. There are good bivouac sites along the ridge about 4m down the S side.
20-30hr on average

133 **NORTH-EAST PILLAR – SCOTTISH ROUTE**
ED3 I MacEacheran, A McKeith and K Spence, 28-31 July 1970.
64 Winter: J Benes and J Krch, 17-21 Jan 1978

The NE pillar separates the N face (Eigerwand) from the NE face. This route climbs the pillar more or less direct whilst the Austrian route ought really to be considered as a NE face route. For a description of the route see Alpine Climbing, the ACG Bulletin 1971 Page 31.

There is 1800m of climbing; the first 900m is pure rock climbing and the other 900m almost entirely on ice. It is almost entirely free of objective dangers. The rock section rises in three pillars, the first is 240m (VI and A3), the second is 200m (VI and A1) and the third is 220m (VI and A3). There is a fairly good bivouac site at the foot of the second pillar and another at the top of this pillar suitable for four people. A third bivouac site can be found above the third pillar.
See also photos 65 and 66

134 **NORTH-EAST PILLAR – AUSTRIAN ROUTE**
TD T Heibeler, R and G Messner and F Maschka, 30 July–1 Aug 1968
66

A safer way up the NE face (and with more mixed climbing) than the Lauper route in that it is not so exposed to the avalanches which sweep down the latter. It has about the same amount of climbing as the 1938 Eigerwand route but is not nearly so serious. Dougal Haston considered that in good conditions it could be climbed in a day, and would be an excellent training route for N face candidates.

135 **LAUPER ROUTE**
TD+ H Lauper with A Zürcher, J Knubel and A Graven, 20 Aug 1932.
66 Winter: H Trachsel and G Siedhoff, 10-12 Feb 1964

One of the classic ice climbs of the Alps. Quite a serious undertaking, with both stonefall and avalanche dangers, but in good conditions a competent party should be able to avoid a bivouac. It has been descended on skis. The route has ice of 50°-55°, mixed ground of 60° and rock difficulties up to IV.

From Alpiglen get onto the Honysch glacier and climb this, or the rocks on its E side, to just below its upper edge. Move up diagonally R over slabby rock and a few short steps into a steep gully leading through a rock barrier. Climb the gully on the L wall for three pitches, then in the bed and finally on the wall on the R to the top of the barrier. Continue up to the foot of a rock rib (bivouac site).

Climb up three steps on the rib (smooth, brittle and sloping limestone) until forced down R by a rock band into a snow/ice groove. Climb this to the upper icefield then slant Rwards up this to a projection on the N rib, which separates the NE face from the N face.

This is the crux section. Keep just on the R of the rib for several pitches, on very difficult slabby mixed terrain with little in the way of protection, to an often iced-up wall. Climb this by a crack (V, crux) and exit onto steep and probably iced-up slabs. Less steep climbing leads to the Mittellegi ridge. This section is sometimes avoided by following the upper icefield onto the Mittellegi ridge. 12-18hr

136 **NORTH-EAST (MITTELLEGI) RIDGE**
D M von Kuffner with J Beiner, A Burgener and A Kalbermatten,
66 3 July 1885 (in descent). Y Maki with F Amatter, S Brawand and F Steuri, 10 Sept 1921

A superb, exposed route adorned with about 200m of fixed rope (sometimes frozen in or ice covered) and with an excellent snow crest to finish. The climb is much harder if the rope is not used. The first ascent party made use of a 5m pole. The only disappointment is the shortness of the climb. See also photo 62

From the Mittellegi hut go along the ridge for a few minutes to a short but delicate descent down a rocky nose into a gap and the first fixed rope. Follow the crest to the first big step which is climbed on the N side by the longest of the ropes. After two more steps (and ropes) the ridge eases. The final ridge is followed, often on the rocks on the S side (beware of any cornices), to the summit. 4-5hr

137 TD 62

SOUTH-EAST FACE – 1937 ROUTE

O Eidenschink, E Moeller, H Rebitsch and L Vörg, 11-12 Aug 1937. Winter: K Haas, W Müller, E Ott and M Wacker, 21-23 Dec 1972

Most of the climbing is IV and V but is rather spoiled by being subject to stonefall.

From the Eismeer station go out onto the glacier. Turn N and climb to the highest part of the first glacier bay, close to the foot of a couloir in the summit fall-line. About 25m R of the couloir climb a big crack going up Rwards for 4-5 pitches (II-III) to a steepening in the wall. Climb another 40m in the same crack (IV) to where it is possible to traverse R under some overhangs for about 40m.

Get into a chimney and climb this steeply to gain access to a major gully line (probably snow/ice in the gully bed). Climb a few pitches up the gully then exit to the R by a narrow crack (IV). Move up Lwards (V) then R and L again with difficulty (IV and V) to a good stance in the same gully. Two pitches Rwards now lead to a scree covered shoulder (IV, V–). From the R edge of the shoulder climb a crack Lwards to a steep gully (IV). Climb this, with two vertical steps (V–), to a scree filled hollow. Steep broken ground up Lwards leads round an edge on the L. Continue, still Lwards, up good rock for 40m (V–) to a stance. Climb a fine crack for 20m to easier ground. Two pitches up this lead to a deep gully which becomes a chimney (III). Follow this to the Mittellegi ridge. 10-12hr

138 TD+ 62

SOUTH-EAST FACE – 1974 ROUTE

K Moser and W Müller, 24 Aug 1974

More direct than the 1937 route and mainly on good rock. It is best climbed in snow-free conditions, otherwise it is too wet.

Start as for the 1937 Route. 50m up the crack traverse L onto slabs above a small overhang. Climb the slabs for two pitches (IV) to a belay near the central watercourse where the slabs steepen. Move slightly R by a short crack which merges into smooth slabs, then climb these slabs (V–) for one more pitch straight up to the top of a small pillar. An awkward crack now leads diagonally R (piton) onto a sloping ledge under a yellow overhang. Climb this at its weakest point and gain a second ledge by a wet slab (can be avoided on the

R). Climb just R of a 5m high waterfall then under it into a large Rward leaning dièdre (piton). Climb this for 15m (V+) to a belay at the start of the middle zone of slabs.

Climb the slabs direct using cracks. A smooth section at the start can be turned on the L. A second steep section is cut by a deep crack. Where this becomes overhanging move L into a second crack and climb it (IV+) to a ledge. Move R on this to a gap on the edge of the pillar. Climb straight up for a few m, then traverse R on a narrow ledge (piton) until cracks on a broken ramp on the L lead onto the top of this second steep section of the climb. Easier climbing leads to the fore-summit on the Mittellegi ridge. 10hr

Mönch 4099m

S Porges with C Almer and U Kaufmann, 15 May 1857

A much frequented mountain with short routes on the S and E sides and some very fine long and difficult climbs on its N side. This side has a reputation for loose rock but it is really no worse than on other mountains in the vicinity. It is probable that the routes are safer than on the Fiescherwand which has the additional danger of ice avalanches. There are climbs on the W face but nothing of any real interest.

139 **SOUTH-WEST RIDGE**

AD F Wethered with C Almer and C Roth, 24 Aug 1875

67

The SW ridge rises from the E side of the Sphinx by the Jungfraujoch. Half the route is rock, the rest is snow. A good climb and worth combining with the SE ridge as a traverse.

From the Jungfraujoch station exit onto the Jungfraufirn or from the Mönchjoch hut get onto the ridge, about level with the prominent sérac barrier low on the S face, using a slabby couloir just L of an inclined gendarme. Turn a rock tower on the L and reach the foot of a 10m high slab. (If there is a lot of snow it may be possible to climb direct to this point from the Jungfraufirn.) Climb the slab by its R edge (III, 1 piton) then keep more or less to the ridge to where it steepens. Climb direct (rock and snow) until the angle eases then follow the easy snow ridge to the summit. 3-4hr

In descent it is possible (given good enough snow conditions) to descend a steep but easy snow couloir from the top of the highest step on the ridge to join the S face route on the glacier terrace.

140 **NORTH-WEST BUTTRESS – NOLLEN ROUTE**
AD E von Fellenberg with P Egger and C Michel, 13 July 1866
69

A fine long climb (mostly PD) whose difficulty depends on the state of the ice-boss (Nollen). This varies in steepness, may or may not have steps cut in it, and the condition of the ice is variable.

From the Guggi hut traverse Lwards before climbing the scooped face up well-stepped rock and snow to the Mönchplateau (3112m). Now keep to the crest of the ridge to the Nollen. This is climbed direct or in a corner on the L in about 1½ pitches (55°-60°, may even be vertical for a few m. It has taken up to 5hr to climb). From the top of the Nollen cross a small plateau and climb, obliquely R, the snow/ice slope as far as the upper rocks on the R. Climb these easily to the junction with the SW ridge then easily to the summit. 6-10hr

141 **NORTH-WEST FACE – HASTON-EISTRUP ROUTE**
TD+ D Haston and O Eistrup, Sept 1976
69

The route takes the ice couloir between the Nollen and the NW face.

From the Guggi hut follow Route 144 to the foot of the face. Climb the couloir and the upper snow slopes on the W face to the summit. If the lower part of the couloir has insufficient ice use the rocks on the R (W) of the couloir, climbing diagonally from R to L in three pitches to get into the couloir. 7-10hr

142 **NORTH-WEST FACE – 1934 ROUTE**
ED1 Frau Hutton-Rudolph with A Rubi and P Inäbnit, 18 Aug 1934
69

In the lower limestone part of the face there is grade V climbing and on the upper granite parts grade III. Allow about 12hr

143 **NORTH-WEST FACE DIRECT**
ED2 D Renshaw and D Wilkinson, 23-26 Dec 1976
69

The quality of the climbing on this route was found to be excellent, but with poor belays and steep ice on the lower section. Stonefall makes it inadvisable as a summer climb, but in winter, spring or autumn objective dangers are much reduced. The climb generally follows the angle formed between the N face rib and the face itself.

144 **NORTH FACE RIB – LAUPER ROUTE**
TD H Lauper and M Liniger, 23 July 1921
69

An excellent mixed route which is more-or-less free of objective danger.

The climb was originally done from the Eigergletscher and the rib was followed in its entirety. It is more common now to start at the Guggi hut because of the state of the approach glacier on the original line. It was climbed in winter in 1963.

From the Guggi hut follow Route 140 to the Mönchplateau and then make a steep descent E to the glacier coombe below the NW face. Cross the coombe almost horizontally to a snow slope that splits the NE rib. Climb the snow slope to its upper edge and slant up R to get onto the upper of three snow covered ledges crossing the rock wall.

Follow the ledge to its W end and reach a vertical crack. Climb this (often verglassed) to its top (V–) and then move R behind a detached block. Now either traverse L to a second crack and climb this with difficulty (V) or use aid to climb the roof above the block. It is also possible to move down R before climbing mixed ground back Lwards to above these difficulties.

Climb the ice slope for 300m (rock in a warm summer) to a rock rib, leading up L. Climb it (II, III) to get back onto the NE rib itself. Climb the steep snow crest to its top and junction with the NE ridge. 10-12hr

145 NORTH-EAST RIDGE

AD
69

G Foster with H Baumann snr and jnr and F Teutschmann, 31 July 1877

More entertaining than the ordinary, SE ridge route and quite accessible from the Mönchjoch hut. Delicate in places.

From the Mönchjoch hut follow Route 124 to the S Eigerjoch at the foot of the ridge. Climb the snow and rock crest to the bergschrund which is usually crossed on the L on the NE flank. Back on the ridge climb two steeper rock sections (or avoid them on the L) to the final steep snow crest (cornices) leading to the summit. 4-5hr

146 NORTH-EAST FACE

D+

G Hasler and C Jossi snr, 19 June 1904

A short but quite steep (300m, 55°-60°) snow/ice climb. A good introduction to N face ice routes.

From the Mönchjoch or Bergli huts follow Route 124 towards the S Eigerjoch. From Pt 3687m cross to the centre of the face and take a line direct to the summit. 3-5hr

147 **SOUTH-EAST RIDGE**
PD R Macdonald with C Almer and M Anderegg, 29 July 1863
67

This constitutes the ordinary route and is a very short climb from the Mönchjoch hut. Delicate in places but of no real difficulty.

From the Mönchjoch hut cross snow slopes SW to the foot of the S branch of the ridge. Climb the ridge in its entirety on snow and rock. The last section is almost horizontal and corniced. Keep on the S side. 2-3hr

148 **SOUTH FACE**
D D von Bethmann-Hollweg with O and O Supersaxo, 22 Aug 1913
67

Mainly a snow climb but with some delicate rock in dry years. Difficulties can usually be avoided by choice of line. Because of the S facing aspect it is as well to complete the face early in the day.

Reach the centre of the face from the Mönchjoch hut. Climb up to the R of the low sérac band and reach an inclined glacier terrace. Climb as direct as possible to the summit. 3-5hr

Jungfraujoch 3475m

First traverse: H George, J Hardy, H Morgan, L Stephen, A Moore and R Liveing with C Almer, C and P Michel, U Kaufmann, C Bohren, P Baumann and P Rubi, 21 July 1862

Situated between the Mönch and Jungfrau and often referred to when one really means the Sphinx (3569m) which is the rocky point on the ridge just to the E and the point of exit from the Jungfraujoch railway. It is of no great value as a route of access to the Jungfraufirn, since the N side is protected by a long sérac band. The S side is very easy.

149 **NORTH SIDE**
D From the Guggi hut follow Route 152 to the upper snow plateau of the Chielouwenen glacier (3-4hr). Now climb up to the R of the sérac band (55°) and traverse L above it to the col. 3-4hr, up to 8hr in all

Jungfraujoch to the Lötschenpass

A long chain of mountains running NE-SW which actually starts with the Eiger and the Mönch (which are described in another section). The whole chain maintains a height of over 3000m, and is consistently well above this in the NE half, over most of its length. There are no easy crossing points on the whole of the ridge except over the Petersgrat. The climber is thus presented with considerable problems if wishing to return to the valley after doing routes on the Lauterbrunnen wall – the magnificent N side of the chain extending from the Rotalhorn to the Lauterbrunnen Breithorn. The rock quality on the faces leaves much to be desired but on the ridges it is generally quite good. Most of the routes from the S side of the chain are quite easy whilst those from the N are much more demanding and require a great deal of ability and commitment as well as fitness. The major peak in the chain is, of course, the Jungfrau. It was one of the first 4000m peaks to be climbed and is regularly climbed today thanks to the easy access provided by the Jungfraujoch railway.

The chain is delineated on its S and E sides by the Jungfraufirn, and by the Grosser Aletsch glacier on the E side of the Lötschenlücke and by the Lötschental on the W side of this pass. To the N is the Lauterbrunnental to the E of the Tschingelpass and the Gasteretal to the W of this pass.

Map covering this section is: Jungfrau (264)

Jungfrau 4158.2m

J Rudolf and H Meyer with J Bortis and A Volker, 3 Aug 1821. Winter: Miss Brevoort and W Coolidge with C and U Almer, 22-23 Jan 1874

The Jungfrau is to Interlaken what the Matterhorn is to Zermatt. From the N side it has a look of impregnability but from the S it is much more amenable, although not easy to approach unless use is made of the Jungfraujoch railway. Only the ordinary route is short; all other climbs are quite lengthy undertakings and not that easy to retreat from in the advent of bad weather.

150 **SOUTH-EAST RIDGE FROM THE ROTTALSATTEL**
PD First ascent party
68 *A much frequented route in summer and spring since there is easy access to*

the Jungfraufirn from the Jungfraujoch railway. Less wealthy alpinists may prefer to approach from Konkordia. Several parties have come to grief on this climb in the past at the traverse just above the Rottalsattel. This has been made safe by the installation of fixed belay posts. See also photo 70

From the Mönchjoch hut retrace the track to the Sphinx tunnel entrance. Descend the Jungfraufirn Swards (crevasses) to the foot of Pt 3411.1m. Scramble up the rocks (rain gauge) on traces of track to where the angle steepens. Climb another 8m (abseil slings and ring piton) then make a long traverse L onto easy angled snow. Now gain the crest of the broad snow ridge above. Alternatively and more commonly pass round the S side of this point to a steep snow slope which is climbed to the broad snow ridge. Continue on the ridge until it is possible to traverse R (usually a trench) to below the Rottalsattel. Climb steeply up to the col (usually from the L in summer).

Climb about 50m above the col and traverse the snow/ice slope (posts) to the rocks on the L. Climb the rocks and snow patches to the summit. 3½-5hr.

It is sometimes possible (in a very snowy year) to reach the Rottalsattel by ascending SW into the coombe directly below the col. The bergschrund below the col is often impassable. This saves about 1hr.

From Konkordia hut climb the L side of the Jungfraufirn to Pt 3411.1m (2-3hr) and there join the route described above.

151 **INNER ROTTAL RIDGE**
AD F von Allmen with U Brunner, F Graf jnr, K Schlunegger and
70 J Stäger, 21 Sept 1885

The route follows the S branch of the SW ridge. It is a splendid long climb and the only satisfactory route on the W flank of the mountain. It is quite delicate if the rock is snow-covered or verglassed and the best line is not easy to find, especially in descent.

From the Rottal hut follow a track NW to the foot of the crags seen on the skyline above the hut. Climb through these easily by moving L a little way and reach the broad and fairly level part of the Inner Rottal ridge (cairn at Pt 2927m).

Go along the ridge to a steepening then slant L (but not too far) and climb easy slabs to regain the crest of the ridge, above the steep section, at a narrow, smooth rock nose in which there are three iron stakes. It is possible to move well to the L at the steepening and climb slabs and gullies to regain the ridge, but this will always be harder than the route described. Above the nose continue to a snow saddle where the main difficulties begin.

Move L off the ridge and climb a couloir slanting L (two fixed ropes). Slant back R at the top of the couloir to a steep wall (gneiss now after limestone) and climb the wall (fixed rope) to easier ground leading up to the ridge on the L, which is gained close to Pt 3790m. Difficulties in this section are II and III. At this point Inner and Outer Rottal ridges merge.

Continue up the ridge and climb a steep section, via a shallow snow couloir and easy rock steps, to the upper snow plateau from which a steep snow slope and easy rocks lead to the summit. You can avoid the steep section by keeping L and traversing back R onto the snow plateau. 6-8hr

152 **GUGGI ROUTE**
D H George and G Young with C Almer, U Almer snr and
71 H Baumann, 29 Aug 1865

At one time quite frequently climbed, but glacier conditions have changed over the years and it is now a considerable undertaking, whilst remaining a very fine climb in magnificent surroundings. The main difficulties are on ice, but the ability to navigate quickly through jumbled glacier terrain is important. Late in the season the route is probably impracticable. See also photos 70 and 80

From the Guggi hut descend a couloir down ledges and slabs (unpleasant, cables) SW. Still on the rocks traverse S, rising slightly (more cables) to some polished rocks. Turn these and then descend to the Guggi glacier (more cables) at a flat area with few crevasses. Climb the glacier SW to the icefall below the Chielouwenen glacier. Climb the icefall (often complex and difficult) to the snow basin above. Cross this Wwards to the rocks at the foot of the Schneehorn. Climb these direct or slanting up from L to R to a snowy ledge. Either gain the summit or avoid it on the L and enter the upper coombe of the Giessen glacier.

Cross the coombe SW to the foot of the Kl Silberhorn (3543m). Climb the snow/ice ridge to its summit and so reach the snow coombe below the Silberlücke. Cross the coombe in the direction of the col (bivouac site) and climb to it by a steep snow slope. The slope may be icy or protected by a large bergschrund. In this case continue up the NE ridge of the Silberhorn (3695m) and descend the easy, rocky S ridge to the col.

Climb a short rock ridge and an exposed snow crest to the

Hochfirn and then continue up this to the summit rocks which are climbed via a steep snow slope and easy rocks. 8-12hr

153 **NORTH-EAST RIDGE**
D+ A Weber with H Schlunegger snr, 30 July 1911
68

A long ridge with some excellent climbing. Unfortunately the lower part of the ridge has been spoiled by the installation of some telecommunications equipment and, although it is still possible to climb this section, it seems better to avoid it even though this means missing the most difficult part of the ridge. See also photo 71

From the Mönchjoch hut follow the track to the Sphinx tunnel and descend the Jungfraufirn to get under the S side of the ridge. Climb a couloir leading up between the double gendarme of Pt 3809m (if necessary the rocks bordering the couloir can be utilised, III). Follow the ridge over over several steps (excellent climbing on the crest, III and IV), with deviations onto the N face where necessary, to a large gendarme (3992m).

The next section starts with a snow crest and is followed by three high gendarmes. Climb each of these – the first has poor rock in its lower part and is quite delicate (mostly III, one section of IV) – before a steep and exposed wall leads to the Wengen Jungfrau (Pt 4089m). Cross the Hochfirn to the foot of the final rocks and follow the crest (reached by steep snow) to the summit. 8-11hr

Silberhorn 3695m

E von Fellenberg and K Bädeker with C von Allmen, P Michel, H Baumann, P Inäbnit, F Fuchs and C Lauener, 4 Aug 1863

A satellite of the Jungfrau and best climbed in combination with this peak. There are no easy descent routes from the peak.

154 **ROTBRETT RIDGE**
D E Gertsch, Ed Gertsch and F Fuchs, 22-24 Aug 1926
71

The route had been climbed earlier but the key passage had been avoided (H King, A Supersaxo and L Zurbrüggen, 24 Sept 1887). It is a long mixed climb with the major difficulties on rock and low down. The Rotbrett is the 500m high triangular pillar of rock on the NW side of the Jungfrau adjacent to the Silberhorn hut. The climb follows its N edge and has three sections of fixed ropes. Nowhere are the difficulties very great but escape from the route is difficult and it is this which makes it a serious undertaking.

From the Silberhorn hut climb SE across steep and overlapping rocks to snow slopes leading to the crest of the ridge forming the N side of the Rotbrett. Climb the R (W) side of the snow slope and reach a wall via some shattered rock steps (all this section is somewhat variable and is best inspected in the light of day). Climb the wall using a 30m long cable then climb a few more metres before following a stony gangway Rwards for about 50m (delicate with a slight descent at the start). A wide, stepped crack leads easily to a fixed rope. From its top climb the ridge without much difficulty, on the crest or just L of it, and reach the shoulder at Pt 3382m (the top of the Rotbrett).

Follow the less steep ridge to the bottom of a 6m high, overhanging step (the Fellenbergflieli). A fixed rope allows this obstacle to be passed. In very good snow conditions it is possible to pass it on the N side by the edge of the Silberhorn glacier. Just above the ridge turns to snow. Continue up it and over a snow boss (Goldenhorn) and then climb the snow slopes to the summit. 5-6hr

Continue via Route 152 to the summit of the Jungfrau. 8-12hr in all

155 **NORTH-WEST RIB**
D J Hornby and T Philpott with C Almer, C Lauener, J Bischoff and
71 U Almer snr, 10 Aug 1865

Best climbed when the rock is dry. The climbing is a bit more sustained than on the Rotbrett Ridge.

From the Silberhorn hut traverse across rocks to a scree band below the Silberhorn glacier and then go up L (NE) across scree covered loose rocks into a gorge (stone and icefall danger). Now climb the W flank of the ridge to the crest which is followed to a notch. More difficult climbing, either direct or on the L, follows (III) to an easing. Follow the fairly steep snow above to the summit. 6-8hr

156 **NORTH FACE**
D+ J Jenkins and M Taylor, 11 Aug 1939
71

Approximately 50° ice with some stonefall danger in the lower part. Probably a useful route for training or indifferent weather.

From the Silberhorn hut go downhill Wwards onto the snow band at the foot of the NW ridge. Go round the base of the ridge then climb rocks on its E flank before gaining the snowfields on the L. Climb these with increasing difficulty to the summit. A bergschrund has to be crossed near the crest at the top of the NW ridge. 4-6hr

Rottalhorn 3969m

Merely a subsidiary summit of the Jungfrau but probably worth traversing to extend the ascent of this mountain. There are two rock climbs on the SE face (AD and D) but otherwise there is little of interest.

157 **TRAVERSE SOUTH-NORTH**
AD T von Hahn with F Amatter and F Kaufmann, 1 Aug 1907
68

From the Mönchjoch or Konkordia huts follow Route 150 to the foot of Pt 3411.1m. Pass round the S side of this point (large crevasses) and climb steepening snow slopes towards the Louwihorn (3778m). Traverse under this summit to the col at the foot of the SE ridge.

Climb a steep, narrow snow/ice couloir, which cuts through the lower two thirds of the rocks, and then easy rocks to the summit. 3-4hr

Descend the easy snow ridge to the Rottalsattel and rejoin Route 150 to the Jungfrau. 15min. See also photo 70

Louwitor and Louwihorn 3676m and 3779m

These are two snow humps between the Rottalhorn and Gletscherhorn. Quite frequently climbed in spring, and worth considering if travelling between the Hollandia and Mönchjoch huts as an alternative to going via Konkordiaplatz. Some people come this way as a winter approach to the Lauterbrunnen Wall from the Jungfraujoch railway, descending one of the couloirs into the Rottal.

158 **FROM THE EAST**
F From the Mönchjoch hut follow Route 157 to the col at the foot of
68 the SE ridge of the Rottalhorn. Climb the snow slope leading S to the summit of the Louwihorn (it may be possible to ignore the

traverse to the col and climb direct to the summit). Continue easily to the Louwitor. 3hr

159 **FROM THE SOUTH**
F
72
From the Hollandia hut get onto the Kranzbergfirn after descending the Aletsch glacier by Route 205 and climb it straightforwardly to the summit of the Louwitor. The crevassed zone at about 3300m is climbed on the R (E) side. 3-3½hr

Kranzberg 3737.7m

Probably C Freeman with H Zurflüh and A Stähli, 19 Aug 1896

This is a popular ski mountain but is infrequently climbed in summer athough it is not unworthy of attention. It has four distinct tops and a traverse of them is quite satisfying.

160 **TRAVERSE SOUTH-NORTH**
PD
72
From the Konkordia or Hollandia huts reach the SE corner of the mountain (Pt 2740m) and climb the glacier face, passing below the rib S of Pt 3610.6m, to reach the col between this point and the S summit (3666m). Continue along the ridge to the N summit. 3-4hr

It is also possible to climb the SE ridge (D, loose in places) to reach the S summit. 8-10hr

Descend by reversing Route 159 to the Aletsch glacier to return to either hut.

Gletscherhorn 3983m

J Hornby with C Lauener, 15 Aug 1867

The most notable feature of the mountain is its magnificent northern flank, which forms the E end of the Lauterbrunnen Wall and which dominates the view from the Rottal hut. Its S side is much less spectacular but still provides a few worthwhile and not much frequented climbs, each of which requires a good deal of effort to approach.

Climbers attempting routes on the N side can be faced with the problem of returning to that side. This can be achieved at much expense by using the railway from the Jungfraujoch but otherwise there is no easy route (see note to Lowitor for winter approach).

Probably the best solution is to descend to the Hollandia hut and then follow Route 182 to get onto the W flank of the S ridge of the Grosshorn and from here reach the Schmadrijoch. Descend from here by reversing Route 188 to the Schmadri hut.

161 **SOUTH-EAST RIDGE**
D– R Hodel, H Lamper and H Rey, 9 June 1919
72

There are pitches of III and IV in the lower part of the ridge.

From the Konkordia or Hollandia huts reach the foot of the ridge N of Pt 3414.1m. Climb the first step on the S side and then the narrow snow crest to the next step. Climb this on the N side by a groove and wall. Another snow crest is climbed followed by two gendarmes before descending into a snowy gap. Easy rock leads to the summit. 6hr

162 **WEST RIDGE**
PD First ascent party

From the Konkordia or Hollandia huts climb the Gletscherfirn to the Gletscherjoch (3769m). 3-4hr

Climb the snow ridge (cornices) to Pt 3888.7m. In good snow conditions it should be possible to climb direct to the lowest rocks on the ridge without going to the Gletscherjoch. Pass two gendarmes then climb steep rock (II, III) to the W summit. Cross a deep gap and some small gendarmes (exposed) to the main summit. 2hr, about 6hr in all

163 **NORTH FACE RIB**
TD H Etter and E Reiss, 29 Aug 1945
73

The lower part of the rib had been climbed in 1911 (O Williamson, J Maître and H Fuchs) but the party left the rib to reach the Gletscherjoch. The climb takes the extreme R-hand rib on the NW face directly below Pt 3888.7m, where the route ends. A worthwhile climb with no real objective dangers. Most of the difficulties are on ice.

From the Rottal hut cross the Rottal glacier to the foot of the rib coming down from Pt 3888.7m. Cross the bergschrund on avalanche debris at the foot of a snow couloir. On the E side of the couloir get onto the rib at its least distinct section via a snow band. This part of the rib has easy broken rocks. The rib disappears higher up into a solid rock flank which is climbed until it is possible to get onto snow at about 3600m. The snow rib is interrupted by an ice bulge, which is climbed with difficulty, and then becomes less distinct. Continue up snow to another ice bulge which is climbed diagonally Rwards. From the top of the rib follow the W ridge to the summit. 12hr

164 **CARRINGTON-ROUSE ROUTE**
ED2 R Carrington and A Rouse, June 1972
73

The lower half of the route gives some excellent, sustained and serious mixed climbing, then from the 'terrace' at half height the difficulties ease somewhat. The lower part of the climb is threatened by the sérac band on the upper face. It had a winter ascent in the 1980's.

Start in the first gully R of the central couloir and climb this (steep) for 150m to a broadening and easing of the angle. Trend L on icy rock and climb grooves just R of a rock pillar before exiting onto a rectangular icefield. Climb direct to the rock band above and work through this, just R of the continuation pillar, by a series of icy grooves, before trending L again to the crest of the rib above the pillar. Keep on the rib to the 'terrace'.

Move up the icefield and find a way through the sérac band (usually climb diagonally R to the séracs and work back L through a break in the wall). Above the séracs trend R, cross a bergschrund and get onto an ice ridge below a final sérac bulge. Climb the ridge to Pt 3888.7m. 8-12hr from the foot of the face

165 **REISS-ETTER-JAUN ROUTE**
TD+/ H Etter, F Jaun and E Reiss, 16 July 1945. Winter: H Muller and
ED1 H Berger, 12-13 Feb 1971
73

A long (over 1000m) mixed climb with the main difficulties on ice up to 60°. It is the easiest climb on the face and the most direct route to the summit, but is seriously threatened by sérac fall over its entire length.

Reach the foot of the face in about 1hr from the Rottal hut. Cross the bergschrund and immediately traverse R to the rocks. These give steep climbing on good holds (mostly II and III with some moves of IV) straight up to a 60m high icefield. This leads to a very steep ice slope on the first hanging glacier. Slant L up the ice to the rocks in the summit fall-line below the upper hanging glacier. The rocks are steep and often icy and lead to another icefield which, higher up, is blocked by a rock rib.

Climb the ice, turning a bulge on the R, and reach the foot of the icy summit rocks by crossing a slabby groove. Go up Lwards on very steep ice onto an icy bulge directly below the summit. A steep snow slope with another ice bulge allows access to the foot of the ice couloir leading to the summit which can be gained on the L or R. 10-16hr

166 **WELZENBACH ROUTE**
TD+ W Welzenbach, A Drexel, H Rudy and E Schulze, 9-10 Sept 1931
73

The original route on the face. In present lean snow conditions it is not being climbed (at least in summer). The lower part is seriously threatened by sérac fall.

The climb starts at the foot of the central couloir and climbs Lwards towards the prominent rock barrier at half-height. The crux of the climb is a L to R traverse through the top of this barrier. Above this obstacle the route keeps trending L to finish on the NE ridge some distance from the summit.

167 **GRIFFIN-BARTLETT ROUTE**
ED1 L Griffin and P Bartlett, 1977

This climb is a more direct and harder variation of the Welzenbach Route and was considered to be much safer. The start is a couloir below and slightly L of the crux pitch on the original route. After a few hundred metres some quite difficult climbing (Scottish winter IV) is encountered moving R to the icefield below the rock barrier. After crossing the barrier a more direct line is taken (easier climbing now but sustained) to exit on the NE ridge. 8-9hr

168 **BARRY-NICHOLLS ROUTE**
TD J Barry and D Nicholls, Aug 1977

The start is as for the Griffin-Bartlett Route but in this case the couloir is climbed in its entirety. It crosses mixed ground with two or three superb ice pitches (70°-80°). Some of the difficulties can be avoided and the route finishes well down the NE ridge. 12hr

169 **NORTH-EAST RIDGE**
AD Mme and M Gallet with J Kalbermatten and C Kaufmann,
72 26 July 1897

Not greatly popular but could be combined with the W ridge to make a traverse of the mountain.

From the Konkordia or Hollandia huts follow Route 159 to the Louwitor. Make a short descent to a col at Pt 3644m. Follow the crest of the ridge, which is corniced in its central part, to the rocks of the upper part. Climb these direct to the summit (III) or traverse to the S and reach the upper part of the SE ridge to gain the summit. 2hr from the Louwitor

Äbeni Flue 3962m

T Brown with P Bohren and P Schlegel, 27 Aug 1868

On earlier editions of the map it was named Ebnefluh. Its main attraction is its N flank which provides some good and not too serious ice routes. On the S side there are fairly gently inclined snow slopes which provide some interest to ski-mountaineers in spring time, although the ascent is often spoiled by planes and helicopters landing close to the Äbeni Flue-joch.

170 **SOUTH-WEST FLANK**
F First ascent party

An easy outing in fine glacier terrain.

From the Hollandia hut climb the Äbeni Fluefirn. The first part is crevassed, but as the angle eases it is much less so. Follow the obvious curving line to reach the col NW of Pt 3928m. The snowy ridge leads to the summit. 2-3hr

It is also quite common to reach the summit by climbing to the col E of Pt 3811.4m and following the W ridge to the top.

171 **NORTH-WEST (ROTI FLUE) RIDGE**
TD O Hug and H Lauper, 18 Aug 1922
74

This is a good mixed climb, the rock difficulties being no more than III in dry conditions but much harder when verglassed. The lower part of the ridge is the hardest.

From the Rottal hut reach the foot of the ridge at a snowy bay which is climbed to attain the ridge at about 2950m. Climb the crest over a series of ever steepening steps. Avoid a rocky projection on the L (N) side and get back to the crest at a small gap not much below Pt 3811.4m. Traverse into a steep couloir and climb this to reach the corniced ridge just E of the distictive gendarme of Pt 3811.4m. Continue along the ridge to the summit. 8hr

172 **NORTH FACE TO WEST SUMMIT**
TD P Gabarrou and P Steiner, 25 Sept 1980
74 *Probably the hardest route on the N face, this climbs to the ridge just E of Pt 3811.4m by a fairly direct line. It is mainly ice with two steep sections of 80°-85°.*

173 **NORTH FACE**
D+ C Macdonald with P Bernet and C Jössi snr, 2 Aug 1895. Winter:
74 E Friedli, 1964

In good snow/ice conditions (usually in early summer) it is possible to

climb almost anywhere on the face at about the same grade. The face is about 900m high and almost as wide, with an angle of 50°-55°. Choice of route will often depend on where it is possible to cross the bergschrund. Some lines finish on the ridge between Pt 3811.4m and the summit, whilst others finish at the summit. A line up the centre of the face ending on the ridge about mid-way between the summit and Pt 3811.4m is about the easiest, and is sometimes used as a means of descent on this side of the Lauterbrunnen Wall.

From the Rottal hut cross the glacier to the foot of the face and climb the bergscrund wherever possible. Climb as direct as you wish to the ridge or summit. 5-8hr

174 **NORTH RIDGE**
D J Farrar and Miss F Wills with P Almer snr and jnr and P Boss,
74 16 July 1924

A very fine snow/ice ridge up to 50°. The route avoids the rocks forming the lower part of the ridge although these can be climbed at a higher grade.

From the Rottal hut cross the glacier and climb up it on the W side of the ridge, avoiding crevasses on the R. Cross the bergschrund and climb the snow/ice slope on the W flank of the ridge to reach the crest near the last rocks. From here the ridge is steep and narrow until it merges with a bulging glacier slope which leads to the summit. 7-8hr

175 **SOUTH-SOUTH-EAST RIDGE**
AD D Chervet and M Etienne, 23 July 1928

The best climb on the S side of the mountain. It was descended two years prior to its first ascent.

From the Hollandia hut traverse horizontally NE to below Pt 3463m. Climb a snow/scree couloir towards the gap between the last two gendarmes on the ridge until just below the crest. Move L and climb rocks to the top of the gendarme (Pt 3463m). Keep to the crest as far as Pt 3716.6m.

A steepening snow crest leads to the S summit (3928m) then easier angled snow is followed to the main summit. 5hr

C Montadon, A Ringier and A Rubin, 19 Aug 1878

This is a fairly undistinguished mountain, quite easily reached from the Hollandia hut. It has a steep, glaciated and fairly remote S face whilst its N face forms part of the Lauterbrunnen wall. The climbs on the N face are less frequented than those on other parts of the wall.

176 SOUTH FLANK

AD T Danby and H Reade with T Kalbermatten, 2 Sept 1895

Fairly infrequently climbed but it has some interesting glacier terrain.

From the Hollandia hut descend the Lang glacier to the flat Grossi Tola, then pass under Pt 2800m to Chrumme Rigg and get onto the flat part of the Anun glacier. This same position can be reached from Fafleralp by following the path leading to the N side of the Lang glacier and up the SSE ridge of Jegichnubel. Where the path disappears get onto the Anun glacier and climb its W side to the flat central section.

Climb as direct as possible to the fore-summit by the glacier slopes on the W side of the Anujoch. About 4hr from the hut, 6hr from Fafleralp.

177 WEST RIDGE

AD H Dübi with F Fuchs and F Graf snr, 16 July 1880

The easiest route from the N side. Good rock in remote surroundings.

From the Schmadri hut get onto the Vordre Schmadri glacier and cross it Ewards before climbing up it SE to gain the foot of the W ridge (this is the ridge whose top is Pt 3753.6m).

Climb the ridge on the crest with just the occasional detour on the N side (II, III). From the top of the ridge the summit is easily reached by the snow ridge over the W summit (narrow in places). 7hr

178 NORTH FACE OF WEST SUMMIT

ED1 P Zafiropule with H Stähli, 2 July 1977

The face had been climbed earlier by a less direct line (H Kiene, 7 July 1976). The route starts up the Schmadririgg and is 750m high, steepening as it rises. The lower part is about 50° with mixed sections up to 60°, whilst the upper part is about 60° with mixed climbing up to 80°. Most of the difficulties are in the mixed sections which require climbing in crampons at V and V+ in places.

From the Schmadri hut cross the moraine and pass under the N wall of the Grosshorn Lwards up the Vorder Schmadri glacier. At about 3000m get onto and go up the Schmadririgg to its end.

Start by climbing diagonally Lwards up a 50° snow slope to a rock rib. Climb a gully slanting L, then go straight up the rib and again L to its edge before finally moving back R to its top. Climb the snowfield above moving slightly L to the next rocks.

Get into an ice couloir and climb it for 10m then move L on steep mixed ground to a stance. Climb steep rocks moving Lwards to reach the final steep wall. Climb one pitch, 10m Lwards to a rib then 20m straight up to a vertical section, where a traverse R is made to a small snow rib before moving up a few more m to a good stance on the L edge of a snow couloir. Traverse 5m into the couloir then go up it, keeping on the L side, to exit via rocks at the top onto the summit icefield. Climb the gradually easing slope direct to the W summit (3835m). 9-12hr

179 **NORTH-WEST FACE**

TD+ E Feuz and K Dahlem, 4 July 1934

The lower part (about 500m) of the face is a steep snowfield tapering towards the top between icy rock ribs. The upper rock wall has an obvious pillar and the route takes the R side of this. Most of the difficulties are on mixed terrain but there is rock of IV-V with poor protection.

From the Schmadri hut follow Route 178 onto the glacier, but cross this Ewards, climbing slightly, and cross the Schmadririgg at about 2600m to reach the S Breitlouwenen glacier. Climb this to the foot of the wall.

Climb to the highest bergschrund and cross it more or less in the summit fall-line. Climb the snow/ice slope above into the narrow section to reach the upper rocks. Climb the pillar using ribs slanting L to R up it. Two overhangs are turned on the R by the edge of the pillar. From the top of the pillar a snow ridge with a few rocks leads to the summit. 10hr

180 **NORTH RIDGE**

D J Gallet with J Kalbermatten and C Kaufmann, 27 July 1897

A short but interesting climb with one pitch of IV.

From the Hollandia hut follow Route 170 but leave this to reach the Äbeni Flue-Joch. Climb the snow and rock ridge to the summit. About 4hr

181 **SOUTH-SOUTH-EAST RIDGE**
PD First ascent party

From the Hollandia hut climb the Äbeni Fluefirn (crevassed at first on the steeper section) along the obvious ramp to below the Anujoch. Climb to the col (3635m) by a short but steep snow slope. Climb the ridge, mainly snow and narrow in places, to the fore-summit. Rocks between the fore-summit and main summit are delicate if verglassed. 2-3hr

It is possible to climb the Anungrat all the way from the Hollandia hut. It is D and about 4hr to the Anujoch.

Grosshorn 3754m

W Summit: F Wyss-Wyss with F Fuchs and C Gertsch, 29 July 1875
Main Summit: E Burckhardt and O Schifferdecker with J Rubin, P Schlegel and K Schlunegger, 12 Aug 1885

A splendid, remote summit with three distinct ridges and a prominent subsidiary top to the W. The S ridge is mainly snow and offers the easiest route. The NE, between the summit and the Grossjoch, has three steep and quite difficult steps and is rarely climbed (D). The ridge linking the main and W summits is also not often climbed but is described here. The most important feature of the mountain is its 1200m high N face on which there are some quite demanding ice routes.

182 **SOUTH RIDGE**
F First ascent party

From Fafleralp or the Hollandia hut follow Route 176 onto the Anun glacier and from there reach the col, Zem hindri Ligg (3018m), by a steep and partly rocky couloir. Now follow the ridge N to the summit. The last section, between a fore-summit at 3567m and the main summit, is very narrow. About 8hr from Fafleralp and 5hr from Hollandia

183 **WEST RIDGE TO WEST SUMMIT**
PD First ascent party to this summit
76

From the Schmadrijoch, reached by Routes 188 or 189, climb the steep snow and rock ridge to about 3350m, where the angle eases and a snow ridge leads to the W summit at 3671m. Avoid any difficulties on the S side. 3hr

184 **NORTH-WEST RIDGE TO WEST SUMMIT**
TD– H Lauper and M Liniger, 26 July 1921
76

A fairly interesting climb; the rock changes from granite to limestone to gneiss as the ridge is ascended. It becomes progressively steeper as it approaches the W summit and some of the rock is loose.

From the Schmadri hut get onto the start of the ridge (large granite blocks) and climb easily to Pt 2746m. Continue up the steeper crest (limestone) and then snow to a step (gneiss) which is climbed on the crest. The final and steepest section of the ridge can be climbed direct (IV+) by a smooth wall a few metres R of the crest to a small platform. From here rejoin the crest by slanting up L in cracks and chimneys. The alternative is to traverse L a little onto the N face and get back onto the crest via a chimney/couloir. A succession of short steps lead to the W summit. 7hr

185 **TRAVERSE FROM WEST TO EAST SUMMIT**
TD *Although infrequently climbed the rock is good. In descent several abseils*
76 *are necessary.*

From the W summit turn a rock spike on the S side and reach a gap below a vertical step. Climb 30m slanting R on the S side (III) to a sloping belay (piton) below a 25m high vertical wall. Start up the wall (V, pitons) then traverse L to a dièdre which is followed (pitons) until it can be left on the L to reach a flat belay on the ridge crest below another vertical step (abseil piton). Climb less steep rock on the N side then follow the exposed crest (III) to the final snow crest. 2hr

186 **NORTH FACE OF WEST SUMMIT**
TD+ K Grüter and F Villiger, 6 July 1962
76

The difficulties on the route depend mainly on the amount of ice build-up on the rocks. In lean conditions the route is quite unsafe.

From the Schmadri hut follow Route 187 until at about half-height on the N face. Now climb steep snow/ice and the rocks above fairly directly to the summit. It is also possible to follow a line further to the W. 10-15hr

187 **NORTH FACE**
TD W Welzenbach, A Drexel, H Rudy and E Schulze, 25-27 July 1932.
76 Winter: H von Känel and H Müller, 2 Jan 1970.
Direct finish: E Koblmüller and E Lackner, July 1971.
Route described: E Feuz, W von Allmen, 8-9 July 1934

The route described is more direct than the original Welzenbach route and is more frequently climbed. The route is essentially an ice climb of fairly constant angle but with two steeper pitches (55°-60°), and is relatively safe. There is a direct finish, and some other options which can be taken according to conditions. On 27 July 1959 K Diemberger and M Eiselin climbed the face by a line further E.

From the Schmadri hut climb E up the Vordre Schmadri glacier to the steep narrow glacier at the foot of the face. Climb the glacier slope (often several bergschrunds which can be avoided by rocks on the L at II-III) to reach the shallow ice couloir descending from the summit. Climb this until below a rock barrier at about 3200m. Pass this by a traverse L in an icy gully (steep). Now, close to the rocks, reach the upper ice slope and climb this to the summit rock wall. Keep L of this and, still on ice, reach the summit. 8-15hr

Jegichnubel 3124.1m

This minor summit offers the possibility of some entertainment when higher summits are out of condition. It is quite easily reached from Fafleralp. The N ridge is D, quite exposed and with some doubtful rock. The SE ridge is PD and well worth climbing, whilst the SW ridge is AD and highly recommended (some III+).

Approach all the routes via Route 176. For the SW ridge climb up the coombe between the SW and SE ridges and join the ridge at a point E of the snow patch under the S face, by a tricky couloir. Allow 5-6hr from Fafleralp for all the routes.

Schmadrijoch 3337.5m

First traverse: J Hornby, F Morshead and T Philpott with J Anderegg and C Lauener, 4 Aug 1866

Of no great value as a pass but it provides a means of descent for routes on the Grosshorn N face, access to the W ridge of this mountain and to the NE ridge of the Breithorn.

188 **NORTH SIDE**
AD
77

From the Schmadri hut climb the lateral moraine on the E side of the glacier which descends W of the hut (Hindre Schmadri glacier), until it is possible to walk onto the glacier. Climb S towards the lowest rock outcrop. Go up a steep snow slope to the R of this and L of a curving rock rib, and then up rocks to avoid the séracs of the upper branch of the glacier. Continue by climbing part way up an icy couloir between the rocks and the sérac barrier before quitting this for the rocks on the L which lead to the less steep upper part of the glacier. Reach the col by moving R. 4hr

It is sometimes possible to move R before the icy couloir and climb steep snow slopes further W.

189 **SOUTH SIDE**
PD

From Fafleralp follow the path from Guggistafel to Pt 2108m. Now climb N up the valley and at about 2200m go up a couloir, then brocken rocks, to reach scree slopes below the W flank of Jegichnubel. Climb up parallel to the base of the rocks of the Jegichnubel until above the rock island sited below the W side of Zem hindri Ligg. Now traverse the glacier NW to the col. 5-6hr

Lauterbrunnen Breithorn 3784.9m

E von Fellenberg with J Bischoff, P Egger, P Inäbnit and P Michel, 31 July 1865 followed 10min later by J Hornby and T Philpott with C Almer and C Lauener.

A very attractive mountain which seems quite detached from surrounding peaks. It has some high-class routes on both rock and ice. The mountain has three main ridges, each of which is a good climb in its own right, with reasonably sound rock. It is usual to combine an ascent of the NE or S ridges with descent of the W ridge. Of the three faces only the N is of any real interest. It has some of the most serious climbing on the whole of the Lauterbrunnen wall on account of the stonefall danger.

190 **SOUTH RIDGE**
D– Mrs and G Murray with A Supersaxo, 9 Aug 1928

A demanding yet interesting route that is best achieved in combination with a traverse of the Burstspiza, although it is possible to gain the ridge at Pt 3165m (Burstsattel). There are pitches of III.

From Fafleralp follow Route 196 over the Burstspiza to the Burstsattel. Alternatively walk up the Inners Tal to a height of about 2300m. Climb NE, up loose stony ground and a small couloir, to the moraine to the SE of the Inner Tal glacier. The couloir can be avoided a few m on its L (NW) side. Climb to the top of the moraine and from there up to the Burstsattel. 5hr

From the saddle, sustained but not too difficult climbing leads to the top of Pt 3656m (3-4hr). There is now a 100m descent before the final climb to the summit. Go down the ridge until it becomes impossible. Abseil 25m to a ledge on the W side. Leave this by a (usually) snowy couloir to a gap. Follow a narrow overhung ledge on the W side then turn a gendarme on the E side. Make another abseil (30m) on the W side and reach the narrow snow crest at the low point.

Climb the rock barrier diagonally R to L to reach an obvious way ahead. Climb up some slabs to the final snow slopes that lead, steeply at first, to the summit. 3-4hr, 11-13hr in all, 2hr longer over the Burstspiza

191 **WEST RIDGE**
AD– First ascent party
78

A very good climb and highly recommended with difficulties of III–. It is not advisable to try to climb to, or descend from, the Wetterlücke from the Schmadri hut as the Wetterlücken glacier can be quite complex. However if you have done one of the N face routes you will probably not mind making a descent from here.

From the Mutthorn hut climb to the Petersgrat and contour under the S face of the Tschingelhorn to the Wetterlücke (3181m). This can be approached from Fafleralp by following Route 190 to the Inner Tal glacier and then take a curving line up it to the col in 4-5hr.

Pass to the R of the first rocks on the ridge and reach a gap up snow slopes. Traverse 20m on slabby rocks on the same side then move up to the crest. Keep to the ridge over Pt 3403m to the foot of two rock steps. Climb these direct or traverse to a dièdre on the S side and climb this to the crest to avoid the first step. Traverse R again and climb short steps and a short vertical chimney to avoid the second. A final obstacle can also be avoided on the R before a snow crest, which can have a large cornice, leads to the summit. 4-5hr

192 **NORTH FACE: NORTH-NORTH-WEST SPUR**

TD E Feuz and E von Allmen, 31 July 1949

78

A mixed rock and ice climb with much less in the way of objective dangers than the face itself. Highly recommended in good conditions (dry rock on the lower spur, consolidated snow in the middle part and, most importantly, good snow/ice on the upper mixed section which is by far the hardest part). There is some sérac fall danger on the lower part of the route. It would make a good introduction to the more serious N walls in the Oberland. The rock is mainly III with bits of IV and the ice is 55° with one pitch of 60°.

From the Schmadri hut a track leads SW to the Breithorn glacier. Cross this and climb it to the foot of the spur on the R side of the steep glacier bay below the N face. Climb the rib to a steep narrow snow terrace which is followed to the R to within 40m of the séracs. Climb a corner then make a rising traverse R below a rock wall and above the ice cliffs. Now, below another set of séracs, climb the rock wall and then traverse L (mixed) to pass the séracs by their L edge.

Follow a snow/ice slope to mixed ground which is climbed or avoided on steep snow/ice on the R, until one is forced onto an icy ribbon L of the rib crest. This leads to the summit ridge. 8-10hr from the foot of the spur.

193 **NORTH FACE: ORIGINAL ROUTE**

ED1 E Schulze and W Welzenbach, 14 Sept 1932. Winter: R Steiger and H Kallen, Jan 1973

78

Relatively popular at one time, this route suffers from some very poor rock and there is considerable danger from rockfall especially low on the route. Nowhere is the rock very difficult but good protection is not easy to arrange. Possibly best attempted in winter conditions nowadays.

From the Schmadri hut reach the glacier bay at the foot of the face by Route 192. Climb the L side of this bay then move L onto a ramp line cutting the bounding buttress (the ramp can be reached easily from Route 194). From the ramp follow a slabby couloir to its narrowing then trend R and cross the rock band above by a gully (delicate). Move up R to another rock band which is crossed to the lower L edge of a steep ice band.

On the L is a rib which is cut by a chimney/couloir; climb it to a ledge slanting R. The route now keeps more or less to the rib line over mixed terrain to the summit. 10-14hr from the bay

194
TD
78

NORTH FACE: NORTH-NORTH-EAST SPUR

D Chervet and R Richardet, 12 Aug 1924

The first and probably best route on the N side of the mountain. Quite serious but not subject to the objective dangers of the Welzenbach route. The first ascent party joined the route described at the foot of the upper part of the spur. This variation is still popular, but by climbing the lower spur the standard is better maintained throughout. Difficulties on rock are no more than III but it is friable. The difficulties lie on the mixed ground or on the rock sections when they are snow covered or verglassed. Slow parties will not avoid a bivouac. See also photo 77

From the Schmadri hut follow Route 192 to the foot of the buttress on the E side of the face. Three ribs rise from here. Climb easily up the central one to where the rock changes from gneiss to limestone. Now climb a short vertical crack (III–) and a smooth dièdre (III–) to a large overhang. Make a long rising traverse L on debris covered ledges and up short steps, and take the first opportunity to climb up past the overhang. Continue straight up on slabs (III, pitons) and then Rwards to reach the crest of the spur. Climb this (snow) onto the glacier slope above and then to the foot of the upper part of the spur.

The whole of this lower part can be avoided by crossing the Breithorn glacier to the N foot of the Wärmietenhören (2849m) and climbing the snow coombe on its W side, which narrows to a couloir, to the col to its S (some icefall danger). Alternatively climb more directly to the col from the E side of the Wärmietenhören (icefall danger). Both ways are fairly easy and can be climbed quickly. From the col follow the base of a rock step SE to a steep snow couloir which is climbed (or the rocks on its L) to by-pass the obstacle. A second rock step is climbed by a short steep rib on the R before the glacier is reached. Climb this SW to the foot of the upper spur.

Climb over the bergschrund, then directly up the ice slope for about 60m and then get onto the rock on the R (gneiss again). Follow the spur to the summit. 8-12hr

195 **EAST-NORTH-EAST RIDGE**
D J Gallet with G and J Kalbermatten and J Rubin, 2 Aug 1896
78

A very good route on good rock but not easy to reach. It can be climbed from the Breithornjoch (not named on LK but reached by the alternative start to Route 194) or more easily from the Schmadrijoch. If approaching from the S a bivouac at the Zen hindri Ligg is recommended. See also photo 77

Reach the Schmadrijoch by Route 188 or 189. Start up the ridge but avoid the first rocks on the N side and get back onto the ridge by a chimney. Descend a short steep wall to a gap then go easily over Pt 3386m. Descend from here to the Breithornjoch (not marked) and then climb on the crest to Pt 3471m, the last step being avoided on the S side. Keep to the almost horizontal snow crest (cornices) and reach the bottom of a 70m high step. Climb most of this on the crest (III+) but move onto the S flank for the last part. A narrow snow ridge leads first to the E and subsequently to the main summit. 2-4hr, 6-8hr from the Schmadri hut, 8-10hr from Fafleralp

Burstspitza 3195m

A rocky peak at the end of the S ridge of the Lauterbrunnen Breithorn. The rock is quite slabby and forms a saw-toothed crest that gives an entertaining climb and makes a good approach to the S ridge of the Lauterbrunnen Breithorn itself. All the difficulties are N of the Pt 3119.1m.

196 **TRAVERSE SOUTH TO NORTH**
AD E Benecke and H Cohen, 25 July 1894

There are pitches of III, mostly on good rock but a little loose in places. The climb can be accomplished in a day from Fafleralp.

From Fafleralp follow a path to Guggistafel (1933m) and then turn N and follow traces of track on the SE flank to gain the ridge called Gugginburst. Climb this to reach rock then follow the ridge quite easily to the Pt 3119.1m. 4hr

Continue along the ridge (about 50m of descent) and contour round an impossible section on the W side before reaching the summit. Lots of small teeth are now encountered before arriving at the Burstsattel (3165m, neither name nor height marked on the map), just before which a split gendarme is turned on the W side. 3hr, about 7hr in all

If returning to Fafleralp it is probably best to retrace the route from the summit although it is possible to descend from the Burstsattel (see description of Route 190). To continue on the S ridge of the Lauterbrunnen Breithorn see Route 190.

Tschingelhorn 3567m

W Hawker with H Feuz and C and U Lauener, 6 Sept 1865

An attractive snow dome dominating the view from the Mutthorn hut. It has some short pleasant routes which might be attractive to the alpine novice.

197 **SOUTH FLANK**
PD First ascent party
75

From the Mutthorn hut climb snow slopes SW to the col at 3122m. Follow the snow slopes below the SW ridge to a broad snow-filled couloir in the S flank. From Fafleralp reach the same place by climbing the path up the Uistertal and the snow slopes on the W side of the Chrindelspitza to reach the Usser glacier. Climb this to the foot of the couloir.

The couloir is subject to stonefall but in good conditions it can be climbed quickly to the col at its top. Otherwise climb easy rocks on the E side and finally a snow slope to reach the crest of the SW ridge a little above the col. The ridge leads easily to the summit. 3-4hr from the hut, 5-6hr from Fafleralp

198 **SOUTH-WEST RIDGE**
AD K Blodig and W Srauss with G Lorenz snr, 4 Aug 1892
75

The climb follows the SW ridge in its entirety from the saddle at 3214m and traverses the Chlys Tsingelhorn.

199 **NORTH-WEST FLANK**
AD E Häberli, A and W Scabell and Messerli, 28 July 1911

The climb takes the E side of the couloir leading to the col betwen the Chlys Tsingelhorn and the main summit. An alternative route to the col takes the diagonal line across the face of the Chlys Tsingelhorn.

200 **NORTH-WEST FACE**
D B Weibel, W Jecker, K Käch and U Walliser, 22 Aug 1976

The route climbs direct to the summit, mostly snow/ice but with a rock barrier to cross.

201 **NORTH FACE**
D– O Williamson with R Lochmatter and J Mâitre, 14 July 1903

This is a nice short ice climb (55°) starting from the col between the Lauterbrunnen Wetterhorn and the Tschingelhorn. There is sometimes a large bergschrund.

202 **EAST RIDGE**
PD E Bradley with C Jössi snr, July 1892
75

This climbs from the Wetterlücke which is reached by Route 191. The ridge starts with rock and finishes with snow.

Petersgrat 3207m

This is a long snow crest with a few rock outcrops between the Lötschental and Gasteretal which can be crossed almost anywhere in either direction. A roam along the crest is easy but quite rewarding for the views.

203 **CROSSING NORTH-SOUTH**
F

From Heimritz in the Gasterental take the path leading NE to Pt 2411.3m then via the Alpetli glacier get onto the Kanderfirn and continue NE to about 2550m. Turn S and climb loose rock and/or snow slopes as far as Pt 2719.3m. Continue SE, on easy snow slopes, to the crest which is reached near Pt 3207m (a start from the Mutthorn hut shortens the day considerably). 4-5hr

A walk SW along the crest over the Birghorn and Elwertäsch to the col NE of the Sackhorn can be made, before crossing the Tennbach glacier under the Sackhorn to reach the top of the chairlift at Gandegg, SE of the Hockenhorn, by way of the Milibach glacier. Descend by the path to the E of the chairlift to Holz and then use the cablecar to Wiler or take the path to Blatten from Lauchernalp (Berghaus). Alternatively descend from the ridge onto the Telli glacier in the direction of the Tellispitza. Go down the W side of the spur running SW from the highest point (3082m) to the path leading down Im Tellin to Blatten. 2½hr

A return to the Gasteretal can be made by way of the Lötschenpass.

Sackhorn 3212m, Hockenhorn 3293m, Tennbachhorn 3012.9m

These three peaks give some pleasant outings when higher peaks are not in condition.

The Sackhorn is worth climbing by its SW ridge (AD) from the Märliglücke (reached by a couloir). There are five gendarmes on the ridge. The first is easy. Keep to the crest for the next three (III) and make a 20m abseil from the fourth. Climb slightly R to the top of the last (III). About 6hr from Lauchernalp. The NE ridge is easy to descend.

The NE ridge of the Hockenhorn is AD and is climbed from the gap SW of Pt 2996m. The summit rocks can be turned on the N or S. 4½hr from Lauchneralp. Descend the SW ridge to the Lötschenpass. Alternatively descend the S flank, starting down just before reaching the Kl Hockenhorn, over snow patches and slabby rocks, heading W of Pt 3758m.

The Tennbachhorn has good climbing on its E ridge. This is reached from Weritzstafel by climbing N over pastures to stony slopes between the S and E ridges. At about 2500m turn R and climb to the Tellihorn. Follow the crest (slabby rock, some III) to the summit. 3½hr. Descend to the gap between the two summits and climb down the couloir on the E side back to the stony slopes leading to Weritzstafel.

Aletschhorn Group and Peaks South of the Lötschental

In this section climbs described are on the long chain of mountains whose N flanks end either in the Grosser Aletschfirn or in the Lötschental. They form a high-level ridge which at no point falls below 3000m and which has very few easy crossing places. Those peaks in the eastern part are surrounded on three sides by the great Aletsch glacier. Those in the western part descend eventually into the Rhône valley.

The Aletschhorn dominates the whole group although the Bietschhorn in the W of the section stands out as an isolated peak considerably higher than anything close to it.

The climbing varies greatly, but covers good quality rock routes of various grades as well as a whole spectrum of climbs on snow and ice, including some classic and serious routes. The quality of the rock varies enormously from the perfect granite of the Torberg to something much less pleasant in places on the Bietschhorn. Like the rest of the eastern parts of the Oberland there are some long approaches to huts and to routes, especially if you don't use mechanised transport.

Maps covering this section are: Visp (274) and Jungfrau (264)

Lötschenlücke 3178m

An important high level pass, glaciated on both sides, giving access to the central area of the Oberland from the Lötschental. Much less frequently traversed in summer than in winter, when ski parties make frequent crossings of the pass (mainly from E to W). The Hollandia hut is sited about 50m above the pass on the N side.

204 **WEST SIDE**

F

From Fafleralp walk up the path on the N side of the river for about 250m then cross the river at the bridge and continue by a good path above the S bank to the tongue of the Lang glacier. Climb the S side of the glacier to a height of about 2400m before working into the middle of it. Keep in the middle to an easing of the angle at about 2600m then slant a bit L towards the rocks S of Chrumme Rigg. Below these take a direct line towards the pass by climbing the N side of the glacier and so avoiding a crevassed zone below Grossi Tola. From this plateau climb straight up to the pass. 6-8hr

205 **EAST SIDE**
F
80
From the Konkordia hut cross Konkordiaplatz (which can be waterlogged in the afternoon) and climb the L side of the Grosser Aletschfirn to the pass. 2½hr

If coming from the Jungfraujoch, reach the SE corner of the Kranzberg and climb the R side of the Grosser Aletschfirn to the pass. 4-5hr

Olmenhorn 3314m

C Grove and C Townley with F Graf and L Zurbrücken, 29 Aug 1886

A rarely visited summit which may gain some interest with the opening of hut accommodation at Märjela.

206 **TRAVERSE**
AD
SE ridge: C Blum and L Matter, June 1968. SW flank: first ascent party

From Märjela cross the Grosser Aletsch glacier and climb the slopes of Olme at least 300m N of Pt 2443.2m. Continue up grassy slopes to a terrace below Pt 2726m. Move R and climb as high as possible up a couloir in the first step of the SE ridge, where short grassy cracks lead to easier ground. Carry on up the ridge to just below Pt 3211m where, at a gap, it is necessary to move onto the SW flank.

Keep as close to the crest as possible over various rock towers; the last few before the summit are past on the L. A crack on the SW side permits access to the summit itself. 7hr

Cross the crest to the W summit and descend S to the edge of a couloir. Descend into the couloir but climb out again as soon as possible on the W side and continue the descent alongside the deep couloir to about 2800m. Follow a terrace towards the foot of the SE ridge, with a short ascent at the end, to regain the route of ascent. About 5hr, 12hr in all

Dreieckhorn 3810.7m

T Browne with P Bohren and P Schlegel, 26 Aug 1868

An unimportant summit facing the Konkordia hut across the

Grosser Aletsch glacier. It is sometimes included in a traverse of the Aletschhorn. The N face provides some good ice-climbing for the N face novice. The rock on the ridges is loose in places.

207 **TRAVERSE**
PD E flank: first ascent party
80

The climb can be done in either direction but is described here starting from the Konkordia hut. Late in the season it may be preferable to climb the NE ridge in its entirety (PD).

From the Konkordia hut cross the Grosser Aletsch glacier SW to the N foot of Drittes Dreieck (2951.9m). Climb up rubble and snow, keeping this point on your L, to reach the unnamed glacier on the E flank of the mountain. Climb it to the snowy shoulder above Pt 3541m on the NE ridge. Continue up the ridge (steep snow/ice and easy rock) to the summit. 5-6hr

Descend the W ridge to the Aletschjoch. 30min. It is usual to continue to the summit of the Aletschhorn by Route 217 but descent can be made to the Mittelaletsch bivouac hut by this route.

208 **NORTH FACE**
D C Blum and L Matter, 18 Apr 1967
80

Similar climbing is possible on both the N and NW faces, the two being separated by the NNW ridge (which is AD). Both faces are, in effect, steep glacier slopes with variable sérac bands. The angle of each rises to a maximum of about 55°. Numerous variations of the line described are possible.

Reach the foot of the face from the Konkordia hut by crossing Konkordiaplatz and climbing steepening snow slopes to a height of about 3000m. Climb up to the L of rocks protruding from the ice then traverse R above them. Fairly easy slopes lead to a sérac zone which is climbed to steeper slopes. Go up these until forced Rwards onto the NNW ridge from where it is relatively easy to reach the NE ridge and the summit. 5-7hr

Gross Fusshorn 3626.9m

Miss Brevoort and W Little with M Salzmann and two others, 21 Sept 1876

A fairly popular summit but little more than a training peak. There is some good rock on the ridges but the flanks are rotten.

209 WEST-SOUTH-WEST RIDGE AND SOUTH-WEST FLANK

PD Miss J and C Hopkinson, 1894

This is the ordinary route and avoids the more difficult part of the WSW ridge.

From the Oberaletsch hut follow a vague path NE to get onto the ridge oriented W at this point. Just beyond Pt 2953.1m keep on the N side past a gap and several gendarmes but otherwise keep to the crest to a height of about 3230m. Make a descent on the E side for a few m then climb snow/boulder slopes below the ridge to the foot (about 3400m) of a snow filled couloir descending from a gap in the ridge. On the bounding E side of the couloir is an obvious V notch. Climb to this then up the ridge above it for a few m before traversing E onto the upper edge of a snowy bay. Follow this to a small couloir and climb this a short distance then work up R on slabby rocks to the WSW ridge. Follow this to the summit. 4-5hr

210 WEST-SOUTH-WEST RIDGE INTEGRAL

AD+ J Kuhn and H Röthlisberger. 16 Apr 1949

A long climb on good granite and recommended. Pitches of III and IV.

From the Oberaletsch hut follow Route 209 to about 3230m. Now keep mainly on the crest which has some splendid climbing. At one point a large slabby block bars the way. Climb this direct (pitons) or pass it on the R (pitons, a bit easier). Beyond a distinct gap a steep wall is climbed direct to gain the final summit ridge. 5-6hr

It is possible to leave the ridge at about the mid-point to get onto the ordinary route.

211 SOUTH RIDGE

AD G Young with C Ruppen, 3 Sept 1898

What amounts to an alternative finish to the ordinary route. Bits of III. It climbs only the last part of this long ridge.

From the foot of the couloir at about 3400m on the ordinary route (209) traverse E to a snow filled couloir. Climb this to a gap between the last tower on the ridge and the main summit. From the gap climb the S face before slanting R to the ridge which is followed to the summit. 5-6hr

Geisshorn 3740m

W Coolidge and A Walden, 26 Aug 1880

The highest point hereabouts which, although not often climbed, provides a good training route.

212 **TRAVERSE**
AD From the N: L Kurz and H Rieckel with F Graf jnr and C Lauener, 10 Aug 1892

From the Oberaletsch hut walk up the Oberaletsch glacier as far as the unnamed glacier on the W flank of the mountain. Go up this, keeping on the R side of the rocks below Pt 3368m. Pass above this point and reach the crest of the ridge running NW from Pt 3675m. Climb the ridge over this point (good rock) and continue to the next top (Pt 3723.9m, Sattelhorn) turning gendarmes on the W side. Cross a snowy saddle to the Geisshorn. 6-7hr

Descend the SW ridge and continue along the ridge to the summit of the Rotstock. Return to the Oberaletsch glacier by the W ridge of this peak (snow and rock). 3½hr, 10-12hr in all

Aletschhorn 4195m

F Tuckett with J Bennen, P Bohren and V Tairraz, 18 June 1859

The second highest summit in the Bernese Oberland and much sought after. It is a big mountain and much higher than anything close by. There are three principal ridges which separate the three glacier systems that converge on the mountain and bear its name. Most of the climbing is not too demanding but is always interesting. Any two of the ridges can be used to create a traverse of the peak and it is particularly rewarding to combine a traverse with an ascent of the Sattelhorn, from the N, or an ascent of the Dreieckhorn from Konkordia. The mountain has a magnificent glaciated N face.

213 **SOUTH-WEST RIB**
PD+ L Liechti and T Middlemore with A Kummer and a porter,
79 6 Aug 1879

The ordinary route from the Oberaletsch hut, the most convenient hut for access to the mountain. It is fairly steep with adequately sound rock but it can be time consuming if the usual snow section becomes icy. In descent the top of the rib is not easy to locate in mist.

From the Oberaletsch hut walk NE up the Oberaletsch glacier to below Pt 2860m. It may be possible to get onto the rock barrier near here and make a rising traverse L (shortest way); if not continue on the glacier until SW of Pt 3100.9m. From here a track leads back R on the lowest rock shelf. By either way reach a hollow between the rocks and moraine S of Pt 3100.9m. Climb up this for a few minutes and then get onto the crest of the rib on the L. Keep on the rib or its E side over large blocks to Pt 3382m. 3½hr

Snow slopes (possible bergschrund and crevasses) are now climbed, curving gradually to the E before finally turning back W to Pt 3736m. This is the start of the true SW rib which is followed to a fairly steep snow slope below the summit rocks. Climb this and then easily up the rocks to the summit. 3-4hr, 7-8hr in all

In descent: from the summit go down SSW to find the top of the rib.

214 **SOUTH-WEST FLANK AND WEST-NORTH-WEST RIDGE**

AD W Coolidge and W Larden with C and R Almer jnr, 5 July 1894

79

Basically a long snow climb to the ridge with a few obstacles on the ridge itself. See also photo 80

From the Oberaletsch hut follow Route 213 past where it leaves the glacier and continue to a height of about 2700m. Climb up the glacier slope, more or less in the middle, to the snowy col E of the Kl Aletschhorn (3702m). 4-5hr

Climb on snow up the ridge, avoiding the loose rock on its L, to a bergschrund. Now either cross the bergschrund and climb a steep snow/ice slope, or traverse R onto the rocks (now more solid) and continue up these over several steps and so reach a small snowy plateau. Cross this to the final snow crest. 2-3hr, about 8hr in all

215 **NORTH FACE**

D/TD E Blanchet with K Mooser and A Rubi, 9 Aug 1925.

80 In descent: V Ryan with G Lochmatter, before 1914.

Winter: H Gunten and W Moser, 22-23 Dec 1971.

Direct: H Aufschläger and G Mitterer, Aug 1935

The whole N flank of this mountain, from the Sattelhorn to the Dreieckhorn, is a most impressive steep glaciated slope up to 1000m high, interspersed with some rock buttresses which mostly merge into the ice some way below the summit ridge. Various routes have been recorded on the face, which can be climbed almost anywhere, but none has a particularly distinctive line. The one described gives the longest climb and leads directly to the summit. Difficulties will vary according to conditions but there is usually plenty of snow on the easier sections. It is the sort of climb that requires a good sense of terrain in order to find the most efficient line of ascent. The overall angle is about 45° but there could be some vertical or even overhanging steps where sérac barriers cannot be avoided. Some danger of falling ice. Recommended in cold weather.

From the Konkordia or Hollandia huts reach a point at the foot of the face about 400m NE of Pt 3127.7m. Climb the crevassed slope to where, usually, an enormous crevasse cuts across the entire slope at about 3400m. Generally move R to cross this difficulty then climb less crevassed slopes directly in the summit fall-line. This leads to a vertical (or even overhanging) step, barring access to a less inclined terrace. Usually move L to surmount this obstacle. From the terrace climb up L to reach the NE ridge or, better, pass R of the rock triangle and climb direct to the summit which is gained finally by the WNW ridge. 5-8hr from Hollandia, allow 2hr more from Konkordia.

216 HASLER RIB

AD+ F Middlemore with J Jaun jnr and C Lauener, 4 July 1873.

80 Winter: G Hasler with F and A Amatter, 26 Jan 1904

This is the rocky interspersion of the N face below Pt 3718m. It is a good mixed climb and the most popular route on the mountain from the Konkordia or Hollandia huts. The rib has an average angle of 45° with difficulties of II-III and some loose rock, although there are no real objective dangers. It is probably best avoided after fresh snow.

From the Konkordia or Hollandia huts reach the foot of the rib at about 3000m. Climb it direct to a height of about 3550m where it merges with the snow/ice slope. This section can be avoided by the snow/ice slope on the L. Climb another 200m and regain more rocks which are followed to the NE ridge. Climb this easily to the summit. 6-7hr, slightly longer from Konkordia.

217 SOUTH-EAST FLANK AND NORTH-EAST RIDGE

PD First ascent party

Fairly infrequently climbed, it is the shortest route and the quickest in descent from the summit.

From the Mittelaletsch bivouac hut climb NW over the crevassed glacier until under the rock outcrop below Pt 3482m. Less steep slopes lead more or less in the same direction to the Aletschjoch. A fairly narrow snow crest leads to Pt 3718m from where a broad snow slope continues to the fore-summit at 4086.4m. This can be traversed or avoided on its S side. Reach the main summit by the final part of the WNW ridge. 5-6hr

218 **SOUTH-EAST RIDGE**

PD A Eggel, M Jossen and E Ruppen, 15 July 1862

79 *The ridge starts at the Mittelaletschlücke but is normally only climbed from the gap NW of the big gendarme (Pt 3947m). From about mid-season it is often very difficult to actually set foot on the ridge because of the size of the bergschrund. Otherwise it is the easiest route from the Oberaletsch hut. The rock sections are generally loose and fairly unpleasant in descent.*

From the Oberaletsch hut follow Route 213 to Pt 3382m. Now climb the glacier slope NE to the foot of the snowy couloir (may be mostly rock at the end of the summer) leading to the gap in the ridge NW of Pt 3947m. Climb the couloir (45°), which broadens to a snow slope, to the crest of the ridge. Follow the ridge on snow and rock to the summit. 7-8hr

Sattelhorn 3741.1m

K Schulz with A Burgener and J Ritter, 26 Aug 1883

This mountain forms the W end of the great glaciated N flank of the Aletschhorn and has no real character of its own. It is best climbed in combination with a traverse of the Aletschhorn. The N flank is frequently swept by avalanche after fresh snow.

219 **SOUTH FLANK**

PD E Häberli, H Messerli, A and W Scabell, 5 Aug 1911

79 From the Oberaletsch hut climb the Oberaletsch glacier to the S foot of the mountain. Climb up E of Pt 3116.6m to a shoulder and then NE up a snow ridge to where it merges into rock. Scramble up the rock to a gap in the ridge 100m SE of the summit. The rock ridge leads to the summit. About 5hr

220 **WEST WALL: OREON COULOIR**

TD– K Ochsner solo, 23 Apr 1982

The W wall is a large rocky buttress overlooking the head of the Lötschental and is bounded on the R by the broad snow couloir leading to

the Sattellicka. The route starts R of centre and takes a direct line up the front of the buttress in a 600m long, narrow couloir (3-6m wide). The first ascent was made in very snowy conditions in 70 min. It is mostly 45°-50° with one section of 55° and some mixed climbing. Above this there is a 200m slope to the summit. A summer ascent in 1990 found ice up to 80° and rock difficulties of III-IV with some stonefall.

221 **NORTH RIDGE**
AD L and M Dufour, 1 Aug 1900
80

A good approach for a traverse of the Aletschhorn but avoid it after fresh snow.

From the Hollandia hut walk down to the Lötschenlücke and the foot of the ridge. Climb the rocks, or snow on the L, and the snow slopes above to the summit. 2-3hr

222 **NORTH-EAST FACE**
D J Gallet with J Kalbermatten and A Müller snr, 24 July 1900
80

Viewed from the Hollandia hut this looks like a ridge. It is in reality a steepish face about 500m high cut by crevasses and séracs which leads to a point about 400m E of the summit. Avoid after fresh snow. 4-5hr

223 **EAST RIDGE**
PD First ascent party
79

Used in descent or on the traverse to the Aletschhorn.

From the summit of the Sattelhorn follow the snow crest, quite narrow in places, as far as Pt 3629m. A short but steep snow ridge leads to the summit of the Kl Aletschhorn. Easy slopes lead to the col E of this summit. A descent from here via Route 214 can be made to the Oberaletsch hut or continue the traverse by this route.

Distlighorn 3716m

H José with A Walden and C Zurbriggen, 22 Aug 1892

An unimportant summit which nevertheless provides one worthwhile climb. It is usually traversed along with the Schinhorn.

224 **TRAVERSE**
AD+ J Gallet, J Kalbermatten and A Müller snr, 28 July 1900

From the Oberaletsch hut climb up the Oberaletsch glacier under the Distelberg until N of Pt 2733m. Continue up a vague glacier ramp to about 3000m then turn W up crevassed slopes to the E foot of the mountain. Turn N to below a depression in the ridge 150m NE of the snow dome (Pt 3618m). Climb easy rocks and a short but steep snow slope to the ridge. If the slope above 3000m is too crevassed, continue up the ramp towards the Sattellicka and turn W to below the depression in the ridge.

A short snow ridge leads to a 30m high vertical step. Climb a detached flake for 3m then make a big detour R and climb to the top of the step by projecting rocks (IV, piton). Keep to the snowy N side of the ridge over the snow dome and then on the crest with some nice climbing to the summit. 5-6hr

Descend the SW ridge to the marked gap at its foot, the last step being turned on the E side. From here it is possible to descend steep snow slopes to regain the line of ascent, but it is preferable to continue by Route 227 over the Schinhorn.

Schinhorn 3796.8m

J Häberlin with J and A Weissenfluh, 30 Aug 1869

An attractive peak with 5 ridges radiating from its summit. It presents some good climbing in a nice, remote and uncrowded setting. The traverse, in conjunction with the Distelhorn, is a particularly good outing.

225 **SOUTH FLANK**
PD First ascent party in descent

The ordinary route and almost entirely on snow.

From the Oberaletsch hut reach the foot of the S flank W of Pt 2705m via the Beich glacier. Climb up the middle of the glacier face (often very crevassed) or near its W edge; the upper slope below the fore-summit is about 45°. A short snow and rock ridge leads to the true summit. 5-6hr

226 **SOUTH-WEST RIDGE**
AD D Hall and M Pallis with A Michaud, 29 June 1929

From the Oberaletsch hut as for Route 225 to the foot of the S Flank. Gain the ridge at a snow col close to Pt 3282.1m. The ridge is easy to Pt 3662m, where two abseils are made into a gap to the N. Avoid a gendarme in the gap and regain the narrow crest which turns to snow before the summit. 9hr

227 NORTH-NORTH-EAST RIDGE

AD+ J Gallet with J Kalbermatten and A Müller snr, 28 July 1900

Best climbed in combination with Route 224 although it is possible to reach the col at its foot by branching off the first part of that route. Basically a snow/ice climb whose difficulty varies with conditions.

From the Oberaletsch hut reach the col at the foot of the ridge by Route 224. Climb poor rock to a gendarme and then follow the splendid snow/ice crest to the junction with the E ridge. Climb a 20m high step on the L side (III) then follow the near horizontal ridge to the summit. 1hr from the col

228 EAST RIDGE

D– A Bonacossa, Miss R Batsford and U di Vallepiana, 6 Sept 1913

A good mixed route with difficulties up to IV– on sound rock.

From the Oberaletsch hut follow Route 224 to 3000m on the glacier ramp. Slant up W and pass between two sérac bands to the foot of the ridge. Get onto the ridge at a shoulder near Pt 3291m, above a high step which terminates in the glacier. If the glacier is too crevassed above the ramp continue up it towards the Sattellicka then turn SW and eventually descend slightly to reach the shoulder. 3hr

Climb a few small steps interspersed with snow, to a distinct steepening. Just before this traverse three gendarmes (IV–) then climb the step direct (III). The ridge turns to snow and leads to a junction with the NNE ridge 60m from the summit. Climb a 20m high step on the L (III) then the horizontal ridge to the summit. 4-5hr, 7-8hr in all

Wysshorn 3542.2m

E Merian and S Simon with J Tischhauser, 16 Aug 1885

Along with the Distelberg and Torberg, this mountain presents some very good rock climbing in the region of the Oberaletsch hut. The rock is impeccable granite.

229 EAST FLANK

PD First ascent party

A good glacier expedition which makes a nice training climb.

From the Oberaletsch hut follow Route 224 until below the narrow glacier on the E flank. Climb the L-hand of two couloirs for 50m (unpleasant unless snow filled) then traverse S to a stone-covered terrace on the E side of the Distelberg. Climb NW to the glacier and go up it (some big crevasses), with a steep section for 100m, to the saddle between the Wysshorn and Pt 3625m. Reach the summit in a few minutes from here. 4hr

230 **SOUTH-EAST FACE**

TD– A Anliker, C Blum, R Schifferli and H Schneider, 10 July 1967

81 *Highly recommended, the climb takes a direct line to the summit. 350m of climbing, mostly IV-V with a bit of V+ and some aid.*

From the Oberaletsch hut cross the Oberaletsch glacier NW to Pt 2550m. Climb the moraine to the foot of the E ridge of Pt 3325m (Ober Torberg) or ascend a deep couloir further L (which can be followed, unpleasantly, as a means of reaching the summit of the Torberg). Move out R before it narrows and then climb NNE to the foot of the same ridge. Now climb NW up the Distel glacier, passing the foot of the E ridge of the Sud Wysshorn, to the foot of the face. 2½hr

Start directly below the summit at a 50m high trapezoid slab. Climb a dièdre on the R side of the slab to a poor belay. Continue up the dièdre then move 10m R when possible to a piton belay (V+, A1). A few m above the belay traverse 15m R into a couloir which widens below. Climb this for several pitches (V to start) to where it widens to a funnel and becomes less steep under the steep summit wall. Traverse 40m R climbing gradually to a distinct rib. Cross another couloir and climb the next rib to a gap and hence to the summit. 8-9hr

Distelberg 3127m

Probably R Carrupt and two others, 2 Sept 1929

What amounts to a rock buttress at the foot of the E ridge of the Wysshorn.

231 **SOUTH RIB**

D– H Schneider and U Saxer, 28 July 1966

A good varied climb of 300m with difficulties up to IV.

From the Oberaletsch hut follow Route 229 to the stone-covered terrace on the E side of the mountain and follow it S to the foot of the rib. Start a few m R and slant up L, passing a rocky projection, to reach a ledge 50m up the rib via some slabs. Move up R (IV) to the bottom of a grey slab and climb it to a chimney on the R. Climb the chimney and a short wall on the R to the foot of two slabs (easily seen from the hut). Climb the first of these, slanting L, then the higher one, to a piton belay at its top. Get back onto the rib and climb a difficult crack (IV, 3 pitons) up a steep slab, then go straight up for 15m to a belay. Make a gradual descent L to a chimney with a jammed block. Climb this (III), move easily L up a ramp for 30m then move up R to a short dièdre-crack which is climbed to the crest. Easier climbing leads to the summit, one step being avoided on the R (III). 4-5hr

To descend; go along the W ridge to the lowest point. On the N side make a gently rising traverse across snow slopes to some detached blocks. Abseil 20m (slings in place) to a rock band or make a 40m abseil to the glacier. Return to the stone-covered terrace. 1hr

Torberg 3022.8m, 3160m and 3325m

Only the lowest of these three points is named on the LK map. All three amount only to high points on the S ridge of the Wysshorn. The highest is the Ober Torberg, the lowest is the Torberg and the other simply the Mittler Torberg. There are several short but worthwhile climbs on their excellent granite.

232 **OBER TORBERG: EAST RIB**

D C Blum and H Schneider, 31 July 1966

400m of good climbing with some IV+. The rib rises from the Distel glacier to a point just S of Pt 3325m and is prominently marked on the map.

From the Oberaletsch hut follow Route 230 to the foot of the rib. 1½hr

Move up the glacier slope on the N side of the rib, this flank forming a massive slab. Climb a system of cracks (difficult to start if there is not much snow) straight up to a belay in a niche at the upper edge of the slab (IV). Move L to get onto the crest of the rib (III–) and climb 8m up a slab on well spaced holds (IV) to a block belay. By another slab (small holds) and a short wall reach a terrace (IV–). Move up to the start of a dièdre slanting R and climb it before regaining the crest by a short wall and an awkward step (III).

Move 5m R to a chimney and climb this (IV+). The next step

on the rib is mounted by a series of cracks on the L, then follow the crest (III) to a 40m slab. Climb this by a narrow crack (IV+, 5 pitons) then easily Lwards to the summit. 2-2½hr, 4-5hr in all

Descend the S ridge on the W flank, passing below the Mittler Torberg, and from the gap N of the Torberg descend a couloir to the Beich glacier. 2hr to the hut

233 MITTLER TORBERG: SOUTH-EAST RIDGE

TD– H Nievergelt and W Bissig, 16 July 1975

A fine curving ridge to Pt 3160m (not marked on LK, this point is S of Pt 3325m). It is mostly III-IV but there is some V and V+.

From the Oberaletsch hut follow Route 230 to the foot of the E rib of Pt 3325m. Traverse SE across snow slopes to the foot of the rib, which has a shallow dièdre on its L side. Start in this dièdre. Climb 40m (V) up it and then about 5 pitches as direct as possible up the crest (bits of IV+) to a wall. Climb a detached flake on the L then move up Rwards and then back gradually L to a belay (30m, V). Climb a further 20m Rwards to a belay just L of the crest (V). Now a narrow slab (V+) followed by a dièdre-crack (V) leads to the crest. Keep on the crest to a ledge (III-IV) and then, still on the crest, reach some dark and lichenous rocks (V) and, finally, the crest of the S ridge. 4-5hr from the hut

Descend as for Route 232.

234 TORBERG: SOUTH-WEST RIDGE

AD

Another good climb in this region, shorter and easier than the others described. Mostly III, 350m of climbing.

From the Oberaletsch hut cross the Oberaletsch glacier onto the Beich glacier passing S of Pt 2588m, to the foot of a couloir descending from the gap N of the summit of the Torberg. Climb the couloir to where it widens then move out of it to the R and go along terraces (foundations of an old hut) to the slabby foot of the ridge. 1½hr

Climb the R side of a large slab to its upper edge by a crack system. Follow the upper edge Lwards then climb a dièdre to the crest of the ridge. Move up the crest for a few m and then, on the NW flank, climb some steep cracks to a ramp below a split tower. Regain the crest via the ramp and climb it to a wall with good holds. The ridge becomes oriented S and leads easily but excitingly to the summit. 1½hr, 3hr in all

Descend the N ridge to the gap at its foot and then the couloir back to the Beich glacier.

Beichpass c3160m

This is a long established pass allowing passage between the Lötschental and the Oberaletsch hut. The actual pass is about 80m SW of the snowy low point on the ridge and is close to a small rock pyramid. It is not easy to find in mist.

235 **NORTH SIDE**
F

From Fafleralp cross the river at the bridge (1771m) and walk up the valley as far as Pt 1937m. Now get onto and follow the moraine on the E side of the Dischlig glacier to a height of about 2760m. From here either climb the E branch of the glacier (few crevasses) or continue on the the side of the glacier to reach a rock barrier below the col. Climb the barrier on stepped rock (I, II) to the col (slightly tricky if snow covered). 5-6hr

236 **SOUTH SIDE**
F

From the Oberaletsch hut get onto the Beich glacier and climb it to a height of about 2800m directly below the col. Turn N and climb rock (granite) and snow straight up before making a slight movement E to reach the col. 2½-3hr

Nesthorn 3824m

B George and H Mortimer with C and U Almer, 18 Sept 1865

The mountain is more or less hidden from view from most distant points and is consequently not well known. This should not detract from its potential for providing good climbing. It is frequently climbed from both the Oberaletsch hut and the Baltschiederklause hut. Its most notable feature is its N face which offers some quite challenging routes.

237 **WEST RIDGE**
PD First ascent party
82

A pleasant climb from either of the huts, mostly on glacier terrain and frequently ascended by parties traversing between the two huts. See also photo 83

From the Oberaletsch hut follow Route 236 to 2800m then climb up the glacier close under the Lonzahorner. Once above the sérac zone turn SE to reach the Gredetschjoch (3508m). It may be possible to shorten the approach by climbing lines further E but this will depend on the condition of the icefalls. 4hr

From the Baltschiederklause hut descend a little way (approach route to the hut) and get onto the moraine on the W side of the Innre Baltschieder glacier. Climb this to a marked steepening and descend onto the glacier. Curve round in an arc to just S of Pt 2866.4m and from there climb up to the foot of the rocky couloir leading to the Baltschiederlicka (3219m). The couloir is about 100m high and is fairly steep and very loose. Scramble up the bed of the couloir or climb the rocks on its N side to the gap (in descent go down the couloir and abseil the last few m). An easy descent on the E side of the gap, on snow or scree covered ledges, leads to the Gredetsch glacier. Climb this to the Gredetschjoch. 3½hr

From the Gredetschjoch climb the ridge on snow or ice following, if possible, a sort of corridor between rock and snow. There is a short descent after the fore-summit. 1½hr, about 6hr in all

238 **NORTH FACE ORIGINAL ROUTE**

TD/ W Welzenbach with A Drexel and E Schulze, 25 July 1933.

TD+ Winter: R Karl and H Kühn, 8 Jan 1969

82

The face is about 900m high with a slabby rock barrier at about half-height. It is this barrier which causes most of the difficulty. The best conditions for an ascent are when the rock zone is well covered with snow (May-June most commonly and later in very snowy years or in winter). In very snowy conditions the technical difficulty is not very high (about D). There is some danger from stonefall low on the route and there is also danger from the séracs on the NE ridge. The average angle is 55° but it is up to 65° in the central zone. All fairly serious. See also photo 83

Reach the foot of the face from the Oberaletsch hut by way of the Beich glacier (1½hr). Start just E of Pt 2898m by climbing up avalanche debris to the bergscrund and cross this (usually on the R). Now move up L to the snow/ice slopes above some ice cliffs and then climb direct to the highest point in the slabby rock zone. Traverse R below some very steep slabs for about two rope lengths (mixed) then move up (still mixed) to reach the upper ice slopes. Climb these direct to the summit. 8-11hr for the face.

239 **OTHER NORTH FACE ROUTES**

82

In June 1977 L Griffin and P Bartlett climbed a very direct line to the summit on the W side of the face which Griffin considered one of the better routes he had done. It was objectively safe (at the time the lower

part and traverse on the Welzenbach Route were periodically being swept by falling ice). The route was climbed in snowy conditions (fairly essential) and had some excellent pitches up icy runnels with good rock belays. Probably best climbed in winter or spring.

On 12 July 1973 P Boardman and D Barton, in very snowy conditions, took a more direct line on the Welzenbach Route which eliminated the traverse. Conditions were so good that the climb took only 4hr.

On 29-30 Aug 1990 the Yugoslavs V Furdan and Z Pozgaj climbed a line that more or less followed the Griffin-Bartlett Route. The rock zone was fairly snow free. Where the 1977 route climbed straight through the R side of the rock zone the Yugoslavs moved out L and climbed six pitches on rock (up to VI+ and A1) before rejoining the 1977 route (ED2).

240 NORTH-EAST RIDGE

AD+/D R Dumford and T Hammond with A Pollinger and A Ritz,
83 27 Aug 1874

The NE ridge itself is mainly glacier terrain leading down to a rocky section before a col SW of Pt 3440m. Below this point there are three ridges terminating in the Beich glacier. The col can be reached by way of the Nesthorn glacier (only named on older maps) to the S of the three ridges or by any one of the ridges. The glacier route was taken by the Dumford/Hammond party; the S-most of the ridges by E Häberli with A and W Scabell, 9 Aug 1911; the central ridge by C Blum, W Jossi and R Schifferli, 4-5 July 1967 and the N-most ridge by C Blum and W Jossi, 20 Aug 1966. See also photo 82

Reach the start of any of these routes from the Oberaletsch hut by crossing the Beich glacier.

To climb the glacier route reach the snowy coombe SE of Pt 3440m by a wide circling movement. Climb up to the col SW of Pt 3440m by moving Rwards up easy rocks after crossing a bergschrund. 3hr

To climb the S-most ridge (AD+) get onto the ridge from its S side at a shoulder close to Pt 2874m by a short couloir. The ridge is followed more or less on its crest. After a first steep section (II, III) avoid a pyramid shaped gendarme on its S side. Start the traverse by first descending about 20m down a small couloir, which starts at a gap 10m before the gendarme. After the traverse the climb is straightforward for some way until a smooth step is reached. Climb this (IV, 2 pitons), then descend delicately to a gap.

Once out of the gap there are some exposed bits of III and IV, then it becomes easier. Pt 3440m is a slender tower and is climbed on the R of the ridge (III+). Its SW ridge is narrow and jagged and leads down to the col at the start of the NE ridge. It is descended by ledges about 40m below the crest on the SE side before the crest is joined 40m from the col. 4-5hr

To climb the central ridge (D) climb up into the snowy coombe on its S side and get onto the ridge where it becomes less steep, above the first step at about 2850m. Keep on the R of the crest at first, then on the crest to the top of the first tower (IV+). Descend a few m on the S side then abseil 15m on the N side before turning the next tower on the N side by ledges and some unstable blocks. The third tower is climbed on its S side and then the fourth to its horizontal crest. Make a 20m abseil on the N side to the next gap and climb the fifth tower by its crest until 20m below its top. Traverse to the gap before the sixth tower and at this level reach a small square platform on the S side of it (V). Now climb this tower and the seventh (on the S flank) and reach Pt 3440m and the col as for the S most ridge. 5-7hr

The N-most ridge is more sustained with several pitches of IV and IV+ with some V and takes 8-9hr.

From the col climb the initial part of the ridge (II, III) to reach snow. Now keep to the boundary between rock and snow/ice to pass the séracs on the N side of the ridge. It may be necessary to use the rocks on the E face in places. Eventually traverse across a sort of snow funnel and then climb a step by a snowy ramp. Gradually easing slopes lead up to the fore-summit and a corniced crest to the main summit. 3hr

To avoid soft snow on the upper part of the Beich glacier in the afternoon it is possible to descend to the Rhône valley from the Gredetschjoch by way of the Gredetschtal. 4hr

241 **SOUTH-EAST RIDGE**

AD+ In descent: J and E Hopkinson, G Lowe and C Slingsby with a

83 porter, 4 Sept 1895

This long ridge eventually finishes at the Sparrhorn, a popular viewpoint above Belalp, and can be climbed in its entirety from there. However the route described here is much shorter and joins the ridge at Pt 3539m. Excellent granite with numerous pinnacles.

From the Oberaletsch hut follow the glacier route to the NE ridge (Route 240). At about 3200m turn SW, cross the bergschrund and climb up to the col (Pt 3539m) by a steep snow and rock slope. The pinnacles on the first part of the ridge can be turned on the SW side but a particularly imposing tower is turned on the NE side. It can be traversed by climbing a crack on the R to a stance, then descending a gangway to a ledge on the SW side before climbing vertically (few good holds) for one pitch to just below its top. Make a 10m abseil into a gap beyond the tower.

The upper part of the ridge gives some steep and demanding climbing on superb rock with good holds. Some of the difficulties can be avoided on the NE side. A final step, with few holds, is climbed direct. 8-10hr

Lötschental Breithorn 3784.9m

J Häberli with A and J Weissenfluh and J Rubin, 28 Aug 1869

The mountain is called simply Breithorn on the LK map but is distinguished here by name to avoid confusion with the Lauterbrunnen Breithorn a few km to the N. It has three quite different faces. The N face dominates the Lötschental and is steep and icy, the E face is an easy glacier slope whilst the S face forms a high rocky rampart. The rock on the mountain is generally of good quality.

242 **BLANCHET RIDGE**
D E Blanchet and P Zurbriggen, 29 Aug 1922
85

This is the striking ridge projecting into the Innre Baltschieder glacier from the SE ridge of the mountain just SE of Pt 3664m. It is a highly recommended climb on good granite and is probably the best climb on the mountain.

From the Baltschiederklause hut follow Rt 237 onto the Innre Baltschieder glacier and curve round to the foot of the ridge. Move round to its E side onto a scree covered terrace. Easy cracks lead to the crest which is followed as closely as possible (II, III). Just before the S flank (on the R) merges with the ridge climb a 10m step on well spaced holds (IV). The ridge steepens abruptly. After three slim gendarmes, climb a 7m wall (V–, 3 pitons) and then a tower (IV, piton). This section can be avoided after the three slim gendarmes by a traverse on the L side into a slabby couloir which leads back to the crest.

A short wall blocking progress is climbed a bit on the L (IV) then the steep crest of the ridge (III, IV) is followed until it eases. Next cross some small gendarmes (III, IV), followed by a large one. A last very slim one can be turned on the L. Easy climbing now passes another gendarme (L or R) then easy rock, or snow on the R, leads to Pt 3664m. The SE ridge to the summit is easy. 6-8hr

243 **SOUTH-WEST RIDGE**

PD+ G Yeld with F and S Pession, 14 Aug 1898

85

An enjoyable mixed route with good rock and a nice culminating snow crest. See also photo 84

From the Baltschiederklause hut follow Route 237 onto the Innre Baltschieder glacier. Head for Pt 3350m and climb into the glacier coombe by passing just E of the foot of this point. Go up the coombe to a snow saddle close to Pt 3624m. It is also possible to get onto the ridge a little further R by means of a small rock couloir. Another alternative is to climb steep rocks and an icy gully, just on the E side of a yellow rock tooth close to the lowest gap in the ridge.

Once on the ridge keep on its crest to the summit. 6-7hr

244 **NORTH FACE**

TD W von Allmen and E Feuz, 18 June 1936

84

The face is 700m high and in good conditions provides an excellent climb. It makes a good training route for longer N face climbs. There are rock difficulties of up to IV in both rock zones and the ice is 50°-55°. Probably best climbed from a bivouac at the foot of the face.

In 1977 L Griffin and P Bartlett climbed an independent line to the L of the von Allmen/Feuz Route (see photo). They approached the face by scrambling up the ridge on the W side of the Distlig glacier and then climbed the glacier itself towards the top. The final rock wall has various possible lines, each giving two or three pitches of quite difficult mixed climbing.

From Fafleralp cross the bridge then climb SE via Gletscherweng to reach Pt 2336.1m. Continue up rubble slopes to a saddle E of Pt 2783m before following the Loibinbach glacier to the col between the mountain and the Gletscherspitza. 3hr

Climb a short steep snow slope to the rock zone. Climb this, at first straight up then slanting L (III, IV) to reach the central ice slope. Climb this direct to the final rock barrier which is surmounted (IV) to reach the summit. 5-6hr for the face

245 **EAST FLANK**
PD– First ascent party
85 *The easiest route on the mountain and the ordinary route from the Oberaletsch hut. Entirely on snow and ice.*

From the Oberaletsch hut follow Route 237 to above the séracs on the Beich glacier then climb the snow slopes to join the SE ridge. Climb this to the SE summit and then continue NW to a gap before a narrow snow crest leads to the NW rock summit. 5hr

Breitlauihorn 3655m

E Häberli with A and J Weissenfluh, 26 Aug 1869

The mountain has little to distinguish it but it is frequently climbed, in combination with the Breithorn, from the Baltschiederklause hut. The NW face is thought to be comparable with the Lötschental Breithorn N face.

246 **SOUTH RIDGE**
PD P Geny with J Kalbermatten, Aug 1907

From the Baltschiederklause hut follow a path, after a little scrambling, under the walls of the Jägihorn NW to the Ussre Baltschieder glacier. Climb this, curving round to reach a col at the foot of the S ridge and just N of three towers on the N ridge of the Jägihorn. Pleasant climbing up the ridge (II, III) leads to the summit. 3½hr

247 **NORTH-EAST RIDGE IN DESCENT**
AD H Bullock, G Irving and G Tyndall, 19 Aug 1907

There is some delicate and exposed climbing.

From the summit go down the ridge turning the first big gendarme on the N side. Continue along the jagged ridge to another gendarme which is also turned on the N side on a short icy rib. As Pt 3624m is approached more short traverses are made on the N side. 4hr

Jägihorn 3406.5m and 3509m

Highest point: J Gallet with J and G Kalbermatten, 28 July 1896

The two peaks are known as the Nördliches Jägihorn (the highest)

and Südliches Jägihorn, the latter appearing almost impregnable when seen from the SW or NE on account of its steep rock walls. Both peaks can be climbed quite easily from the W. The S Jägihorn has some very good rock climbs on sound granite and the climbs described are on this peak.

248
SOUTH-WEST WALL

TD
R Aubert, A Collini, R Dittert and J Weigh, 9 June 1946

85
A splendidly sustained climb on good and very steep rock, best done later in the season when all the snow has melted, otherwise there is danger of falling rocks.

From the Baltschiederklause hut follow the track under the wall towards the Ussre Baltschieder glacier for about 25min to a big black water streak (a waterfall when there is melting snow). L of this is a chimney/crack over 100m high leading to some very steep slabby walls. Climb on the L of the chimney on small rounded holds, then get into the chimney and climb it for about 60m with one quite awkward section to a ledge (more or less vertical to here). Traverse L for 10m then straight up (piton). Climb a big slab by slanting up L before a delicate stride L (piton) leads to easy grooves. Climb these (broken rock) to a spacious shoulder at the foot of a steep wall.

Traverse R and pass behind an enormous detached block, then descend an easy ramp before climbing the wall above it to reach a series of steep slabs that form the R wall of a wide couloir (water course). Climb these slabs directly for several pitches, first on the L then on the R, to reach the top of the couloir (stonefall) where the R wall is overlooked by a big vertical wall. Climb fairly easily for another 60m then mount an overhang before a second overhang blocks further progress.

Small holds and a small flake allow progress up a slab on the R wall (8m, piton) to beneath an overhang. Climb this directly (2 pitons, étriers) to reach a terrace. Here there is a 12m high smooth wall with an overhanging chimney on each side. Climb the one on the R, which starts 3-4m above the terrace (use aid to get into it), by jamming (hard). A flake offers respite and a belay.

A chimney (possibly icy) is next climbed (easier) to where it can be left on the R. Easier, but still vertical, climbing follows on rough rock with good holds. Eventually move R to a gap at a small shoulder on the face from where the climbing becomes very easy. Keep moving up broken rock and short walls Lwards to reach the SE ridge. Follow this to the summit. 8hr

249 **WEST FLANK AND NORTH RIDGE**
PD A, J and P Siegen, 27 Sept 1869

From the Baltschiederklause hut follow Route 246 onto and up the Ussre Baltschieder glacier and reach a couloir in the W flank close to the N Jägihorn. Climb the couloir (snow early in the season) to the upper edge of a slabby section then slant R and climb on easier angled slopes over large blocks to the N ridge. Follow this, level at first, easily to the summit. 3hr

250 **SOUTH-EAST RIDGE**
D– D Chervet and W Richardet, 10 June 1924
85 *A very enjoyable climb on perfect rock.*

From the Baltschiederklause hut scramble up directly behind the hut to where the rock steepens. Climb Nwards (no specific line, III and IV) to reach easy ground. Follow this round onto the SW flank, all the time rising steadily, to where a broad gully leads to the SE ridge. Follow the crest, traversing two yellow gendarmes (IV–) which can be turned on their W side. A 14m high smooth dièdre in another tower is climbed on the R (IV, piton) or avoid the tower on the E side. This is followed by a 25m high step. Start on the crest then traverse R (IV) to a dièdre which is climbed to regain the crest. Continue to a yellow wall facing W which is partly overhanging. Climb this direct (IV+). The next gendarme is climbed direct or turned by a traverse on its E wall (few holds) into a steep 15m high couloir. Climb this, the difficulties then ease to the summit. 4-5hr

Baltschiederjoch 3204m

First recorded crossing: D Freshfield and C Tucker with F Devouassoud, 9 July 1866

The pass gives access to the Baltschiederklause hut from the Bietschhorn hut or the reverse, thus connecting the Lötschental with the Baltschiedertal. Unfortunately the climbing on the N side is rather unpleasant.

251 **NORTH SIDE**
PD
86 From the Bietschhorn hut climb a little before traversing NE to cross the ridge descending from Schafbärg. Descend onto the Nest glacier and cross its tongue to reach the col below Pt 2581.7m. Keep

traversing and cross the Birch glacier to the foot of a steep couloir (usually snow filled). Climb it, following its R bank. From the top of the couloir traverse horizontally SE to the pass. 3½hr

252
F
85

SOUTH SIDE

From the Baltschiederklause hut follow a track NW as for Route 246 and get onto the Ussre Baltschieder glacier on the R side of a sérac zone. Continue NW to the pass. 2hr

Bietschhorn 3934.1m

L Stephen with J and A Siegen and J Ebner, 13 Aug 1859

A big mountain which, like the Eiger, fails to top the 4000m mark by only a few m, and as a consequence, does not receive the attention that it deserves. Its appearance from the S is mostly of rock whilst from the N it looks mainly snow and ice. Viewed from almost any angle it is a magnificent sight, standing proud of all the adjacent peaks. It has three principal ridges, each of which is quite narrow, the SE one in particular being quite jagged. None of the routes is easy and the rock is quite variable in quality but by no means is it all bad, as is sometimes thought to be the case.

253
D+

SOUTH FACE

G de Rahm and A Tissières, 21 Aug 1947

The S face is comprised of a series of ribs and couloirs. The route described climbs the face via the rib above Pt 3040m. The approaches to the start, from the Bietschhorn hut via Shafbärg or by the Bietschtal, are long and a bivouac near the foot of the rib is advisable. The rock is good.

From the foot of the rib climb up to a ramp on the W side (stone or snow covered) and follow it to its W end. Climb easily up to the foot of a massive couloir. 1½hr

Climb up Rwards for one pitch to a hidden chimney which leads Rwards for three pitches (II, III) to the crest of the rib. Follow the rib (III–) to where it becomes slabby and very steep and is overhung by a red gendarme. Climb diagonally Rwards to the foot of a chimney-crack (three pitches, III, 2 pitons). Climb for 20m on the R of the chimney and then in it (vertical and exposed, IV, 4 pitons) to a hollow below a projecting edge.

Cracks now lead to a gap behind the red gendarme (V–,

4 pitons) from where the crest is followed for two pitches to some more gendarmes. Turn these on the R. Easy ground leads to a step which is avoided on the R in a big couloir. Easy but delicate climbing (loose rock) for about 5 pitches leads to a saddle. On the R is a wet couloir which is climbed to the foot of the final vertical wall. On the L climb a chimney to a gap (III, piton) and then follow the undulating crest and a couloir on the R, leading to a small saddle (one pitch, III). Another chimney and some loose blocks lead to the summit (II). 8hr in all

254 **WEST-SOUTH-WEST RIDGE**
AD– E von Fellenberg with P Egger, P Michel and A and J Siegen,
86 19 Aug 1867

A fairly unpleasant climb, much of the rock being quite loose. It is, however, the easiest route to the summit and is frequently climbed and used in descent during a traverse of the peak.

From the Bietschhorn hut follow traces of path up the slopes of Schafbärg to the Bietschjoch (3165.7m). Cross the Bietsch glacier to the foot of the W subsidiary ridge and climb this to the main ridge.

Climb up the ridge to the base of a grey tower. Traverse this then descend a little way down the S flank and traverse Rwards under the crest before rejoining it via a rock rib on this side. Keep mainly on the crest now, with just an occasional detour onto the S flank (poor rock), until a longer traverse on snow leads to a section of gendarmes. Traverse these on the crest to a narrow and exposed section of the ridge which in turn leads to a red tower. Start this by moving up 2-3m on the S side then climb directly up the W face on good but small holds to the top. A narrow crest now leads to the N summit. Reach the main summit over a number of gendarmes. 6-8hr

255 **NORTH RIDGE**
AD From the Bietschhorn hut: first ascent party. From the
86 Baltschiederklause hut: D Freshfield and C Tucker with
F von Allmen and F Devouassoud, 10 July 1866

The N ridge can be approached from either the Bietschhorn hut or the Baltschiederklause hut, the two routes joining at Pt 3706m. Both approaches are frequently used but the latter is more reliable. The rock is not perfect but is much better than on the WSW ridge. See also photo 87

From the Baltschiederklause hut follow Route 252 to the Baltschiederjoch. Now climb gentle snow slopes SSW to the foot of a rock rib. Climb this (loose rock) to the narrow snow crest, commencing at Pt 3477m, and climb this to Pt 3706m. 4-4½hr

From the Bietschhorn hut follow Route 254 to the Bietschjoch then traverse NE on snow to reach the ridge between the Kl Nesthorn and Pt 3706m. Cross a bergschrund then climb an ice slope to the rock. Climb the ridge (broken rock on the S side) to join the N ridge a little below Pt 3706m. 5½hr

Follow the narrow snow crest or a narrow but easy rock ledge a few m below the crest on the W side to the N summit. Traverse several gendarmes to the main summit. 2hr, about 6-8hr in all

256 **EAST RIB**

AD+ C Dent and J Oakley Maund with J Jaun and A Maurer,

87 25 July 1878

This is the rib running E from the summit and provides a very direct route to the summit from the Baltschiederklause hut. Nowhere is the climbing very difficult but it is fairly sustained on quite good rock and requires a positive attitude.

From the Baltschiederklause hut follow Route 252 onto the Ussre Baltschieder glacier and climb this NW to about 3100m before turning S to reach the foot of the rib. Start on the N side and cross a bergschrund, close to the rock, where it is easiest. Climb up to a snowy saddle then traverse or turn (on the R) a wide gendarme. The rib steepens and the climbing becomes more difficult. Keep on the crest all the way to the summit. 7-8hr

It is possible to get onto the rib from the S side by entering the glacier coombe on that side and climbing up to the ridge where it becomes steep.

257 **SOUTH-EAST RIDGE**

TD– F Kast and W Stösser, 9-11 Aug 1932

87

Probably the best climb on the mountain and mostly on good rock. The climb can be compared with the nearby S ridge of the Stockhorn which is similar in style but technically more difficult. However the commitment required to climb the Bietschhorn is much greater. First, the approach to the climb and the descent are much longer and much more equipment must be carried (snow and ice gear). In addition, once above about half-height it is impossible to abandon the climb. On the Stockhorn it is rare to encounter wet rock, but certainly high on the route, wet or even verglassed rock is a possibility on the Bietschhorn. Most of the difficulties are III and IV with the crux at V low down and on good rock.

From the Baltschiederklause hut follow Route 256 to the foot of the rib and continue S into the glacier coombe. The ridge can be started at various points but it is probably best to climb up the coombe to directly below the first big step in the ridge. Climb up easy but sloping rocks to join a ramp leading L to the ridge (possibly snow). 4hr

Climb the first big step direct by moving up steep walls Rwards into a crack which curves L and is topped by an overhang (V–). All this is on compact rock with few possibilities for protection. Less difficult climbing leads to a 25m high gendarme, narrow at the bottom and overhanging. Climb it direct for 8m then move L on a slab to a crack which is slightly overhanging but has good holds. Climb the crack to the top of the gendarme. Now keep to the exposed crest, turning a sharp gendarme on the L side, to the end of the first part of the ridge at about 3780m.

Make a 10m abseil on the S side to a gap at the top of a big couloir on the S side. Follow the easier and less exposed crest for several pitches (deteriorating rock) or turn the first three gendarmes on the L side before returning to the crest via a couloir (slightly easier). Avoid a group of forbidding looking gendarmes by a ramp on the E side and rejoin the crest by an icy couloir and a difficult wall (two pitches of IV). It is also possible to traverse the gendarmes (IV and V) or turn them on the W side. Easy rock and snow slopes lead to the summit. 4hr, about 8-10hr in all

Stockhorn 3211.6m

J Gallet with G and J Kalbermatten, 7 Aug 1884

Situated at the end of the long SE ridge of the Bietschhorn, this is a fine rocky peak most notable for its excellent S ridge, which is amongst the best ridge climbs in the Oberland. The installation of a bivouac hut has made this climb, unfortunately, very popular.

258 **SOUTH RIDGE**
TD– R Aubert, A Collini, R Dittert, R Lambert, F Marullaz,
88 G de Rham, C Thévenaz, A Tissières and J Weigh, 17 June 1945

The ridge is comprised of five towers separated by gaps of various depths. The rock is perfect granite and the difficulties increase as height is gained. Highly recommended. There are various alternatives to the route described, especially on the last tower.

From the Stockhorn bivouac hut traverse W to the foot of the ridge.

Climb the first tower directly up the crest (300m, two steps of IV). From the top descend the steep but easy W ridge then traverse into the gap below the second tower. 2½hr

From the gap climb the ridge direct to the foot of a narrow 15m high crack. Climb this (IV, 2 pitons), moving L at an overhang, and then a chimney. Traverse easily L from the chimney into a couloir and climb this to where it steepens. Now traverse R to the crest and follow this (exposed) to the top of the tower. Scramble over a few blocks and make a 10m abseil into the next gap. 1hr

Keep on the crest to the top of the third tower then descend steep but easy rock to the next gap. 30min

Climb the fourth tower by the crest until 8m from the top. Now make a traverse on the W side (exposed) to an abseil point. Make two abseils into the gap before the fifth tower. 45min

From the gap climb direct for 8m then slant up R for 5m to a good belay (V, 6 pitons). Continue in steep cracks for 30m on the R side of the crest then get onto the crest to belay (III, IV). Follow the crest for 10m (II) to where it merges into slabs and then traverse 5m L, close to red and black stained rock, before climbing on the L side of a crack to a belay (IV). Go straight up for another 4m then move Lwards on a steep and exposed rib to a belay by a projection (IV+, piton). Less steep climbing for two pitches in a crack system leads to the bottom of a chimney (III, IV). Climb the chimney back to the crest of the ridge (III+) and then climb just on the L side of this to the top. 1½hr

Follow the crest, passing some difficult gendarmes on the W side, to a shallow gap, then keep on the crest to the summit (III,IV). 1hr, allow 8-10hr

259 EAST RIDGE IN DESCENT

AD– First ascent party

88

Descend the ridge, first on the N side then on the S, to a noticable broadening (II). Now descend a couloir on the S side, at the top of which, on the R side, there is a big red slab. The couloir leads down to a scree slope. Be careful not to descend a couloir starting higher on the ridge. 1½hr

Doldenhorn and Blüemlisalp Group

These mountains, of modest height, are situated on the N side of the Gasteretal but are rarely climbed from this side. Their N flanks are mainly snow and ice apart from the Gspaltenhorn, which is quite rocky. Despite their lack of grandeur they offer some excellent climbing, especially in the middle grades of difficulty. A traverse of the group from the Gamchilücke (excluding the Gspaltenhorn) to the Doldenhorn would make an excedingly fine three day outing.

Maps covering this section are: Wildstrubel (263) and Jungfrau (264)

Doldenhorn 3643m

E von Fellenberg with A Roth, C Lauener, J Bischoff, K Blatter, G Reicher and two porters, 30 June 1862

A very fine mountain with a great variety of good routes on both rock and snow. It is the W-most summit of the group and dominates the view from Kandersteg.

260 **SOUTH RIDGE**
D W Baumgartner and W Deihl, 15-16 Aug 1942
90

A rarely climbed route but no worse for that. The problem is the difficulty of approach and the need to bivouac. The situations encountered both at the bivouac and on the route are superb.

From Pt 1415m in the Gasteretal climb the scree slope on the W side of Silleregrabe. At the top of the slope find traces of a track which zig-zags up the steeper hillside before crossing the torrent. Continue up mixed grass and stone slopes, on the E side of the torrent, to glacier polished rocks which in turn are followed to the level of the tongue of the Sillere glacier. There are a number of bivouac sites in the vicinity of Pt 2521m. 3hr

From the bivouac climb ESE over stone and/or snow covered slopes until just short of the S ridge. Climb a rock step on the L to gain an adjacent snow slope which is followed to the ridge. Move up the ridge, turning the step below Pt 3354m on the W side on debris strewn and overlapping slabs to reach a gap above this point where the main difficulties commence.

Follow the ridge to a gendarme. Contour this at half-height on the W side (shattered rock) and continue on the ridge to a big slabby step at about 3500m. Descend gradually on the L side to the upper edge of a snow slope and follow this round a rock pillar to a steep chimney-couloir. Climb this (IV, some loose rock) and slant R near the top to regain the crest. Excellent climbing on the crest, up a series of steps, leads to a near horizontal section. Keep mainly on the crest, with just an occasional detour onto the W side, to the summit. 8-9hr from the bivouac

261 **NORTH-WEST FLANK**

PD First ascent party

91

The ordinary route but quite long and with a tedious approach from the Doldenhorn hut. It can be climbed from the Fründen hut but this approach is infrequently used as the lower part of the Doldenhorn glacier can be problematical.

From the Doldenhorn hut follow the track SE to Bim spitze Stei. Contour round this on the W side and get onto the Doldenhorn glacier at a small plateau S of Pt 2973m.

If coming from the Fründen hut follow Route 262 across the Fründen glacier. Get onto the Doldenhorn glacier and cross it to its W side. Climb this side to reach the small glacier plateau S of Pt 2973m.

Climb the glacier to the col between the Kl Doldenhorn and the Doldenhorn. Large crevasses may be a problem especially late in the season. A snow/ice slope, which becomes a ridge, is followed to the summit. 5-6hr

262 **NORTH FACE**

D/D+ M Bachmann and S Plietz, 8 July 1954

91

Frequently climbed especially early in the season. the face is 650m high with a fairly constant angle (50°-55°). It is almost entirely snow/ice with just a short rock band below the summit. This can be avoided.

From the Fründen hut cross the W branch of the Fründen glacier in a big arc starting Swards and ending up on the W bank. At about the level of the hut a rock ramp fitted with cables leads onto the long rib descending from Pt 3480m. Climb up this or on its W flank to a height of about 2800m then slant R up the Doldenhorn glacier to the foot of the face. Take a direct line to the summit. At the rock band either climb it (III, difficult if verglassed) or avoid it on the L by exiting onto the E ridge. 5-8hr

263 **GALLET RIDGE**

AD J Gallet with J Kalbermatten and A Müller, 19 July 1899

91

The route climbs the N rib to Pt 3480m and the E ridge to the summit.

Much of the climbing is on snow, with a few rock steps, and there is a splendid snow crest leading to the summit. There is some danger from stonefall in the couloir at about 3300m if there are other parties ahead.

From the Fründen hut follow Route 262 onto the N rib. Climb the rib or its W flank, passing a rock step at 3034m on the R side, to a gendarme about 100m below Pt 3480m. Either traverse R into a narrow couloir and climb this (stonefall if not snow-filled) or climb fixed ropes on the L, up the first rock step of the gendarme and get into the upper part of the couloir (on the R) via a snowy terrace. By either way reach a gap above the gendarme (fixed belay points on this section).

From the gap a short but exposed ridge and a steep snow slope lead to Pt 3480m. Follow the E ridge (often corniced) to the summit. Care should be taken on the rocky barrier below the summit if the snow is soft. 5-7hr

264 **EAST RIDGE**
D+ E and O Bürke, 5 Aug 1923. Winter: P Allenbach, H Grossen,
91 G Siedhoff and H Trachsel, 19-20 Jan 1964

A slendid narrow ridge, mostly rock to Pt 3480m where it joins Route 263. It is quite safe from objective dangers and is best climbed when the rock is free of snow (late season). There are some excellent pitches with difficulties up to V, although it is mostly III and IV. A classic route. Start early to ensure good snow conditions on the upper part.

From the Fründen hut follow Route 266 to the pass. 1½hr

From the pass climb a scree or snow slope to the top of the first step on the ridge. Now on the crest or just on its R side, in a series of short cracks, climb to a shoulder (III, IV). The ridge steepens here (the Grey Nose). Climb up overlapping slabs to a vertical wall which is climbed on its L edge (V, exposed). It is possible, but not recommended, to avoid this step by a traverse of about 15m on the N side into a widening crack. This leads to a narrow ledge which allows the ridge to be rejoined above the Grey Nose.

Keep on the ridge (IV) with just a few detours to the next steep part (the Kanzel). This is 25m high. Climb the crest to where it begins to overhang (piton) and make an exposed rising traverse on the S face and then climb straight up to the top of the step (good holds, IV+). The ridge is easier now and is followed to Pt 3480m where Route 263 is joined. 6-8hr, about 8-10hr in all

Fründenjoch 2987m

First traverse: Mrs and M Dübi with C and H Heri, 18 July 1885

Of no great importance as a pass, it does make a good climb from the Gasteretal and can be used to reach the Fründen hut from the Mutthorn hut. Starting from Heimritz there are two possibilities; one route is more direct and more difficult (AD).

265 **SOUTH SIDE**
PD
91

Reach the Alpetli glacier from Heimritz in the Gasteretal as for Route 203 or by descending from the Mutthorn hut. Cross it, at a height of about 2480m, in a wide arc to reach the rocks on its N side near to Pt 2555.4m. Slant up Lwards on easy ground then straight up more steeply to reach the suspended glacier under the SE face of the Fründenhorn, near to its NE corner. Traverse the glacier Lwards and, by easy rocks above, gain the SW ridge of the Fründenhorn. Descend this to the pass after a short ascent over a pronounced point. 5-6hr from Heimritz, about 3hr from the Mutthorn hut. See also photo 92

The alternative approach from Heimritz follows the N side of the Kander to Pt 1814m. Here a big couloir originating under the Doldenhorn is followed on its E side until it is possible to slant up R to Pt 2284m. Now cross a deep, narrow ravine by a horizontal traverse R then, on the other side, climb up grassy slopes with a detour R before regaining the E side of the ravine at about 2500m. Keep on this side of the ravine and get onto a scree slope via a short rock couloir. Move up to a short steep rib and climb it (III). Then, a bit to the R, move up to a last step (III) and climb it Lwards (III) to the edge of the tiny glacier under the Fründenjoch. Climb the glacier and a steep couloir to the pass. 6-8hr

266 **NORTH SIDE**
F

From the Fründen hut climb the Fründen glacier, avoiding the séracs above the hut on the E side. 1½hr

Fründenhorn 3368m

E Ober and F Corradi with P Rubi and F Ogi, 8 July 1871

Although of only modest altitude it has some good climbs to offer, a combination of any two of its ridges making an excellent traverse.

267 **SOUTH-WEST RIDGE**
D H Lauper and M Liniger, 18 July 1921
92

An attractive ridge, rising in steps from the Fründenjoch, which for some reason has been rather neglected. An excellent climb.

From the Fründen hut follow Route 266 to the Fründenjoch. Climb the crest of the ridge Ewards to a pronounced point where it turns NE before a short descent. Still on the crest reach the first steep step.

A ledge system on the S side leads for 30m into a corner and then for another 15m to an easy couloir. This is climbed up to the R to regain the crest before the next step. Climb this direct (III+) then continue on the crest to a gap below an overhang. Get over this on the L (IV/IV+, strenuous) and then back to the crest by slanting up R. The remaining short steps are all taken direct (III) to reach a horizontal section (maybe snow) which leads to the summit. 4½-5½hr

268 **NORTH-WEST RIDGE**
PD First ascent party
92

The ordinary route and quite popular. The line of the route can be picked out from the Fründen hut and should be examined beforehand by parties intending to use it in descent after climbing one of the other routes. The lower part is difficult to follow in mist.

From the Fründen hut climb SE up the Fründen glacier to a snowy indent in the rocks at about 2600m. Climb this then a winding path on the W flank (cairns, pitons and cables), passing to the R of a vertical wall, before finally turning E to reach the snow/ice crest of the ridge. Follow this to the summit. 3hr

269 **EAST RIDGE**
D J Berger and A Carter with K and O Ogi, 12 July 1931. In descent:
92 Mrs and J Gallet with A Müller and D Wandfluh, 14 July 1900

Like the SW ridge this route has been sadly neglected despite it being a very worthwhile climb.

From the Fründen hut descend a little to the E and cross the E branch of the Fründen glacier to the rocks of the NW ridge. Climb a step (possible verglas) to reach slabs which lead horizontally L (fixed ropes and waymarking). Follow these to get onto the moraine of the Undere Oeschinen glacier. Climb the L side of the glacier then its middle and finally a steep snow slope to the Oeschinenjoch (3172m). 2hr

Now climb easily up the E ridge to the first steep step which is climbed direct (III–, 20m abseil in descent). A narrow snow crest leads to a second step. Start this on the R (IV) and then climb a slabby couloir slanting L back to the crest (IV–, two abseils of 20m in descent). A third step is climbed direct (III, 20m abseil in descent) before the ridge eases to the summit. 3hr, 5hr in all

Oeschinenhorn 3486m

H Dübi and E Müller with C Hari and F Ogi, 30 Sept 1874

This is little more than a shoulder of the Blüemlisalphorn but is worth climbing by its NW ridge in combination with the SW ridge of the Blüemlisalphorn. A description of the SW ridge is included for the benefit of parties wishing to make the long traverse of the entire ridge.

270 **SOUTH-WEST RIDGE**
D F Kast and W Stösser, 21 Aug 1932
92 From the Fründen hut follow Route 269 to the Oeschinenjoch. Follow the ridge (shattered rock) and turn a group of gendarmes on the L to reach a big step in the ridge. Reach a well marked gap by a traverse L (IV–, few holds) then climb a chimney-crack (IV+, exposed) to reach another gap. From the gap slant up R (easier) back to the crest. A few more short steps (III+) are taken direct. 3-4hr from the pass

271 **NORTH-WEST RIDGE**
AD– First ascent party not known

From the Fründen hut follow Route 269 onto the Undere Oeschinen glacier. Slant up this Lwards to the bottom of the W face of the mountain at about 2800m. Climb NE up rocky slopes (no specific line but traces of track) which are delicate in places, to get onto the ridge. Climb the ridge a little on its N side (steps of II) to the summit. 4hr

Blüemlisalphorn 3663m

R Liveing, L Stephen and J Stone with M Anderegg, F Ogi and P Simond, 27 Aug 1860

On older maps the 'e' is omitted from the name. The mountain is the highest of three summits collectively known as the Blüemlisalp (Wyssi Frau and Morgenhorn are the others). It has a particularly attractive N face and its three ridges provide first class climbs. The SW ridge combines well with the NW ridge of the Oeschinenhorn whilst the ENE ridge is always climbed in conjunction with an ascent of the Wyssi Frau and quite often the Morgenhorn.

272 **SOUTH-WEST RIDGE**
AD– W Borchardt with D Gyger and S Ogi, 19 Sept 1886
92

The only sensible way of climbing this ridge is to include an ascent of the Oeschinenhorn (usually by the NW ridge). The climb, although quite short, has a remote feel to it.

From the Fründen hut follow Route 271 to the summit of the Oeschinenhorn. Descend the easy E ridge to the col at the foot of the SW ridge. The ridge is mixed rock and snow. A gendarme in the upper part is climbed by a chimney-couloir (III–). About 6hr from the hut

273 **NORTH-WEST RIDGE**
AD First ascent party
93

The ordinary route, of no great difficulty, but care must be exercised on the slabby limestone terrain on the lower part of the ridge. This can be quite trying if icy.

From the Blüemlisalp hut climb the E branch of the Blüemlisalp glacier to reach the snow saddle on the S side of Ufen Stock. Descend into the snow bowl below the N face and cross the bowl before climbing a steep snow slope to the col at Pt 3179m. Climb the rocky lower part of the ridge somewhat on the R side (iron belay posts) and then the snow crest to the summit. 4-5hr

274 **NORTH FACE**
D W Amstutz, W Richardet and H Salvisberg, 1 July 1924.
93 Winter: F Herpich and R Meier, 6 Feb 1966

This is a 500m high glaciated face with a few sérac bands but no rock barriers. The average angle is only 45° but it steepens to 70° for some short sections. It is a very pleasant climb in good snow conditions and just about the quickest way to the summit. A good introduction to N face climbing.

From the Blüemlisalp hut follow Route 273 to the snow bowl below the face. The exact line varies with the condition of the séracs.

Usually start on the L and climb up to the lowest sérac band and cross it by a snow/ice ramp before moving Rwards to directly below the summit. Climb as direct as possible, turning séracs as necessary. The final section can be avoided by moving L onto the ENE ridge. 4-5hr

275 **EAST-NORTH-EAST RIDGE**

AD H Hoare with J von Bergen, Sept 1879

93

This is a magnificent narrow snow crest, quite delicate in places and often corniced. It is started from the summit of the Wyssi Frau and an ascent of the Morgenhorn is frequently included. In fact the traverse of the three summits makes for one of the best climbs of this standard in the Alps. It is a much finer climb than the Rochefort ridge.

From the summit of the Wyssi Frau follow the near horizontal ridge SW then make a steep descent to the lowest point on the ridge. Now keep more or less on the the crest, over a number of steps, to the summit. 2-4hr

Wyssi Frau 3650m

E von Fellenberg and A Roth with J Bischoff, K Blatter and C Lauener, 2 July 1862

The central peak of the Blüemlisalp, it has some fine short routes. It is usually climbed in combination with the Morgenhorn and/or the Blüemlisalphorn.

276 **NORTH-WEST RIDGE**

AD First ascent party

The route is considerably easier than the grade given if the ridge is entirely cramponable snow. However it is frequently icy, even early in the season.

From the Blüemlisalp hut climb the E branch of the Blüemlisalp glacier to the snowy saddle S of Ufen Stock. Now climb the rocks at the foot of the ridge and then follow the steep snow/ice crest to the summit. There are belay stakes in place on the upper part of the ridge. 2½-3½hr

277 **NORTH FACE**

D+ First ascent party not known

Although somewhat shorter, it is more difficult than the Blüemlisalphorn

N face on account of its steepness and regular angle (55°). It is a plain snow/ice slope about 300m high.

From the Blüemlisalp hut climb the E branch of the Blüemlisalp glacier to the foot of the steepest part of the face, directly below the summit. Cross a bergschrund where practicable, then take as direct a line as possible to the summit. 3-4hr

278 **EAST-NORTH-EAST RIDGE**
AD E Cardinaux and G Moilliet, 6 Aug 1898

The climb is started from the summit of the Morgenhorn. It is entirely on snow, except in very dry summers, narrow in places and is often corniced.

From the summit of the Morgenhorn follow the ridge on or near the crest all the way to the summit of the Wyssi Frau. 1-2hr

Morgenhorn 3627m

H Baedecker with J Bischoff and U Lauener, 14 Aug 1869

The E summit of the Blüemlisalp, possessing a magnificent N face. It is most frequently climbed by its NW ridge and combined with a traverse of the Wyssi Frau and Blüemlisalphorn. It is the only peak of the three which is worth climbing from the S side.

279 **NORTH-WEST RIDGE**
PD First ascent party
94

A much frequented climb but of no great interest. It is useful as a means of descent or as a start to the traverse of the Blüemlisalp.

From the Blüemlisalp hut climb the E branch of the Blüemlisalp glacier into the glacier bowl below the Morgenhorn and Wyssi Frau. Climb up Lwards to the ridge (one icy step) then follow it or its NW flank to the summit. Any crevasses on the upper part of the ridge are usually turned on the N side. 3-4hr

280 **NORTH FACE**
TD+ M Aurich and E Stauffer, 10 Aug 1933. By the route described:
94 G Siedoff and H Trachsel, 16 Sept 1962

The N face, about 1300m high, is big and complex with several slanting rock bands interspersed with steep ice. Directly under the summit is a band of séracs which makes routes on this part of the face potentially

dangerous. In general the rock is poor and most of the routes on the face suffer from stonefall, although this appears to be at a minimum on the route described. The climb follows a fairly direct line to the fore-summit. The rock sections (up to IV+) are on sloping and overlapping rock on which protection is not easy to arrange. It is best attempted when the rock is dry and free of verglas (hence the late season first ascent) since friction on the rock is fairly essential. Other routes on the face are shown on the photograph.

From the Gspaltenhorn hut follow the track S onto the Gamchi glacier and cross this to the W towards Pt 2254.3m. Climb up the snowy bay just short of this point and, on the L, climb a ramp 80-100m high onto a rib (III, IV–). Climb the rib for about 200m to where it steepens then move R onto a parallel rib. Climb this to the base of a big rock band. Go up this Lwards (IV+) and then continue straight up to a vertical rock band. Surmount this in a couloir for two pitches and then on its edge (IV+). Mixed ground and the upper ice slope then lead directly to the fore-summit. Reach the main summit by the E ridge. 10-15hr

281 **EAST RIDGE**

D G Hasler and Miss H Kuntze with J von Allmen, 31 Aug 1903.

94 From the Gamchilücke: E Bürki and E Krall, July 1925

This is a long ridge giving fairly sustained climbing on quite good rock. It is usually attempted from the Mutthorn hut, the ridge being reached close to Pt 3306m, but it is also possible to start the climb at the Gamchilücke.

From the Mutthorn hut cross the Kanderfirn and climb up the glacier tongue below Pt 3306m. There are now two possibilities. The easier option is to move R to a deep couloir and climb this (delicate) to its vertical upper walls before traversing R to a gap on the ridge SE of Pt 3306m. Cross this point to reach a section of snow. The other option is less prone to stonefall. Climb the steep slabby couloir starting directly below the summit of Pt 3306m and slanting L. Exit onto the ridge at the snowy section.

To start at the Gamchilücke reach this point by Routes 283 or 284. From the pass climb steep rocks on the R of the crest (III) then the crest itself to reach snow. Traverse the snow horizontally Lwards (S flank) and continue in this line round a rib to reach the glacier tongue below Pt 3306m.

Climb the ridge over or round several gendarmes to a vertical step below the fore-summit. Traverse below the step on the S side to a rib and climb this to the fore-summit. Fairly easy climbing now leads to the summit. 6-8hr, about 2hr more for the Gamchilücke start

282 **SOUTH FACE RIB**
AD– W Gerber and A Müller, 8 Sept 1933

The Blüemlisalp group has an extensive S wall but this is the only climb on the whole wall that is worthwhile. There is some stonefall danger low on the route.

From the Mutthorn hut cross the Kanderfirn and climb into the snowy bay above Pt 2740.5m. From the top NW corner of the bay climb rocks to the foot of the rib. On the rib itself avoid a vertical step on the upper part by a couloir on the W side. 4-5hr

Gamchilücke 2837m

A useful pass between the Gspaltenhorn hut and the Mutthorn hut. There is a precariously sited shelter for about eight people on the S side.

283 **SOUTH SIDE**
F

From the Mutthorn hut cross the Kanderfirn to the Tschingelpass and then contour the Tschingelfirn to the base of a rocky couloir below the col. Climb this (chains) to the col. 1hr

284 **NORTH SIDE**
F

From the Gspaltenhorn hut follow the path S to the Gamchi glacier. Climb the glacier to the col. 1½hr

Gspaltenhorn 3436.1m

G Foster with J Anderegg and H Baumann, 10 July 1869

Basically a rock peak with two principal features: the NE face, one of the highest faces in the Alps, and the SW ridge, a very jagged crest usually referred to as the Rote Zähne ridge (Roti Zend on the map). The rock is not perfect but is usually sound enough.

285 **SOUTH-WEST (ROTE ZÄHNE) RIDGE**
TD S Herford and G Young with H Brantschen and J Knubel,
96 14 July 1914. Winter: P Girardin, J Hengelin and M Perrenoud, 15-16 Feb 1959

A splendid historical expedition with some good rock climbing. However it is not a classic route. The climbing is of variable quality and there is a lot of poor rock. It should only be attempted when the weather is settled since escape from the ridge is dangerous. Once past the first tooth, it is more difficult to return than to continue. The climb can be started at the Gamchilücke but it is more usual to reach the ridge at Pt 3275m.

From the Gspaltenhorn hut head SE towards a tiny glacier then turn S up snow slopes to cross the ridge descending W from Pt 3275m. Get into a wide snowy couloir to the S of the ridge and climb this. Leave the couloir in its upper part by easy rocks on the L to a gap. Follow rocks to a second gap and then snow slopes to Pt 3275m.

Go along the ridge, then follow a narrow ledge for 10m on the S side to the foot of the first tooth. Climb easy rocks for 20m then a snowy couloir and a chimney before traversing R into another couloir. Climb this to the crest and follow it to the top of the tooth (III). 4-6hr

Descend a little couloir on the N side (poor rock) then make a 30m abseil. Climb down to a gap before two gendarmes and descend the couloir below the gap (poor rock) to an exposed ledge. Cross the ledge and make another abseil (15m) before easy rock leads to the base of the second tooth. On the S face climb slabs then traverse R to the second of three cracks. Climb a small overhang then the crack to a belay (IV). Now climb a small couloir before slanting L to the S summit of the tooth.

Move down into the gap before the N summit and keep descending on the L to stony ledges. Follow these N to the first of a number of small gaps. On the other side of the ridge make a 20m abseil to the foot of the third tooth.

It is usual to avoid this tooth by making a 20m abseil on the L side of the gap and then traversing round on ledges before climbing a few m to a scree-covered terrace. From the terrace a steep crack (poor rock) leads to the N side of the tooth. (It is possible to avoid climbing the steep crack to the gap by following a rib on the L to the crest.) The tooth can be climbed from the previous gap (on the W side) by a narrow crack and chimney (IV). Descend by a steep and narrow chimney on the N side (good holds). Either way the crest is followed to the summit. 4-6hr, 8-12hr in all

From the Gamchilücke climb the ridge easily to the first tower. Turn this on the R by a narrow ledge followed by a couloir back to the ridge. Snow leads to Pt 3095m (Kamel). Climb this by a chimney-crack (III) then follow the crest to Pt 3275m. 2hr

286 **NORTH-WEST RIDGE**
AD– First ascent party
95

The ordinary route and a pleasant enough climb once the ridge is reached. Fixed ropes have reduced the difficulties once encountered. See also photo 96

From the Gspaltenhorn hut follow a track NE (rocks and snow patches) until under the S wall of Bütlasse. Follow scree slopes under the wall to the col at Pt 3020m. Now head SE (track) to a cockscomb part of the ridge. Traverse this (II) before descending by a crack to a broad, scree-covered col.

Continue up the ridge on scree then rock and snow to the 'bad step'. Climb this using the fixed ropes, then the narrow snow ridge to the summit. 4-4½hr

287 **NORTH-EAST FACE DIRECT**
ED1 R Schatz, E Reiss and E Haltiner, 29-30 July 1951.
95 Winter: H von Känel, H Müller and R Allenbach, 21-24 Dec 1972

The face is comparable with the Eiger in height (c 1600m) and has no distinct line of ascent. On the R side of the face there is a long ridge (the Chilchbalmgrat, see photograph) which was climbed to the col at 3020m by W Amstutz and G Michel, 9 Sept 1929 and is AD with pitches of III+. W Welzenbach, A Drexel and E Schulze, 7 Sept 1932 climbed part of this ridge then veered off onto the face. Details of their route are not exactly clear but the route is subjected to stonefall (TD). L of the Chilchbalmgrat is a big avalanche-chute, then the face becomes quite complex with slabs, ribs and rock walls, all with snow and ice intermingled and the whole topped by a hanging glacier. The lower rocks are of quite good quality but they become quite friable higher up. The lower part of the route is mostly III–IV with bits of V. The crux is at about mid-height and is V+. There is ice up to 60°. A serious route. There is a somewhat safer line further L (H Bichsel and W Munter, 2-3 Sept 1964) which joins the Schatz party route above its crux. It has difficulties of mostly III and IV and is TD (see photograph).

For all the climbs it is probably best to start from a bivouac cave at Chilchibalme. There is also a bivouac cave about 30m diagonally R above the crux in some yellow rocks. The easiest approach to the face is from Grimmelwald, otherwise walk from Stechelberg up the Sefinental.

From the bivouac climb slabs on the L of the big avalanche-chute working Rwards to where the wall steepens. Climb a dièdre then move R to the middle of a big slab and climb up this, then up a rib (fourth from L, IV) to easier ground. Move up Lwards to a 20m high step and climb it to reach the middle of a higher (60m) and more difficult step (crux).

Climb a crack slanting up from L to R and with an overhang to a small terrace (V+). Next climb a vertical crack to a smooth slab and move L to belay (V+). The bivouac cave is up R from here.

Now follow a fairly direct line trending slighly R towards the couloir descending from the summit. All this is quite difficult mixed ground. Climb the L side of the rib which bounds the R side of the couloir and then the snow/ice slopes above to the summit. 12-18hr

Bütlasse 3192m

C Montadon, 26 Aug 1877

A modest summit, with an impressive S wall, situated N of the Gspaltenhorn hut. The W ridge, which forms the upper edge of the S face, makes a reasonably pleasant outing at grade III (some shattered rock).

288 **WEST RIDGE**

AD– E Köchli and L Mani, 8 July 1934

From the Gspaltenhorn hut follow a track round onto the lower part of the ridge at Tragegg. Climb the easy angled ridge (rock and grass) to the first small step. Climb this by a chimney and continue to a taller step. Climb this, by an S-shaped chimney, to a platform then go straight up over some small overhangs. The next high step is vertical on all sides and is started on the L of the ridge (good holds) followed by grooves and a chimney.

A fairly horizontal section leads to yet another step. Keep on the crest for this then climb the next one on the S side. The following step is climbed by a 30m high wall on well spaced holds and leads to a deep gap. Descend into this then follow the crest (loose rock) to another gap. The step above the gap can be taken direct or on the N side and leads to a final snowy section. 4-5hr

289 **NORTH RIDGE**

F– First ascent party

A very easy climb that any fit walker could undertake. Worth climbing for the summit views.

From Griesalp follow the waymarked track to the Sefinenfurgge

(2612m). Just before the last steep slope turn S and cross scree slopes to the broad ridge running due W from the Vordere Bütlasse, which ends at the col E of Pt 2631.5m. A vague track leads up this ridge to the main ridge which is followed, over the Vordere Bütlasse, to the summit. The last part is on snow. 5-6hr

Lötschenpass to Les Diableret

The mountains described in this section are widely separated, apart from the small group situated between the Lötschenpass and the Gemmipass. The other mountains described are fairly isolated peaks which, in the W, are on the border between the Cantons of Vaud and Valais. Apart from those close to the Lötschenpass, which are comparable in height with those described in the previous section, the peaks are of very modest altitude.

Maps covering this section are: Montana (273), Wildstrubel (263) and St Maurice (272)

Lötschenpass 2678m

A long established glacier (on the N side) pass between the Gasteretal and Lötschental. There is a privately owned hut on the pass (see Huts).

290 **SOUTH SIDE**

P From Ferden in the Lötschental follow the waymarked track (or road) via Kummenalp to the pass. 3½hr

From Kippel a lift can be used to Holz. Walk up to Lauchernalp (Berghaus) then take the long traverse track via Sattlegi. 2hr

291 **NORTH SIDE**

PE From Selden in the Gasteretal follow the path SSW to reach the Lötschen glacier at Pt 2403m (Berghaus at Gfelalp). Climb the glacier finishing on its E side. 3-4hr

Rinderhorn 3453m

G Studer with A and J Grichting, 6 Sept 1854

Situated just E of the Gemmipass its main feature is the tiered glacier system on its N flank which, in effect, is three separate glaciers with rocky escarpments between. The E ridge is D and has some attraction. It is reached just W of Pt 3235m but is a bit loose.

292 **NORTH RIDGE**

PD First ascent party

A much frequented route, ideal for an alpine novice. It is mostly snow and quite easy in good conditions.

From Schwarenbach follow the path towards the Gemmipass as far as Pt 2229.4m. Climb up the valley on the S side of the Chli Rinderhorn as far as the Rindersattel (traces of track over grass slopes and scree). Scree-covered slopes above the saddle lead up the N ridge to snow slopes. Follow these in an arc to the R as far as the final snow slope below the summit. About two pitches of steeper snow/ice lead to the top. 4-5hr

Balmhorn 3699m

F, H and Miss L Walker with M and J Anderegg, 21 July 1864

The N face of the Balmhorn (and Altels) makes a fine sight on the drive up the Kandertal towards Kandersteg. The crest joining the two summits is a classic expedition. On the E side of the face is the NE ridge which makes a good approach route to the interconnecting ridge and is a good climb in its own right. The SE ridge, rising from a point close to the Lötschenpass, is a good rock climb. Of least interest is the ordinary route which climbs the SW ridge.

293 **SOUTH-WEST RIDGE**

PD First ascent party

A rather tedious climb on account of the low starting point. There is over 1600m of height gain.

From Schwarenbach follow the track running E round the base of the Chli Rinderhorn to get onto the Schwarz glacier. Climb this (steep at the top) to the col W of Pt 3117.6m. 2½-3hr

Follow the ridge (traces of track if not snow covered) to about 3300m from where easy slopes lead to the fore-summit (3669m). Follow the crest E to the main summit. 2-3hr, 5-6hr in all

294 **NORTH-WEST RIDGE**

AD– H Löhnert, F Wyss-Wyss and A von Steiger with F Ogi and

89 H Hari, 8 July 1874

This interconnecting ridge between the Balmhorn and Altels is highly recommended in either direction but is much more frequently done from the Balmhorn to Altels.

From the Balmhorn summit follow the snow crest W to the fore-summit. Continue WNW down snow slopes, which soon become a ridge, and reach a saddle. A narrow snow crest, corniced in places, is followed over two steps. The second is usually climbed on the W side, to the rocks of Altels. At first traverse on the W side then, by an easy couloir, get back onto the ridge and follow it to the summit of Altels. 1½hr

295 **NORTH FACE**
D– P Desaules and E Seiler, 14 July 1937
89

The face is broad and glaciated, almost entirely snow and ice, and is about 1200m high but not very steep. The séracs vary from year to year but usually there is a band of séracs below the summit which must be climbed or turned on the L. Although it may be possible to climb the face direct from the bottom, the narrow section (see photograph) is usually impassable. The route is objectively fairly safe.

From the Balmhorn hut get onto the R lateral moraine of the Balmhorn glacier. Climb this and then the glacier to a height of about 2500m, a bit below the NW rib (this is the rib descending from Pt 3402m on the NE ridge). Climb up the N side of the rib then cross it at its narrowest point (II-III, cable) to reach the E side of the face.

Move diagonally R into the middle of the face and climb as direct as possible to the summit. 7-10hr

296 **NORTH-EAST (WILDELSIG) RIDGE**
AD H Biehly and H Seiler with A Müller snr and jnr, 12 July 1901
89

A good route but more for the situations experienced than for the quality of the climbing. Well worth combining with a traverse of Altels.

From the Balmhorn hut follow a track generally SE onto the first part of the ridge and climb it easily to where it narrows considerably near Pt 2821.7m. Continue up the ridge, turning the first gendarme on the E side, to the bottom of a big step where there is a commemorative plaque. On the E side follow a stony terrace for about 100m (gradual descent) to a small cairn. A steep couloir (III–) leads back R to the crest (stonefall from other parties). It may be better to climb on the R side of the couloir to start.

Follow the crest to a snowy step. Climb this on the E side using shattered rocks then, once above the step, continue up the ridge to the final big step (Pt 3402m). Climb this on the E side and then follow the ridge over two short but steep snow steps to a little plateau from where a corniced ridge leads to the summit. 5-7hr

It is possible to reach Pt 3402m by its NW rib (D) by following Route 295 to the E edge of the N face and then climbing the rib between the crest and the glacier face. Same time

297 **SOUTH-EAST (GITZI) RIDGE**
AD H Dübi and L Liechti with C and H Hari, 29 July 1886

Seen in profile, the ridge looks like a giant staircase. The rock is not particularly good but handled carefully it is safe enough. Well worth doing, the difficulties are mostly III with two sections of IV.

From the Lötschenpass hut climb easy snow slopes to the Gitzifurggen (2915m) and then turn N up more snow slopes and some rocks to the foot of the ridge. Go up the ridge to a ladder and use this to gain a platform and the start of the real climbing. Keep to the crest on the first step (III+, II) and climb the second direct (III–). The third step is overcome by a dièdre and a chimney (both III+/IV–). Above this get into a couloir on the L of the ridge and climb this to reach a narrow ledge line on the E side. From the end of the ledge climb straight up then slant L to the base of the fourth step. Start this at a rib on the R then work L to a small couloir which leads back to the crest (III+). The step can be avoided on the W side.

The ridge becomes less steep and leads to the fifth step. Climb this one direct (IV) or turn it 20m L of the ridge and then climb direct (III). Finally a few small teeth and a snow crest lead to the summit (there is one small overhang, IV). 5-7hr

Altels 3629.4m

Local people in 1834

The most notable feature is the triangular NW face which appears as a big smooth snow slope contrasting well with the more dramatic N face of the Balmhorn. There is little of interest in climbing Altels for its own sake but it is always worth doing in combination with the Balmhorn.

298 **NORTH-WEST FLANK**
PD First ascent party
89

Mostly used in descent after traversing from the Balmhorn. Rather monotonous in ascent.

From Schwarenbach follow Route 293 round the N foot of the Chli Rinderhorn then cross the moraines of the Schwarz glacier to the bottom of the NW ridge (vague track). Climb the ridge to Pt 3418m. Above this, climb a steeper slabby section, then follow the steep snow crest to the summit. 5-6hr

Wildstrubel 3243.5m

E von Fellenberg and J Tritten, 16 Aug 1856 but possibly J Tritten and M Schmid in 1855

There are two summits of the same altitude on the long curving and almost horizontal ridge with a third top only slightly lower. Collectively they are called Wildstrubel. The peak at the SW end of the ridge takes this name whilst the second top, of the same height, is called Mittelstrubel and the E most top is the Grossstrubel. The N and W flanks are quite precipitous, whilst the enclosed E and S flanks form a gently sloping glacier bowl.

A pleasant and easy outing is a traverse of the main crest which can be combined with a longer traverse starting at the Daubenhorn or the Schneehorn. From the Grossstrubel a descent on the N side can be made to Adelboden. The mountain is popular with ski-tourers.

299 **SOUTH FLANK**
F First ascent party

An easy walk across an attractive glacier with rewarding views from the summit.

From the Wildstrubel hut climb a path to the lowest col on the S side of the Weisshorn. Descend from here onto the Plaine Morte glacier and cross this until directly below Pt 2910m (a yellowish rock nose). A good track leads from here to the summit. 2½hr

300 **EAST FLANK**
F T Hinchliff and L Stephen with M Anderegg, 11 Sept 1858

An easy climb up the glacier bowl that can be convieniently turned into a circular tour of the tops.

From the Lämmeren hut head SW to turn the Lämmerenhorn on its W side. Get onto the central moraine of the Wildstrubel glacier and follow it in a big arc until heading W close to the rock buttress below Pt 3172m. Pass through the narrow section of the glacier (crevasses) then either head SW to the Lämmerenjoch and climb the

SE ridge easily to the summit or take a direct line to the summit. 2½hr

301 **TRAVERSE FROM THE DAUBENHORN**

AD– *Running SE then E from the SW summit of the Wildstrubel group is a long ridge terminating at the Daubenhorn (2941.7m), whose E face soars above Leukerbad. The traverse can be joined at the Schneejoch (3020m) by climbing the Lämmeren glacier. It is a mixed climb, easier than the grade suggested if the E ridges of the Daubenhorn and Schwarzhorn are omitted. Some of the rock is very loose. Viewed from the Lämmeren hut, the route follows the skyline seen to the S, as far as the Wildstrubel summit.*

From the Wildstrubel hotel walk down to the lowest point of the Gemmipass, then go up stony slopes and easy rocks to a band of light coloured rock. Climb this about 100m from the ridge on the L and continue up rock steps to get onto the E ridge of the Daubenhorn. Follow this to the summit. There is a 50m step of III on good rock and another step of III close to the summit. 3hr

To avoid the E ridge, reach the flat valley of Lämmerboden from the Lämmeren hut or the Wildstrubel hotel and climb the stony band slanting up SEwards towards the summit. 2½hr

From the summit climb easily down to the col S of the peak. Turn W towards Pt 2973m and pass round the S side of a tower to reach the point. Now either climb the ridge to Pt 2993m (III, loose) or turn it on the S side. From the col on the W side of this point climb up towards the Schwarzhorn. The first step reached is climbed direct (III). The one below the summit is climbed, initially up the second chimney on the L and then by the third chimney on the L, before finishing on the crest (II-III, good rock). 2hr

It is possible to turn the Schwarzhorn on the S side by a big detour round the foot of the S ridge.

Descend the easy W ridge to the col at 3005m then make a pleasant climb up the NE ridge to the top of the Rothorn (II). Snow and stony slopes lead down to the Schneejoch (3020m). 1hr

To reach the Schneejoch from the Lämmeren hut get onto the Lämmeren glacier by climbing steep slopes up the sérac zone (PD). This is usually done by keeping close to the rocks on the W side to start and then crossing to the E side of the glacier. Once up this section climb up under the Rothorn then traverse W to the pass. 2hr

Now climb the Schneehorn by its SE ridge and continue over three more tops to the Lämmerenjoch and thence to the Wildstrubel summit. 2hr

From here it is possible to descend to the Plaine Morte glacier (Route 299) or the Lämmeren hut (Route 300) or to continue along the ridge to the other summits of the Wildstrubel. This latter is very straightforward and easy to the Grossstrubel. 1½hr

From the Grossstrubel return to the col at Pt 3092m. To descend to the Lämmeren hut go down the broad couloir on the S side (40°) on snow and unpleasant shale, and join Route 300 back to the hut. If the couloir is icy or the snow is too soft, it is possible to descend rocks 50m E of the couloir bed. To descend to Adelboden head NW down snow slopes then follow traces of track NE to the broad col SE of Pt 2827m. Descend onto the Strubel glacier and follow this NW towards Schönbüel where a path is joined which leads to Engstligenalp (berghaus). 2hr, allow 8-12hr in all from the Wildstrubel Hotel to Engstligenalp, about 6-7hr if the Schneejoch is reached direct from the Lämmeren hut

Wildhorn 3247.6m

G Studer with A Schäppi and a local shepherd, 10 Sept 1843

This is an attractive and fairly isolated peak situated N of Sion in the Rhône valley. It is popular among ski-touring parties but at the same time has some enjoyable routes for the summer alpinist. From the summit the vista to the S is reward enough for climbing the peak, irrespective of the pleasure experienced during the ascent. The rock on the ridge crests is quite good but on the flanks it is loose.

302 **NORTH (WILD) RIDGE**

PD A von Bonstetten and Fr Streckeisen with C and J Jäggi, 27 July 1882

Quite straightforward with nothing more than II on rock.

From the Wildhorn hut head SW, passing Pt 2495m and then the small lake at Pt 2465m before climbing the scree slope to the ridge itself at Pt 2738m. 1-1½hr

Follow the ridge, broad at first then narrow, to Pt 2949m. Climb down into a gap beyond this point and next climb a gendarme on its R side before reaching stony slopes and a track. Go over several short steps, making one short climb slanting L, to reach the fore-summit. Cross easily to the slightly higher main summit. 3hr, about 4½hr in all

303 **NORTH RIDGE BY ITS NORTH-EAST RIB**
D K Germann and W Dürrenmatt, 16 July 1924

A nice rock climb on the crest of the rib, mostly III with one step of IV–. The rib is the obvious one descending NE from Pt 2949m.

From the Wildhorn hut follow Route 302 to the lake at Pt 2465m, then climb direct to the foot of the rib. Start on the L and follow a stony ramp slanting up R. On the L, just short of the crest, climb up easily to where the rock steepens. Either climb the step direct, on the crest or by a slab. Either way take care with the rock (good belay after 25m). Pleasant climbing then for about 200m up the crest leads to a comfortable stance.

Start the next section direct, or on the R and climb a slab by slanting R (IV–) before reaching Pt 2949m. Continue to the summit by Route 302. 2-2½hr for the rib, about 6hr in all

304 **NORTH-EAST FLANK**
PD First ascent party

The ordinary route, almost entirely on snow. There are various possibilities for getting onto the upper part of the Tungel glacier depending on the state of its lower part. The most reliable way is described.

From the Wildhorn hut follow a track SW leading onto the moraine of the Tungel glacier and follow this to the N side of Chilchli. Keep on the rocks on the E side of this rock island as far as its SE corner and here get onto the glacier. Climb up past Pt 2912.2m (go either side) onto the Ténéhet glacier and follow this SW to the summit (crevasses). 3hr

305 **FROM THE COL DU BROTSET**
PD Hubler with J Schwitzgebel, about 1879

The easiest route from the Gelten hut.

From the Gelten hut follow the track, starting NE, onto the terrace called Rottal. Cross the stream then, on the R side of the terrace, reach a stream coming from the R. Now head up past Pt 2425m (crossing a few streams) before turning E to Pt 2578.5m (traces of track). Climb easy snow slopes to the Col du Brotset (2759m).

From the col follow traces of track on the N side of rocks situated just E of the col, and reach the ridge beyond these rocks. Climb the ridge easily to a rocky obstacle a little way below the summit. Move R on steep brown rocks for a few moves and climb a

2m wall to a stone-covered ledge. Go N along this as far as a steep couloir which leads to the ridge above the step. The summit is now attained easily. 5-6hr

Les Diablerets 3209.7m

G Studer and M Ulrich with J Ansermoz and J Madutz, 19 Aug 1850

This is the highest summit in the Vaud Alps and near the W limit of the peaks described in this guide book. The name refers to a relatively complex group of summits, the highest point indicated on the map being called Sommet des Diablerets. This top appears to be about 5m lower than a rocky point some 60m to the E. There is also a snowy top to the NE of this which is sometimes higher. In simple terms the massif is mainly snow on the N side and mostly rock on the S side. The mountain has been spoiled to some extent by the incursion of ski-lifts, but it is still able to provide a good day's sport.

The mountain has been the scene of some spectacular landslips over the years, the best known being those in 1714 and 1749, and it is well worth making a slight diversion to have a look at the results.

306 **TOUR OF THE MASSIF**

PD

The route takes in some varied terrain although most of the ground covered is glacier. There is a nice contrast between this and the rocks of the Tour St Martin and the pyramid of the Oldenhorn (also called the Becca d'Auden). There are some strikingly different views to be admired, especially the landslips. The route can be done in a day from the Col du Pillon by utilising the lift system, otherwise start from the Diablerets hut.

From the Diablerets hut follow a track S onto the Sex Rouge glacier and climb this to the Col de Tsanfleuron (2839m). 1hr

The col can be reached from the top téléphérique station by a path descending ESE. 10min

Climb easy snow slopes SW over Pt 3016m (the Dom) and along a snow crest to get onto the Diablerets glacier. Follow this to the summit. 1½hr

It is worth making a short detour to the SE top of the Sommet des Diablerets (Tête de Balme, 3185m but not marked on the map) to see the debris left by the land slips to the SE (Eboulement des Diablerets).

Descend from here back to Pt 3016m then, first E and then SE, descend gently to the base of the Tour St Martin (2908.1m). Start on the NW side by climbing a short wall from L to R (III) to the NW ridge. Now go up slabs and a bulging wall to a vertical chimney. Climb this (II, some dubious blocks) then more slabs to the summit. About 45m in all. 1hr

Descend by two abseils back to the Tsanfleuron glacier and cross this Nwards to the col E of the Oldenhorn (Pt 2737m). Follow the E ridge (traces of track) to the Oldenhorn summit. 1½hr

To return to the Col de Tsanfleuron either descend the SW ridge (abseils on the last step) or go back down the E ridge to the col and walk under the S flank. 1hr, allow 6-8hr in all

Grand Muveran 3051.1m

A rock peak well seen from the Rhône valley, which offers some good rock climbing even though the quality of the rock is not particularly good. The summit is well worth a visit for the views alone.

307 SOUTH FLANK

F

The easiest route and only a short climb from the Rambert hut. It is quite easy to do the route in a day from the valley.

From the Rambert hut climb a grass and scree slope Nwards up the crest of the S rib, which is in the middle of the S face and directly above the hut. Cross a few short rock bands Rwards (avoid going L) to reach a wide chimney with a yellow tower on its L. Climb another 30m then follow a terrace Lwards, climbing gradually for about 250m (cairns and traces of track), to reach a couloir. Follow this to the summit. 1½hr

308 SOUTH-SOUTH-WEST (SAILLE) RIDGE

D+ Probably R Chevalley and M Francey, 1937

Climbed earlier than the date given but the crux section was avoided. It is a good climb with good rock where it matters. It is possible to do the route in a day from the valley starting at Pont de Nant (NW of the mountain). There are pitches of III and IV with one of IV+ and another V–.

From the Rambert hut follow a track to the foot of the ridge and ascend it to the first difficulties. Climb the first step direct for a few m then make a 6m traverse R before slanting up R to the foot of a dièdre. Climb this using a slab on the L at first, then in the bed of the dièdre to a piton. Now move R onto the rib bordering the dièdre and climb this for a few m (30m, IV, exposed). Less steep slabs lead back to the crest of the ridge.

Climb the next step on the R of the crest by an overhanging chimney-crack (piton) followed by a slab on the L (IV). Take the third step direct at first, then avoid a wall on the R (III) before slanting back L and finishing by a ramp to the R (III). Easier climbing on loose rock, then in a chimney-couloir leads to a small saddle at the foot of a big overhanging wall (good views across the W face).

Climb a vertical wall to an obvious niche and good belay. Now move Lwards to a vertical dièdre which leads to a delicate traverse L (20m, IV+, exposed). A slab leads back R then a short but overhanging wall is climbed to another vertical dièdre. Climb this (V–) then an easy couloir to the top of the step. Easier slabs with some short walls (III) are now followed to the summit. 4-5hr

The crux section can be avoided by a long traverse R followed by a short ascent up three chimneys (II and III) then a long traverse L back to the ridge.

309 SOUTH RIB

AD

A short but pleasant climb, quite delicate in places.

From the Rambert hut follow Route 307 to the chimney and yellow tower. Instead of going L continue up the slabby rib to the final step below the E ridge. It is best here to go L and climb a chimney-couloir with a few short walls (III) to reach the E ridge. Follow this easily to the summit. 3hr

Rock Climbing Areas

On the fringes of the Oberland Massif and in the Cantons of Vaud, Fribourg and Bern there are numerous cliffs which, in recent years, have had their potential for rock climbing realised. The climbing is generally on sound limestone or on excellent quality granite, and many of the routes will be as good as are found anywhere else in the Alps.

On most of the cliffs described the routes are equipped with pitons and/or bolts and it is left to the climber whether or not to use the in situ gear for aid. Sometimes it is essential to use aid but at other times, by doing so, it will bring many of the routes into the realms of the possible for the average climber who does not normally attempt E grade climbs.

Of necessity only a selection of climbs are described on a selection of cliffs, most of which are fairly easily accessible. Most of the routes do not have a written description but a topo diagram, and usually a photograph, is used to indicate the line of ascent. On some of the cliffs there have been so many routes developed that care must be taken to avoid taking the wrong line. A line of pitons/bolts does not always mean that the route you are climbing goes that way. It is not uncommon for a route to finish below the top of the cliff. Usually in these circumstances there will be an equipped abseil descent line. This is also the case on many routes which do climb to the top where the descent might otherwise be tedious or difficult. It is not uncommon, especially among continental climbers, for only one pitch of a climb to be done before abseiling back to the ground.

On practically all the cliffs described, new routes are continually being developed and the use of aid on existing routes is being eliminated.

Although not in the Oberland massif this splendid mountain is not to be missed by climbers visiting the Grimsel/Handegg area since it can be easily reached by a drive over the Sustenpass. The quality of the rock is similar to that found at Handegg although access to the routes is more of an undertaking. See the huts section for the approach to the Salbit hut and the bivouac hut from the Göschenertal W of Göschenen. The classic route is the S ridge but climbs are also described on the W ridge and on the Zwillingsturm (the last tower on the S ridge) S face.

On the way over the Sustenpass you will pass under the Tellistock and Wendenstock. Both of these are quite spectacular and have a number of existing routes and potential for more. It is also possible to cross the Furkapass, which has a wealth of granite faces, to Andermatt. From there descend the superb Schollenen gorge to Göschenen.

Map for this area is: Sustenpass (255)

1 **SOUTH RIDGE**

D A and O Amstad with G Masetto, 16 Aug 1935

97

A sustained rock climb comparable with, but more difficult and more sustained than, the N ridge of Piz Badile. The hardest step is V and A0 or V+ free. A Friend 2 is useful as well as wedges.

From the Salbit hut follow the track leading to the grassy couloir below the end of the S ridge. Climb the couloir to an indistinct saddle. Start a little way R on the E side. 1½hr

Easy climbing at first then steeper ground for a few m leads to mixed grass and rock before a dièdre (V) leads onto the crest. Move up R to a chimney and climb this (20m, can be avoided on the L) then the ridge to another chimney. Climb this (steep) then up R to a slab. Above the slab make a traverse R below the crest to a small gap and from here reach the top of the first tower. Abseil 20m into the gap beyond.

Just below the crest on the L side climb 20m then go up a short chimney to a gap. Go straight up for 6m then slant up R to a corner which leads to a small gap on the crest (IV+, a fine pitch). Now climb a short slab then a long one to a block (sling). Make a short descent on the N side then climb parallel to the crest to a gap. Keep on the crest (easier) to a good stance before a 15m pitch up the crest followed by a smooth slab leads to another gap below a slabby wall. Climb this for 4m then, on the L side of the ridge, move up a thin crack (pitons, V and A0) back to the crest and follow this to a stance (40m in all). Move round the L side of the ridge and climb a dièdre back to the crest and follow this to a smooth slab. Move L into a corner then climb up to the crest again and follow it to a ledge below a fine pinnacle (cairn).

Start up the pinnacle then traverse its L side to a gap on its N side. Climb the step above to the top of the tower (V). It is easier half-way up this step to traverse L then back up R on the other side of the tower. A 20m abseil leads to the next gap, then climb the crest to the top of the tower (called Zwillingsturm, 2920m). Cross the two summits and descend to the next gap without difficulty.

From this gap move up L to reach a short dièdre. Climb this then a 20m dièdre to a grassy terrace. On the R climb a 6m crack and a short corner to reach the ridge above. Move onto the N side and climb the summit block. 6-8hr in all

Descend by going about 150m down the E ridge passing one gap to another very prominent one. Now follow a gully down the N side onto the small glacier on this side of the mountain. Cross the glacier to its N side (few or no crevasses) then follow the slope down to a snow/scree couloir which in turn leads to a scree slope and a track back to the hut. 1½-2hr

2 **WEST RIDGE TRAVERSE**
ED1 E and B Favre and I Henchoz, 1948
98
5

There are five towers on the ridge and the route traverses each of them, the climbing being quite sustained. The rock is excellent throughout on this, one of the hardest rock ridges in the Alps. The climb can be abandoned after the second tower, and after the fourth tower by abseil on the S side (descent on the N side leads into a dangerous gully). At the gap after the third tower there are good bivouac sites on the N side of the ridge. Pitons are in place where needed. The bivouac hut can be reached from the Salbit hut by following a Via Ferrata style path constructed by the hut guardian. Ask at the hut for details. See also photo 99

South Face of Second Tower

The towers of the W ridge have seen a good deal of development in the way of rock climbing in the late 70s and throughout the 80s,
99 although it was as early as 1959 that the first of the routes was
6 climbed on this face (SE Pillar). All the routes are fully equipped with in situ protection, but wedges and camming devices should be carried. Approach from the bivouac hut in about 15min.

3 **BGA** VIII– or VI+ and A1

4 **GKG** VIII– or VII and A0

5 **KGB** VII+ and A0

6 **HAMMERBRUCH** VII or VI and A0

7 **IRON MAN** VIII– or VII– and A0

8 **SOUTH-EAST PILLAR** VII– or VI– and A0

Zwillingsturm South-East Face
Zwillingsturm is the uppermost tower on the S ridge with a steep ribbed face on its SE side. A deep cleft in the ridge separates it from the summit. The face offers some excellent climbing on perfect rock with routes of between 300m and 400m. The first routes on the face were climbed in 1959 and 1962 respectively, but more recently the Remy brothers, among others, have been active and at least four
97 more routes have been added. Fixed protection is in place but
7 wedges and camming devices should be carried. The foot of the face is reached in about 75min from the Salbit hut.

9 **JATZI** VII– with one point of aid or VI and A0

10 **LICHT UND SCHATTEN** V/VI with one step of VII–

11 **JIMMY** VII–

12 **CLOG AND STOCK** IV/V. Abseil down Jimmy

13 **VILLIGER PILLAR** VII or VI and A0

Handegg and the Grimselpass area

On the N side of the Grimselpass there are two areas of cliffs for climbing. In the Haslital, described by Claude Remy as the Llanberis pass of Switzerland, are a number of roadside crags of which three have become very popular and on which a large number of routes have been developed. The other area is on the N side of the Grimselsee. Several cliffs have been developed of which three are described. Two of these, especially Eldorado, require a little more effort to reach but that effort will be justly rewarded. There is a proposal to raise the level of the Grimselsee, and if this is accepted by the Swiss authorities it could have serious consequences for climbing here. All the more reason to make a visit if you are not already familiar with the area.

The rock on each of the cliffs described is excellent, slabby granite – the best in Switzerland. Some of the lines become water courses after rain but others dry very quickly.

Neither camping nor bivouacing is permitted in the Haslital other than on recognised campsites, nor are they permitted in the Grimselsee region although at Eldorado, where the descent path joins the main path, there is an excellent bivouac site under an overhanging boulder. Use of this appears to be tolerated but it can be crowded. There are four campsites in and around Innertkirchen, and bivouacing on the terraces below the Grimsel Hospiz appears to be tolerated. Accommodation is available at the Handegg Hotel and at the Grimsel Hospiz (reduced rates for SAC members).

Maps for this area are: Sustenpass (255) and Nufenenpass (265)

Oelberg 666.8/163.5
Park at the power station just below the first hairpin bends on the road to the Grimselpass, about 6km S of Guttanen. The cliff is about 15min walk E from here and is comprised of three main areas with routes of up to about 250m in length.

All the routes are well equipped with in situ bolts and pitons,
100 but it is necessary to carry wedges and camming devices and a
101 minimum rope length of 45m. Descent from most routes is by abseil
102 and a number of routes have been equipped for this purpose.
Descent from the N most crag is by the tramway.

8 Below is a list of climbs referred to in the topos and
9 photographs with the grade of the hardest moves. Routes that are
10 particularly recommended are 1, 3, 5, 9, 13, 14, 15 and 18.

1 **HERRENPARTIE** VI–

2 **SCHIEFER TRAUM** VI–

3 **SPIEGELWEG** VII+ or VI and A0

4 **CHATZENFAD** V no topo

5 **SIEBEN SCHAFER** VII or VI and A0

6 **ENGELIWEG** V

7 **EILE MIT WEILE** VII+ or VII and A0

8 **JIM KNOPF** VI+ with 4 aid points or VI and A0

9 **BOULDER HIGHWAY** VIII– with one aid point or VI+ and A0

10 **MISSISSIPPI** VIII–

11 **NOLI ME TANGERE** VII+ or VI and A0

12 **FRED FEVERSTEIN** VIII– or VII and A0

13 **HANDEGG VERSCHNEIDUNG** VI– or V and A0

14 **QUARTZ RISS** VI or V+ and A0

15 **STATUS QUO** VII+ or VI– and A0

16 **TOTENWEG** VII or VI and A0

17 **BIOWEG** VI and A2. Two good initial pitches of V+

18 **FAIR HAND LINE** VI/VI+ or V+ and A0

Bügeleisen 666.2/163.4

Park as for Oelberg. The cliff is about 10min NW from the parking area on the W side of the main road and has routes of up to 150m in length.

103
11
All the routes are equipped with pitons and bolts, but carry wedges and camming devices and at least 45m of rope. Descent is by abseil and equipment is in place.

19 **RAPUNZEL** VI+ or VI and A0

20 **HORIZONT EXPRESS** VII or VI+ and A0

21 **EISTEIGESVARIANT** VI or VI– and A0

22 **BÜGELEISEN** VI or VI– and A0

Gelmerfluh 668.3/180.9
About halfway up the pass from the power station, parking is at Pt 1596m at the start of the path to the Gelmersee. The cliff is about 10min walk to the SE and has climbs of up to 200m in length.

104 All the routes are equipped with pitons and bolts but wedges
12 and camming devices should be carried as well as a minimum of 45m of rope. Descent is by abseil, mostly down or alongside the route of ascent.

23 **DON'T PANIC** VII+/VIII–

24 **BANANEN SPLIT** VI+

25 **GREEN APPLE** V+

26 **MELODIE** VI+

27 **EISENFRESSER** VI+

28 **WILDHEUERWEG** VI+

29 **MOBY DICK** VI

30 **KURZSCHUSS** VIII

31 **VIA BIRRA** V

32 **BALANCE** VII

Marée 668.2/158.3
Park at the Grimsel Hospiz at the E end of the Grimselsee. The cliff rises from the waters on the N side of the reservoir close to the dam

wall and has routes up to 150m in length. Approach the cliff by crossing the dam wall then climb steps and a path on the other side to a tunnel through the cliff. Routes on the E side of the cliff are reached by abseil from just before the tunnel entrance whilst those on the W side, below the path, are reached by descending steep vegetated slopes from the tunnel exit. Three climbs are located on the walls adjacent to the tunnel exit.

105 All the routes are equipped with pitons and bolts but some
13 wedges should be carried. HWT = High water traverse.

33 **RISS** VI or V+ and A0

34 **PAPILLON** VIII– or VII+ and A0

35 **SEEKOMEL** VI+/VII–

36 **MISTRAL** VII+ no topo

37 **LES PIEDS ET LES MAINS** VI+/VII– or VI+ and A0 Friend 1½ useful

38 **SCIENCE FRICTION** VIII– no topo

39 **EUREKA** VI+/VII– or VI+ and A0

40 **LES OS** VII no topo

Cascade 667.3/158.6
This is quite an extensive cliff although routes have only been developed on one section of it. It is situated W of Marée and somewhat higher on the hillside. After exiting from the tunnel through the Marée cliff continue to the bridge below the cascade (obvious). The cliff is 15min scramble up the hillside on the E side of the torrent and the climbs are located on the steep buttress just R of a deep chimney.

The climbs are about 200m in length and are a little easier
106 than the majority in the area. Only Razmataz is fully equipped with
14 in situ protection and belays. Descent to the foot of the cliff is by walking W towards the cascade then down grass slopes, or it is possible to descend to the E back to the dam wall.

41 **LES PETITS BAINEURS** V+ and A2

42 **RAZAMATAZ** V+/VI

43 **FOREIGNER** VI

Eldorado 664.3/157.3

Situated at the W end of the Grimselsee above its N shore and about 1½hr walk from the Grimsel Hospiz on the route to the Lauteraar hut (Route H5). Without doubt this is the major cliff in the area and one of the finest in the Alps. It has classic routes, of 500m length, in a much more varied style than can be found in the other cliffs of this region.

Only Routes 2, 3, 4, 5, 6 and 8 are fully equipped with in situ protection and belays, but even on these routes wedges and
107 camming devices should be carried. 45m of rope should suffice. The
15 descent is on the E side of the cliff and takes about 30min to the foot (or abseil down Motörhead).

44 **GENESE** V+/VI–

45 **DJAMSMODELE** VI+ Etriers needed

46 **MARCHE OU CREVE** VII+

47 **SEPTUMANIA** VI+

48 **MOTÖRHEAD** VII– or VI+ and A0

49 **VENON** VII or VII– and A0

50 **FRANZ BENELLI** VII+

51 **METAL HURLANT** VII or VII– and A0

52 **SIMPLE SOLUTION** V+ and VI

53 **RADIO SONDE** V and VI

54 **BALAI AERIEN** V– and VI

Engelhörner and Klein Wellhorn South-East Face

This area of magnificent limestone peaks at the NE corner of the Oberland massif is within easy striking distance of Meiringen, the Haslital and of Grindelwald, from where a post bus can be taken to Rosenlaui on the E side of the Grosse Scheidegg pass. It is well worth a visit when the higher mountains are out of condition, or as a bit of variety from the granite slabs of Handegg.

There are many long established easy climbs, on good rock, to the summits of the various peaks, whilst in recent years many harder climbs have been created.

The obvious base for many of the climbs is the Engelhorn hut (see huts section) although many routes are quite feasible undertakings from the valley. Note however that there is no camping in the valley. All the climbs described here are easily accessible from the hut which is at the foot of the Ochsental on the E side.

Maps for this area are: Interlaken (254) and Sustenpass (255)

Gross Simelistock 2482m

One of the finest peaks in the group with a very impressive SW face on which have been developed several modern routes.

1 **TRAVERSE**

AD H Brog, O Neiger and N Kohler, 16 Aug 1913

108

It is usual to include the Kl Simelistock in the traverse, which is one of the most popular excursions in the area. There are rock pitches of III and two steps of IV.

From the Engelhorn hut head SE up the Ochsental to reach a band of rock crossing the coombe (10min). Now turn L on a well-worn track up scree to reach a grassy terrace below a steep wall. At the end of the terrace climb a grassy couloir to reach a small col and from there attain a more obvious col on the NW ridge of the Kl Simelistock.

Climb a couloir leading slightly L to get onto the E flank of the ridge, then continue in the same direction for about 35m up rocky ledges and short steps. A deep slabby dièdre leads R to the ridge crest which is followed to a slight depression. The ridge becomes more interesting and turns towards the R. Follow the crest for a little way, then slant L to a rib and climb this back to the crest of the main ridge just L of a fine tower. Climb down into a gap then follow the crest to another couloir (III+) Climb slabs on the R of the couloir and so gain the top of the Kl Simelistock. 1½hr

Descend ledges to the gap beyond then climb fairly easily up the ridge to reach the final wall. Traverse some slabs to a fault line parallel to the crest and climb this to a projecting block before making a short descent on the R side. Go 2m along a narrow ledge then climb up L onto the block. Descend into the next gap. A terrace leads Rwards and is followed to its R end where it joins the SW ridge (piton belay). Climb the wall above direct for about 10m (IV–) then the crest of the ridge (IV) before slanting R to the summit. 1½hr

To descend go NE at first then down a grassy crack on the R to an abseil point. Make three short abseils to reach the Simelisattel. Now go down a stone-filled couloir on the W side to a smooth step (piton). Abseil or climb down this then continue in the couloir to a second piton. Now descend a couloir with overlapping steps at the bottom, then a short vertical step. Move L onto a grassy shoulder (cairn). A steep couloir on the L leads onto slabs which are followed Lwards to the spur below the W rib of the Vorderspitze. Go down grassy slopes (vague track) then head across L to reach the S-most of three couloirs (there is a snow patch at the top of the central couloir). Keep on the L side of the couloir as far as a rocky projection, then traverse delicately into the couloir before following it down into the coombe. Easy slopes lead back to the hut. 1½hr, allow about 6hr in all

2 **MACDONALD CHIMNEY**

D+ C Macdonald with P and R Almer, 20 Aug 1898

10m above the level of the Simelisattel is a small rubble-covered terrace. From the terrace a steep chimney leads directly towards the summit of the Gross Simelistock. This provides a strenuous climb of about 100m with moves up to V.

From the saddle climb vertical rocks (IV) to the terrace. A smooth narrow chimney is climbed to a piton before exposed moves up Rwards over a smooth bulge (V) leads to a piton belay. Continue up the steep but easier chimney before moving R above a vertical wall to a belay on a rib on the R (abseil point for descent). Easy climbing up the chimney follows, but it is better to continue straight up from the belay over a smooth step and a grassy crack slanting R.

Gross Simelistock South-West Face

108
16
All the routes, which are up to 250m in length, are fully equipped with in situ protection, but wedges and camming devices should be carried.

3 **SILBERFINGER** VII

4 **SILBERMAGIC** IX or VII– and A0

5 **DECUBITUS** VIII+ or VII– and A0

6 **AGONIE** IX or VIII– and A0

7 **LIMITE** VIII– or VII– and A0

8 **SUDPILIER** V+

Vorderspitze 2619m

G Bell with U and H Fuhrer, 3 Sept 1901

This is the peak SE of the Gross Simelistock and the Simelisattel. Its most attractive feature is its W ridge.

9 **WEST RIDGE**

D+ *A long (400m) and demanding climb, one of the best in the Engelhörner. The upper part of the ridge is steep and very exposed. The rock is good and pitons are in place. Aid is used in places and the grades given allow for its use. Use of a double rope is recommended in view of the sharp nature of the rock.*

From the Engelhorn hut walk up the Ochsental to its flat part and continue to the foot of the R-hand of three couloirs (route to the Simelisattel). Climb the couloir to where it widens and becomes less steep then move R out onto its bounding edge across smooth slabs. Continue up to the foot of the ridge over grassy slabs. On the R is a subsidiary ridge. Climb to its crest by a grassy dièdre (III, delicate) then follow the crest to a steep wall. Slant up R (III) to an exposed stance, then climb vertically for 10m (III+) before following a couloir Lwards for 60m (II) to a distinctive gendarme on the W ridge itself.

Follow the crest for a little way then move L and climb on this side to reach a good belay below a steepening of the ridge (IV–).

Climb a short dièdre on the L and then slabs (III+), all the time on the L of the crest, then move up the crest (III) for a few m before a traverse R leads to another good belay. Move up R to a ledge (IV) then, from its R end, climb a vertical dièdre for 8m to a niche. Continue upwards by first moving R then back L (IV) to reach a steep crack which leads to a cramped belay (IV). Climb a grey bulge using a leaning crack (IV) which widens into a couloir. Follow this to the upper part of the climb.

Climb a vertical crack for 10m (IV+) to a narrow ledge which is followed R for 15m (IV) to a niche (don't belay). Continue up exposed slabby rock (IV) to another niche and belay (about 40m in all from the foot of the crack). Take care on this pitch to avoid rope drag on account of the number of pitons and the changes in direction. Now climb a crack (III) to a ledge which is followed to the L to a chimney-crack. Climb this (III) to the summit ridge which is followed (III–) to the top. About 5 hr from the hut

Decend on traces of track across scree slopes on the E side to a rocky shoulder. Climb down rocks, or turn them on the R in a yellow couloir, to reach a saddle above a section of pinnacles on the ridge. Descend a few m on the Ochsental side to an abseil point and make a 20m abseil down slabs towards the Simelisattel. Keep moving down slightly Lwards then descend a couloir before reaching the Simelisattel. Continue as for the descent from the Gross Simelistock (Route 1).

Kingspitz 2621m

H King with A Anthamatten and A Supersaxo, 13 Aug 1887

Undoubtedly the finest peak in the Engelhörner and particularly impressive on its N side where one finds the classic NE face route. The face has attracted some attention from the modern rock climber and a route by D Anker and M Piola is described.

10 **NORTH-EAST FACE CLASSIC ROUTE**
TD H Haidegger and M Lüthi with H Steuri, 26 Sept 1937
109
17

A classic and frequently climbed route which has all the necessary pitons in place. The middle section of the climb is quite sustained. The rock is good but there is danger of stonefall created by other parties on the route. There is over 500m of climbing, aid is used but étriers are not really necessary. The foot of the face is reached in about 30min from the

Engelhorn hut by walking up the Ochsental. Start at a band of yellow rock a few m L of the summit fall-line and below detached rocks at 60m.

11 **ANKER-PIOLA ROUTE**
ED1
109
17

First climbed in 1988. Considered to be worthwhile but at the same time serious. The rock is not completely reliable everywhere and additional protection to that in place should be carried. VII+ or VII and A0. The route is equipped for abseil.

12 **WEST FLANK COULOIR**
PD First ascent party

The ordinary route, quite easy but with some interesting climbing, and the usual route of descent. Stonefall in the couloir is a problem when other parties are above and this is not a nice place to be in a storm.

From the Engelhorn hut follow the approach path to a scree slope rising on the NW side of the Rosenlauistock. Follow the track towards the Rosenlauistock then make a short descent to reach grassy slopes interspersed with short rock steps. Climb this slope Lwards (tracks) then cross a couloir descending from the gap S of the Rosenlauistock. Keep moving almost horizontally to a very obvious grassy shoulder. 45min

Climb steep grassy slopes above the shoulder (track) to below a yellow wall at the foot of a ridge (leading up to the Engelburg summit). Now traverse horizontally R until a short descent can be made into a scree-filled couloir (cairn – look for this in descent). Slant up R on grassy slopes then straight up to a conspicuous gendarme. More grass and scree lead to the col above (Ochsensattel, c 2299m). 45min

The pleasant climbing begins here. Follow a slightly descending track R to a horizontal rib. This can be reached from the conspicuous gendarme without going to the Ochsensattel. Descend into a wide couloir (descending from Kastor and Pollux). Climb the couloir on its R side (track) to a small col (cairn). Now climb up slanting R under a steep wall, then climb the R side of a steep slab (good but small holds, III–) to a piton on the crest of a rib. Traverse horizontally R to another piton in the couloir descending from a gap in the ridge above. Climb the smooth couloir (exposed) for two pitches keeping on the R side (II+). The couloir opens out and easy stepped and stone-covered slopes lead Rwards to the steeper summit rocks. Climb a reddish-yellow couloir up Rwards (good holds) and gain the W ridge. Follow the ridge on its R side to the summit. 2hr, allow 4hr from the hut

West Group

A group of fairly low peaks NW of the Kingspitz offering relatively easy climbing that can be attempted soon after poor weather.

13
AD+

TRAVERSE

First climbed in two stages: W ridge of Rosenlauistock and E ridge of Tannenspitze, H Kuntze, G Hasler and U Fuhrer, 22 June 1902: W ridge Engelburg and W ridge Sattelspitzen, H Kuntze, G Hasler and M Kohler, 12 July 1902

Entertaining climbing, nowhere harder than IV unless the Rosenlauistock ridge is climbed direct, and mostly III. The climb can be abandoned at the Grasspass.

From the Engelhorn hut follow Route 12 to the couloir coming from the gap S of the Rosenlauistock. Climb up the couloir to a grassy terrace leading L. Follow this to reach the crest of the ridge above a steep step. Climb R at first (II) then up to a grassy platform. Enter a gully on the R and in it climb a 6m step (IV) leading to a rib. Continue to a cave before moving up R to a ledge on the crest. Climb a crack (IV+) to overcome the next step, then continue more easily up the ridge before moving L into a deep couloir which leads back to the crest (III+).

Move up L to a small stance under an overhang. Move L onto the NW face and climb a smooth slab, first 3m horizontally L (III+) then up to the ridge. Now climb up Lwards to a gap between the W and main summits of the Rosenlauistock. Follow the crest to the top. 2-2½hr

To climb the ridge direct: from the ledge on the crest after the cave, climb a smooth slab to reach a deep crack (V). This leads R to an exposed dièdre (V) which slants R and leads to a series of steep slabs. Climb another crack (IV–) to reach a niche and then climb gradually L to reach the summit ridge.

Descend, on the SW side, a chimney leading to a terrace. Follow this to the lowest gap before the Tannenspitze. From the gap climb the narrow ridge, avoiding a steep step on the R, to reach the main steep section. Move R into a narrow dièdre and climb this on good holds to a small shoulder. From here move up to a ledge on the crest. Now climb the crest direct to a shoulder below the final step. Move gradually L up the crest to the summit of the Tannenspitze. 1hr

Descend the E ridge for a little way then the S face to a piton. Make two abseils to a grassy col (Grasspass). The climb can be left here by descending on the W side.

From the col follow easy slopes to a shoulder on the W ridge of the Engelburg then follow the crest to a steep step. Move up L into a couloir and follow this to a grassy ledge and then climb the crest on the L to the summit of the Engelburg (IV). 1hr

Descend on the SW side to the saddle before the Sattelspitzen. Keep on the ridge to below a big step. Climb down R to a stone-covered ledge and then climb a chimney slanting R across the S face of the NW summit. Move up easily to this summit and then into the gap before the main summit. Climb to this direct (III) or more easily from the L (it is possible to climb the big step direct (IV) to the NW summit). 30min

Descend on the SE side to a terrace then slant down Lwards over short steep steps to reach a small platform. Now descend a couloir and slabs (II) to reach the Ochsensattel. 30min

Probably the best finish to the traverse is to descend to the Ochsental. Follow traces of track, rising slightly, to a short rock rib. Climb this then step R (S) to a chimney-couloir and descend this to a grassy shoulder. Leave this on the R and traverse a steep wall to a scree-filled couloir. Go down the couloir to a short rib and an abseil point. Make one abseil of about 20m then continue down the couloir on the L side over a few slabby steps before being disgorged into the Ochsental. 1hr to the hut, allow 6-8hr in all

Tannenspitze and Rosenlauistock North Faces

The two faces merge to form a steep, almost triangular slab about 350m high with easy access from the Engelhorn hut, from which it can be clearly seen. It is conveniently sited just above the path to the hut from Rosenlaui. Routes are equipped with in situ protection but wedges and camming devices should be carried.

14 NORTH FACE DIRECT

V+

110

A good climb first done in 1977, V+ with three steps of A2.

Start 25m R from the widest rocky gully at the foot of the cliff. First climb up cracks in a dièdre (50m, II). Now go up L to a small jagged spike (25m, III) before some easy, partly grassed, slopes lead to a steep wall (15m). Continue L over slabs for 30m (III). Climb a 10m crack before stepping 3m R and then up to the next belay. Continue in a dièdre for 45m (V) then over a step before working up R to belay after 30m (III). Climb two more dièdres and a steep slab (30m, IV+). Next move up R then L, then gain the crack above which leads to a belay (25m, IV+). Continue via a slab, moving L at the top to belay (30m, V and A2). Now climb a bulging wall before traversing R into a small gully (30m, V and A2). Go straight up at first from here then L via a crack (25m, V+ and A0). Climb straight up again then move R over the edge (junction with Route 15) before moving L again to a prominent overhang. Pass through a gap and climb slabs to below the next overhang (40m in all, IV+). Climb the overhang then traverse 10m R before climbing up to the next belay (45m, V+ and A2). Move up Lwards, finally over slabs to the last belay (30m, V, route book). Reach the summit via a chimney (IV). 5hr

15 **GROSSE NORDVERSCHNEIDUNG**

V+ *An enjoyable free climb with one pitch of V+. First climbed in 1956.*

110 Start some way R of the line of the dièdre (verschneidung) by climbing easy rock for 20m onto a slab. Traverse Lwards to a wall below the dièdre and climb this by a crack until forced to exit R into the great dièdre. Climb it to its top and a big overhang (V–). Climb the overhang by a deep crack to reach the large niche above after 25m (V+). Traverse L over short but difficult steps to reach a scree gully and finally climb vegetated slabs (delicate), keeping R, to gain the ridge joining the two summits. 4-5hr

110

18

16 **NORDÜBERHÄNGE** VIII– or VII–/A0 Fine slab climbing but not sustained

17 **NORTH-WEST FLANK** IV Nice slab climbing

18 **NORTH-WEST FLANK CRACK** IV+ Awkward, the poorest route here. No topo

Descent from the Tannenspitze is as for Route 13. Descent from the Rosenlauistock is from the gap between the two summits direct to the Grasspass by way of the SE flank (I and II).

The SW face of the Rosenlauistock has a number of worthwhile routes with easy access from the Engelhorn hut.

Klein Wellhorn South-East Face

Climbs on this mountain have been described earlier in this book; one of these is on the SE face (Route 45). Two modern style routes have been added (1987 and 1988), each of about 750m in length, which are fully equipped with pitons and bolts although K Ochsner, the instigator and leader on the first ascents, has a reputation for fairly well-spaced gear so carry some wedges and camming devices. Route finding relies very much on following the lines of in situ gear. Approach the face as for Route 45.

Map for this area is: Interlaken (254)

19
VII

ADLERAUGE VII or VI+ and A0 belays are all equipped with 2 bolts. Allow 7-10hr

Start 30m R of Route 45 (start is marked).

1 25m. Direct over an overhang. VI
2 25m. Move up first R then L and finally L again to an overhang. Over this then belay on the L at a flake. V+
3 45m. More or less straight up the wall to a short crack slanting R and to a thread belay on a L sloping ramp. VI+
4 40m. Up R to a thread then back Lwards to a bolt then up to the belay. VII–
5 35m. Up R then L past a line of bolts and pitons to a thread before moving straight up to the next belay. VII–
6 20m. Straight up then L before trending back R to belay. VI
7 42m. Ramps and grooves lead up Lwards to a belay on a ramp. IV
8 25m. Straight up over an overhang then past a thread to the next belay (thread). VII
9 35m. Diagonally L past one thread to a second thread then direct to an overhang with a belay above this. VI+
10 40m. Follow a crack Lwards then straight up passing a ramp leaning L before trending slightly R to a belay. VI
11 40m. Straight up then trend slightly R to a thread on the R of a bulge then up to the belay level with the top of the bulge. VI+
12 45m. Climb the wall fairly direct to reach easier ground. VII
13 35m. Just L of the belay climb the wall direct. VII–
14 45m. Diagonally L to a flake and above it move L to belay. VI+

15 30m. Up to a ledge above the belay then slant L to an overhang. Over this to belay a few m higher. VII
16 25m. Traverse R then straight up and R again to belay. VII
17 40m. Straight up passing a thread and a spike. VI–
18 35m. Move Rwards then straight up to a thread belay on a ramp. VII–
19 20m. Above the belay move L then back R to a thread and belay on the ledge above. V
20 30m. Up to the ridge. V–
Descend by abseiling down the route or follow Route 43 (main section) in reverse.

20
VII+

GLETSCHERSINFONIE VII+ or VII– and A0; belays are all equipped with 2 bolts. Allow 8-10hr

The start is L of Route 45 and involves moving 100m up the glacier and crossing a bergschrund. Start at an obvious niche with a bolt belay below a big groove and system of corners.

1 35m. From the R side of the niche straight up. VI–
2 15m. Over the overhang above the belay to belay at the top of a flake. VI+
3 40m. Up L to a slanting overhang. Over this near it L end to ledges. VII+
4 45m. 10m to the back of the ledges then up past a thread before moving L to the next belay. VI
5 40m. Diagonally L to a thread and the next belay above this. VII
6 30m. Move R then up past two threads to belay on a ramp. V–
7 15m. Up to a belay below an overhang. VI
8 40m. Move R and then up to join Route 45 and reach the big groove. I (Route 45 continues up the groove)
9 35m. Climb the L wall of the groove past two threads to a thread belay below an overhang. VI+
10 45m. Traverse R up to a ramp line then follow this L then move up to a thread and a belay on its L. VI–
11 20m. Easy ground leads up L. III
12 45m. Straight up the wall to a thread. Above this move L then up to belay on a ramp. VII+
13 35m. Traverse R then move up to a boss. Pass R of this to a belay. VI

14 35m. Climb up to and over an overhang then keep moving gradually L before a traverse R leads to a belay. VI
15 30m. Straight up a crack to belay on a ledge. VI+
16 15m. R on the ledge then up R to belay at a thread. VII–
17 40m. Up diagonally R past two bolts, then up moving slightly L to gain a belay on a ledge on the R. VI
18 45m. R for a few m then straight up to gain a groove on the L. Follow this to a ledge on the R then straight up over an overhang to belay on the edge of easy ground. VI+ Follow easy ground for 70m.
19 20m. Straight up past two threads to belay at a third. IV
20 40m. Straight up for 20m then make a descent Rwards before climbing up to the next belay past a thread. VI
21 40m. Straight up past a slight bulge. VII
22 30m. Move up R to a gap in the ridge above (easy) or climb up L to pass a flake on its L then over an overhang to reach the ridge. VII+

Descend by reversing Route 43 (main section) or abseil down Adlerauge or this route.

Bernese Fore-Alp region

This is a large region of limestone hills/mountains with a profusion of cliffs on which climbing is practised. The region extends from the Jaunpass in the W to Meiringen in the E. Its S border is the main Alpine chain and its N border is roughly a line running E and W from Thun. Climbs on a few of these cliffs are described here. Apart from the climbing the whole of this area provides wonderful walking country.

Maps of the area are: Gantrisch (253), Interlaken (254), Wildstrubel (263) and Jungfrau (264)

Rothorn 2410.1m
From Matten, which is NNW of Lenk in the Simmental, a side valley (Fermental) leads NE before curving back SSE. The peak is on the N side of this valley and the crags (Rote Fluh) face S onto it. The rock is steep and compact orange coloured limestone offering

five routes of about 300m each which were developed in the late 60s and 70s. The routes are equipped with in situ protection but it would be wise to carry wedges and small camming devices. The aid grades can be reduced for climbers prepared to use hooks.

Park on the road below the crag and take the path from Büel to reach its foot. Below the crag are three ledge systems. Climb to the
111 highest of these via cracks, dièdres and short walls in about 150m of
21 climbing. About 1½-2hr from the road

1 **DIRECT ROUTE** ED Steep and sustained climbing, the main feature is the 6m high roof which is A3.

2 **BERNER ROUTE** TD+ A fine route with an appreciable amount of aid climbing.

3 **DIAGONAL ROUTE** TD The easiest of the climbs on the face and mostly free. Well worth doing to get a feel for the place.

4 **GEMEINSCHAFTSWEG** TD+ The route uses a lot of aid in the lower half but above that it is mainly free climbing.

5 **FRUTIGERWEG** ED1 The best route on the crag and worth a visit for its own sake. It takes a direct line to the summit and is mostly free.

Descend by the W ridge, turning the fore-summit on the N side, to reach a grassy shoulder. Turn S down the second couloir to reach the track leading to the valley.

Gastlosen 1996m

Not strictly in the Bernese Fore-Alps as it is in the Canton of Fribourg on the W side of the Jaunpass. Camping is possible at the Jaunpass and this is the only site close to the crag. It is also a suitable base for climbs on the Chemiflue and Trümelhorn. Other camp sites are at Lenk in the Ober Simmental, at Zweisimmen and at Oey in the Nieder Simmental. This, and the two crags described next, can be reached from Interlaken or Kandersteg in about 1½hr in addition to the walk-in time.

The peak overlooks the town of Jaun from the S and is at the end of a very extensive ridge, which has multiple summits, running roughly NE-SW. There is an enormous potential for new routes, of up to 300m, along the whole length of the ridge. To reach the climbing from Jaun take the road towards the Jaunpass but leave it for a minor road following the river (Jaunli) SE. After about 4km take a R turn leading to Grat. There is parking here (and a bar) and a little way before this where another road leads to Oberberg.

The main interest here is a traverse of the peak by its fine crenellated ridge. There is also a small crag at the foot of the E face and only 10min walk from the parking area. It has short rock climbs ranging in difficulty from VI– to IX+. Most have gear in place but a few require a selection of wedges to be carried.

6
D
113

TRAVERSE SOUTH TO NORTH

The ridge has numerous teeth and towers in its 1km length, some of which can be avoided if necessary, which gives some varied and very entertaining climbing without ever being too difficult. The upper limit of difficulty is about IV+ but much of the route is III. A single 40m rope should suffice.

From the car park climb up steep wooded slopes (track) to the col at the S end of the ridge (Col de l'Oberberg – not marked on the map). 45min

The first big tower is called Eggturm. Start up this a few m L of the crest at a crack. Climb this to the crest and follow it to a belay (40m, III+). Next climb a slab and a short wall to a rib (30m, IV). Climb 8m up a wall (IV+) then follow the ridge for about 30m. Next climb a short chimney and leave it Rwards to gain the summit of the tower (40m, III). Descend on the NE side then scramble across to the the foot of a narrow gendarme (Petit Pouce). Climb to a gap then follow the crest to the top (IV). Abseil to the gap below the Grand Pouce, the next tower.

From the gap start on the R then move Lwards onto the steep crest. Climb this to the summit (40m, IV+ and the crux of the traverse). Descend on the NE side. Turn the next gendarme and climb it by its N rib (20m, III-IV). Abseil 15m to the foot of the next tower (Pyramid) and climb it by its SW rib (III). Descend easily to a further gap then climb a couloir to the bottom of an open dièdre (II). Climb this to an overhang then move L to reach the highest point (Marchzähne, 40m, III).

The remaining three teeth of the Marchzähne and the following gendarme are usually turned on the E side (easy). A final tower in this section is climbed on the W side (III). Two 20m abseils on the N side are made and lead to a lower gendarme (Chemigüpfe) with three separate towers. Climb the three towers on their S sides making 10m-12m abseils between towers. Descend to the E in a couloir then turn N and pick up a track leading back towards the alps of Obere Gastlosen. About 6-7hr for the round trip

A little further S is the Wandfluh where there are about 30 mainly short routes at about grade VI and above. The crag is reached by driving along the valley road below Gastlosen, passing Unt Birren (Pt 1425). The road rises towards Pt 1647m. Make a sharp R turn just before this point and park directly below the crags, two of which are only 5min from the parking area.

Trümelhorn 1981.6m and Chemiflue 1878m

On the 1:25000 map the Trümelhorn is named Trimlenhorn and this is the name given in the SAC guide book to the area. See the introduction to Gastlosen for camping details.

On the E side of the Jaunpass, in the Simmental, is the village of Riedenbach and just NE of this is Boltigen. The two crags are to the W of the villages. There are two approaches. From Riedenbach take the minor road to Schwarzenmatt and continue to the road head at Chlus. The two crags can seen from here and are reached by the steep vegetated slope to the NE (vague track). The alternative approach is from Boltigen. Take the road leading N through Adlemsried which leads finally into Alp Ramseren at 1365m. Take the path from here leading round the S side of the Mittagflue to Alp Nüschleten. There is an obvious gap in the ridge to the W which is immediatetely S of the Chemiflue. Pass through the gap to reach the climbs on the W and SW faces of the Chemiflue or traverse under these faces Nwards to the buttress of the Trümelhorn. 1-1½hr

On the Trümelhorn there is only one route of any real interest and that is the NW spur, a superb steep buttress seen in profile from Chlus. The finest line is the direct one climbed by H Trachel and A Grossen in 1966. The original route was climbed first in 1960 by E Friedli and U Greber.

7 **NORTH-WEST PILLAR**

TD 112 20

The direct route is mainly free, after the initial aid section, on good sound rock. The original line on the R is shown in the photograph. Some gear is in place. There is about 200m of climbing. Descend by going E to a gap

then down a couloir Swards to Alp Nüschleten or climb down on the N side (II, III) to return to the foot of the climb.

The Chemiflue (593.9/164.9) has a steep triangular two-faceted face on the W side providing a number of interesting climbs. The classic route here is the original one on the face dating back to 1937 (O Theikäs with F and W Tschabold). There is also an interesting
114 climb up the S ridge starting at the gap described in the approach.
19 This is mostly IV with one step of V.

8 TD **NORTH-WEST SPUR** An interesting climb with pitches of V and some sections of aid. Some in situ gear. About 200m of climbing.

9 TD **WEST FACE** The classic climb which ascends the obvious crack system. Fully equipped with in situ gear, all that is needed are slings and carabiners. Mostly free, about 200m.

10 TD **SOUTH-WEST CRACK** A worthwhile climb utilising some aid. Most of the necessary pitons are in place. About 200m.

11 TD **SOUTH-WEST FACE PILLAR** A good climb on excellent rock joining the SW Crack route for the final two pitches. It is equipped with in situ gear but requires some large camming devices. About 200m.

Buufal and Niderhorn

These are two mountains SE of Boltigen in the Simmental, but the easiest approach to the climbs is from the Diemtigtal which runs SW from Oey (campsite) in the Simmental, 5km from Wimmis. 9km from Oey, at Zwischenfluh, a road branches off R at Pt 1041m. Pay a toll at the house on the L (W) of the turning, before the gate. Follow this road up the valley to where it crosses the bridge at Pt 1515m (car park). The Buufal cliffs can be seen on the N side of the valley from here. To reach the cliffs of the Niderhorn, continue along the road taking the R fork. There is a car park at the second hairpin bend on the rough road below the cliffs. There is a Verboden sign on the road ahead.

Both the cliffs are limestone with good quality rock. At Buufal there are two sections of the cliffs that are of interest but by far the best climb here is on the Meniggrund Pfeiler (600.8/161.5). This is the original route dating from 1965. Adjacent to this route is one climbed in 1985 (Anker and Köchli) which is VII+ (Zytischda).

Reach the cliff from the car park by a path through the wood which peters out on a scree slope above. Climb this, then a grass slope which leads to a chimney slanting up from L to R. When dry this is climbed on the inside, otherwise turn it on the R. Gain the foot of the pillar by a couloir on the L.

To descend, scramble through trees to reach a grassy couloir which provides a way to the alp of Hefuess (1745m). From here a couloir with a fixed cable leads into woods where a faint track leads back to the bridge at 1515m.

12 **MENIGGRUND PFEILER – THUNERWEG**

TD+ 130 23 *A fine climb of about 230m on good rock. One pitch of V+ and another VI– with short sections of A1. Find the start of the route behind a block on the terrace (piton).*

Further L, E of the car park is another steep crag with a distinctive roof (600.6/161.3). Several one, two and three pitch climbs exist here at grades VI-VII which were opened in the late 1980s. All are fully equipped with in situ protection and abseil points and follow lines of bolts and pitons.

115 22

13 **RISBISI** VII The start is marked

14 **LÜCKEBÜSSER** VI+

15 **KAKADU** VIII+/IX–

16 **POLTERGEIST** V+

17 **STÖRNSTUND** VI+

18 **SPION** VII

19 **TOPAS** VII+

For the climbs on the Niderhorn (SE flank) follow the road from the hairpin bend S for about 500m then climb up scree to a path below the cliffs. Turn L on this for a further 100m; finally grassy slopes lead to the foot of the Schmetterlingspfeiler.

The cliff, about 100m high, consists of pillars and towers

broken by grassy ledges and separated by couloirs. The routes described , mostly quite short, are below the highest point of the mountain on good rock. They are all fully equipped with in situ protection and have mostly been free climbed at VIII/IX. About 100m S there are some buttresses on which exist short modern routes. Along the whole length of the cliffs there exist possibilities
116 for new routes.
24 The easiest descent is by a marked couloir 300m N from the summit.

20 **K B F WAND** IV+, A1 and A2 Mixed aid and free climbing

21 **SCHMETTERLINGSPFEILER** IV+ or V A delightful little climb, V and A0 on the first pitch

22 **EAST WALL** V+ and A0 Follows a system of cracks

23 **K B F PFEILER** V and A1 Mostly free but with some aid on most pitches

Ueschenen, Wyssi Fluh and Ärmighorn

A few cliffs with easy access from Kandersteg have been developed since the 1960s but most extensively in the 1980s. The most notable activists have been H Grossen, W Hofer, J von Känel, M Trachsel and M and M Stettler. All the climbing is on good quality limestone. Although not all strictly in the Bernese Fore-Alps the three cliffs described are included here for convenience. Of the three, the most important is that of Ueschenen. It is one of the best known cliffs in Switzerland and has over 70 routes varying in difficulty from grade V– to X.

Kandersteg itself has only one campsite which is often full in summer. There is another campsite in Frutigen.

Ueschenen is just beyond the S end of the Kandertal. The valley splits into three; the Gasteretal running E, another, high valley, leading SSW to the Gemmipass whilst to the SW rises the valley of Ueschenen. The extensive cliffs, facing SE and overlooking the valley from its NW slopes, are up to 150m high.

There are two approaches: from the end of the public road S of Kandersteg it is possible to drive into the Ueschenen valley on

payment of a toll at the bar adjacent to the Stock lift station. Park near the road head, after taking a R turn, at Pt 1595m. The cliff is
117 30min uphill from the car park. Alternatively take the Allmen lift
118 on the W side of Kandersteg and walk S to reach the cliff.

119 All the routes shown in the topos and photographs are fully
25 equipped with in situ protection but it is usually necessary to carry a
26 few wedges and camming devices. As is usual, most routes can be climbed with the use of aid, thus lowering the grade. Several routes
27 are fixed for abseil descent, otherwise this is by walking NE to turn the end of the cliff.

24 **WAGE ZU TRÄUMEN** IX– or VII/A0

25 **ARGUS** VI/VI+

26 **QUO VADIS** VII+ or VI/A0

27 **KNOW HOW** VII+ or VI+/A0

28 **FRITZ UND ROLF** VIII– or VI+/A0

29 **TYPHON** VII+ or VII–/A0

30 **ZÜRCHER-SPORT-WEG** VII or VI/A0

31 **GRAUE WAND** VI or V/A0

32 **DIAGONAL** VI+ or VI/A0

33 **BAUMROUTE** VI+ or VI–/A0

34 **AURIKEL PRIMULA** V–/V 4 pitches of IV/IV+ and 2 top pitches V–/V, no topo

35 **PFILERWÄDLI** VII+ A one pitch climb

36 **TÖFFLI** VI+ or V/A0 A two pitch climb

37 **ALIEN** VII– or VI+/A0

38 **HANNIBAL** VIII– or VII–/A0

39 **JOKER** VII/VII+ or VII–/A0

40 **FUSION** X–/X A one pitch climb

41 **FILIDOR** VII+ or V+/A1

42 **UPATOPIE** VIII or VIII–/A0

43 **LAMPENFIEBER** VII+/VIII– or VI+/A0

The Weisse Fluh is an unremarkable peak at the S end of the Ueschenengrat and N of the Schwarenbach hotel (see hut section). However on its SE side there is an impressive cliff about 150m high and 400m wide on which there are a number of hard routes.

Approach from the Schwarenbach hotel by the path to Schwarengrätli in about 30min. Walk under the crag (avoiding nettles) to its R side where the climbs are located. All the routes are fully equipped with in situ protection but some wedges and Friends
120 1½-2½ should be carried. Descent is by abseil from fixed points or
28 by an easy walk to turn the cliff on its S side.

44 **PANORAMA DIRECT** VII+/A0

45 **PANORAMA** VIII–/VIII

46 **TACHO EXTRA** VII+/VIII–/A0

47 **TACHO** VIII+ or VII/A0

48 **MELCHIOR** VII–

49 **SATELLIT** VII+ The start is marked

50 **KENTAUR** VIII–

51 **MAUER LÄUFER** IX or VII+/A0

The Ärmighorn is on the E side of the Kandertal above the village of Mitholz. From the summit of the mountain a ridge runs S before throwing out a spur running SW. On this spur is the S summit (2583m, but not marked on the map). The climbs described are on the SW flank of this summit. At the foot of the flank are three distinct towers, the highest of which is Pt 2403m. The cliff can be seen on the NE skyline from the centre of Kandersteg. It can be approached on foot from the Kiental or from Mitholz but the easiest way is to use the private lift from Mitholz to Alp Giesenen at 1660m. This can be arranged (ideally beforehand) by asking at the last house on the L in Mitholz on the road towards Kandersteg. This is just before the railway bridge. At the time of writing the charge was 10SFr. The crag is about 75min walk from the top of the lift and is approached from the W side of the three towers in a couloir.

The climbs shown in the topo and photograph are equipped with in situ protection. It is usual to finish on the summit and make a descent to the foot of the cliff on the E side but it is quite an easy matter to reach the main summit from the top of the climbs.

To reach the foot of the climbs themselves it is necessary to climb to a scree-covered bay behind the highest tower by way of the W ridge route.

Descent from all the routes is from the saddle 40m NE of the
129 S summit where fixed ropes lead down the E flank. These are
29 followed by grassy slopes and rocks into the bowl of Hächlere.

52 **WEST RIDGE**
D H Grossen and H Trachsel, 23 Sept 1962.

Used as an approach to the harder climbs but enjoyable enough in its own right. Difficulties are up to grade IV, belays are equipped.

Start at the foot of the ridge which rises from the couloir on the W side of the three towers at the foot of this flank of the mountain. Keep more or less on the crest all the way, any deviations being obvious. On the third and fifth pitches detours to the R are somewhat easier than keeping on the crest. 2-3hr

53 **GLATTE PLATTEN** VII+ or VI/A0

54 **GRAUE PLATTEN** V or IV+/A0

55 **SÜDWÄNDLI** VII– or V+/A1

56 **NEUES SÜDWÄNDLI** V

Lobhorner 2566m

This impressive limestone peak overlooks the Soustal from its W side. The Soustal itself has the Schilthorn at its upper S end. The classic outing here is the traverse of the various towers forming the crest of the mountain. It is a popular climb with pitons cemented into place. There are also two established steep routes of about 130m on the stratified S wall of the main summit, which is a bit broken and fragile in places.

Approach from the Lobhorner hut (see huts section) by a path to the E end of the summit ridge (1½hr) or from the Soustal which
122 is most conveniently reached from Lauterbrunnen.

Descent from the summit is by abseil on the W side.

57 **TRAVERSE EAST-WEST** III and IV with several variations

58 **SOUTH FACE ROUTE** IV+ and V

59 **NEW SOUTH FACE ROUTE** IV and V with one section of V+

Alpes Vaudoises

The Canton of Vaud has a large number of quite easily accessible limestone crags offering some first rate climbing on sound rock. These will be found attractive to the dedicated rock climber and by the alpinist looking for a bit of variety or an alternative pursuit when higher peaks are out of condition.

Many of the climbs described here come into the modern route category but there are plenty that might be attempted by those who only feel comfortable on more traditional routes. Many of the routes are equipped, at least partially, with in situ protection and even the climber of modest ability can enjoy some of the routes if prepared to use a bit of aid.

The maps of the area are: Rocher de Naye (262), St Maurice (272) and Montana (273)

Tour d'Ai 2330m

This is a popular peak above Leysin on the N side. It has a long crest descending from the summit in a SSE direction up which goes the tourist route of ascent. The peak is surrounded on all sides by steep cliffs with only one easy break on the R side of the S face. Climbs have been developed on all the cliffs, many by staff and students of the nearby ISM.

Reach the Tour d'Ai from Leysin on foot in about 1½hr or by the lift to La Berneuse. From here the WSW face and the Sphinx are clearly seen and can be reached in 30min and 20min respectively. Climbs are described on three separate parts of the mountain, on the WSW face, on the Sphinx and on the ENE face.

The West-South-West Face varies in height from about 70m at its Rhand end to 150m on the L. The climbing here is less popular than on the Sphinx and therefore less crowded but has recently seen a lot
123 of new development. Most of the climbs are partly equipped with in
30 situ protection but parties should carry some pitons as well as the
31 usual wedges and camming devices. Most of the routes described have been climbed free or have now merged with other routes.

1 **VOIE DES VIRES** V Classic 150m equipped

2 **VOLOVAN** V and A1 Large camming device useful instead of an old wooden wedge

3 **MILLE BRIQUE** VI and A2 Requires a good selection of pitons

4 **DIEDRE BLEU** VI or V and A0 Carry some large hexentrics

5 **GONZO** V+ and A1

6 **LA CHEMINEE** V+ Interesting free climb; carry some big wedges

7 **GARDE-BARRIERE** V

8 **DIEDRE DU VAGABOND** V+

Descent is by the tourist route from the summit.

The Sphinx forms the angle between the WSW and S faces and has climbs of about 100m on excellent rock, many in the modern idiom,

124
125
32

and virtually all fully equipped with bolts and pitons. Several of the routes have become classics. A major problem on a cliff like this, which is crammed with routes, is following the correct line. The profusion of in situ gear can be quite misleading.

9 **NEZ DU SPHINX** mainly artificial

10 **SPHINX COULOIR LEFTHAND ROUTE** V+

11 **SPHINX COULOIR RIGHTHAND ROUTE** VI–

12 **HARLIN-ROBBINS ROUTE** VII or VI– with aid

13 **VOIE DES LAUSANNOIS** VII+ or VI– with aid

14 **VOIE DES CHAMANS** VII+

15 **LA FOLIE D'GLANDEURS** VIII–/VIII or VII+ with aid

16 **DIVA** VIII or VII+ with aid

17 **ZILISSE VARIATION** VII+ or VI+ with aid

18 **DESIR BRULANT** VIII or VII+ with aid

19 **NAUTILUS** VII+/VIII– or VII with aid

20 **PILIER SONNEY** VII+ or VI– with aid

21 **APOPLEXIA** VII+ or VI– with aid

22 **HITCHCOCK** VII with three aid points

23 **LES 40 MOUVEMENTS** VIII+ or VII with aid

24 **ALI BABA** VIII–/VIII or VII with aid

25 **DESPERATE REALITY** IX

26 **HALF-MOON CRACK** V

Descend by abseil or join the tourist path near the top of the crag.

The East-North-East Face is reached by walking E along the path below the S face then turning up the valley between the Tour d'Ai and the Tour de Mayen. 30-45min. This same path can be reached easily from the lift to Mayen from Leysin. 15-30min

The cliff is 100m-120m high and has some interesting climbs, but one problem is that the rock does not dry quickly after rain. The
126 climbs described are on the R side of the face starting R of the
33 obvious cave. Routes are only partially equipped if at all.

27 **LA GROTTE, PLUM DUFF** A3 Entirely artificial

28 **LA CHEMINEE HERBEUSE** V Partly equipped

29 **SPIATNIK** VI and A1 Mostly free, carry pitons

30 **FINAL SOLUTION** V+ and A1 Mostly free, carry pitons

31 **KOR ROUTE** V and A1 Not equipped

Descent is by the tourist route to the summit. This can be reached by scrambling up to the summit from the top of routes, or make a long traverse L to join it near the top of the gully leading through the S face cliffs.

Tour de Mayen 2326.4m

More massive than the Tour d'Ai but not quite so impregnable. Its main features are the enormous overhanging N face and, on its S side, the splendid cliff called the Diamant. It has a fine triangular shape and is situated above the Lac de Mayen.

The Diamant cliff is about 130m high and faces S. On the L side is the Petit Tour and L again is a short wall which has numerous possibilities. The rock is excellent and several of the routes here
127 have become classics. Some routes are completely equipped with in
128 situ gear and others partially so. As usual carry wedges and
34 camming devices.

35 The crag is most easily reached by using the lift from Leysin to Mayen (on foot this takes about 75min) then descend to the lake and reach the cliff in about 5min.

32 **VOIE PUITS SANS FOND** VI and A1 not sustained Carry some pitons

33 **VOIE PAREGORIQUE** VI and A1 Fully equipped

34 **LA PHALANGE BELZEBOTH** VI and A1 Fully equipped

35 **VOIE DU SUD** V and A1 classic and fully equipped

36 **VOIE DE LA DIAGONALE** V+ classic and fully equipped

37 **VOIE DES ENRAGES** Mainly artificial

38 **VOIE DU SOUVENIR** VI and A2 One of the best routes, partly equipped

39 **VOIE DE LA CROISIERE** V and A2 Interesting, carry large camming devices

40 **VOIE CENTRAL** V+ and A1 Classic and fully equipped

41 **VOIE DU DIEDRE** V+ Classic and fully equipped, some vegetation

42 **ENCORE PLUS PRES OU..** VI+ with one aid point or VI– and A1 Fully equipped and for abseil

43 **VOIE DU BEL AUTOMNE** V and A1 Mostly equipped, not sustained

44 **SEPTIEME ART** VIII–/VIII or VII with aid

45 **CHERCHEZ PAS D'EXCUSES** VIII or VII with aid

46 **LES PIEGES DE LA PASSION** VII+ with two aid points or VI+ and A1

47 **ICE–CRIME** VII+ with one aid point

48 **ARD A Z** VII+ with three aid points

49 **NERINE** VIII–/VIII or VII with aid

Descent can be made on either side of the cliff.

Argentine Miroir

The Argentine is a long ridge running roughly E-W between the Diableret massif to the N and Grand Muveran to the S. There is a lot of climbing available, but of most interest and best known is the massive slab on its N side below Pts 2323m (Cheval Blanc) and 2325.2m, Haute Corde, called the Grand Miroir. The slab is about 400m high and roughly the same width, and is slightly convex.

In the valley below the cliff is the hamlet of Solalex (bars/restaurants), which gets very crowded at week-ends when you will have to pay for car parking. Solalex is reached from the Bex (Rhône valley) to Villars road by taking the turning E at La Barboleusaz (campsite). The foot of the cliff is a steep 50min walk from the car park.

The rock is limestone and is particularly slippery if at all damp, but is quite sound. At one time there were a number of serious accidents here but now most routes have plenty of in situ protection and belay points. Once embarked on a climb it is quite easy to to lose the way, as there are many tempting variations and, because of the convex nature of the slab, reference points are not easy to locate. This is compounded by the step in the slab at half-height.

A main feature of the cliff is the E chimney which rises from the snow patch and was the first route climbed on the cliff. From a point just R of its foot a rising ramp called the Vire Inférieure cuts across the face below the Grand Miroir itself and the steep lower wall. The Vire has broken but easy rock and is crossed by most routes. A short way up the ramp is another chimney which bifurcates. This is the famous Y after which the classic climb takes its name. The slab to the R of the Y is the one with the step at half-height. Just below this step is the Vire Supérieure which leads R to the foot of a steep wall below the summit of Cheval Blanc. Below the main slab and further R is the Dalle Bleue which is a smaller slab above a distinctive shoulder.

Don't be tempted to climb here too early in the season as a cornice often develops at the top of the cliff. At week-ends an early start is advised.

Carry wedges and camming devices as well as plenty of slings and karabiners for the in situ protection on all the routes.

Below the cliff the hillside is cut by a number of gullies. The line of ascent (path) follows the line of the gully R of the one with the snow patch.

Descent from the top of the cliff is along the crest Ewards, skirting round the S side of the summit of Haute Corde. Follow the path which leaves the crest and heads NE to a saddle at Pt 2044m. This can be a bit tricky to locate in mist, which often occurs in the afternoon. Now continue in the same direction then bear N to Anzeindaz from where a rough road leads back to Solalex. Alternatively and more difficult, from the saddle turn L and make a steep but more direct descent to Solalex. This alternative way crosses some quite loose shaly ground but is easy enough to follow.
121 Don't be tempted into the stream bed from the ridge; the route
36 stays fairly close to the ridge after the section of undergrowth.

50 **NARROW ARETE** IV and IV+ to the top of the slab then V/A1 and A2

51 **CENTRAL ROUTE** IV+ and V sustained, recommended, slight stonefall danger

52 **Y ROUTE**

IV+/AO *The classic route of the crag but by no means the best route. There are 14 pitches with all the belays fitted with two anchors. Each of the serious pitches has pitons in place. The climb is not sustained, IV+ and A0 for one step, otherwise mostly III and IV.*

1. A few awkward moves up R then scramble L up the rocky gangway.
2. Climb a steep crack above the belay, passing a piton, then trend R at the top to reach the long diagonal ramp.
3. Scramble up the ramp then up a pillar using chock-stones.
4. Climb the impending wall by a crack R of a piton then step on it and with aid from a hand ring move to easier ground on the L. Belay further L. This pitch is V done free.
5. Up cracks on the L side of the slab with a delicate step R. The best pitch on the route.
6. Move up the broken chimney past two chock-stones.
7. Keep in the chimney past a bulge to a belay below some flakes.
8. The chimney forks R. Take this fork and get into the upper of two crack lines.

9-12. Four very good pitches following the crack line diagonally R.

13. Leave the crack line and climb towards the notch in the summit ridge on the L side of an overlap (one or two thin moves).

14. Climb up to the wall below the notch and climb this direct (strenuous) or move L to climb a groove to the notch.

53 **SUPERDIRECTE** V and V+ with some short sections of A1 and A2 A fine route

54 **ZYGOFOLIS** VI/VI+ and A0 A Remy brothers climb, good

55 **DIRECTE** V One of the best climbs here, much more sustained than 52

56 **DIRECTE DU CHEVAL BLANC** VI and A1 with one section A2

57 **GAMMA** VI and A1 one section A2 A Remy brothers climb, equipped as far as the final wall

58 **HYPERZODIAQUE** VI and A1 and A2 A Remy brothers climb, fine and sustained climbing, exposed

59 **DIRECTE DE LA DALLE BLEUE** VI and A1 with one section A2

Sanetsch

This is an attractive limestone climbing area close to the border between the Cantons of Bern and Vaud but is actually in the Valais. A road leads from Sion through Chandolin to cross the river Marge at the Pont du Diable before eventually reaching the Col du Sanetsch (2251m). Access is usually possible from the end of June until October. On the N side of the col the road descends to a reservoir (Lac de Senin) where there is parking and camping is possible. There is accommodation available at the restaurant by the dam, and on the road between Sion and the Col de Sanetsch at the Auberge de Zanfleuron (dortoir).

The cliffs are extensive, facing SE across the reservoir but also extending a further 2km SW, overlooking the valley of Creux de la Lé. Many of the routes on the SW section of the cliffs the routes are 2 or 3 pitches long but the cliffs above the reservoir have considerably longer climbs of up to 300m.

Much of the development here can be attributed to the Remy brothers, with routes dating back to 1982. In recent years other

131 practitioners have entered the scene and there currently exist well
132 over 50 routes with plenty of opportunity for further development.
133 From the Dent Blanche (Gstellihorn, 2817.7m) in the SW the
134 cliffs extend unbroken to the summit of Les Montons (2566.7m).
135 NE of this summit there is a steep couloir which provides a means of
37 descent. NE again rises another steep crag which rejoices in the name of Orphée.
38 All the harder routes are fully equipped with in situ protection
39 but other protection should be carried on all the routes. Many of the
40 routes are equipped for abseil descent and these are indicated on the topo diagrams.

60 **PLUS TU RUSES, PLUS TU T'USES** VI with 2 steps A1 Equipped

61 **VOIE DE LA RAMPE** V– Not sustained

62 **DESCENDONS** V+ A1 (A2 on first pitch) Carry pitons, descend 61

63 **HOT COKE** V+ A1 and A2 Carry pitons, descend 61

64 **ALI BABA** V+ and A2 for one overhanging crack, carry pitons. Abseil descent from 5m below crest. The variation is less sustained

65 **GREATIME** V with a short section of A1 Equipped. Descend 64

66 **ROCK AND ROLL** VI– and A0 or VII+

67 **VOIE DU FIL A PLOMB** VI+ but V after the break with 66. Carry pitons

68 **TSINGY** VII and A0 or VIII This and all following routes are equipped

69 **COEUR A CORPS** VII and A0 or VIII

70 **DOUCE VIOLENCE** VII and A0 or VII+

71 **EUFRATE** VII and A0 or VIII

72 **AXIS** VII and A0 or VIII

73 **AU BORD DU VIDE** VI– and A0 or VII+

74 **COUP D'AUDAGE** VI– and A0 or VIII

75 **LES ZEROS SONT FATIGUES** V and A0 or VI+

76 **L'ANGE BLEU** VII and A0 or VII+

77 **PAS PERDU** V and A0 or VI–

78 **FANTASIO** V+ and A0 or VI–

79 **ESPRIT DU JEU** VII and A0 or VII+

80 **MEDUKANDIRATION** VI/VI+ and A0 or VIII–

81 **GRANDFINAL** VI/VI+ and A0 or VIII

82 **ESPACE DU DESIR** VII and A0 or VII+

83 **FACE A FARCE** VII+ and A0

84 **SOMBRE CONFUSION** VII and A0 or VII+

85 **TOUT OZZY MUT** VII and A0 or VIII+

Minor Crags

There are guite a large number of low altitude crags within the area described in this guide, which are ideal for a day's bouldering. They are what are called in German, Klettergarten, and in French, école d'escalade. Mostly these crags have in situ protection and belay anchors. In many cases route grades are indicated on the rock. Included here is a list of some of these crags and their access route.

Rotsteini

Map: Sustenpass (255) 176.5/656.3

Just N of the campsite in Meiringen on both sides of the road to

Hohflue there are several small crags with plenty of middle grade climbs from 1 to 4 pitches in length.

Schilligsflue

Map: Interlaken (254) 177.6/653.7

On the N side of the Aare river between Meiringen and Brienz (take the Brünigen road from Meiringen). The approach is a bit difficult to locate but probably the best starting point is the bend in the road below Pt 812m. There are about 10 routes, mostly of two pitches, which are equipped and vary in grade from IV+ to VI and A1.

Brunigflue

Map: Interlaken (254) 177.9/654.4

Just N of the last crag described between Meiringen and Brienz. From Meiringen take the road to Hohflue and then on to the Brunigpass. The crags, which extend for about 1km, are reached from the road about 400m E of the road tunnel. Routes exist of up to 80m at about grade VI.

Leen

Map: Interlaken (254) 170.7/629.2

On the outskirts of Interlaken. Park at the bridge over the Lombach river at Pt 590m. Follow the path on the W side of the river as far as a wooden seat. The crag is directly above. There are about 50 routes, mostly grade VI to IX with just a few easier ones.

Wilderswil

Map: Interlaken (254) 167.5/632.2

From Wilderswil (S of Interlaken) take the road towards Saxeten. Just after crossing the river there is a hairpin bend below Pt 735m. Park here and follow a path which runs below the crag. There are about 40 routes of grade VI to X, nothing easier.

Grindelwald (Hintisberg)

Map: Interlaken (254) 167.2/639.0

About 4km W of Grindelwald, at the Restaurant Stalden, a toll road zig-zags N and then NW to Oberlager (Pt 1782m). Two cliffs, NW and N of this point, on the Stellihorn and on Burg, each have a number of routes, mostly bolted, in the grade VI-IX range. The crags can be reached in 20mins to 30mins from the parking area.

Abendberg

Map: Gantrisch (253) 163.3/605.9

In the Diemtigtal just off the route to the cliffs of Buufal and Niderhorn. Take the road (toll) as for Buufal but leave this, at the second R turn, for Rinderalp. Park at the end of the road running SSW from Rinderalp. Tracks from here lead onto the top of rock promontories on which the climbs are located. There are numerous routes of 1 to 3 pitches on good limestone at grades VI to IX. Abseil from the top to reach the climbs.

Carrières de St-Triphon

Map: St-Maurice (272) 127.2/564.5

This is just W of the village of Ollon in the Rhône valley. There are quarried limestone cliffs up to 50m high although some are only about 10m high. There are aid climbs and free climbs to suit most abilities.

Dorénaz

Map: St-Maurice (272) 110.3/569.8

Just SE of the village of Dorénaz in the Rhône valley. Coming from the village on the road to Fully there is a parking place, on the N side of the river, a little way beyond the bridge that crosses the Rhône. There are several crags scattered about the hillside on the Fully side and the Dorénaz side of the bridge. The rock here is excellent gneiss with routes fully equipped so no gear need be carried (it's bad for the rock). Routes vary in difficulty from about IV to VI, the grades being marked on the rock.

Gérignoz

Map: Rocher de Naye (262) 148.9/578.7

On the road between Granges and Gérignoz is a tunnel. The climbs are on the cliff through which the tunnel passes. Access is from the Château d'Oex to Rougement road which is left just E of Granges village. Park at the bridge crossing the river. There are eight routes up to 25m varying in grade from IV+ to VI and A1.

A Walking Tour of the Massif

A delightful, if somewhat strenuous, way of getting a feel for the Bernese Oberland is to undertake a walk along its N side. This can be taken in either direction although the W-E direction saves some of the finer views for the later stages. The walk described here traverses the various ridges and valleys extending roughly N from the main mountain chain. The walk is comparable to the Tour de Mont Blanc, but is generally less crowded, and can be accomplished in six days although most people will prefer to split the fourth stage. Many variations are possible and extensions at either end are quite feasible.

As on any high mountain walk good quality footwear should be used and regard must be taken of the possibility of having to cross snow, especially if the walk is undertaken early in the season. Adequate warm clothing should be carried as well as waterproofs as mist, which often forms on ridges, can be quite cold even at the relatively low altitudes encountered, or there may be a rapid change in the weather with the possibility particularly of afternoon storms.

Overnight accommodation on the route is available in hotels in the valley resorts or in mountain hotels (Berghaus) which usually have dormitory accommodation. Bivouacing or high mountain camping is an attractive alternative or valley campsites can be used.

The walk can be abandoned almost anywhere and the start regained by means of the excellent public transport system.

The Swiss Tourist Office have available a very useful guide to hiking in the Jungfrau region of the Bernese Oberland which is written in English.

Maps required are: Wildstrubel (263), Jungfrau (264) and Interlaken (254).

Start at Gsteig, heading NE up the valley of Uss Saligrabe to the pass at 1659m (Chrine). Descend in roughly the same direction to the village of Lauenen (1241m). The way now leads E, first to Rütschi before turning SE to Flue, then up the long ridge of the Vordere Trütlisberg. After passing through the short section of forest take a L fork to the Trütlisbergpass (2038m). The day finishes with a long downhill walk to Lenk after a total of about 20km and over 1200m of ascent.

There is a campsite just S of the village and another at the valley roadhead about 3½km SE of the village. Dormitory accommodation is available at Stoss (on the lift system SE of Lenk) and at the valley roadhead (Simmenfälle).

Day two starts at the valley roadhead (Pt 1102.8m). Take the path E through the woods, avoiding the path to the waterfalls (Simmenfälle). The path turns SE and then NE to reach the Ammertentäli. Follow this stony valley, quite steep in places, past Pt 1931.7m to reach the Ammertengrat at Pt 2443m where you will have a splendid close-up view of the Wildstrubel's N flank. Descend steeply on the E side of the ridge to Schönbüel then more easily to Engstligenalp where the hotel offers dormitory accommodation. The alternative is wild camping or bivouacing. The day has involved almost 1400m of ascent in its 14km (from Lenk village).

Stage three starts SE across the valley floor to Märbenen before climbing steeply to the Engstligengrat, which is reached just S of the Chindbettihorn. Fine views to the E are reward for the effort. On the E side of the ridge descend towards the tongue of the Tälli glacier before turning L (N) to reach the Tälliseeli. More adventurous spirits might like to to take the path on the E side of the Tälli glacier which crosses the ridge N of Pt 2628.3m before descending by way of Rote Chumme to the shores of the Daubensee.

The way forward from the Tälliseeli is to head N at first towards the Uschene valley, but shortly take a R fork and a spectacular traverse path to the Schwarzgrätli. Descend from here to the Schwarenbach Hotel (dormitory). A pleasant detour from here is to the Gemmipass by way of the Daubensee. Accommodation is available there (Wildstrubel Hotel – dormitory). The detour can be continued to the Lammeren hut (see hut section).

From the Schwarenbach Hotel the walk continues NE to Sunnbuel. A lift from here will whisk you to the valley but the preferred way is to descend the steep path NE into the Gasteretal which is reached at Waldhüs (dormitory). Camping is possible in Kandersteg but not in the Gasteretal. If you arrive in Kandersteg early enough a start can be made on the next section by walking up to the Oeschinensee where there is a Berghotel. The day has (without detours) entailed about 18km walking and 700m of ascent.

An early start is advisable if the fourth stage is to be completed in one day. From the Gasteretal walk into Kandersteg from where the high pass of Hohtürli (2778m) is reached (the highest point on the walk). See the hut section of the guide book for the route to the Blüemlisalp hut. There are fine views to the S on the whole of this part of the walk, giving ample excuse for rests. Once at the col of Hohtürli a short deviation can be made to the Blüemlisalp hut.

From the col there is quite a steep descent Nwards. Keep close to the rocks on the L, thus avoiding any snow, for about 500m then cross the ridge and continue on the path towards Bundläger. (There is accommodation a little further on at Oberi Bundalp.) Now take the traverse track SE and pass through a gate on the edge of the ridge (Pt 2033m on older maps) before descending to Gamchi. A detour here to the Gspaltenhorn hut is worthwhile and an overnight stop can be taken there. If you choose this option ignore the signs to the hut in the coombe below the gate and walk to the hut from Gamchi. It is also possible from Bundläger to descend to Griesalp for an overnight stop.

From Gamchi the walk continues NW to Bürgli before turning E again to make the long climb to the Sefinenfurgge (2612m). The consolation for reaching this point is the view E towards the Eiger, Mönch and Jungfrau. There remains the long walk to the valley at Stechelberg. From the col take the path NE to Pogaggen (dormitory). Now either follow the path to Murren and take the lift down to Stechelberg or descend via Obenberg into the Sefinental and reach Stechelberg by following the valley road along the Sefinen Lütschini.

There is camping at Stechelberg and a hotel but no dormitory. This has been a long day covering about 30km and climbing about 2600m.

If you split the fourth stage by stopping at the Gspaltenhorn hut a more direct route to the Sefinenfurgge can be taken. From the hut a path leads across the lower part of the W ridge of Bütlasse to Trogegg. From here follow the path NE to the pass.

Stage five begins with a walk along the road N to Sandbach from where a path leads up the S side of the Trümmelbach falls. Follow this to Preech then take the contouring path Nwards towards

Stalden. After about 1km take the track turning sharp R to Mettla and hence reach the path alongside the railway leading finally to Kl Scheidegg. An overnight stop can be made at the Station Buffet (dormitory) or descend to Grindelwald by way of Alpiglen and the path below the railway (camping and hotels but no dormitory).

About 10km to Kl Scheidegg and just over 1000m ascent plus a further 9km to Grindelwald.

The final stage has two alternatives. The first begins by walking through Grindelwald (or use the bus) to the Wetterhorn Hotel at the public roadhead near the foot of the Ober Grindelwald glacier. A path from there leads to Gr Scheidegg. The second possibility is to walk, or use the lift, to First from where a magnificent panorama to the S can be enjoyed. From First a contouring path heads E towards Gr Scheidegg (dormitory accommodation available here). From Gr Scheidegg it is possible to descend directly to Rosenlaui, but a more pleasant way is to take the track heading N (fork R at Pt 2006m) to the small summit of Cheerhubel. From here there are fine views of the Engelhörner peaks and of the Wellhorn. Descend by the path on the E side of the Pfannibach to the road at Schwarzwaldalp.

There is now little alternative to following the road through Rosenlaui and on towards Meiringen (bus service). On the last stretch a fairly direct line close to the Reichenbach falls can be taken.

It is about 22km from Grindelwald to Meiringen and a bit further if the alternatives to First and Cheerhubel are taken. The direct route involves about 900m climbing whilst for the alternatives it is nearer 1400m.

GENERAL INDEX – ERRATA

The page numbering in the General Index and in the Index of Climbs is out of sequence.

Please add 1 extra page from pages 113 to 138
add 2 extra pages from page 139 to 182
add 3 extra pages from page 183 to 194
add 4 extra pages from page 195 to 236

General index

Index of climbs

Lauteraarsattel and Unders Studerjoch to the Aletsch Glacier and Jungfraujoch

Jungfraujoch to the Lötschenpass

Aletschhorn Group and Peaks S of the Lötschental

Alpes Vaudoises

Minor Crags

1

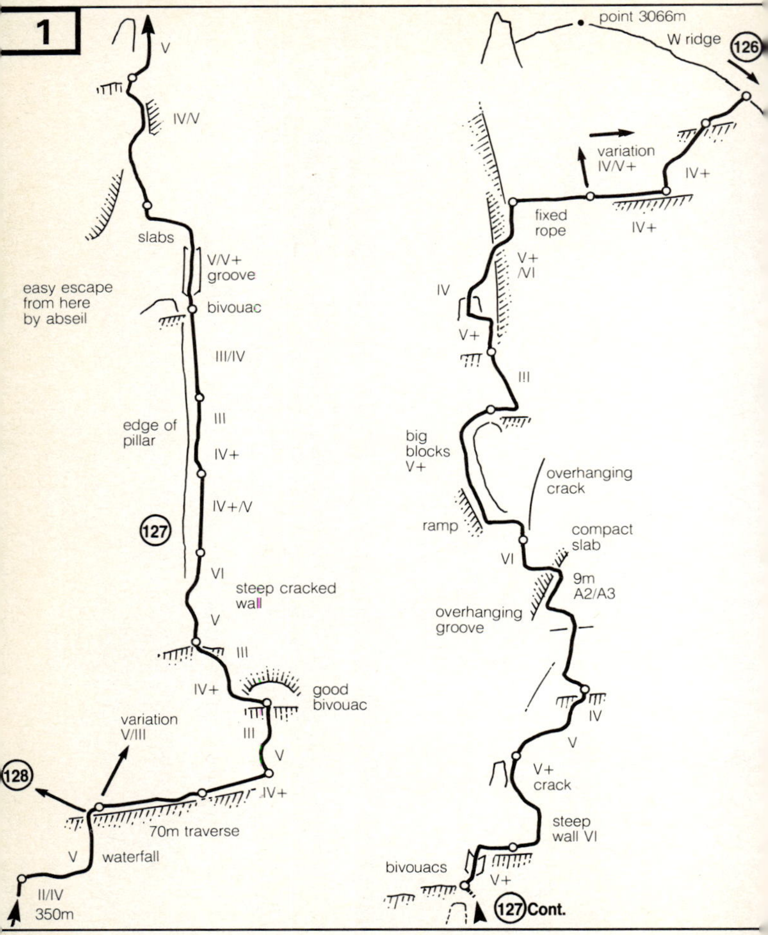
V
IV/V
slabs
V/V+
groove
easy escape
from here
by abseil
bivouac
III/IV
III
edge of
pillar
IV+
IV+/V
127
VI
steep cracked
wall
V
III
IV+
good
bivouac
III
V
variation
V/III
128
IV+
70m traverse
V
waterfall
II/IV
350m
point 3066m
W ridge
126
variation
IV/V+
IV+
fixed
rope
IV+
V+
/VI
IV
V+
III
big
blocks
V+
overhanging
crack
ramp
compact
slab
VI
9m
A2/A3
overhanging
groove
IV
V
V+
crack
steep
wall VI
bivouacs
V+
127 Cont.

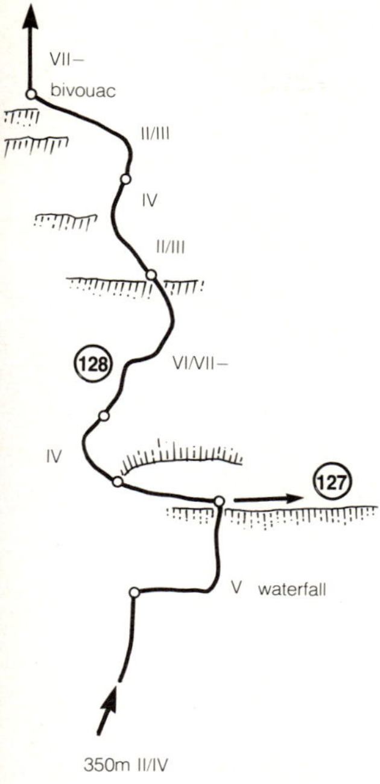
VII–
bivouac
II/III
IV
II/III
128
VI/VII–
IV
127
V
waterfall
350m II/IV

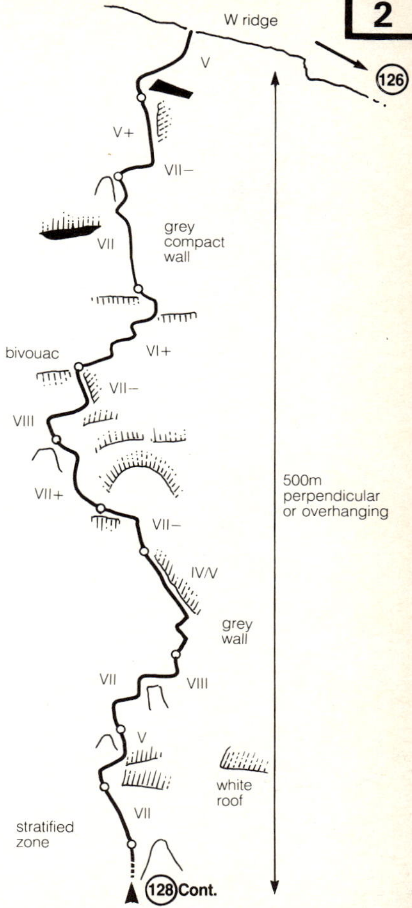
W ridge
V
126
V+
VII–
grey
compact
wall
VII
bivouac
VI+
VII–
VIII
VII+
500m
perpendicular
or overhanging
VII–
IV/V
grey
wall
VII
VIII
V
white
roof
VII
stratified
zone
128 Cont.

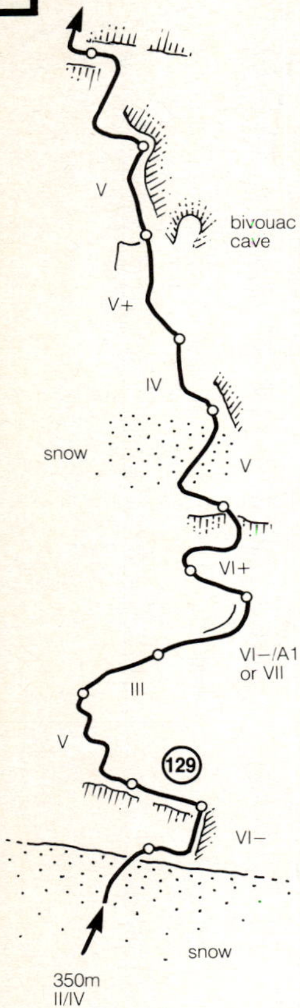
V
bivouac
cave
V+
IV
snow
V
VI+
VI–/A1
or VII
III
V
129
VI–
snow
350m
II/IV

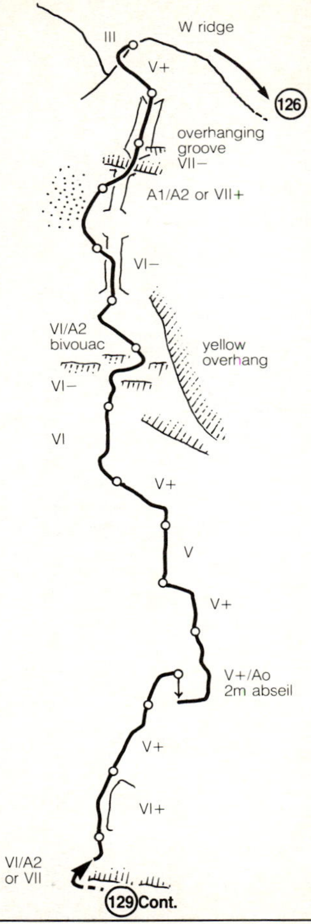
III
W ridge
V+
126
overhanging
groove
VII–
A1/A2 or VII+
VI–
VI/A2
bivouac
yellow
overhang
VI–
VI
V+
V
V+
V+/Ao
2m abseil
V+
VI+
VI/A2
or VII
129 Cont.

4

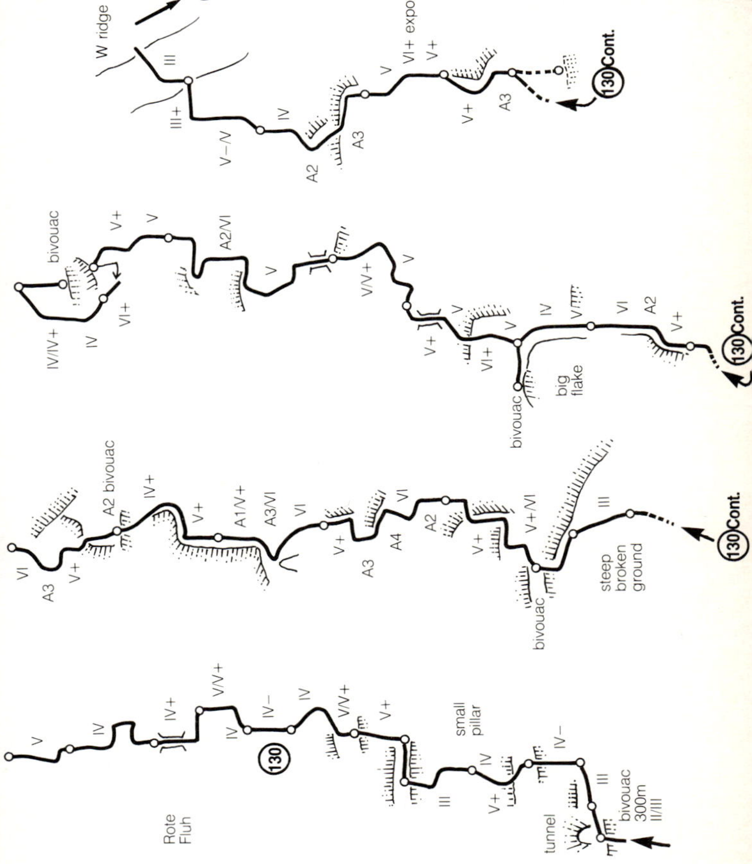
W ridge
126
VI+ exposed
130 Cont.
bivouac
big flake
130 Cont.
A2 bivouac
bivouac
steep broken ground
130 Cont.
130
Rote Fluh
small pillar
tunnel
bivouac 300m II/III

5

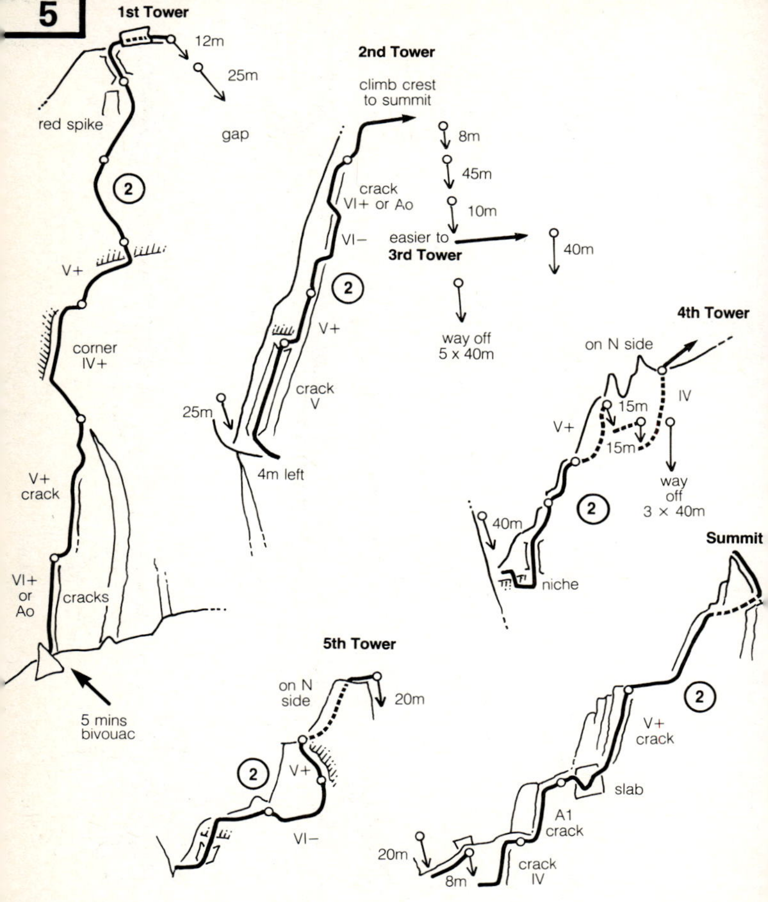
1st Tower
12m
25m
red spike
gap
2
V+
corner
IV+
V+
crack
VI+
or
Ao
cracks
5 mins
bivouac
2nd Tower
climb crest
to summit
crack
VI+ or Ao
VI–
2
V+
crack
V
25m
4m left
8m
45m
10m
easier to
3rd Tower
40m
way off
5 x 40m
4th Tower
on N side
IV
15m
15m
V+
way
off
3 × 40m
40m
2
niche
Summit
5th Tower
on N
side
20m
2
V+
VI–
2
V+
crack
slab
A1
crack
20m
8m
crack
IV

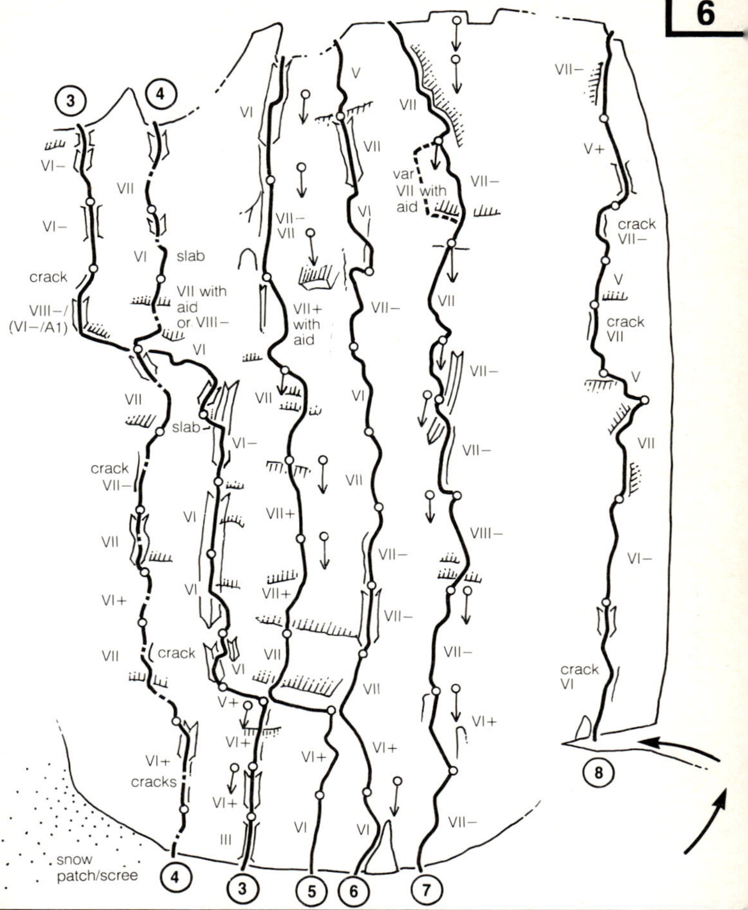
3
4
VI–
VII
VI–
VI
slab
crack
VII with
aid
or VIII–
VIII–/
(VI–/A1)
VI
VII
slab
crack
VII–
VI–
VII
VI
VII
VI+
VI
crack
VI
VII
VI+
cracks
VI+
snow
patch/scree
VI+
VI+
III
4
3
VI
V
VII
VII–
VII
VII+
with
aid
VII
VII+
VII+
VII
VI+
VI
5
VII
VI
VII–
VI
VII
VII–
VII–
VII
VI+
VI
6
VII
var
VII with
aid
VII–
VII
VII–
VII–
VIII–
VII–
VI+
VII–
7
VII–
V+
crack
VII–
V
crack
VII
V
VII
VI–
crack
VI
8

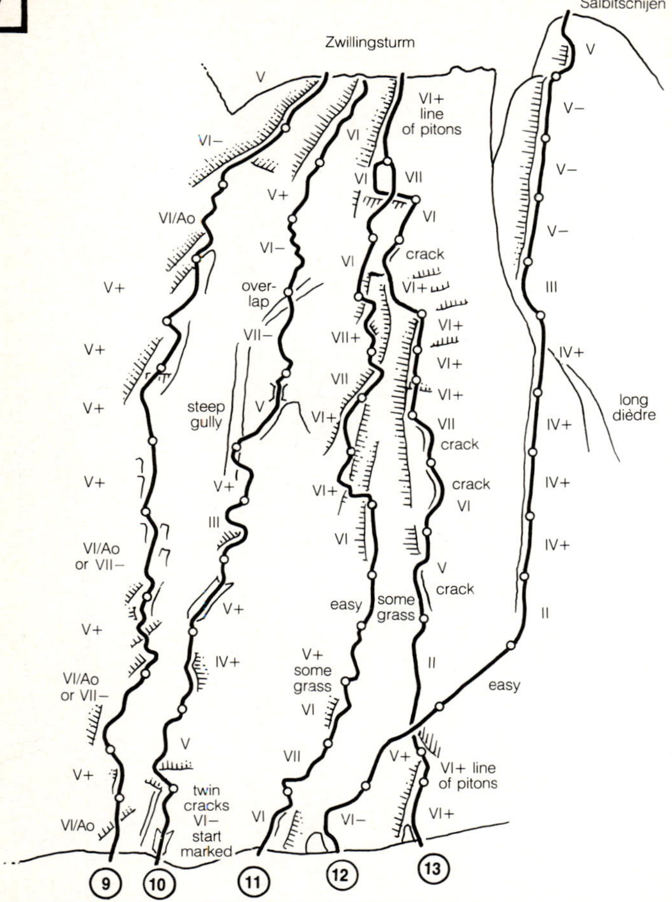

Salbitschijen
Zwillingsturm
V
VI–
VI/Ao
V+
V+
V+
V+
VI/Ao
or VII–
V+
VI/Ao
or VII–
V+
VI/Ao
V+
VI–
over-
lap
VII–
steep
gully
V
V+
III
V+
IV+
V
twin
cracks
VI–
start
marked
VI
VI+
line
of pitons
VI
VII
VI
crack
VI
VI+
VI+
VI+
VI+
VII+
VII
VI+
VII
crack
crack
VI
VI+
VI
V
crack
easy
some
grass
V+
some
grass
VI
VII
VI
II
VI–
V+
VI+ line
of pitons
VI+
easy
V
V–
V–
V–
III
IV+
long
dièdre
IV+
IV+
IV+
II
9
10
11
12
13

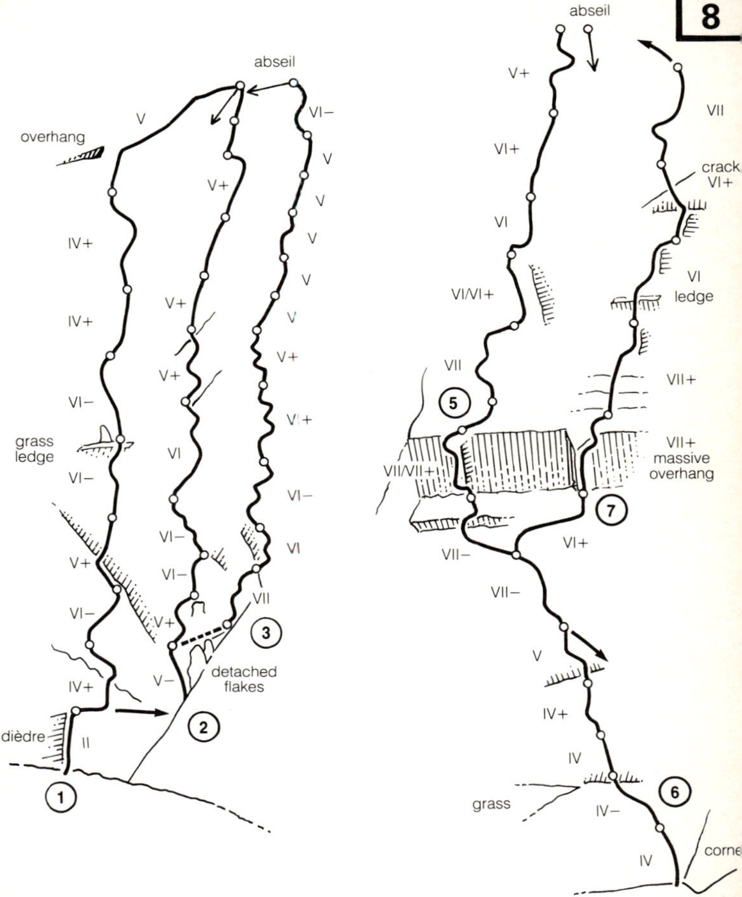
abseil
V
overhang
IV+
IV+
VI–
grass ledge
VI–
V+
VI–
IV+
dièdre
II
1
V+
V+
V+
VI
VI–
VI–
V+
V–
2
VI–
V
V
V
V
V
V+
VI+
VI–
VI
VII
3
detached flakes
abseil
V+
VI+
VI
VI/VI+
VII
5
VII/VII+
VII–
VII–
V
IV+
IV
grass
IV–
IV
6
VII
crack VI+
VI
ledge
VII+
VII+ massive overhang
7
VI+

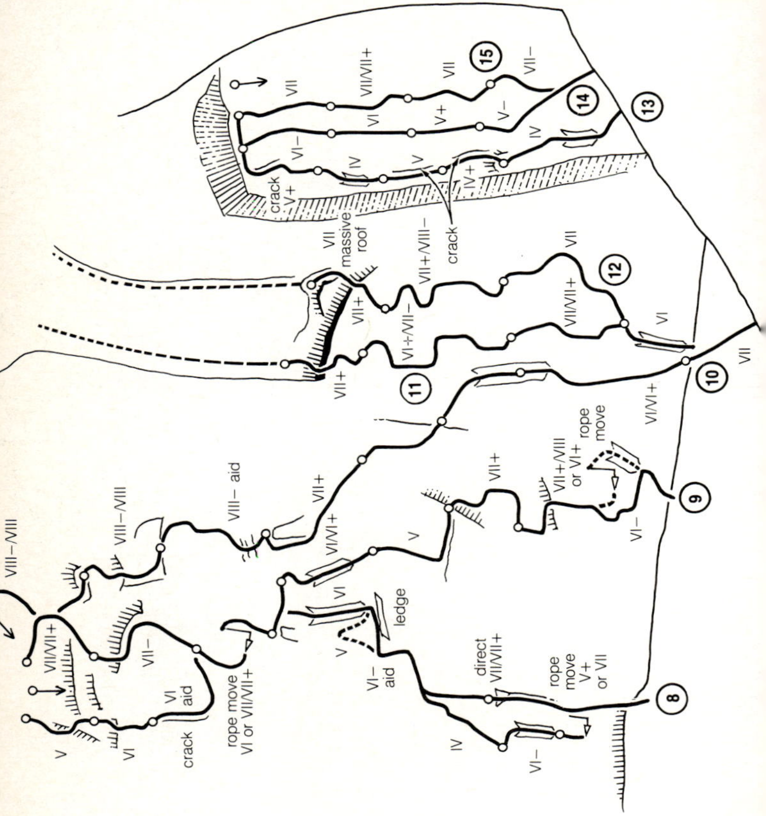

15
14
13
12
11
10
9
8
VII/VII+
VII
VII–
V+
V–
VI
VI–
IV
V
crack
V+
IV+
VII
massive
roof
VII+/VIII–
crack
VII+
VI+/VII–
VII/VII+
VII+
VI/VI+
rope
move
VII+/VIII
or VI+
VIII– aid
VIII–/VIII
VIII–/VIII
VII/VII+
VI/VI+
ledge
VI– aid
direct
VII/VII+
rope
move
V+
or VII
rope move
VI or VII/VII+
VI
aid
crack

10

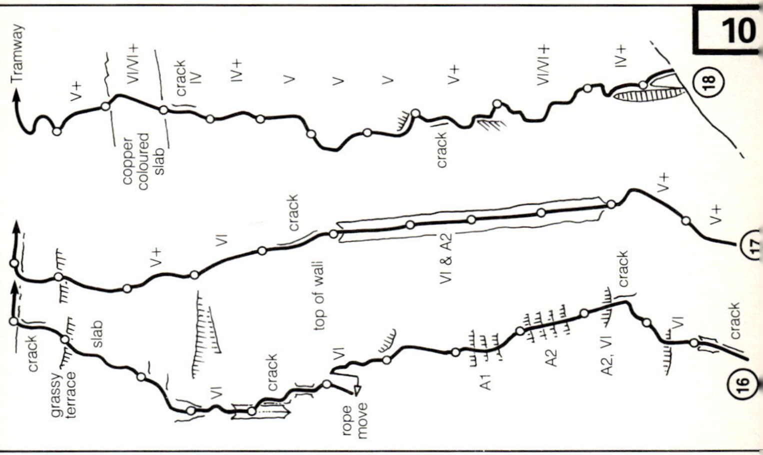
Tramway
V+
VI/VI+
copper coloured slab
crack IV
IV+
V
V
V
V+
crack
VI/VI+
IV+
18
crack
V+
VI
V+
VI & A2
top of wall
V+
V+
17
crack
grassy terrace
slab
VI
crack
rope move
VI
A1
A2
A2, VI
crack
VI
crack
16

11

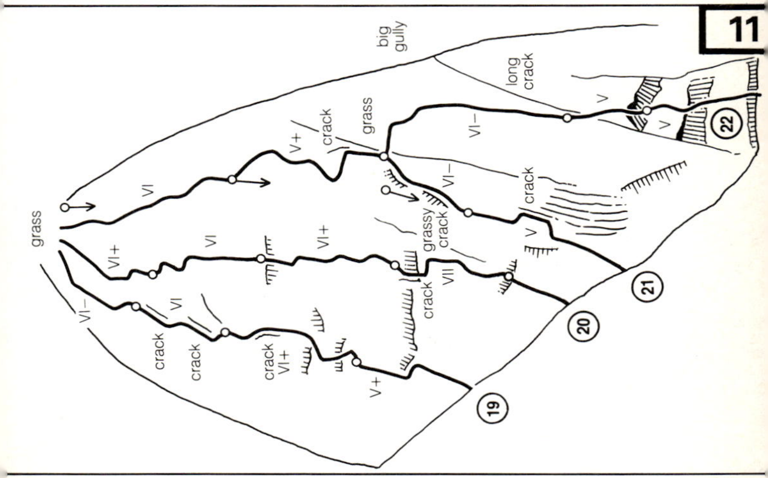
big gully
long crack
grass
V
V
22
grass
VI
V+
crack
VI–
VI–
crack
grassy crack
V
21
VI+
VI
VI+
VII
crack
20
VI–
VI
crack
crack
crack VI+
V+
19

12

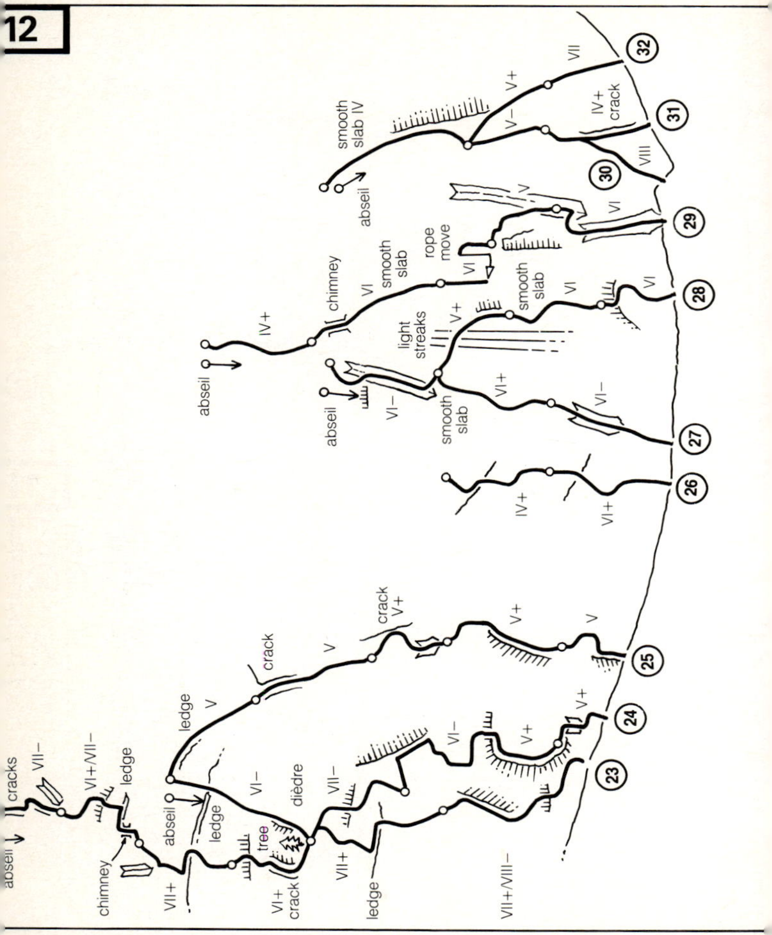

23
24
25
26
27
28
29
30
31
32
abseil
cracks
VII–
VI+/VII–
ledge
chimney
VII+
ledge
abseil
tree
VI+
crack
VI–
dièdre
VII–
VII+
ledge
VII+/VIII–
V
crack
VI–
V+
smooth slab IV
IV+
crack
VIII
VII
V–
rope
move
VI
smooth
slab
chimney
light
streaks

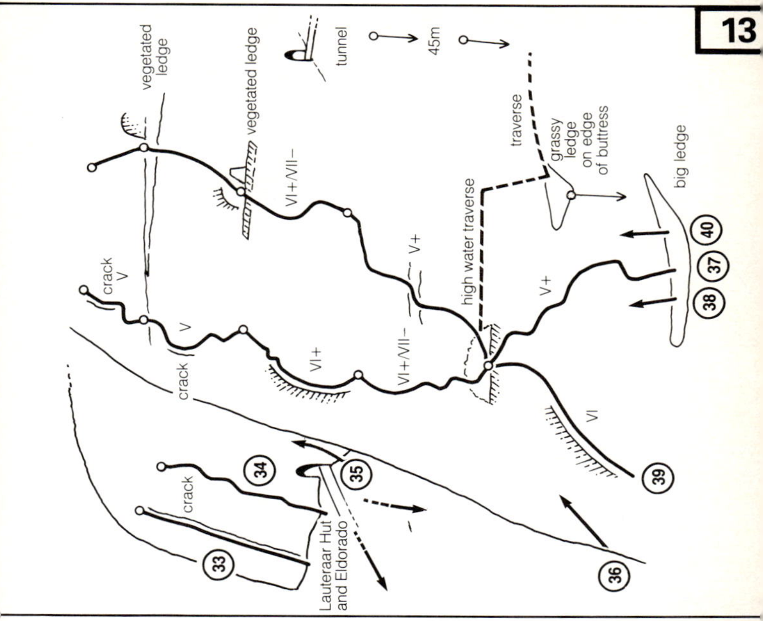
13
vegetated ledge
vegetated ledge
tunnel
45m
traverse
grassy ledge on edge of buttress
big ledge
high water traverse
crack V
V
VI+/VII−
V+
VI+
VI+/VII−
V+
crack
VI
crack
33
34
35
36
37
38
39
40
Lauteraar Hut and Eldorado

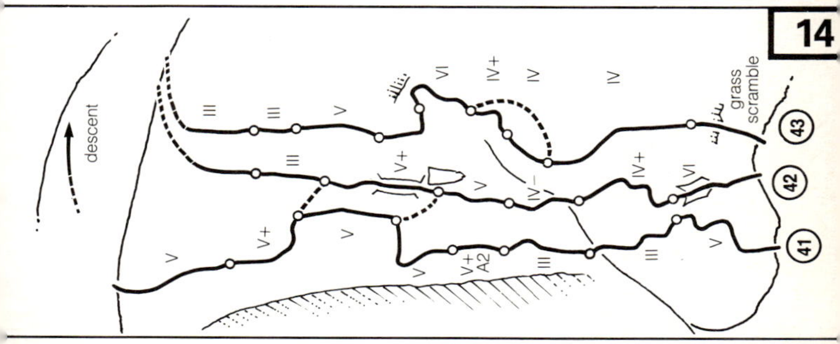
14
descent
grass scramble
III
III
V
VI
IV+
IV
IV
III
V+
V
IV−
IV+
VI
V+
V
V
V+ A2
III
III
V
41
42
43

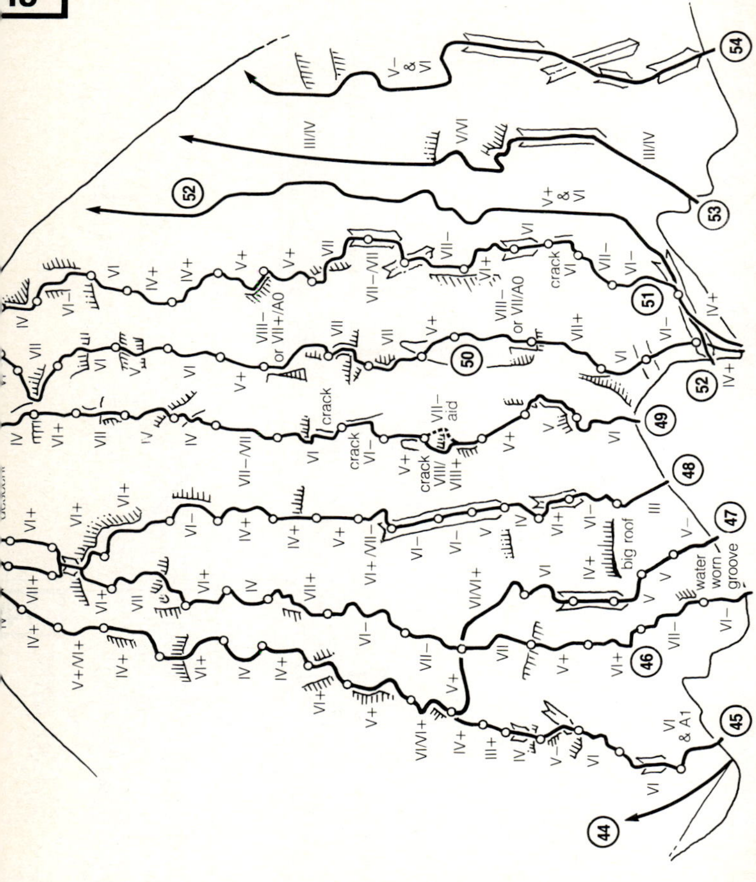
44
45
46
47
48
49
50
51
52
53
54
crack
big roof
water worn groove
aid
or VII/A0
or VII+/A0
VI & A1

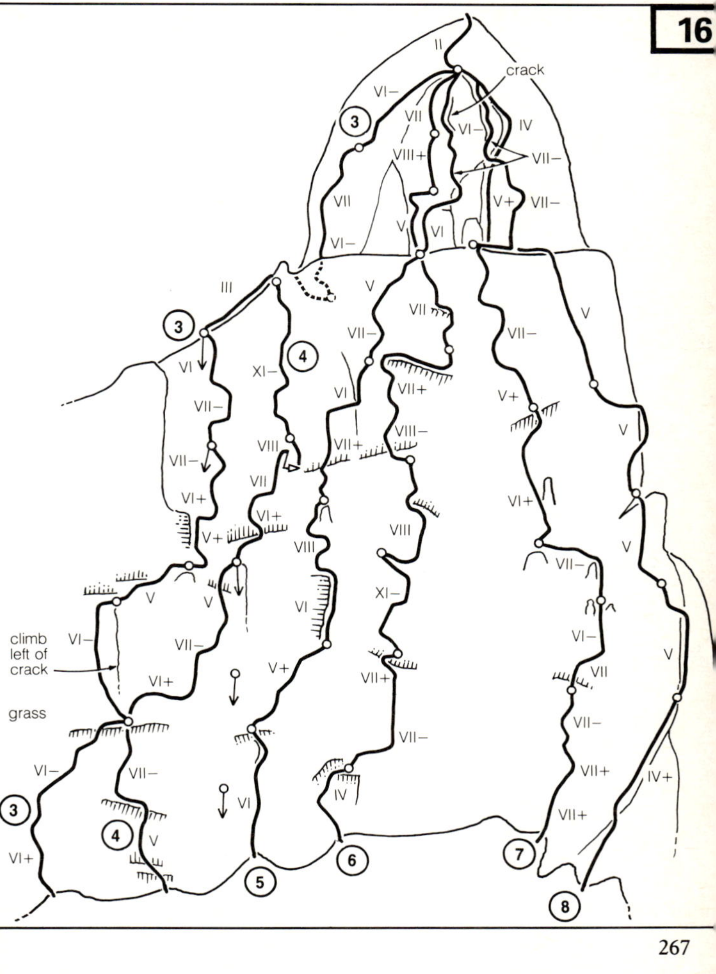
II
crack
VI–
3
VII
VI–
IV
VIII+
VII–
VII
V+
VII–
V
VI
VI–
III
V
VII
3
VII–
VII–
V
4
VI
XI–
VI
VII+
VII–
V+
V
VIII–
VIII
VII+
VII–
VII
VI+
VI+
VI+
VIII
V+
V
VII–
V
V
VI
VI–
climb
left of
crack
VII–
VI–
XI–
VII+
VII
V
VI+
V+
grass
VII–
VII–
VI–
VII–
VII+
IV+
3
VI
IV
VII+
4
V
VI+
5
6
7
8

Kingspitz NE Face

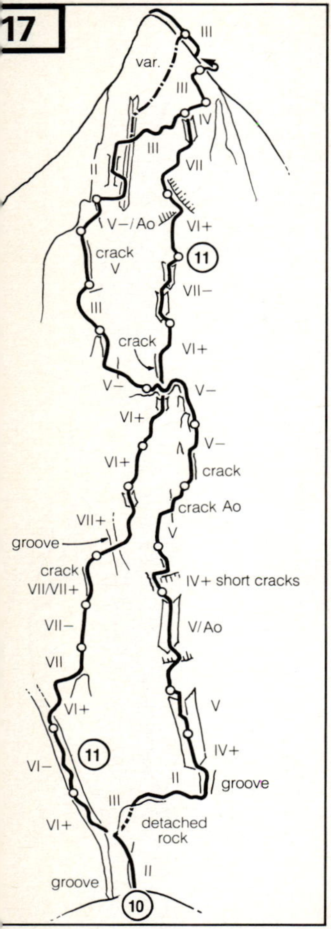

Rosenlauistock N Face

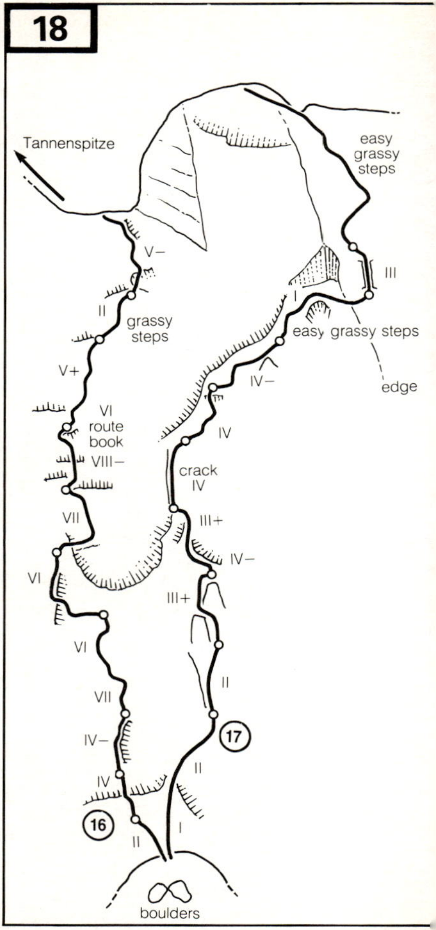

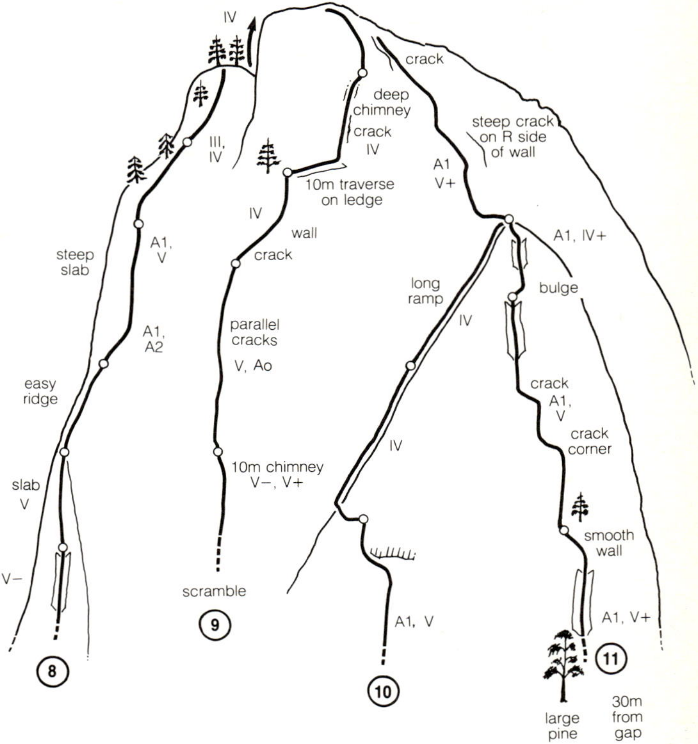
IV
crack
deep
chimney
crack
IV
steep crack
on R side
of wall
III,
IV
10m traverse
on ledge
A1
V+
IV
wall
A1,
V
crack
A1, IV+
steep
slab
long
ramp
bulge
IV
parallel
cracks
A1,
A2
V, Ao
easy
ridge
crack
A1,
V
IV
crack
corner
10m chimney
V–, V+
slab
V
smooth
wall
V–
scramble
A1, V
A1, V+
9
8
10
11
large
pine
30m
from
gap

20

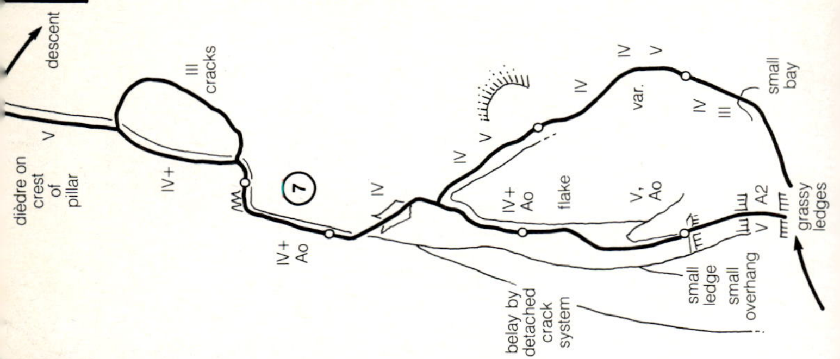
descent
dièdre on crest of pillar
V
IV+
III cracks
7
IV+ Ao
IV
IV
V
IV+ Ao
flake
V, Ao
IV
V
var.
IV
V
IV
III
small bay
A2
V
grassy ledges
small ledge
small overhang
belay by detached crack system

21A

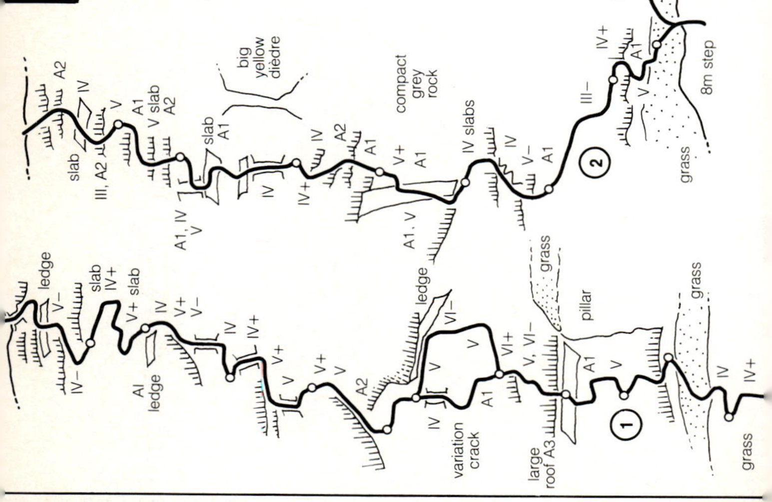
3
IV+
A1
8m step
III–
V
grass
2
IV slabs
IV
V–
A1
compact grey rock
big yellow dièdre
A2
A1
V+
A1
IV
IV+
A1. V
slab A1
A1, IV V
A2
IV
V
A1
V slab
A2
slab
III, A2
ledge
V–
IV–
slab
IV+
V+ slab
IV
V+
V–
Al ledge
IV
IV+
V+
V
V+
V
A2
ledge
VI–
V
V
IV
variation crack
A1
VI+
V, VI–
grass
pillar
large roof A3
A1
V
1
grass
IV
IV+
grass

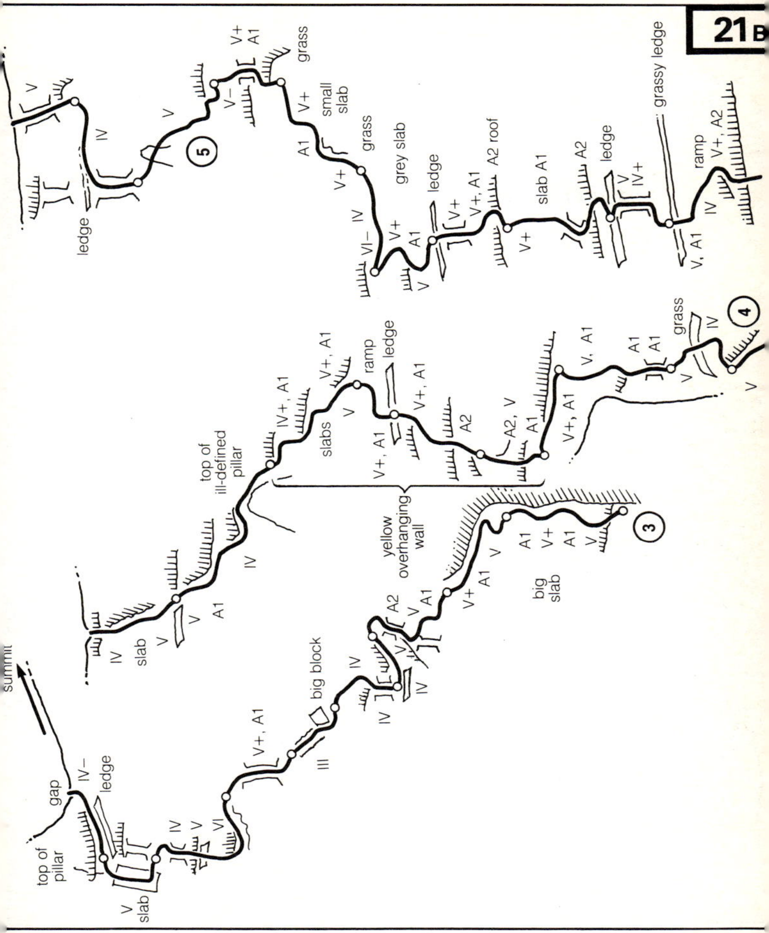
summit
top of pillar
gap
IV–
ledge
V
slab
top of ill-defined pillar
slab
big block
yellow overhanging wall
big slab
slabs
ramp
ledge
grass
grassy ledge
ramp
grey slab
A2 roof
slab A1
small slab
3
4
5

22

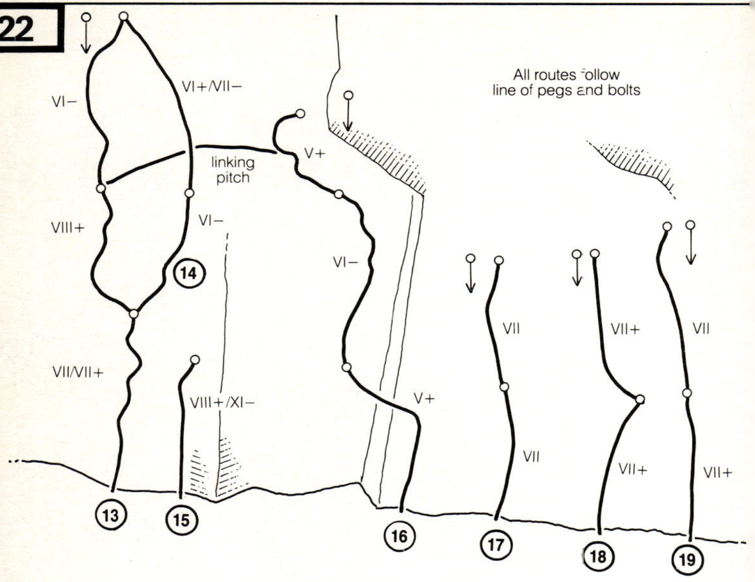
VI–
VI+/VII–
linking
pitch
V+
All routes follow
line of pegs and bolts
VIII+
VI–
VI–
14
VII/VII+
VII
VII+
VII
VIII+/XI–
V+
VII
VII+
VII+
13
15
16
17
18
19

23

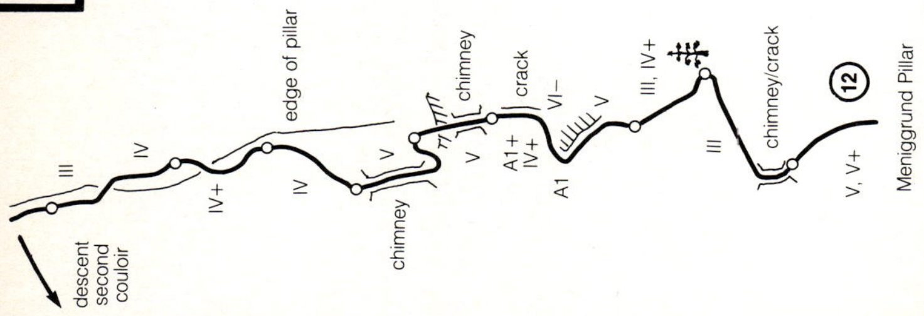
III
IV
edge of pillar
IV+
IV
V
chimney
V
chimney
crack
A1+
IV+
A1
VI–
V
III, IV+
III
chimney/crack
12
V, V+
Meniggrund Pillar
descent
second
couloir

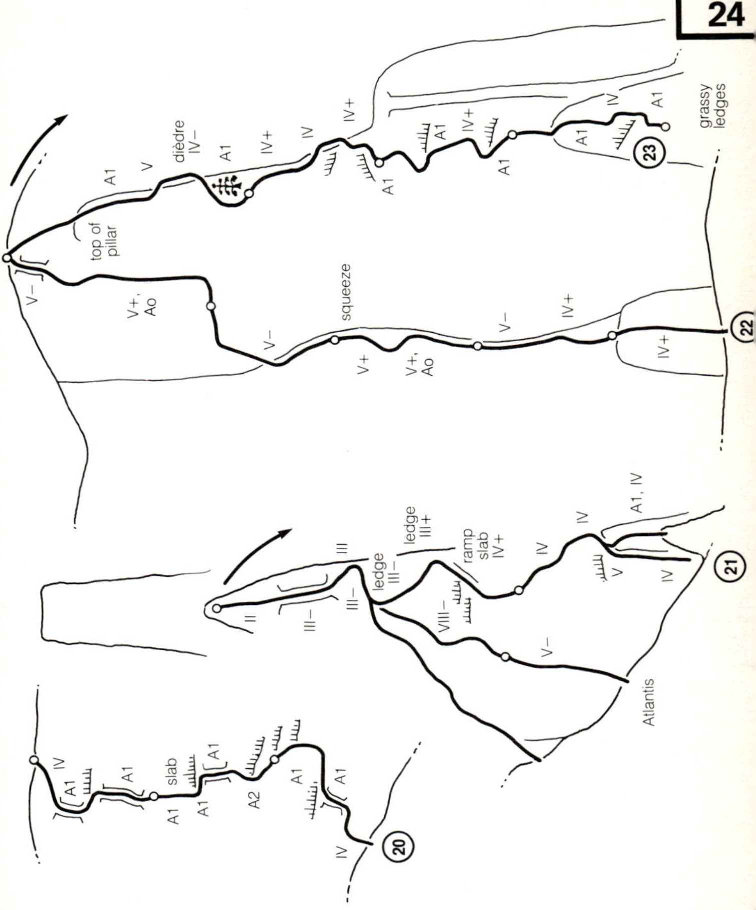
23
22
21
20
grassy ledges
top of pillar
dièdre IV–
squeeze
V+, Ao
ledge III–
ledge III+
ramp slab IV+
VIII–
Atlantis
A1, IV
slab
A2

25

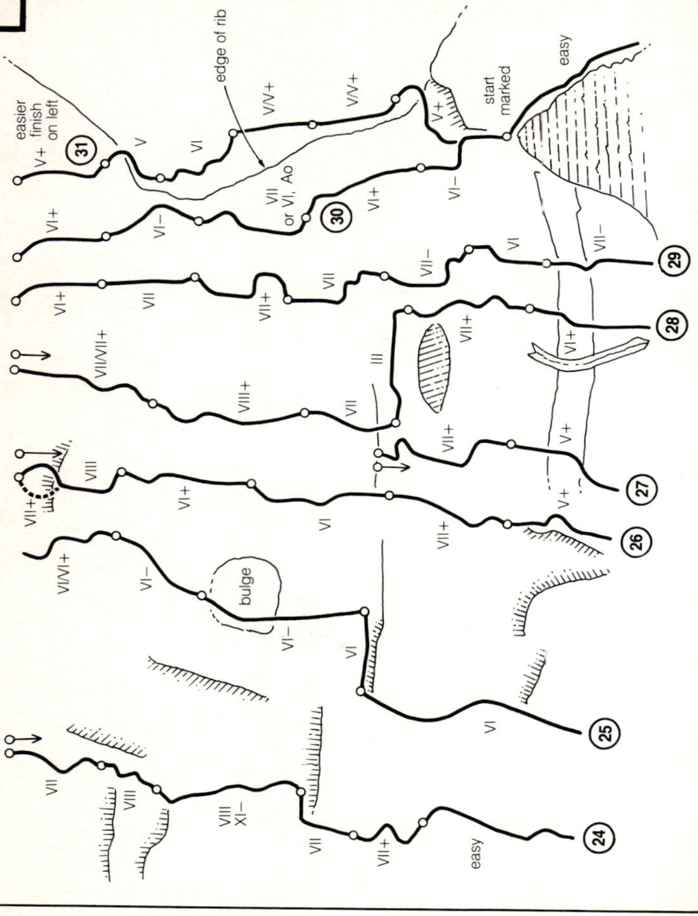
easier finish on left
edge of rib
start marked
easy
bulge
V+
31
V
VI
V/V+
VI+
VI–
VII or VI, Ao
30
VII–
VI
29
VII
VII+
28
VII/VII+
VIII+
III
27
VIII
VII+
26
VI/VI+
25
VII
VIII
VIII XI–
24
VII+
easy

26

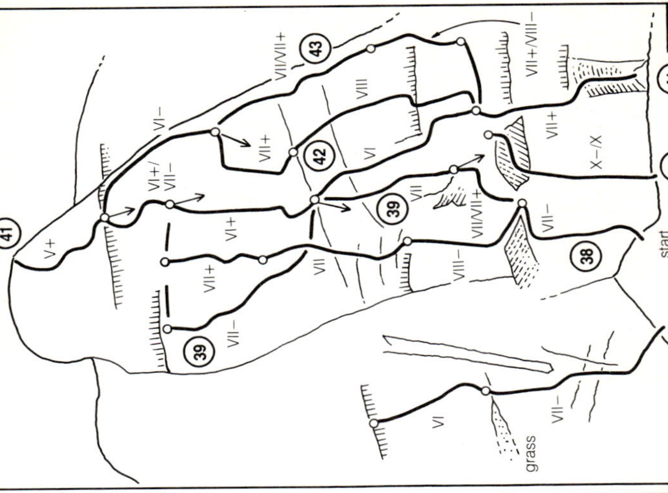
41
V+
VI–
VI+/
VII–
VI+
VII+
VII–
39
VII
VII+
42
VII/VII+
43
VIII
VI
VII
39
VII/VII+
VIII–
VII+/VIII–
VII+
X–/X
VII–
41
40
38
start
marked
37
VI
VII–
grass

27

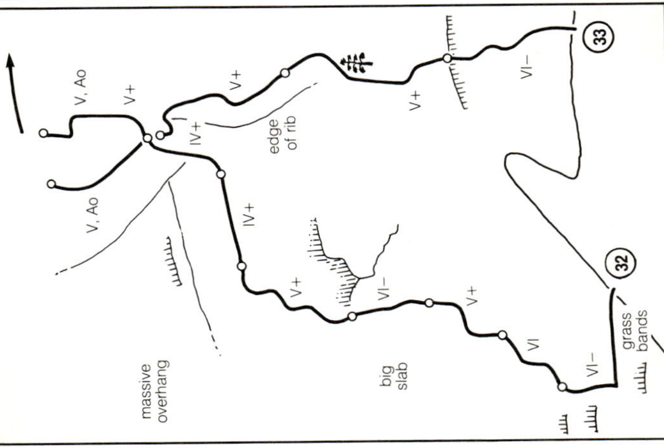
V, Ao
V+
V, Ao
IV+
V+
edge
of rib
IV+
V+
VI–
V+
VI–
33
32
VI
VI–
grass
bands
massive
overhang
big
slab

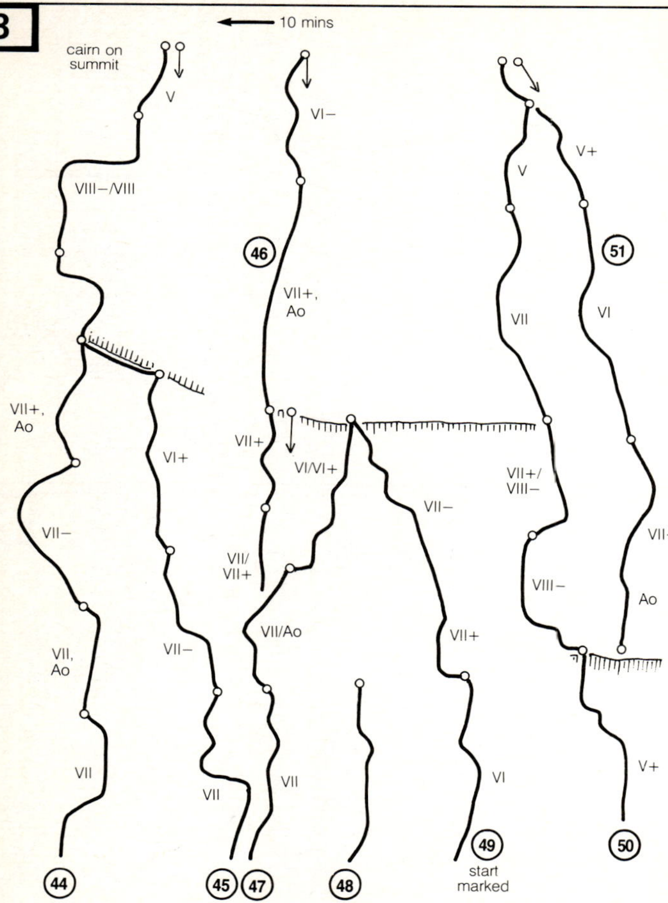
10 mins
cairn on summit
V
VIII–/VIII
VII+, Ao
VII–
VII, Ao
VII
VI+
VII–
VII
VI–
46
VII+, Ao
VII+
VI/VI+
VII/ VII+
VII/Ao
VII
VII–
VII+
VI
V
VII
VII+/ VIII–
VIII–
V+
51
VI
VII+
Ao
V+
44
45
47
48
49
start marked
50

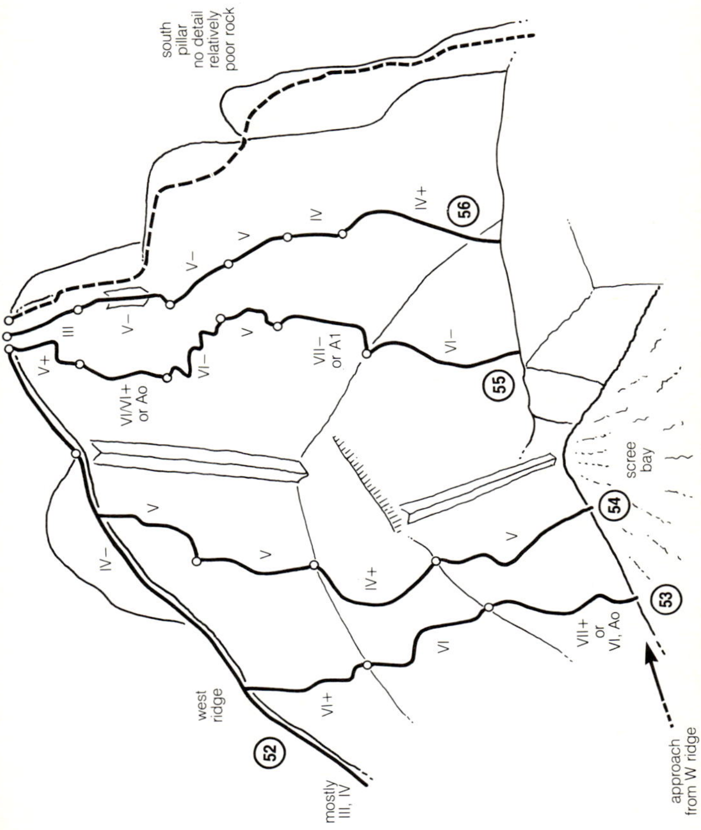
south pillar
no detail
relatively poor rock
56
IV+
IV
V
V–
V–
III
V+
VI/VI+
or Ao
VI–
V
VII–
or A1
VI–
55
scree
bay
54
V
V
IV+
V
IV–
53
VII+
or
VI, Ao
VI
VI+
west
ridge
52
mostly
III, IV
approach
from W ridge

30

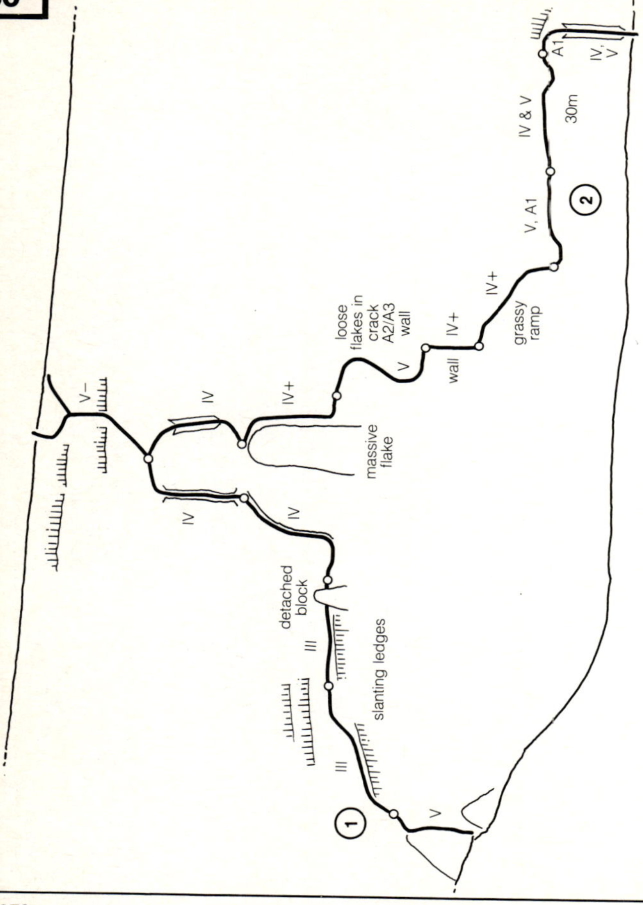
V–
IV
IV+
loose flakes in crack A2/A3 wall
V
wall
IV+
IV+
grassy ramp
V, A1
IV & V
30m
A1
IV, V
massive flake
IV
IV
detached block
III
slanting ledges
III
V
1
2

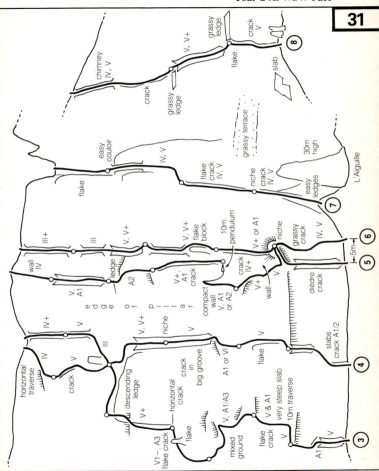

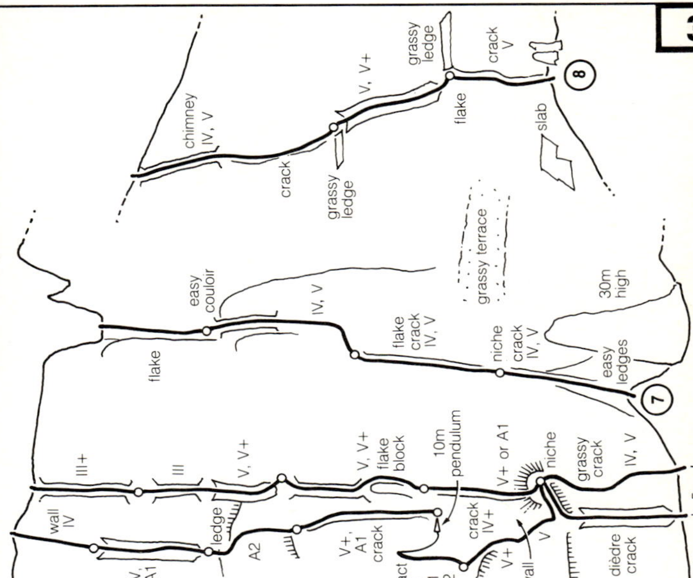

chimney IV, V
V, V+
grassy ledge
crack V
flake
slab
crack
grassy ledge
grassy terrace
easy couloir
IV, V
flake crack IV, V
niche crack IV, V
easy ledges
30m high
L'Aiguille
flake
III+
III
V, V+
V, V+ flake block
10m pendulum
V+ or A1
niche
grassy crack
IV, V
wall IV
ledge
A2
V+, A1 crack
crack IV+
V
V+
wall
V, A1
edge of pillar
compact wall V, A1 or A2
dièdre crack
5m
IV+
V
III
V, V+
niche
V
V
slabs crack A1/2
horizontal traverse
IV
V
crack
descending ledge
crack in big groove
A1 or VI
flake
horizontal crack
V+
V, A1/A3
V & A1
very steep slab
10m traverse
V1–, A3 flake crack
flake
mixed ground
flake crack
V
V
A1
3
4
5
6
7
8

32

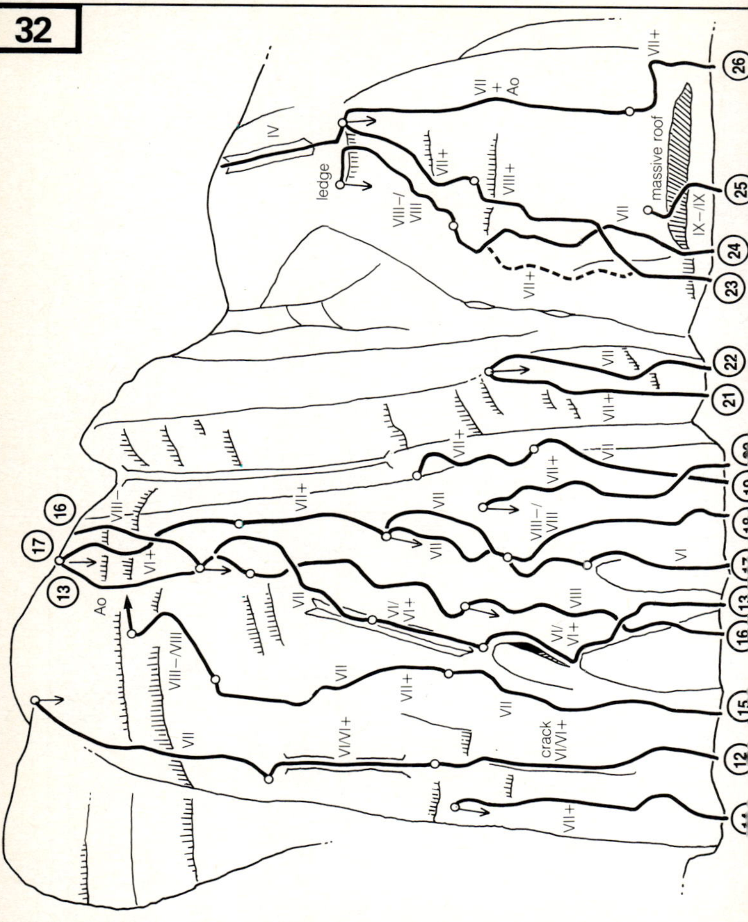

ledge
massive roof
crack
Ao
IV
VI
VI+
VI/VI+
VII
VII+
VII + Ao
VIII
VIII–
VIII–/VIII
VIII–/VIII
IX–/IX

33

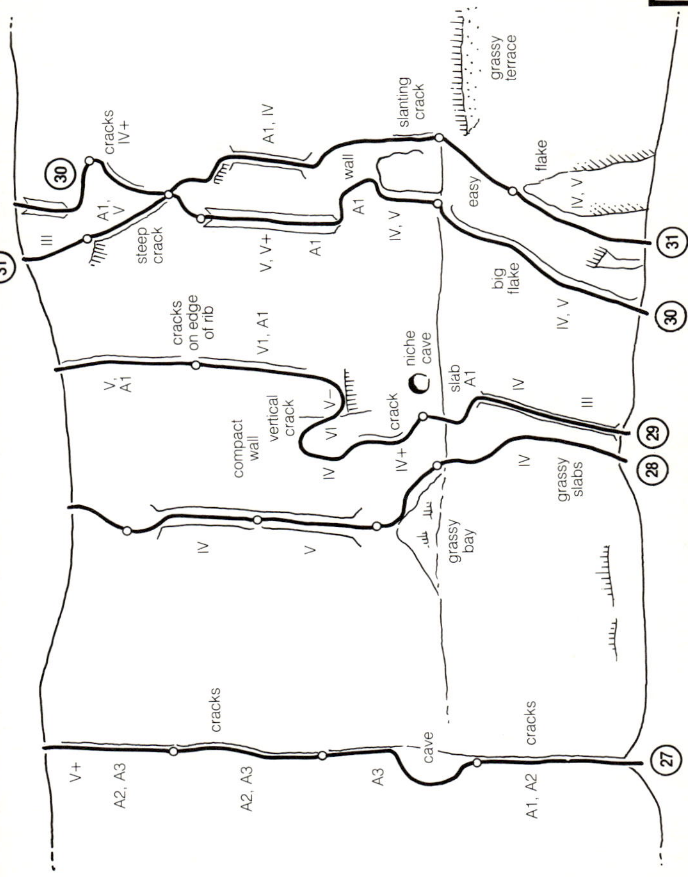
31
30
cracks IV+
A1, V
III
steep crack
A1, IV
V, V+
A1
wall
A1
IV, V
slanting crack
grassy terrace
easy
flake
IV, V
big flake
IV, V
31
30
cracks on edge of rib
V1, A1
V, A1
niche cave
slab A1
IV
III
V–
vertical crack
compact wall
VI
crack
IV
IV+
IV
grassy slabs
29
28
IV
V
grassy bay
cracks
V+
A2, A3
A2, A3
A3
cave
cracks
A1, A2
27

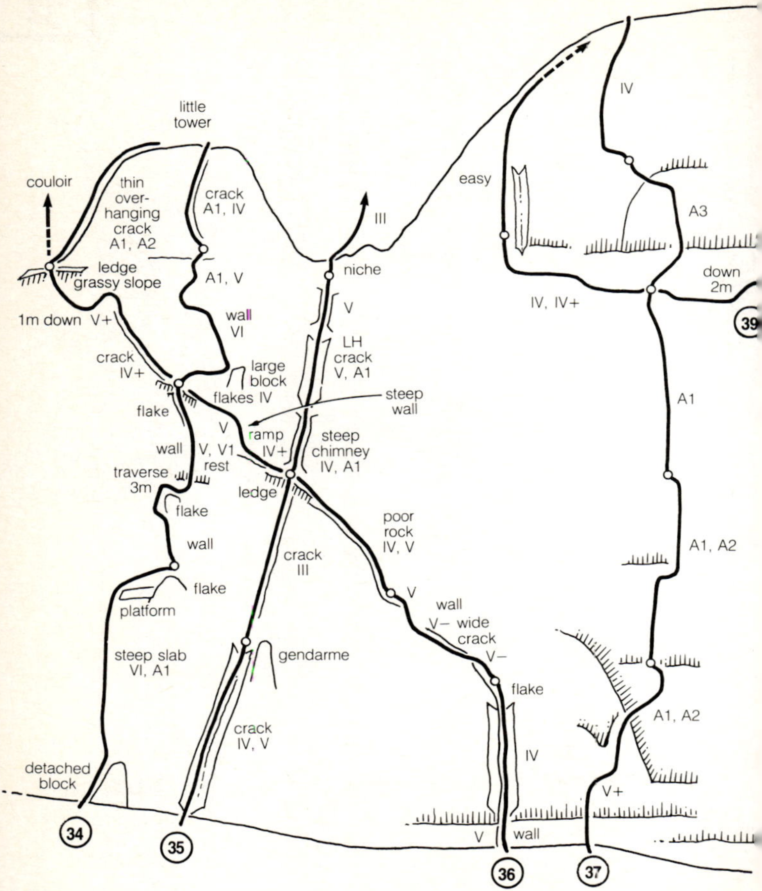
little
tower
couloir
thin
over-
hanging
crack
A1, A2
crack
A1, IV
III
easy
IV
A3
ledge
grassy slope
A1, V
niche
down
2m
IV, IV+
1m down V+
wall
VI
V
39
LH
crack
V, A1
crack
IV+
large
block
flakes IV
steep
wall
A1
flake
V
ramp
IV+
steep
chimney
IV, A1
wall
V, V1
rest
traverse
3m
ledge
flake
poor
rock
IV, V
wall
crack
III
A1, A2
flake
V
platform
wall
V– wide
crack
V–
steep slab
VI, A1
gendarme
flake
A1, A2
crack
IV, V
IV
detached
block
V+
V
wall
34
35
36
37

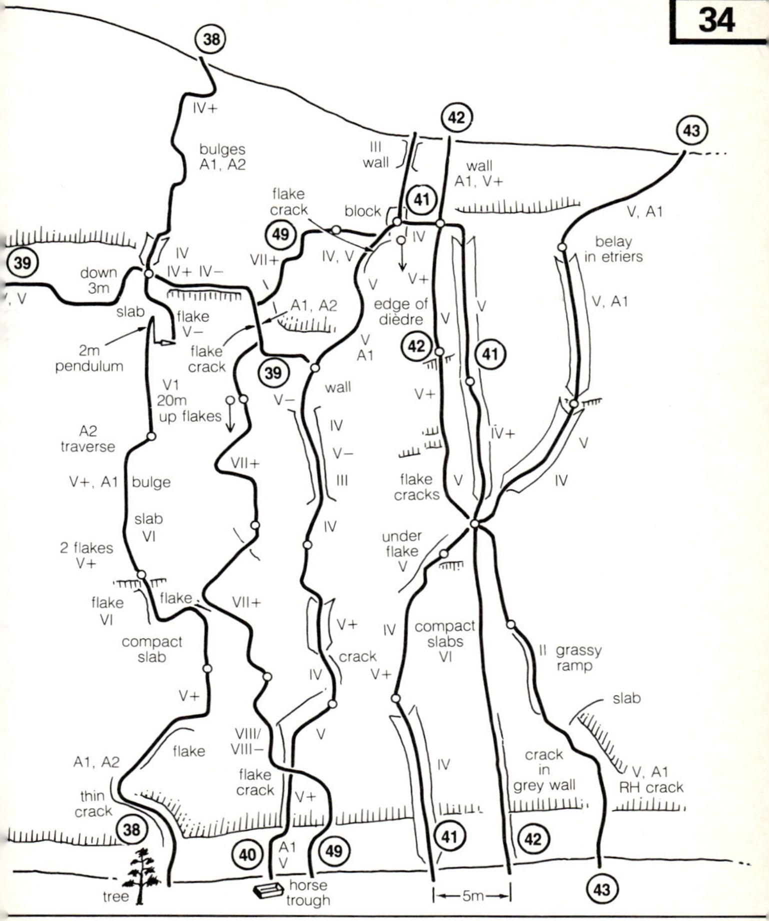
38
IV+
bulges
A1, A2
42
43
III
wall
wall
A1, V+
flake
crack
block
41
V, A1
49
belay
in etriers
39
down
3m
IV
IV+ IV−
VII+
IV, V
IV
V+
V
V
V, A1
slab
flake
V−
A1, A2
edge of
dièdre
V
2m
pendulum
flake
crack
V
A1
42
41
39
wall
V1
20m
up flakes
V−
V+
A2
traverse
IV
V−
III
IV+
VII+
V
V+, A1
bulge
flake
cracks
V
IV
slab
VI
IV
2 flakes
V+
under
flake
V
flake
VI
flake
VII+
compact
slab
V+
IV
compact
slabs
VI
crack
II grassy
ramp
IV
V+
V+
slab
VIII/
VIII−
V
flake
A1, A2
IV
crack
in
grey wall
V, A1
RH crack
thin
crack
flake
crack
V+
38
40
A1
V
49
41
42
tree
horse
trough
5m
43

35

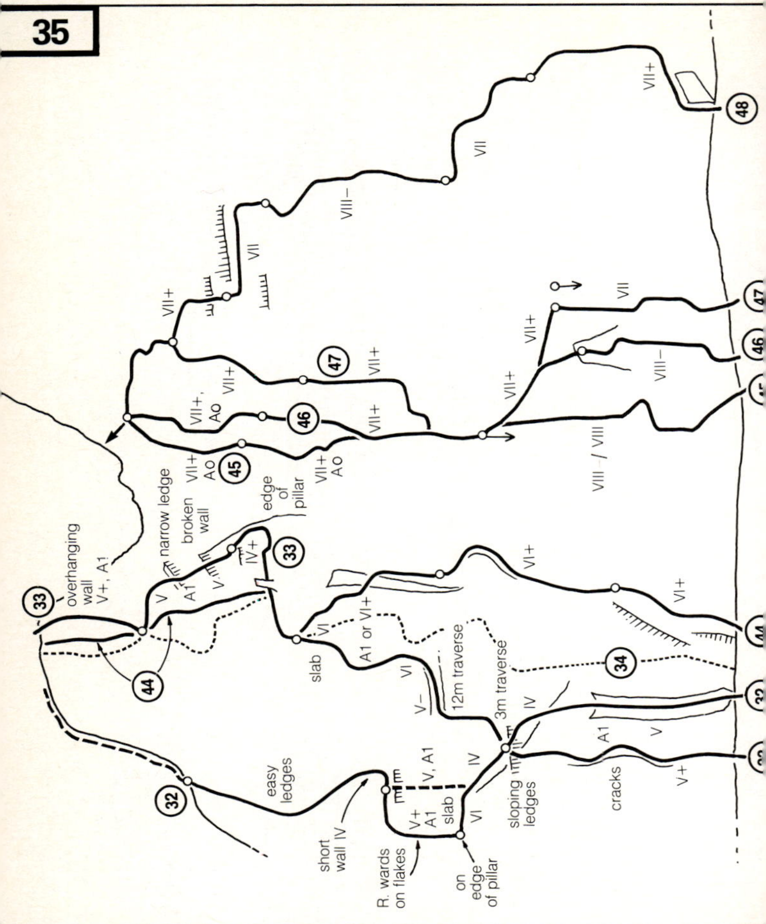
overhanging wall V+, A1
narrow ledge
broken wall
edge of pillar
easy ledges
short wall IV
R. wards on flakes
on edge of pillar
slab
sloping ledges
cracks
12m traverse
3m traverse
A1 or VI+
VII+, Ao
VIII– / VIII
VIII–
VII+
VII
VI+
32
33
34
44
45
46
47
48

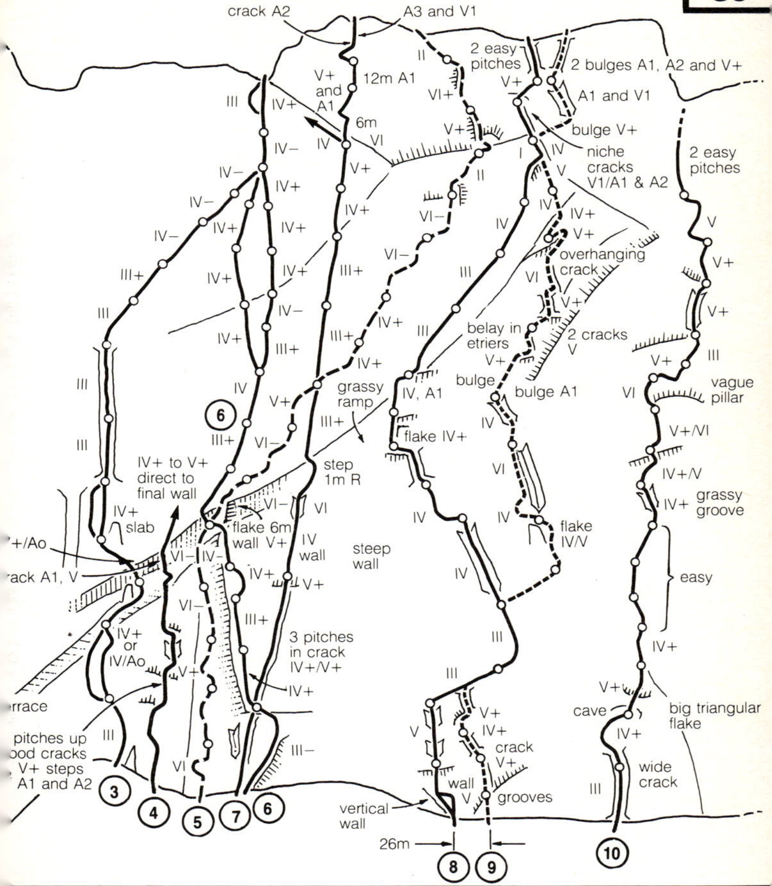

crack A2
A3 and V1
2 easy pitches
2 bulges A1, A2 and V+
A1 and V1
bulge V+
niche cracks V1/A1 & A2
2 easy pitches
12m A1
V+ and A1
6m
overhanging crack
belay in etriers
2 cracks V
bulge
bulge A1
vague pillar
grassy ramp
step 1m R
flake IV+
grassy groove
IV+ to V+ direct to final wall
slab
flake 6m wall V+
IV wall
steep wall
flake IV/V
easy
+/Ao
ack A1, V
IV+ or IV/Ao
3 pitches in crack IV+/V+
errace
pitches up ood cracks V+ steps A1 and A2
big triangular flake
cave
crack V+
wall V
grooves
wide crack
vertical wall
26m
3
4
5
7
6
8
9
10

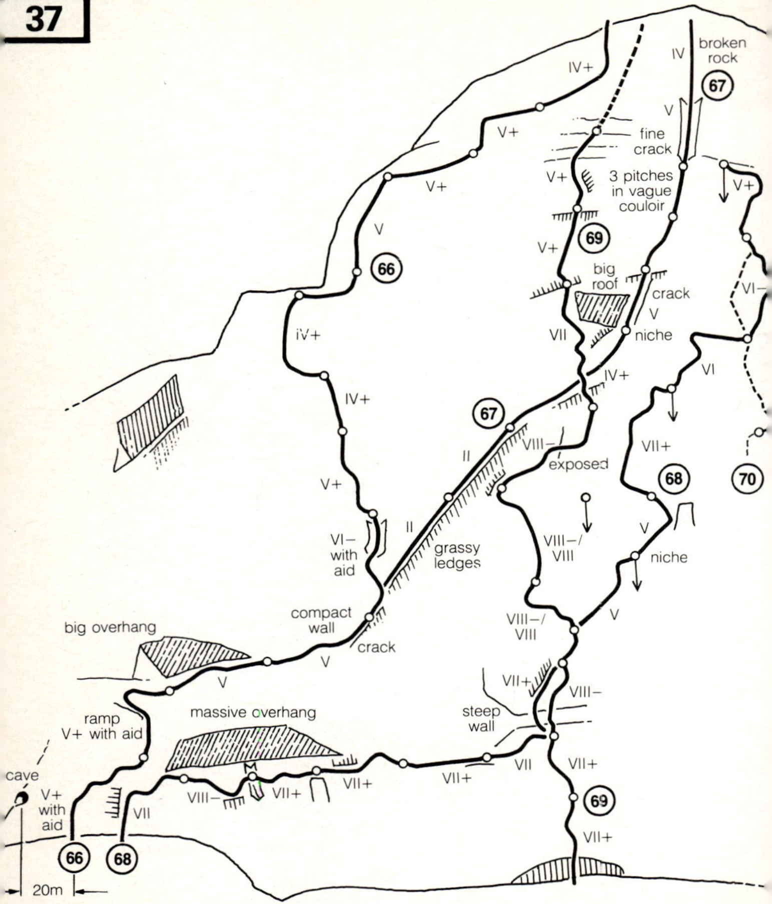
IV+
IV
broken rock
67
V
V+
fine crack
V+
3 pitches in vague couloir
V+
V
69
V+
66
big roof
crack
V
VI–
IV+
VII
niche
VI
IV+
IV+
67
II
VIII–
exposed
VII+
V+
68
70
VI– with aid
II
grassy ledges
VIII–/ VIII
V
niche
compact wall
VIII–/ VIII
V
big overhang
crack
V
V
VII+
VIII–
ramp V+ with aid
massive overhang
steep wall
VII
VII+
cave
V+ with aid
VII
VIII–
VII+
VII+
VII+
69
VII+
66
68
20m

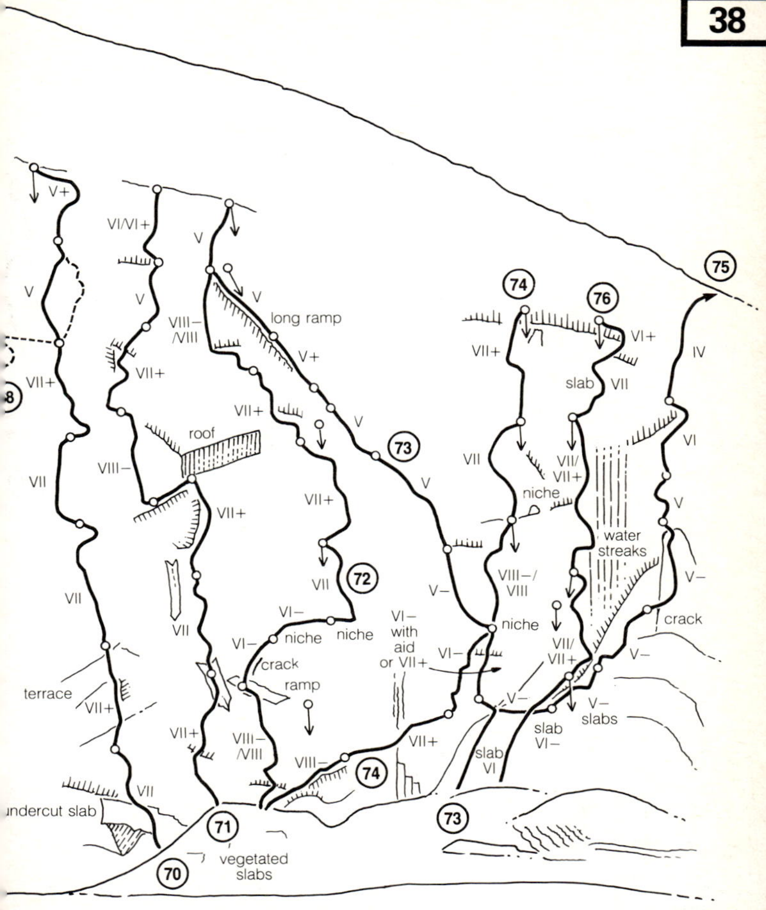

75
74
76
73
72
74
71
70
73
8
V+
VI/VI+
V
V
V
long ramp
V+
V
VIII–
/VIII
VII+
VII+
VII+
roof
VII+
VIII–
VII
VII+
VII+
VII
VII
VII
VI–
niche
niche
VI–
crack
ramp
VIII–
/VIII
VIII–
VII+
VII+
terrace
VII+
VII
undercut slab
vegetated
slabs
VI–
with
aid
or VII+
V
V–
VI–
VII+
VI+
slab
VII
VII
VII/
VII+
niche
VIII–/
VIII
niche
VII/
VII+
water
streaks
IV
VI
V
V–
crack
V–
V–
V–
slabs
slab
VI–
slab
VI

39

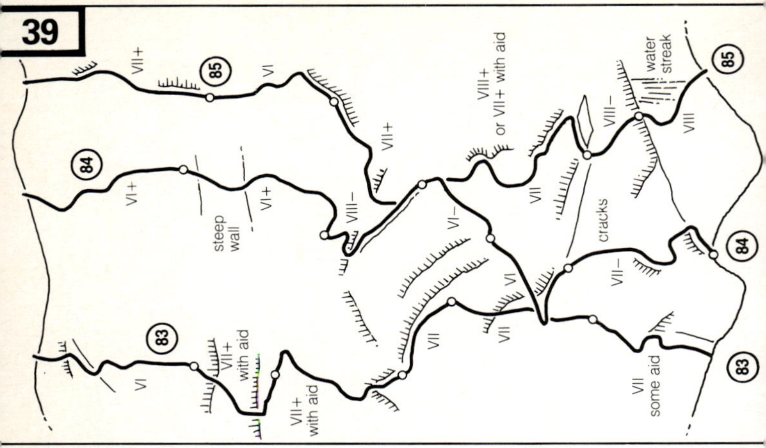
85
84
83
VII+
VI
VI+
steep wall
VIII–
VII+ with aid
VIII+ or VII+ with aid
water streak
cracks
VII
VI–
VII–
VIII
VII some aid

40

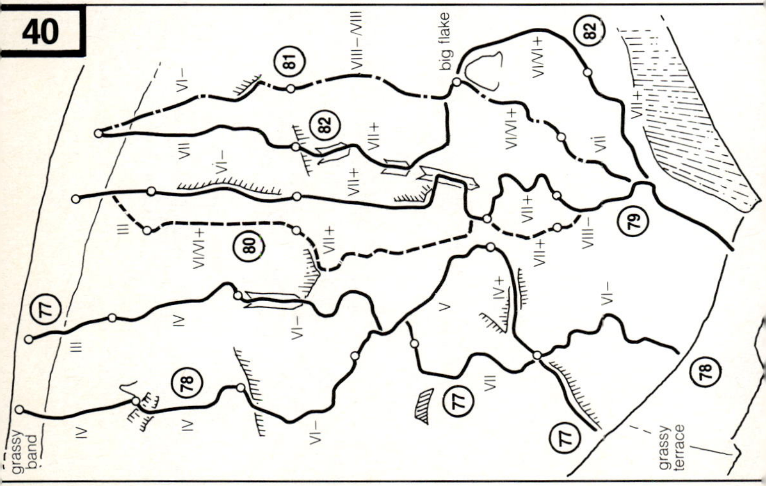
77
78
79
80
81
82
VIII–/VIII
big flake
VI/VI+
VII+
VI–
VII
III
IV
V
IV+
VIII–
grassy band
grassy terrace

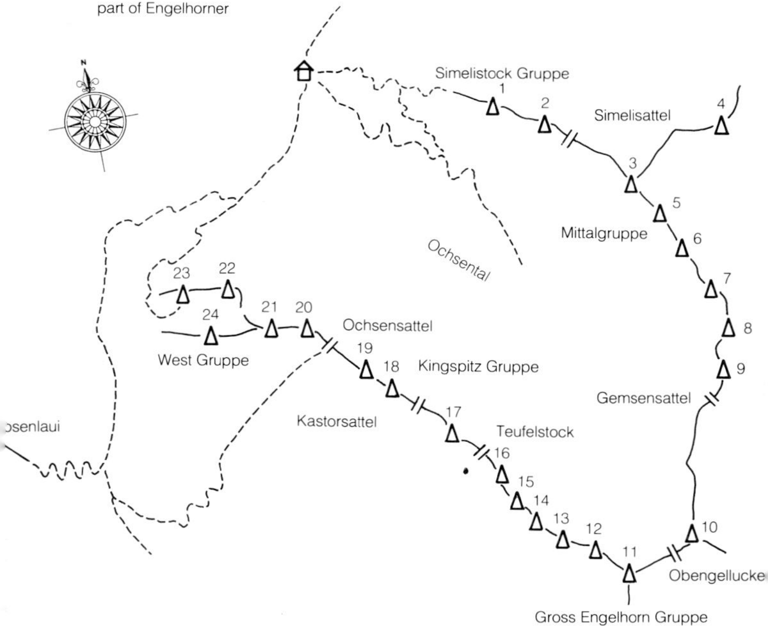

1.	Kl. Simelistock	13.	Niklausspitze
2.	Gr. Simelistock	14.	Froschkopf
3.	Vorderspitze	15, 16.	Prinzen
4.	Hohjägiburg	17.	Kingspitz
5.	Gertrudespitze	18.	Kastor
6.	Ulrichspitze	19.	Pollux
7.	Mittlespitze	20.	Sattelspitzen
8.	Kl. Engelhorn	21.	Engelburg
9.	Gemsenspitze	22.	Tannenspitze
10.	Urbachengechorn Fore-Summit	23.	Rosenlauistock
11.	Gr. Engelhorn	24.	Breitenbodenturm
12.	Maubenstock		

Hinter and Vorder Galmihorn and Wasenhorn N Flank

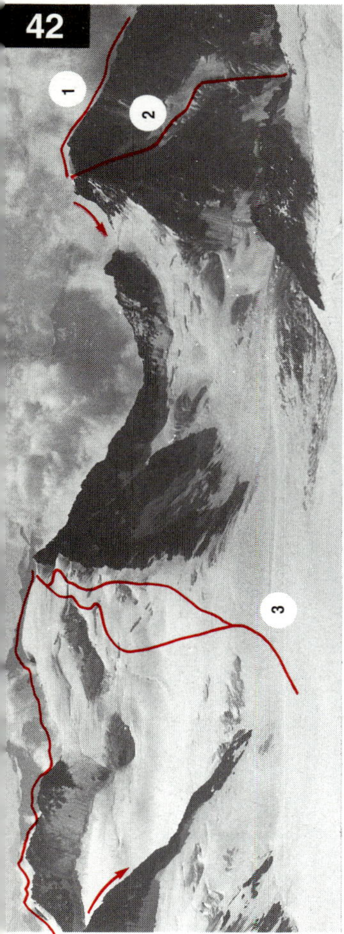

Bächlistock and Gross Diamanstock E Side

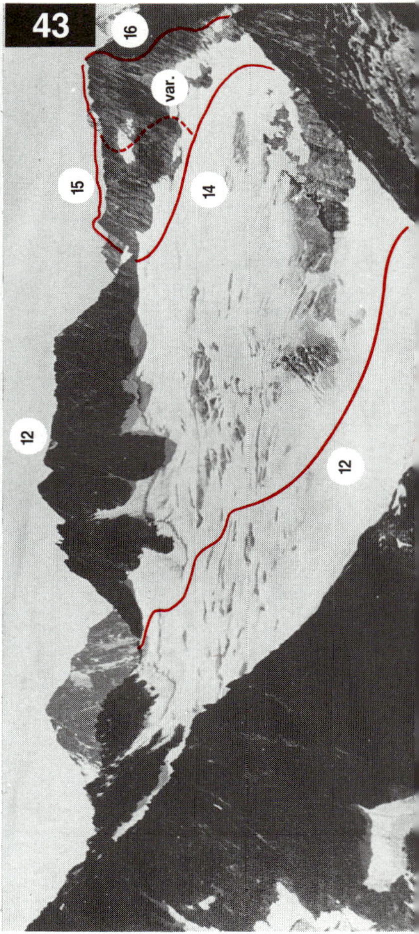

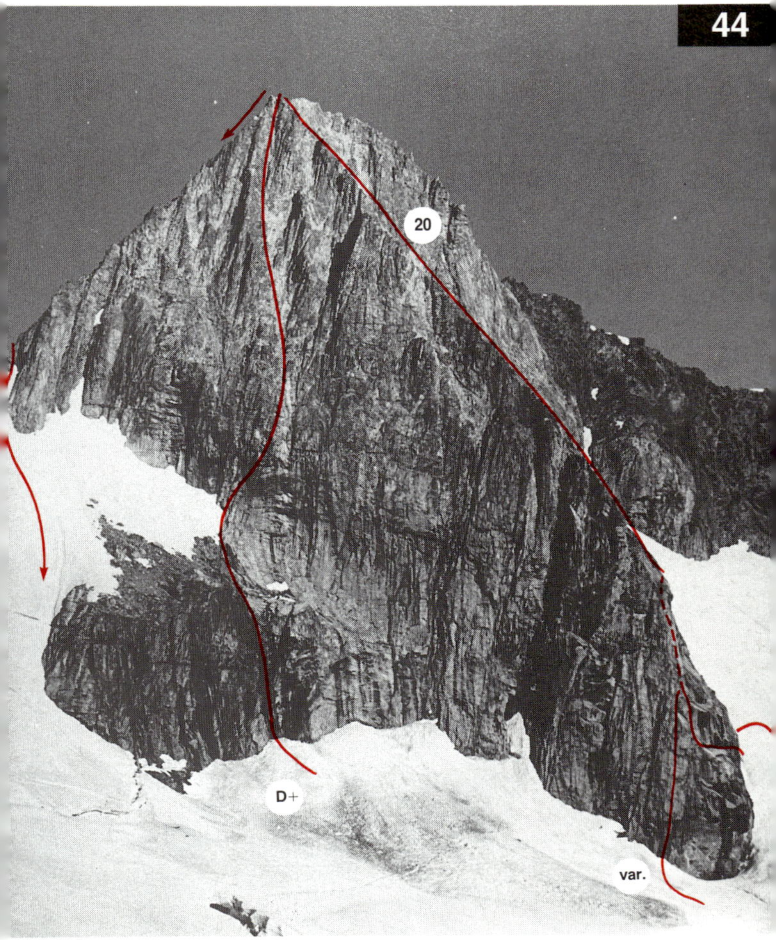
20
D+
var.

45

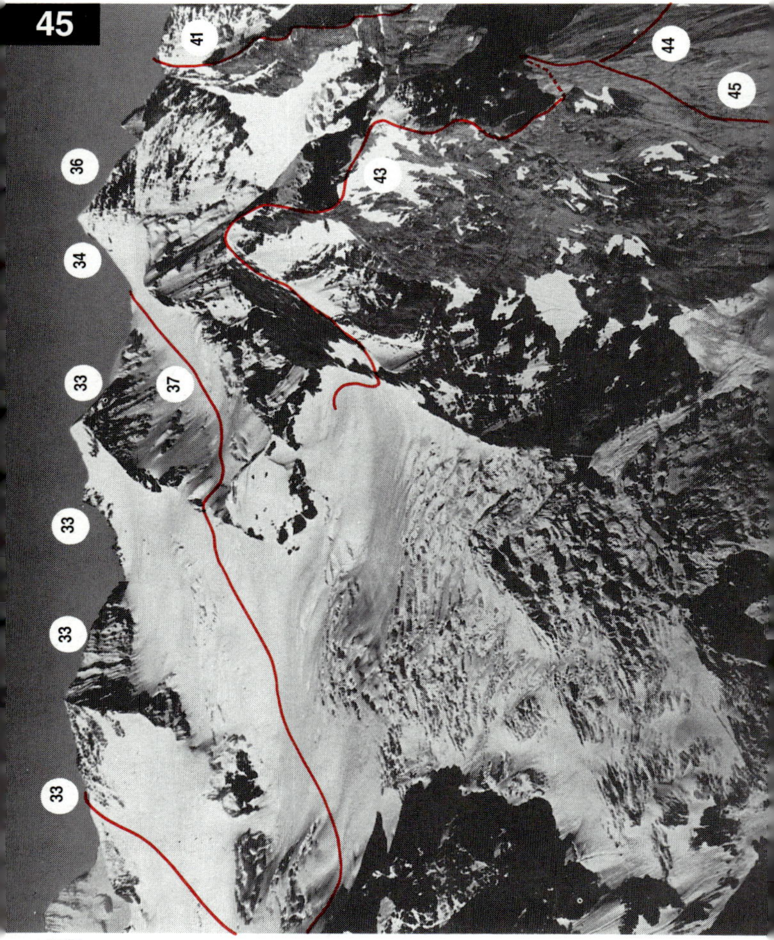

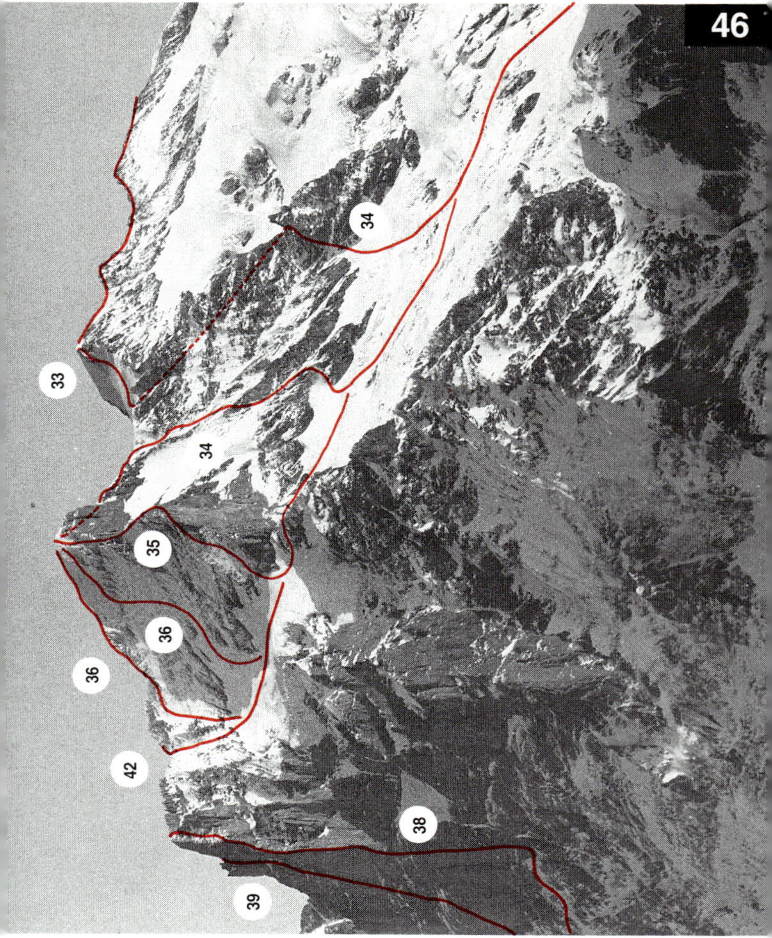
46
34
33
34
35
36
36
42
38
39

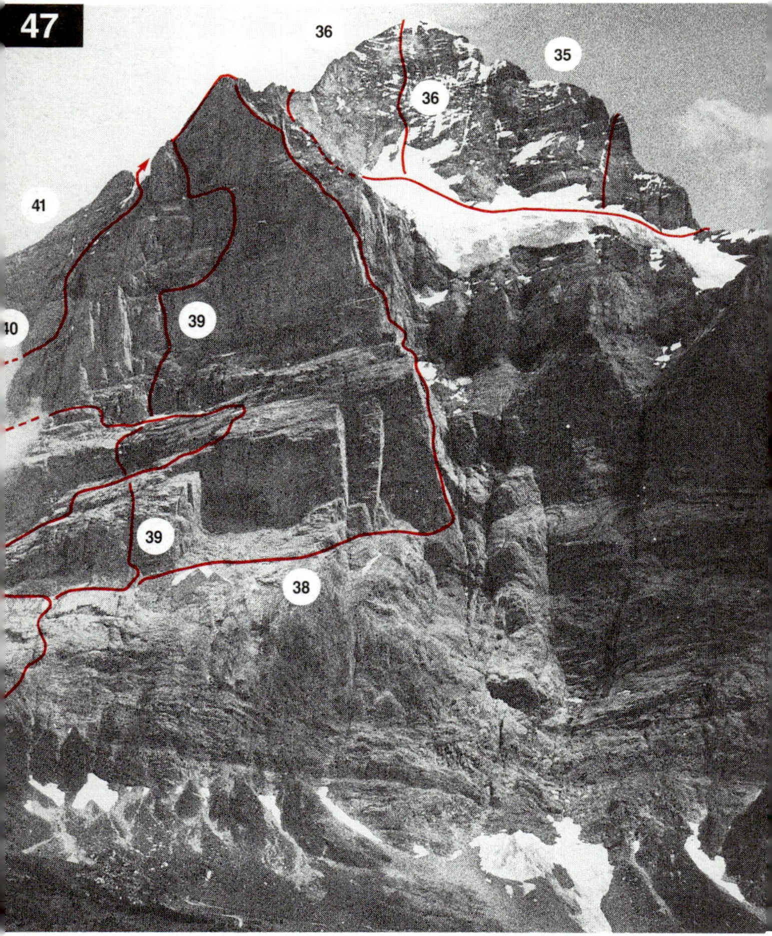
47
36
35
36
41
40
39
39
38

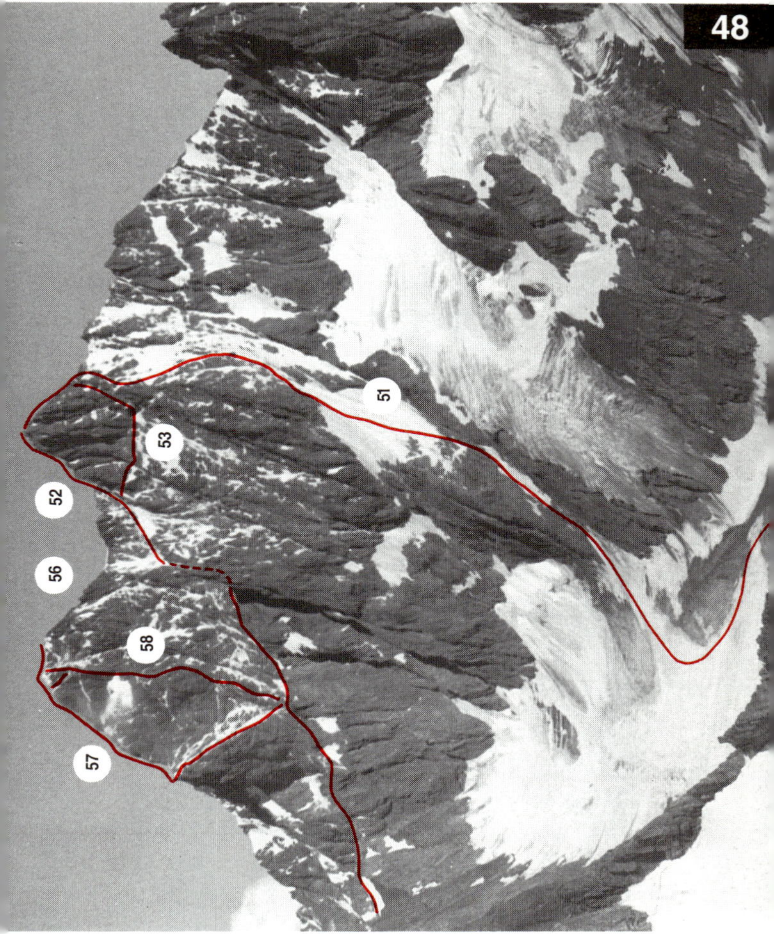
51
53
52
56
58
57

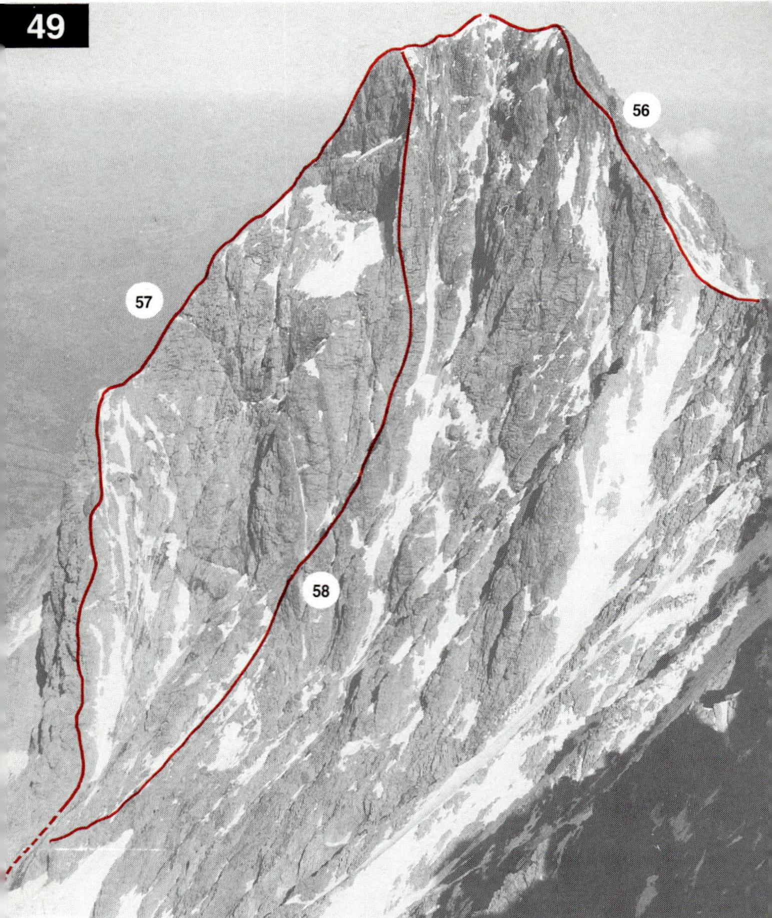
56
57
58

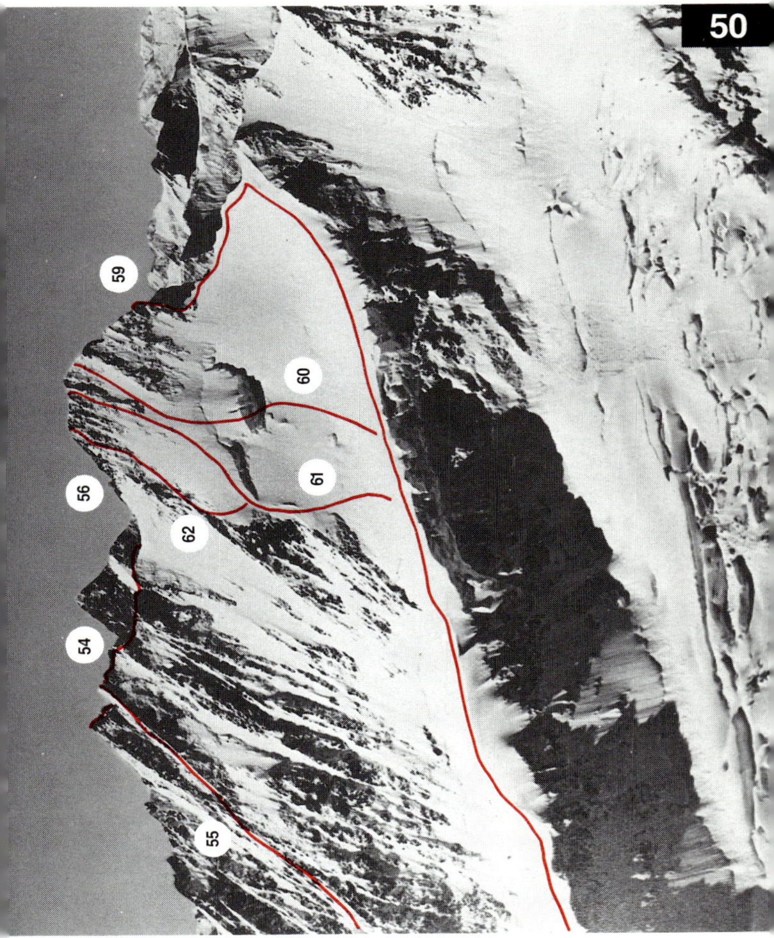
59
60
61
56
62
54
55

51

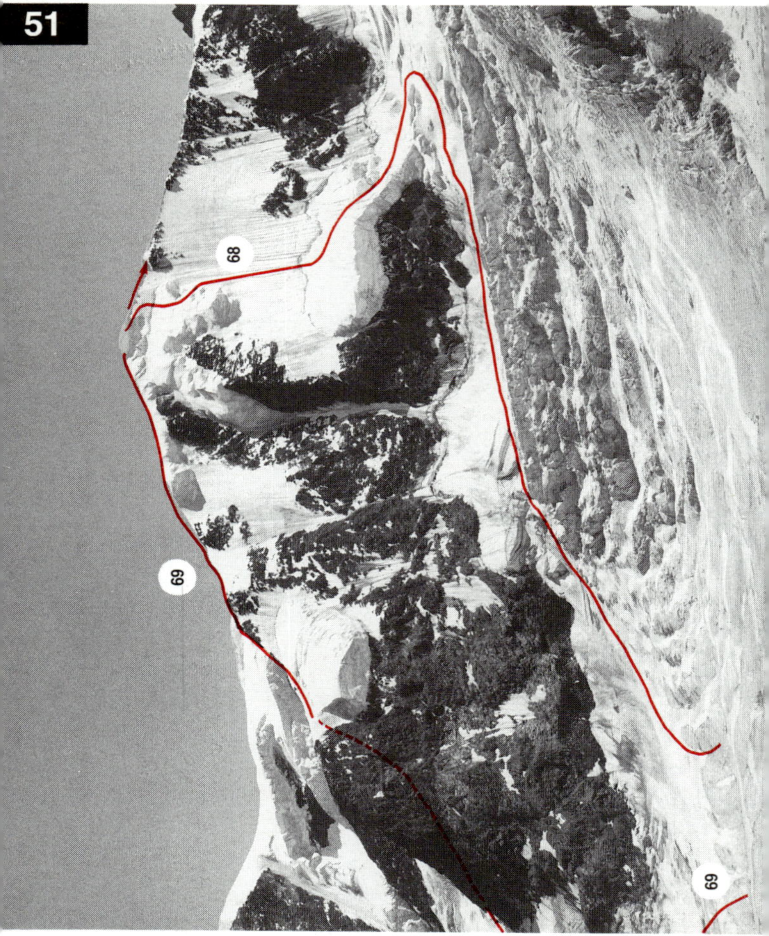

Altmann and Oberaarhorn S Flank

Studerhorn S Flank

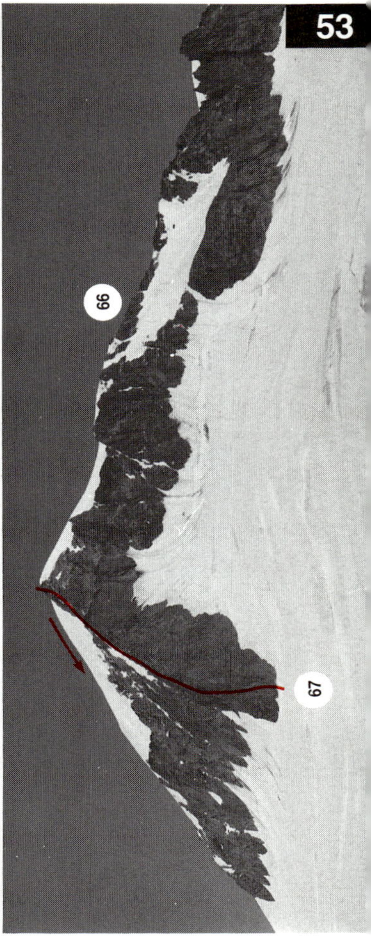

54

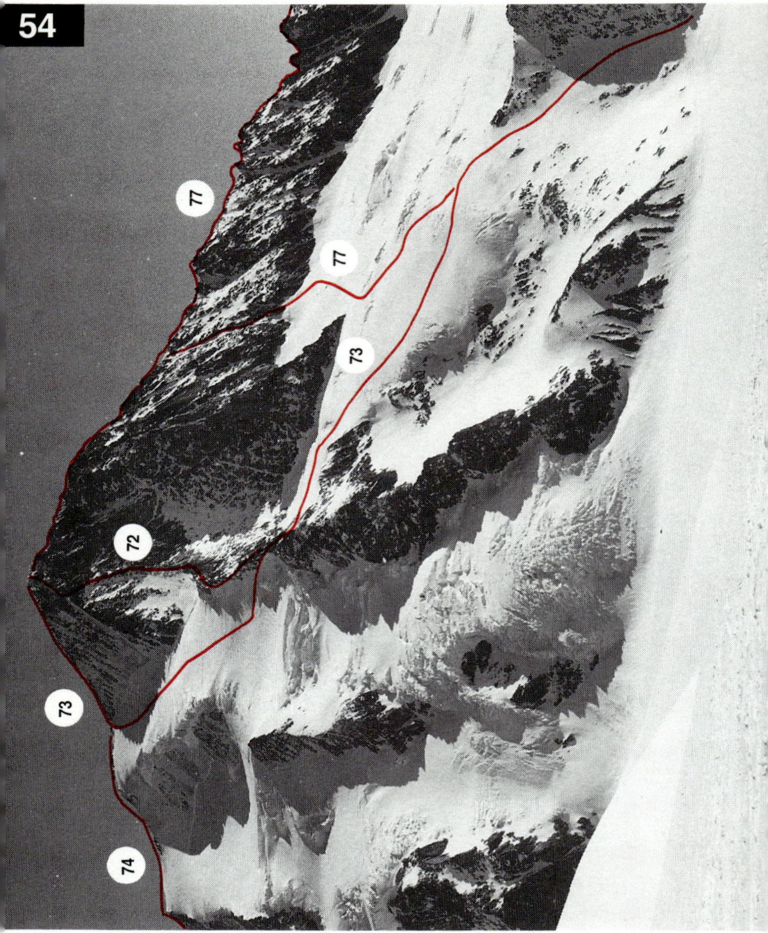

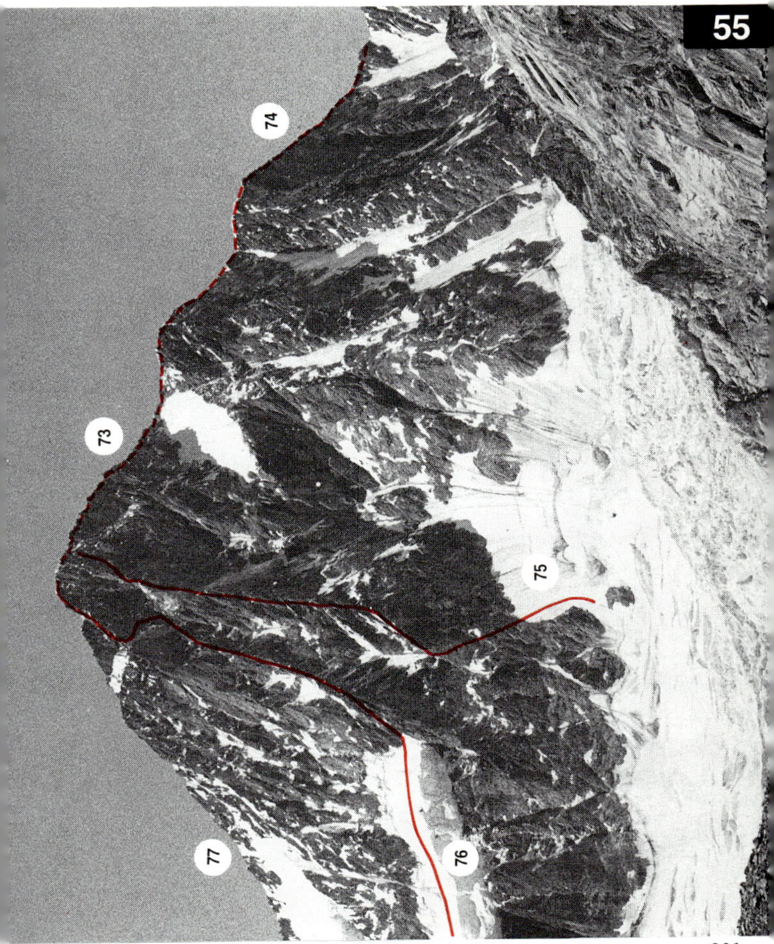
74
73
75
77
76

Finsteraarhorn SE Ridge

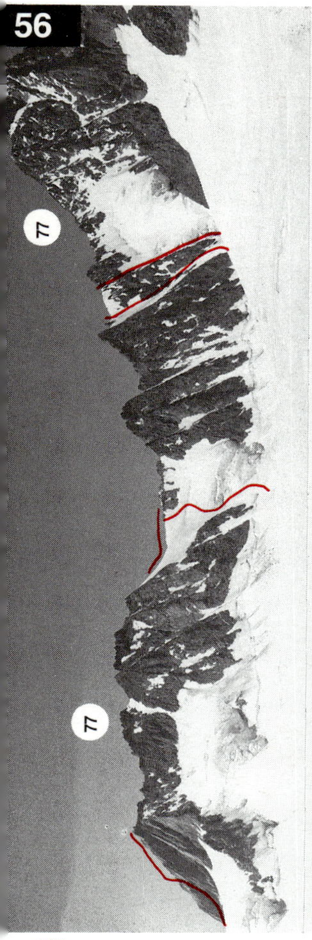

Gross Wannenhorn, Schönbielhorn and Fiescher Gabelhorn E Flank

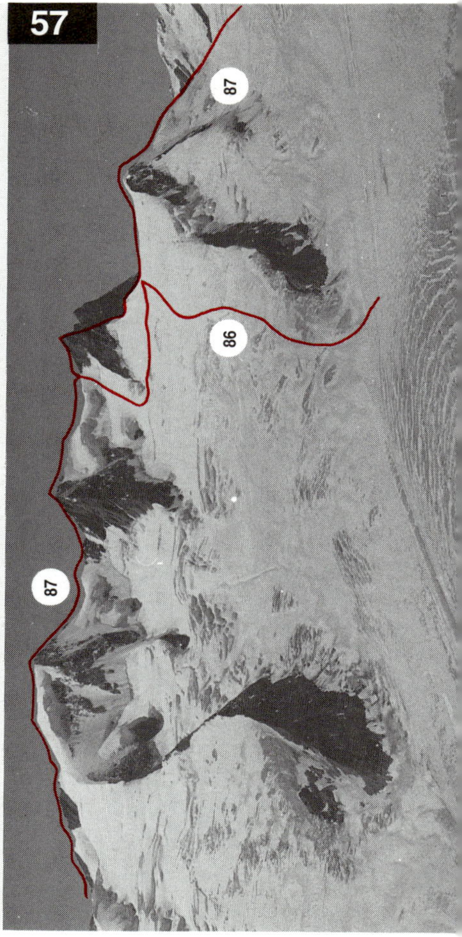

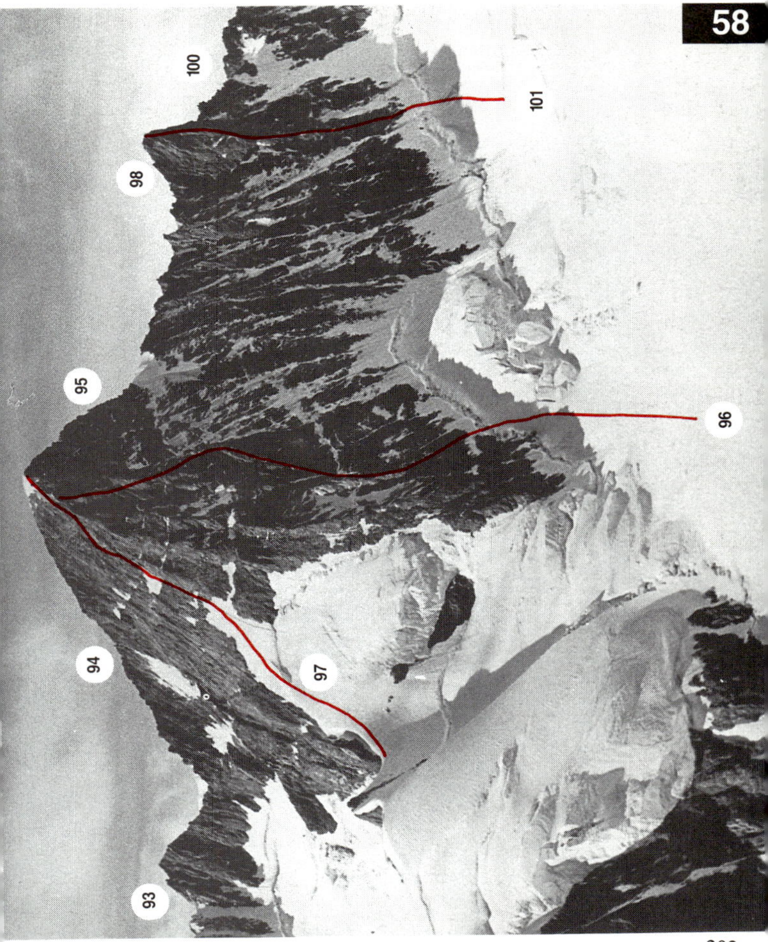
100
101
98
95
96
94
97
93

Gross and Hinter Fiescherhorn NW Flank

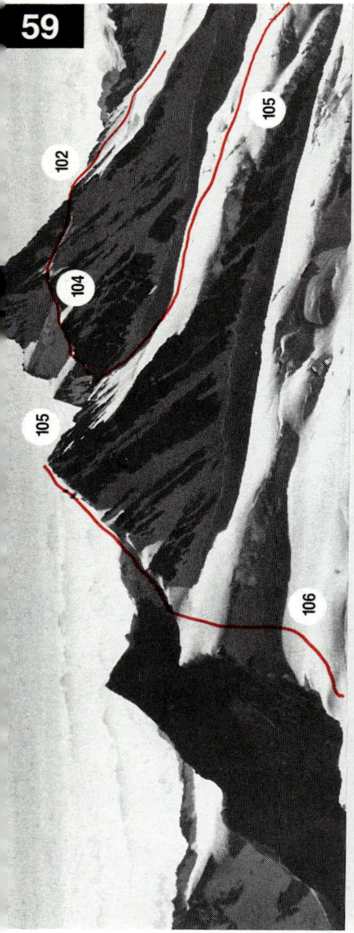

Fiescherwand

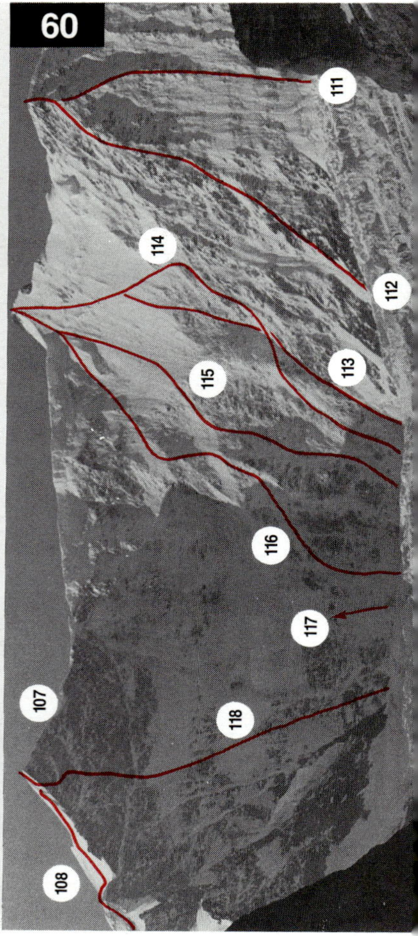

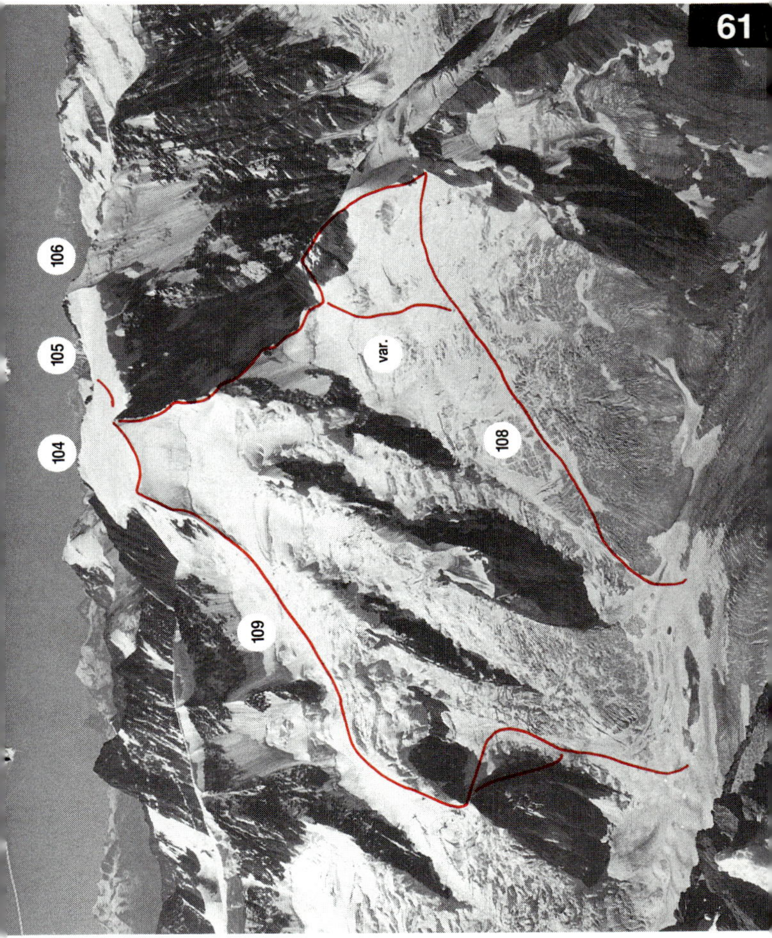
106
105
104
var.
108
109

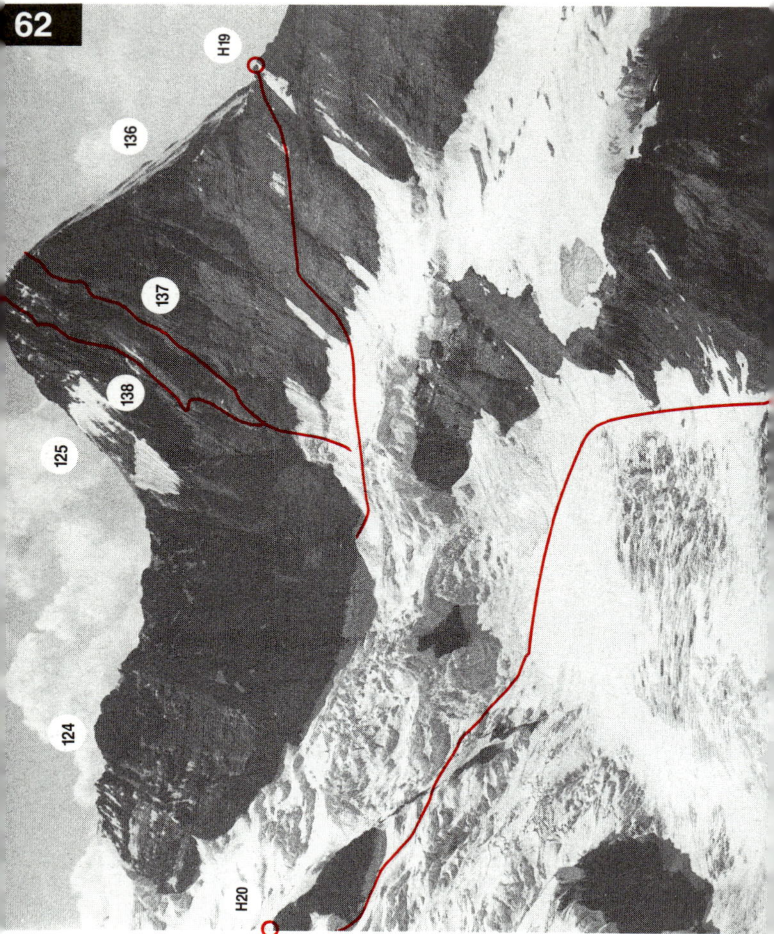
62
H19
136
137
138
125
124
H20

63
126

64

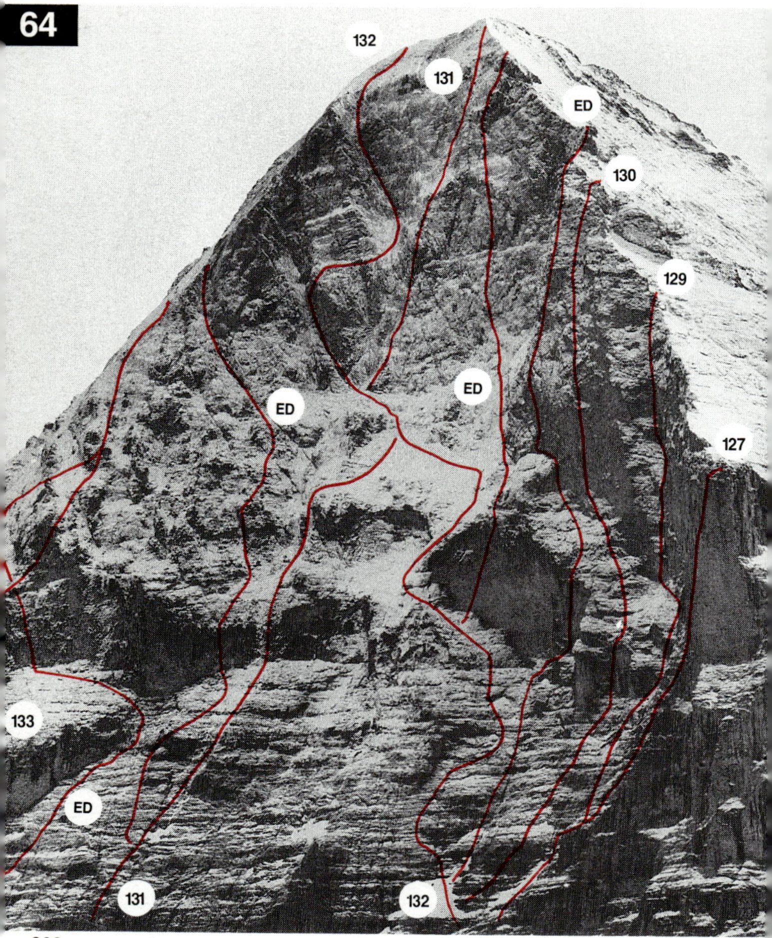

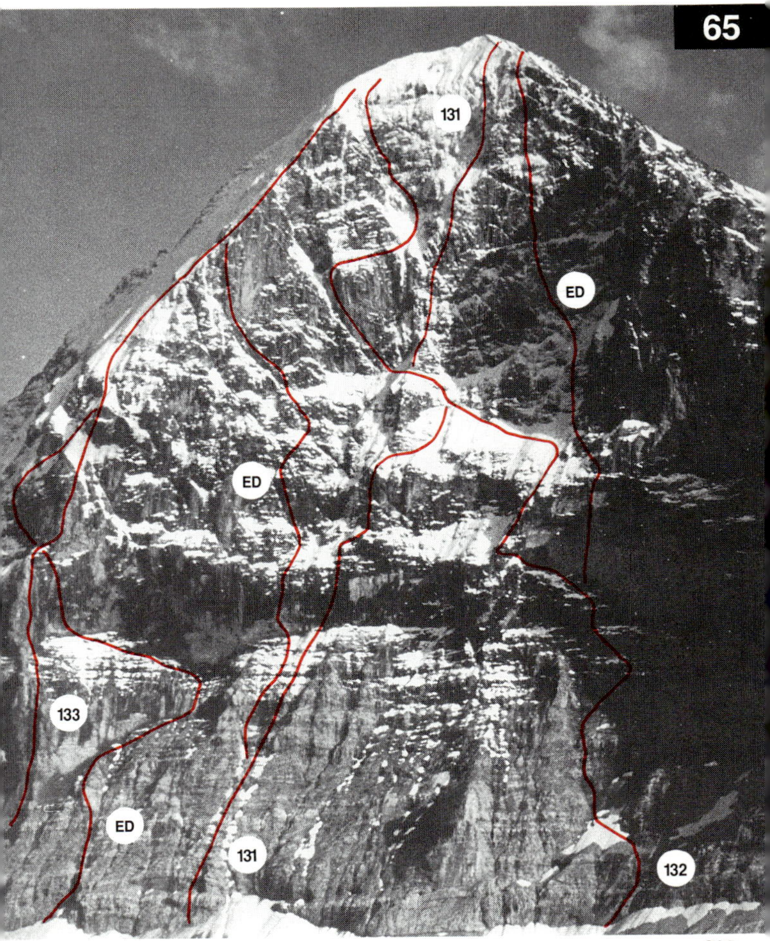
131
ED
ED
133
ED
131
132

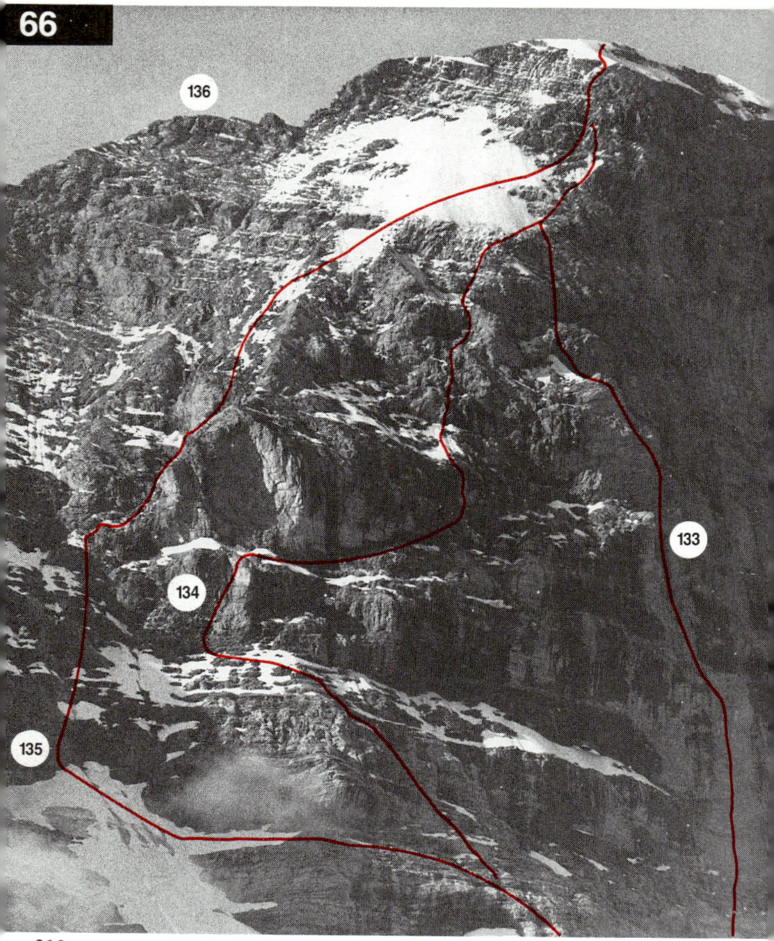
66
136
134
135
133

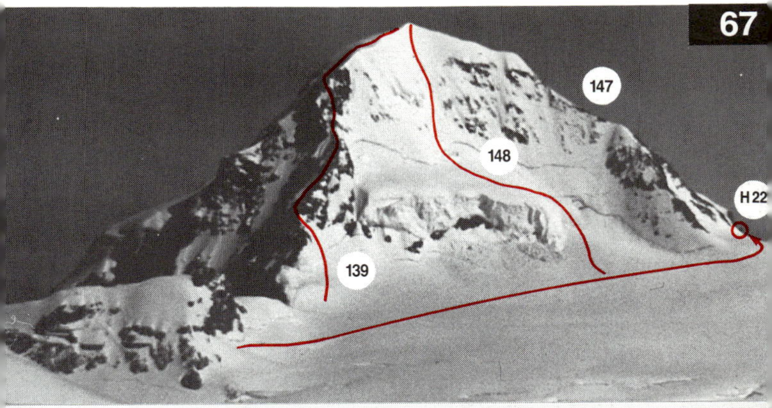

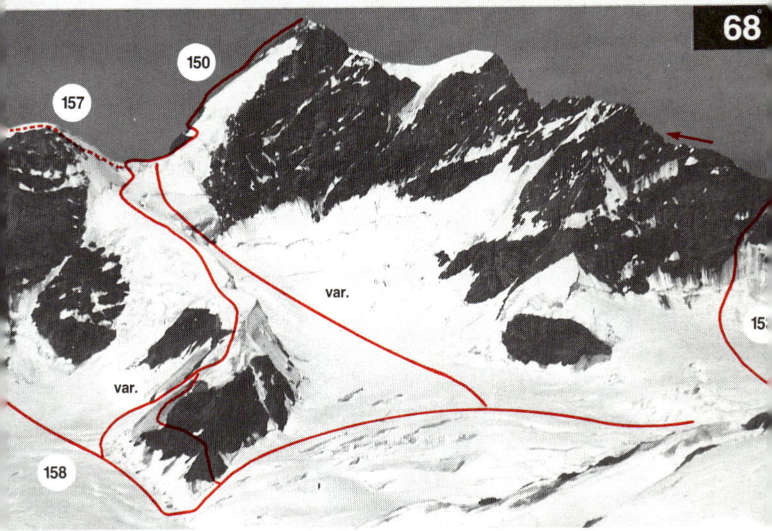

Jungfrau S Flank

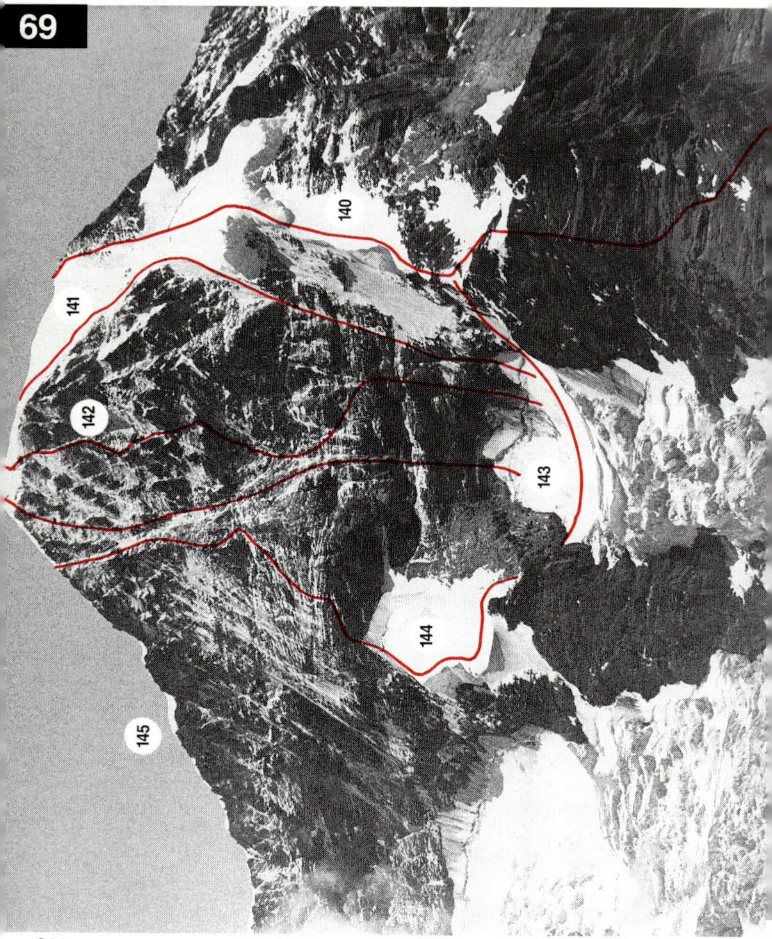
69
140
141
142
143
144
145

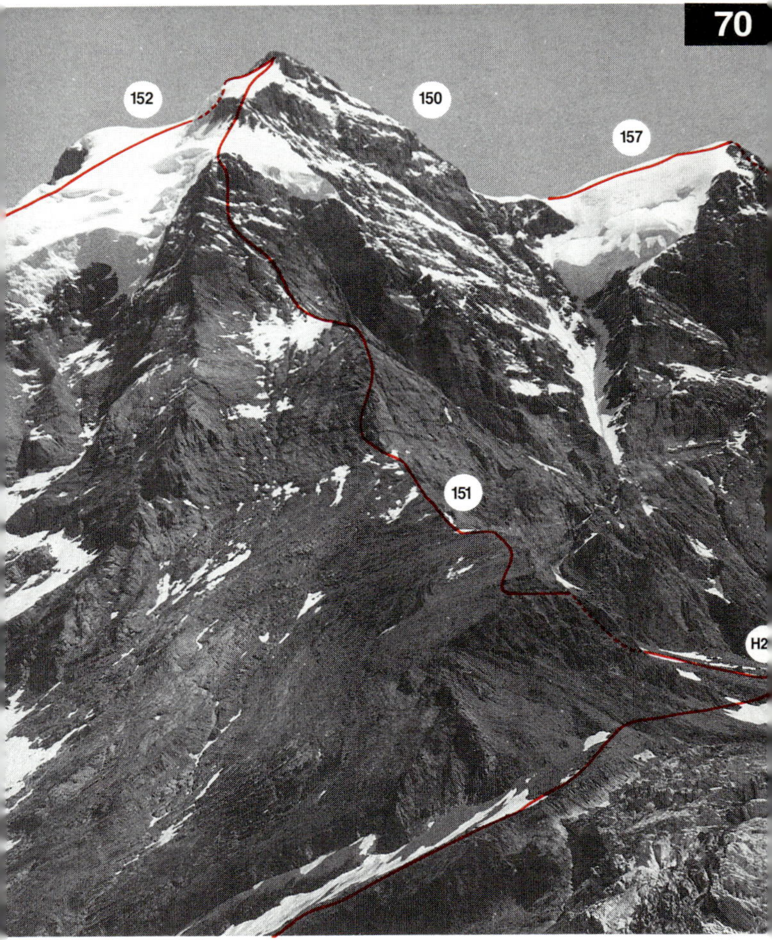
70
152
150
157
151
H2

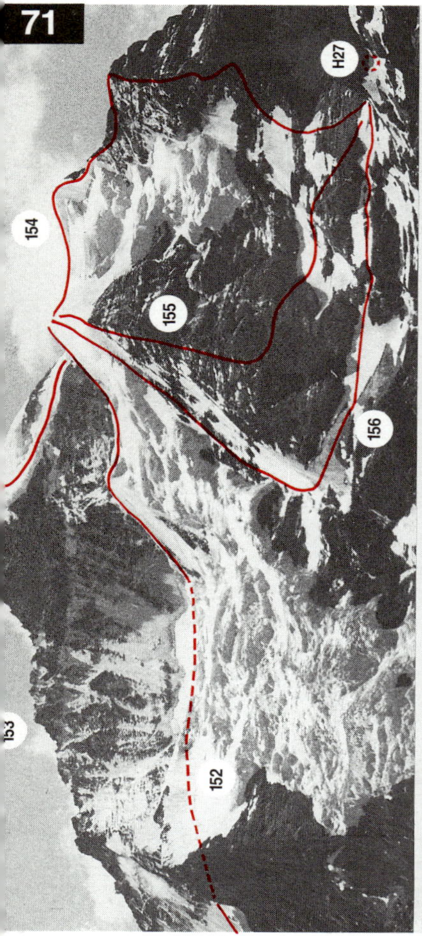
71
H27
154
155
156
153
152

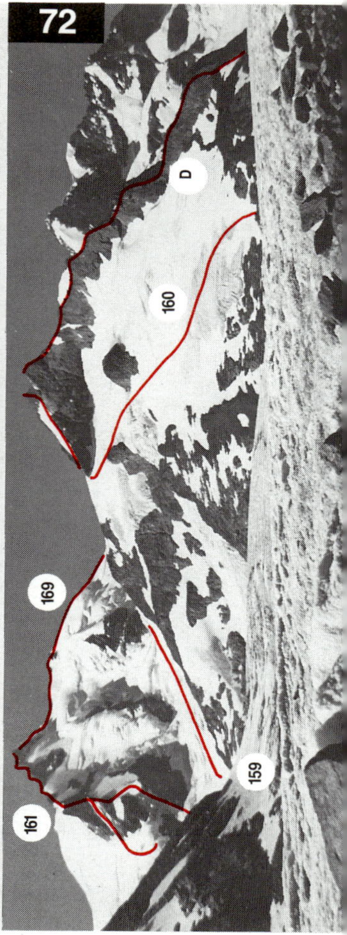
72
D
160
169
159
161

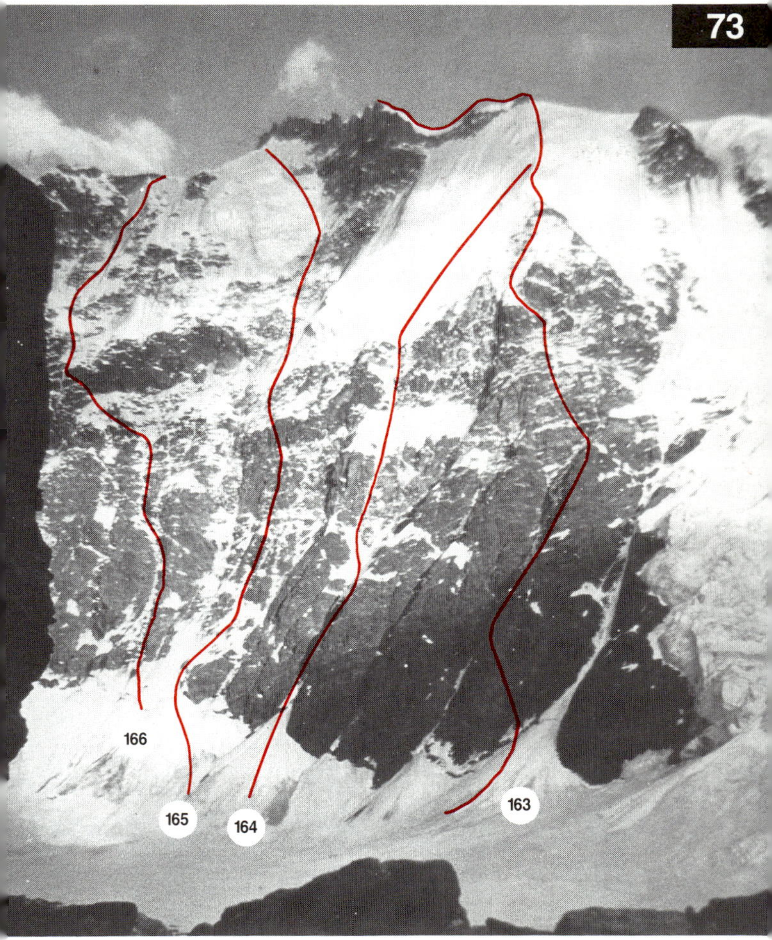
73
166
165
164
163

Äbeni Flue N Face

74

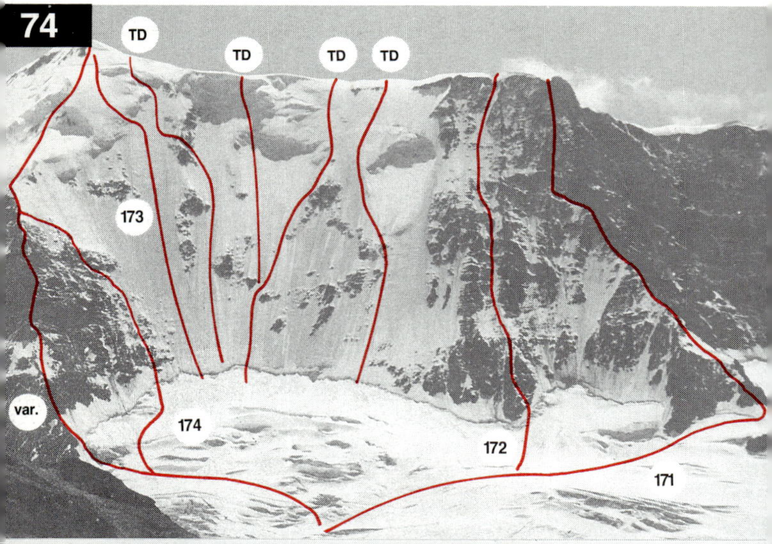

75

 Tschingelhorn S Flank

76

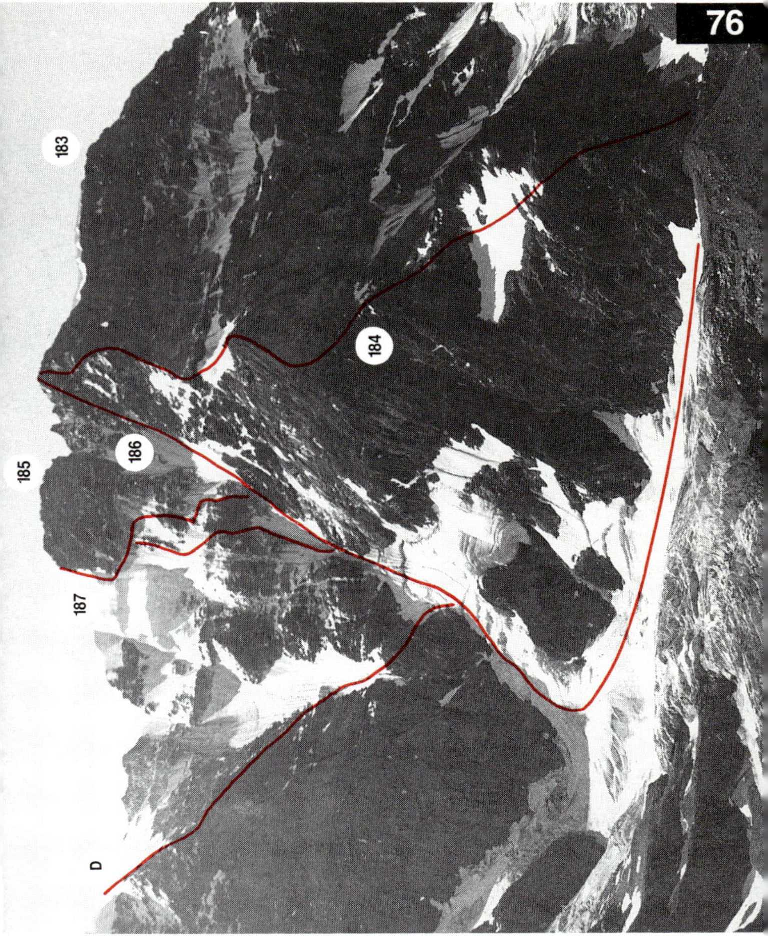

Lauterbrunnen Breithorn N Face (E Side)

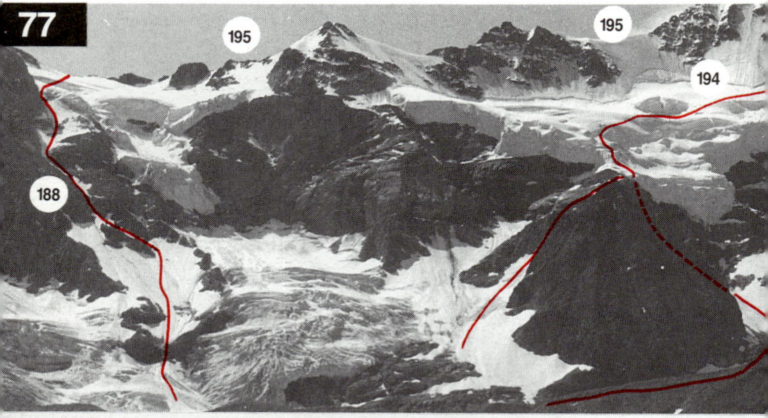

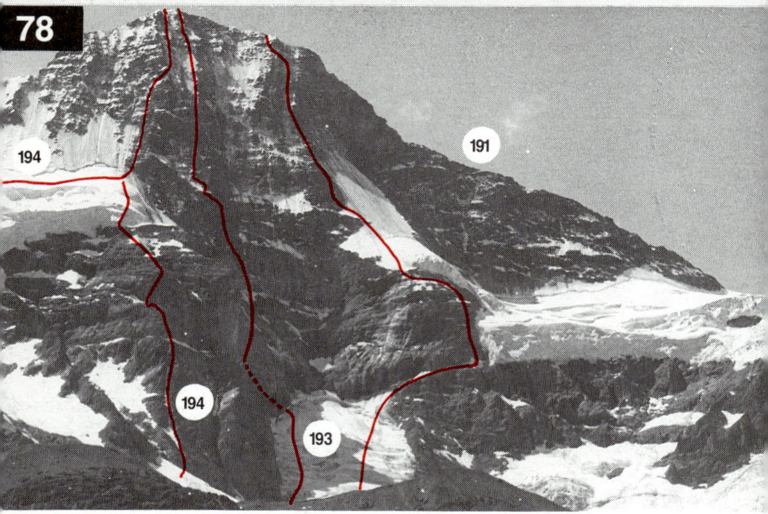

 Lauterbrunnen Breithorn N Face (W Side)

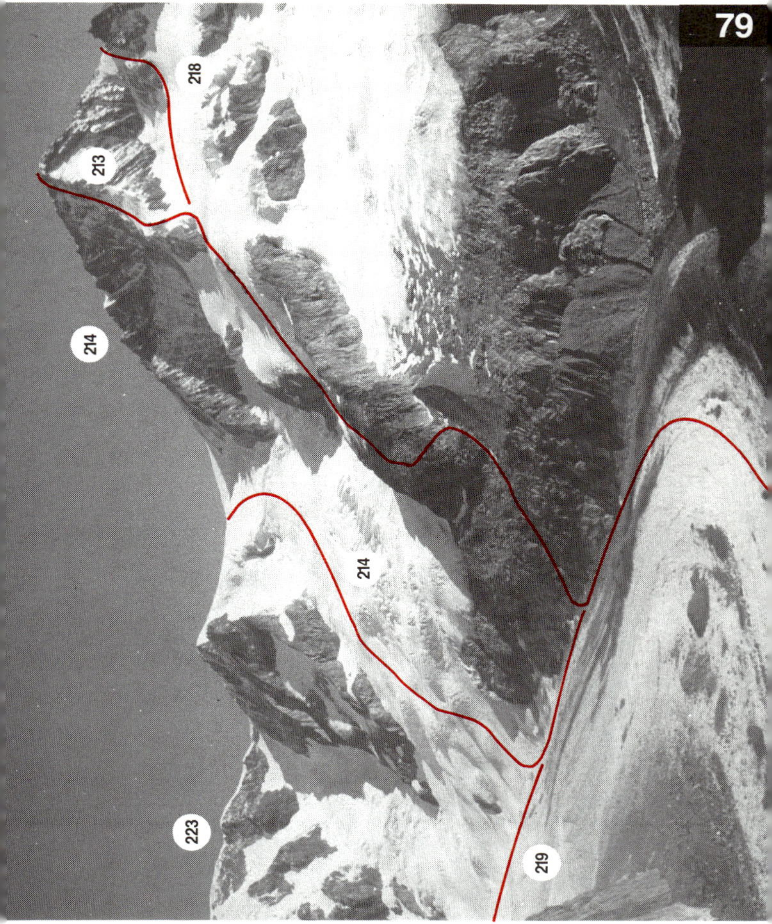
79
218
213
214
214
223
219

Aletschhorn N Face (Winter)

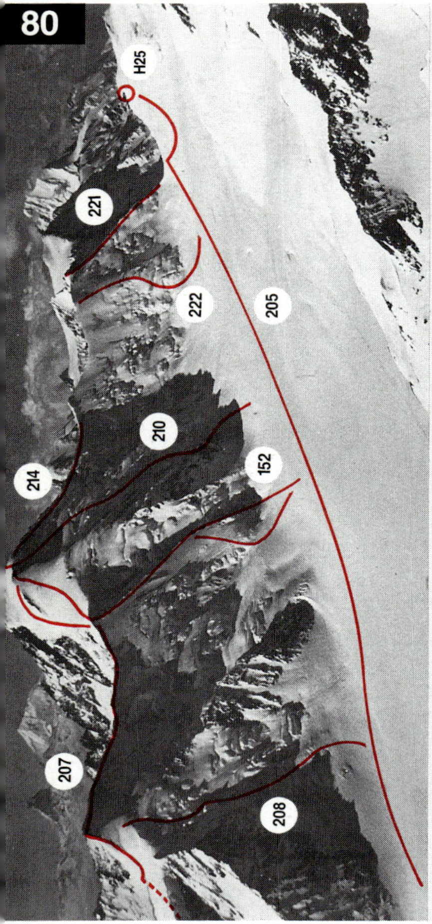

Wysshorn S Face

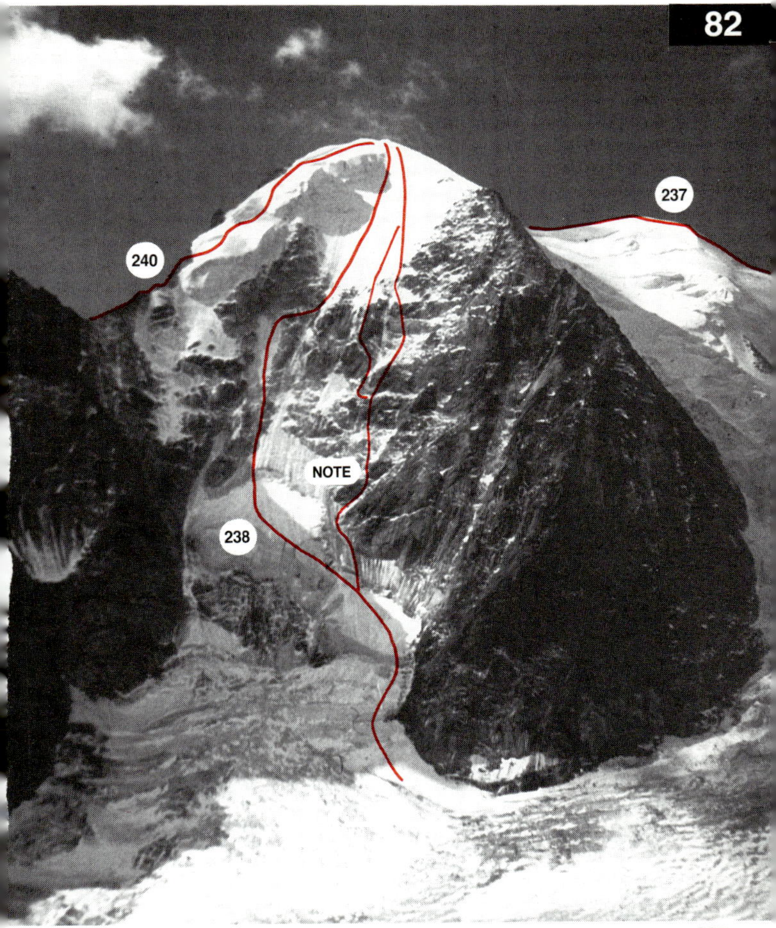
82
237
240
NOTE
238

83

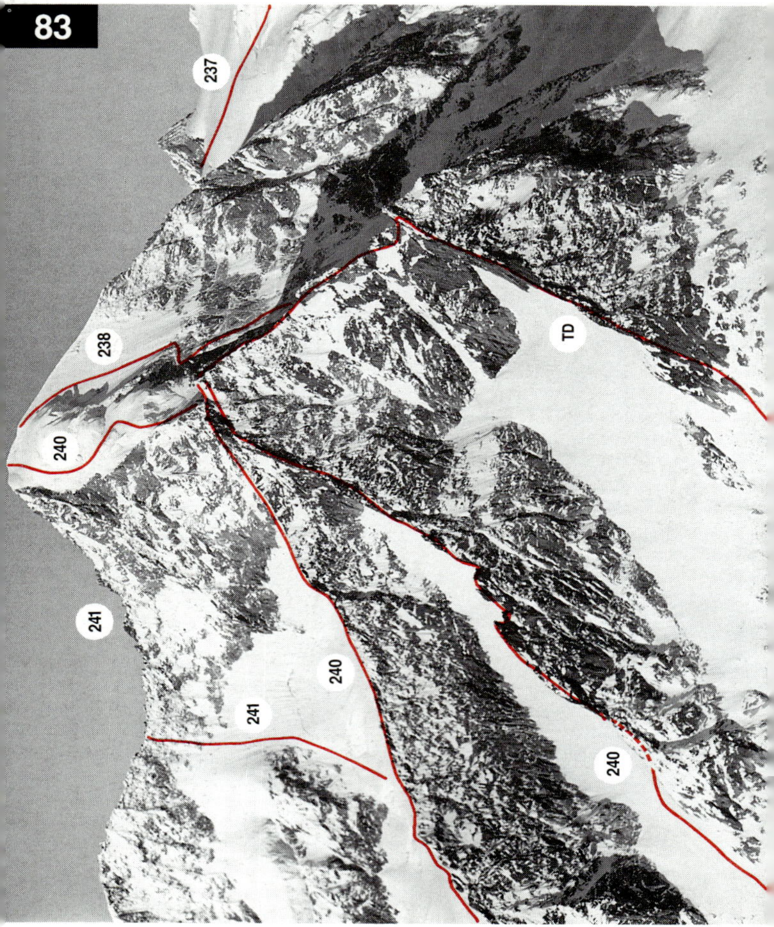

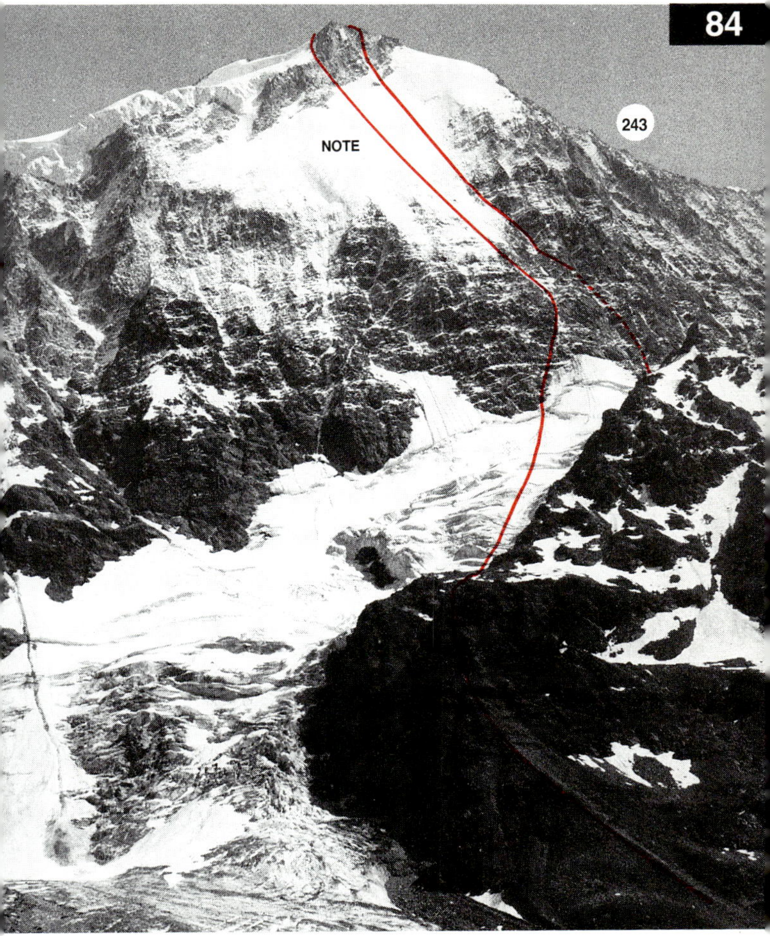
243
NOTE

85

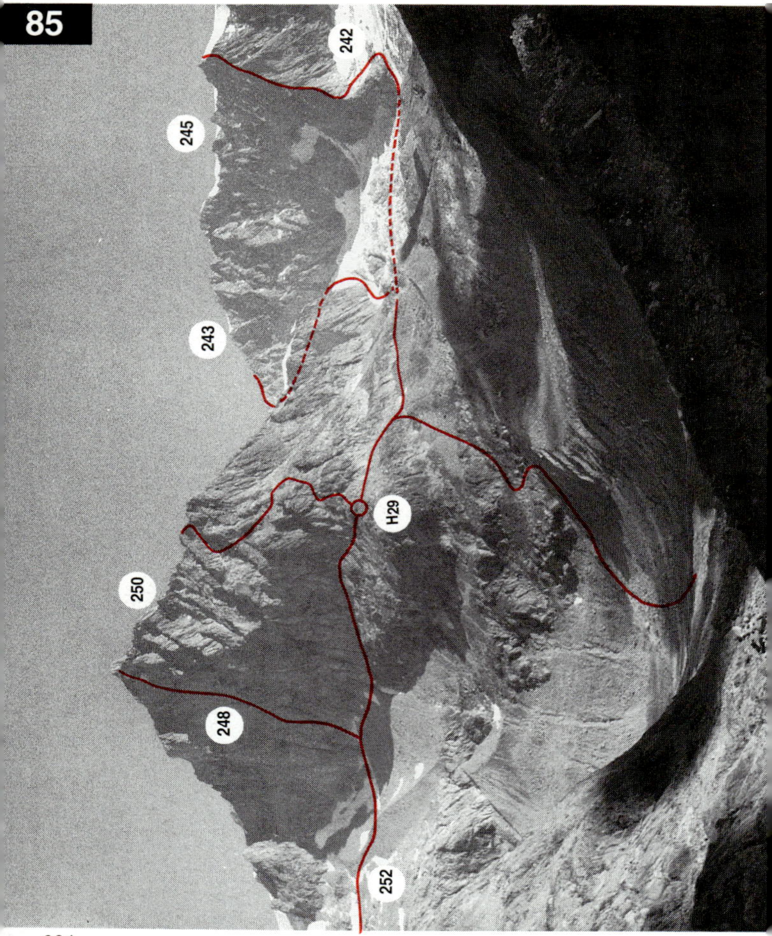

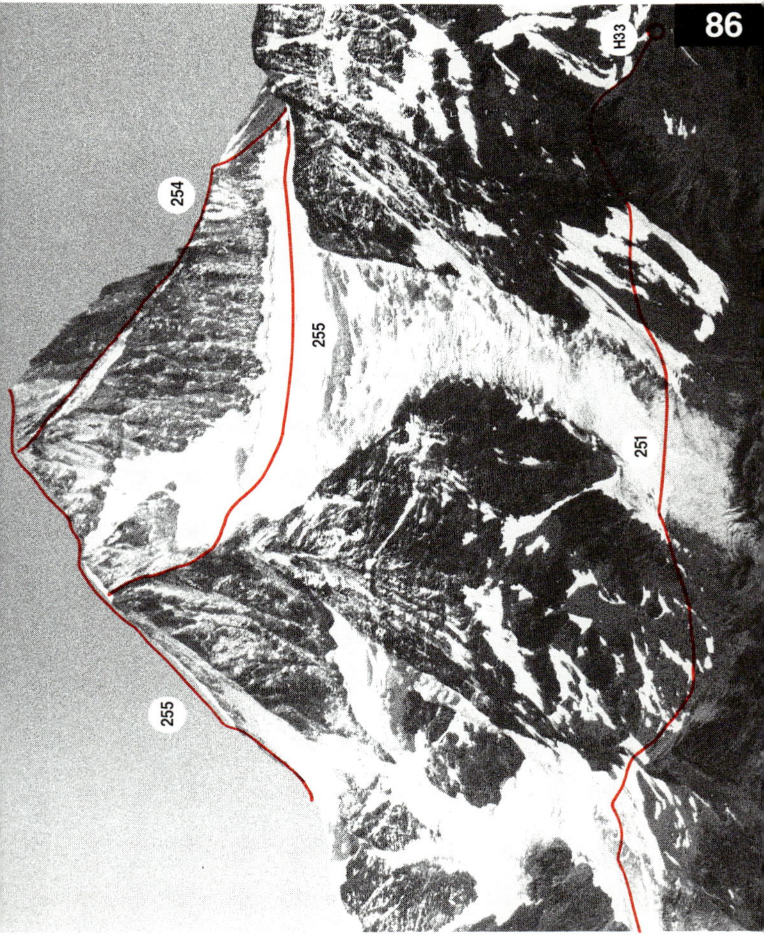
86
H33
254
255
251
255

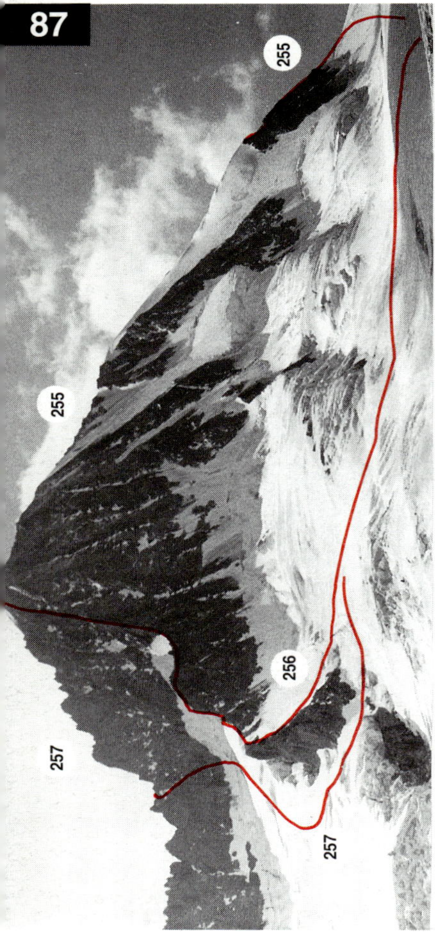
87
255
255
256
257
257

88
259
258

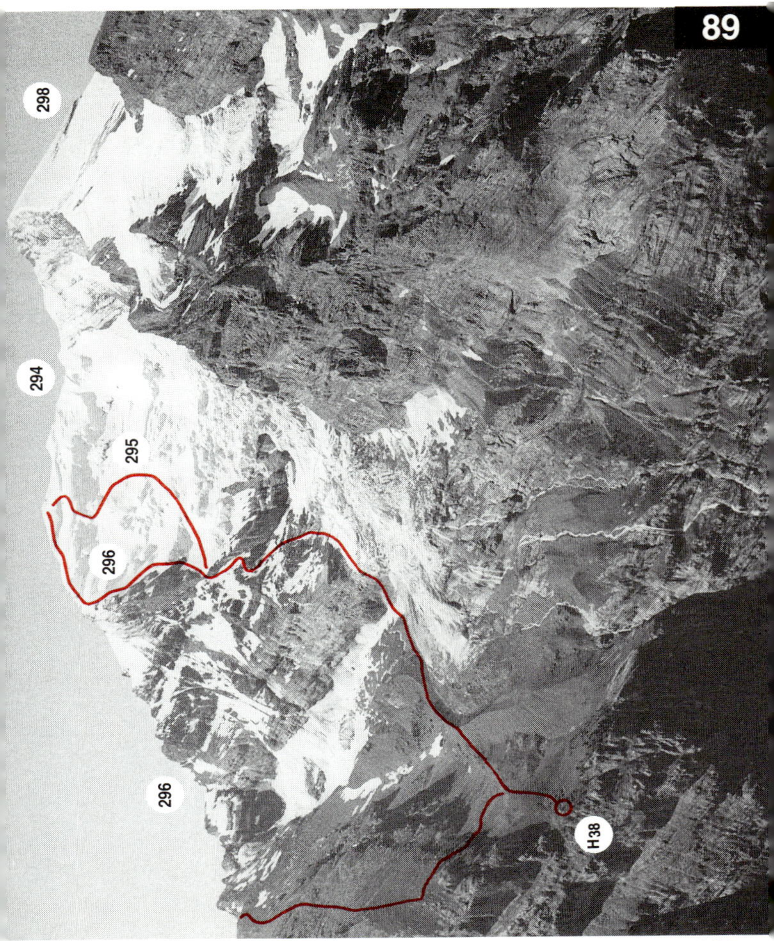
298
294
295
296
296
H38

90

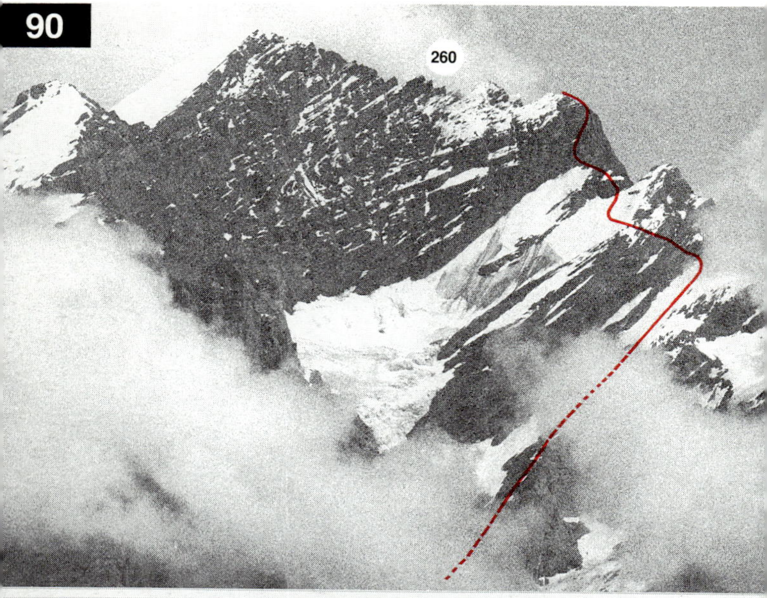

91

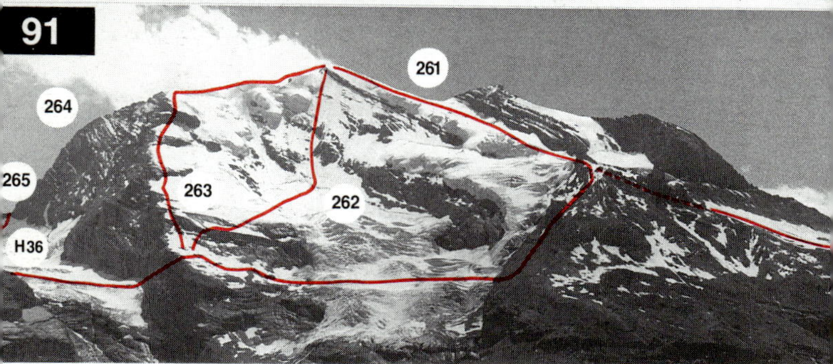

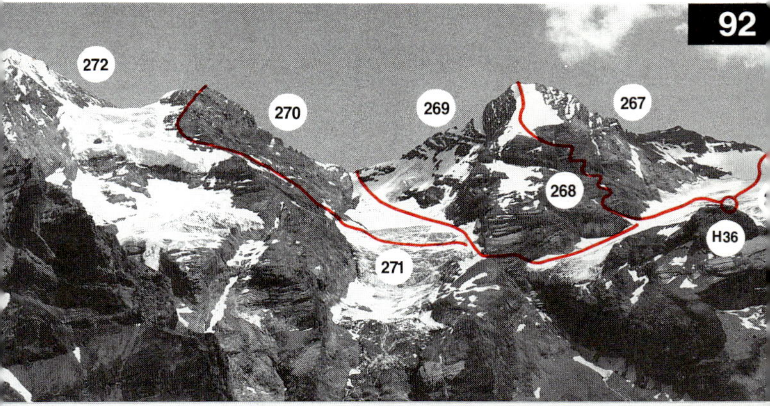
92
272
270
269
267
268
271
H36

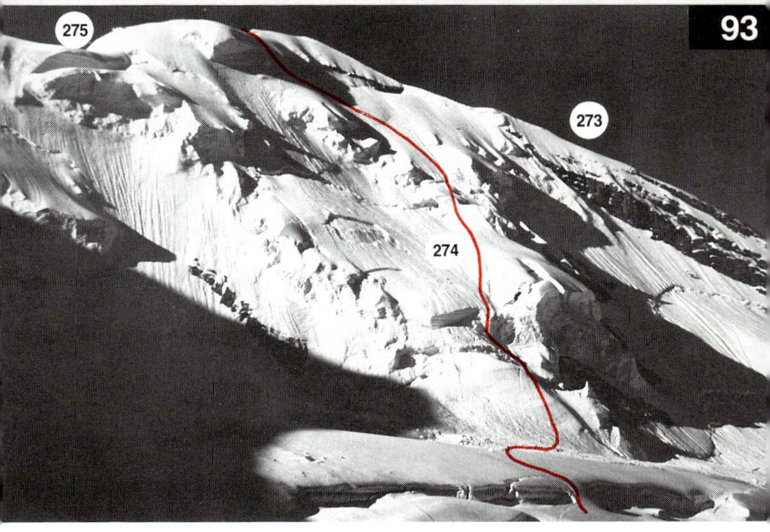
93
275
273
274

94

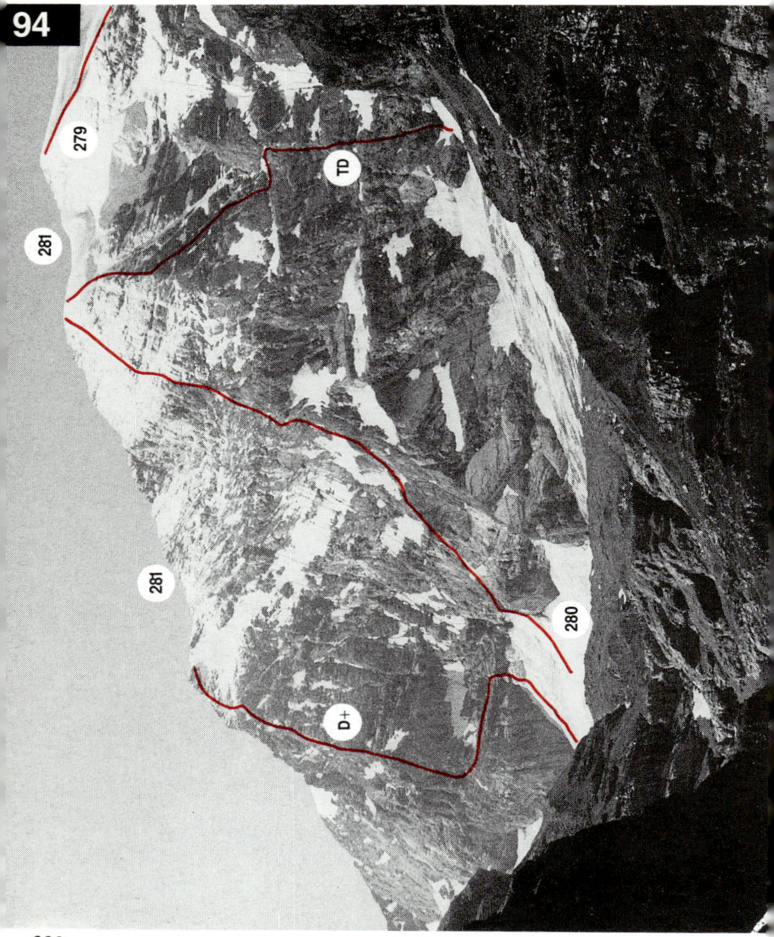

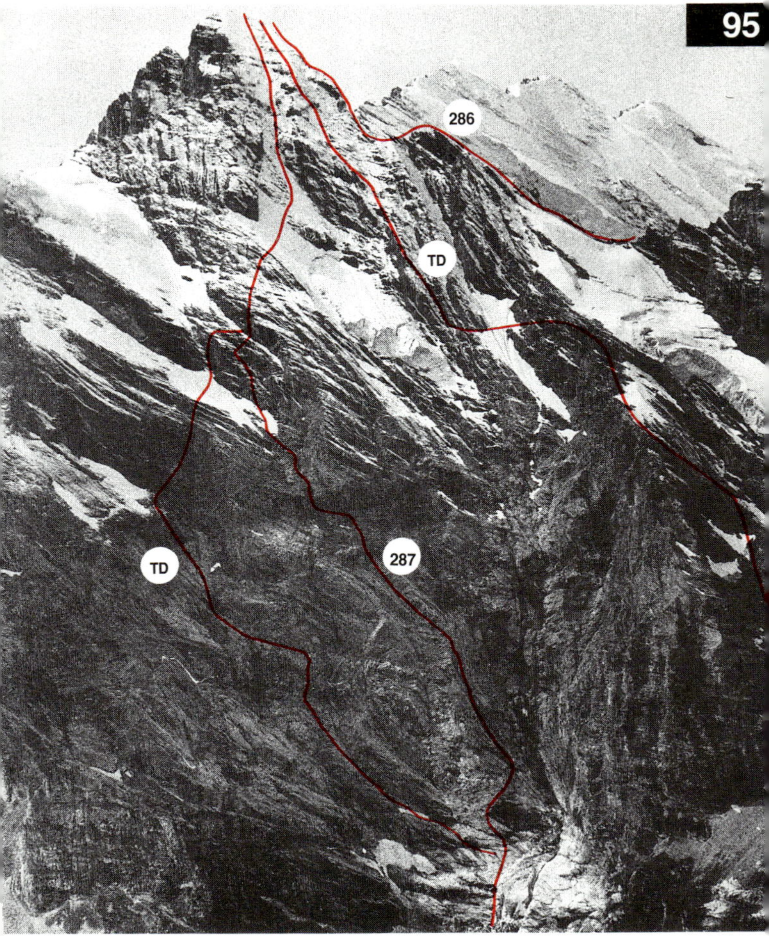
286
TD
TD
287

96

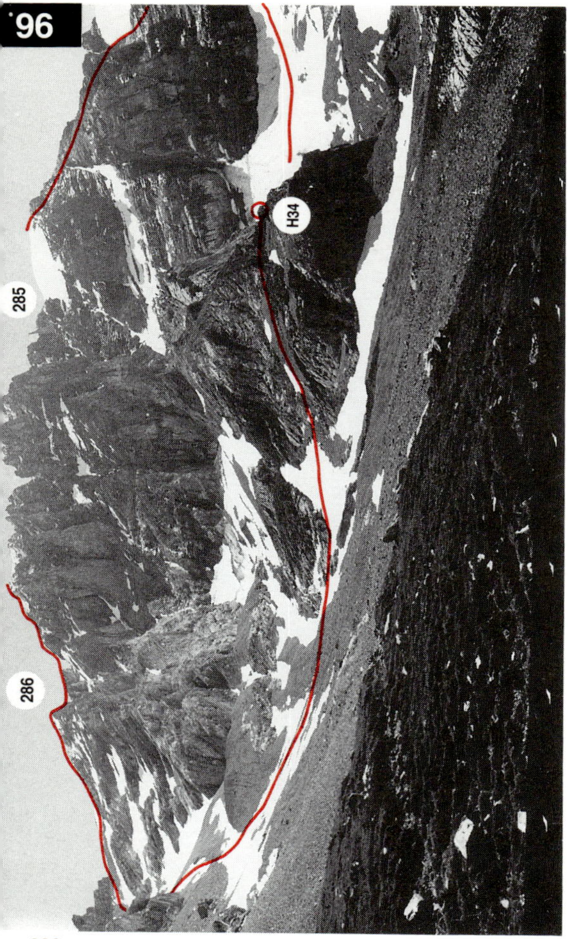

Rock Climbing Areas

97

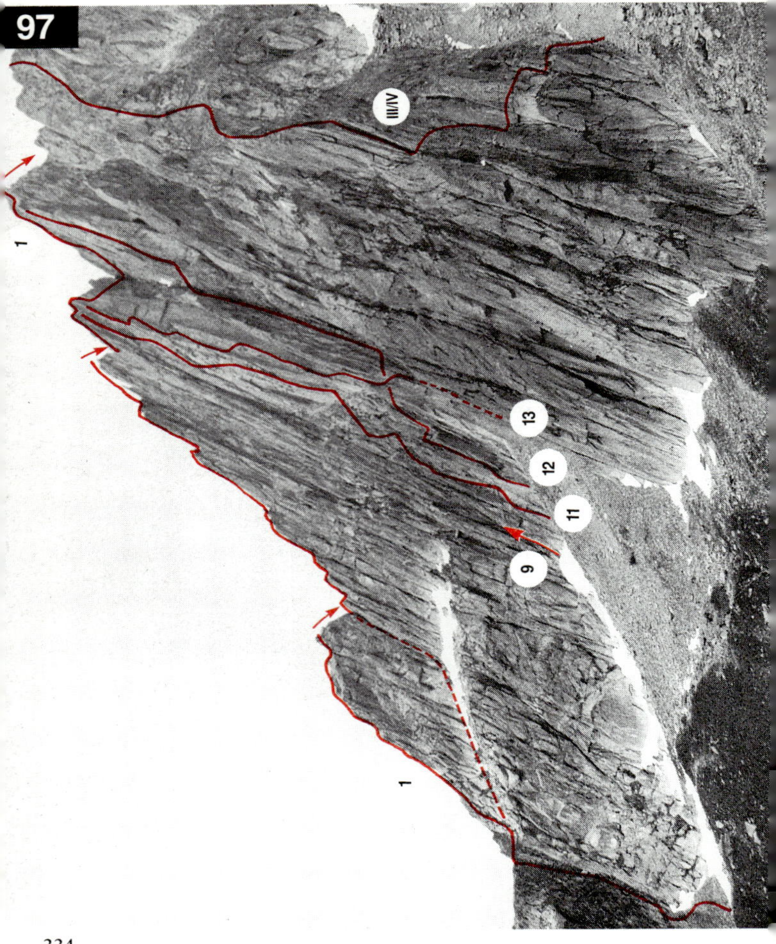

2
2
2
2
2

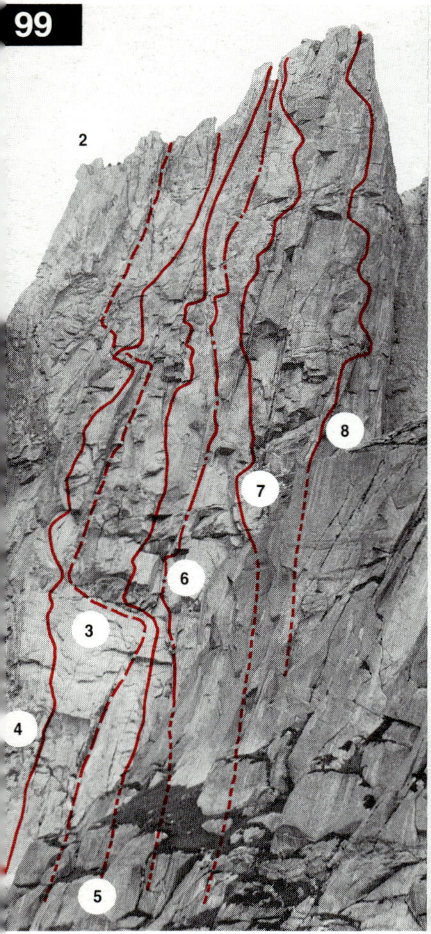
99
2
8
7
6
3
4
5

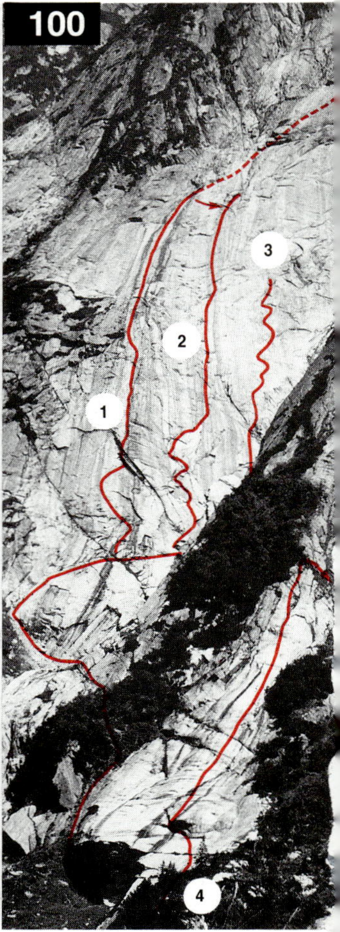
100
3
2
1
4

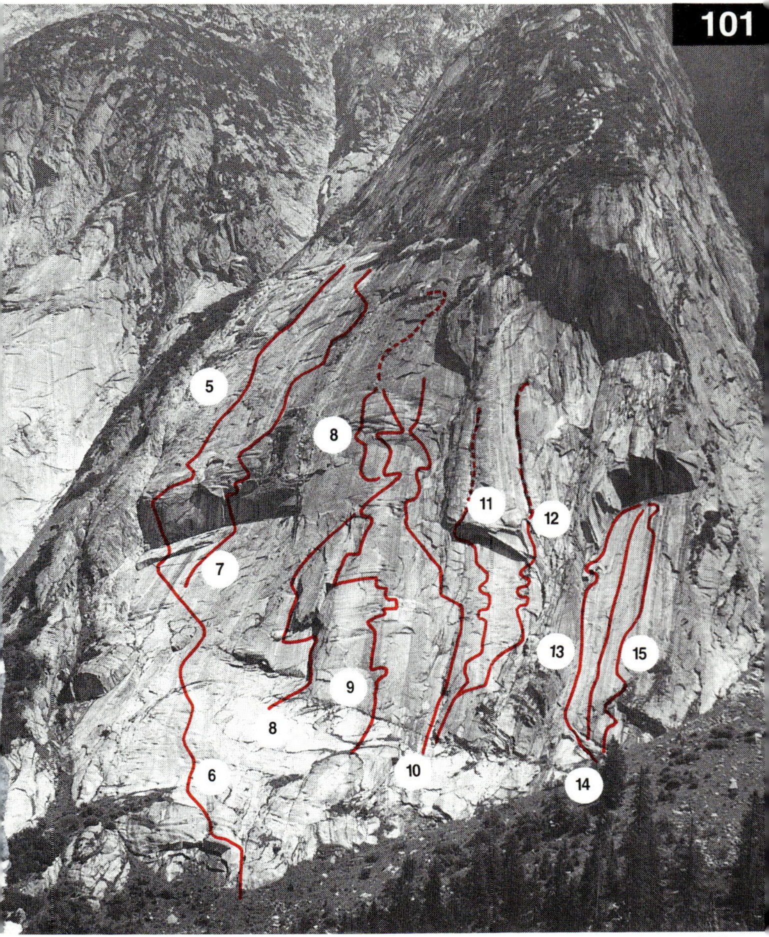
5
8
7
11
12
13
15
9
8
6
10
14

102

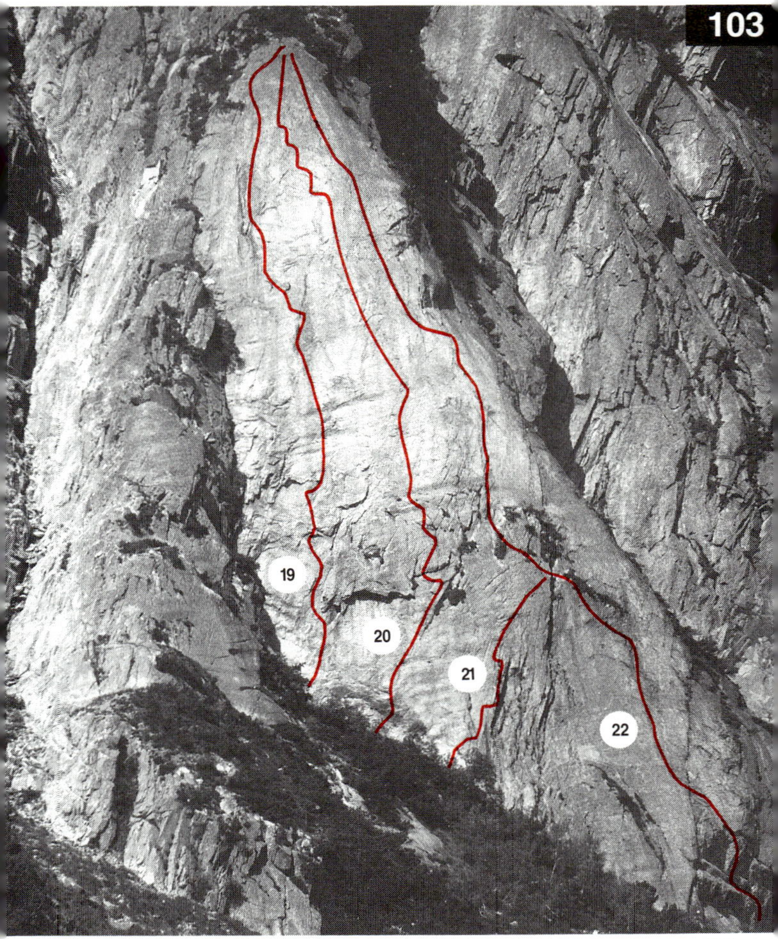
103
19
20
21
22

104

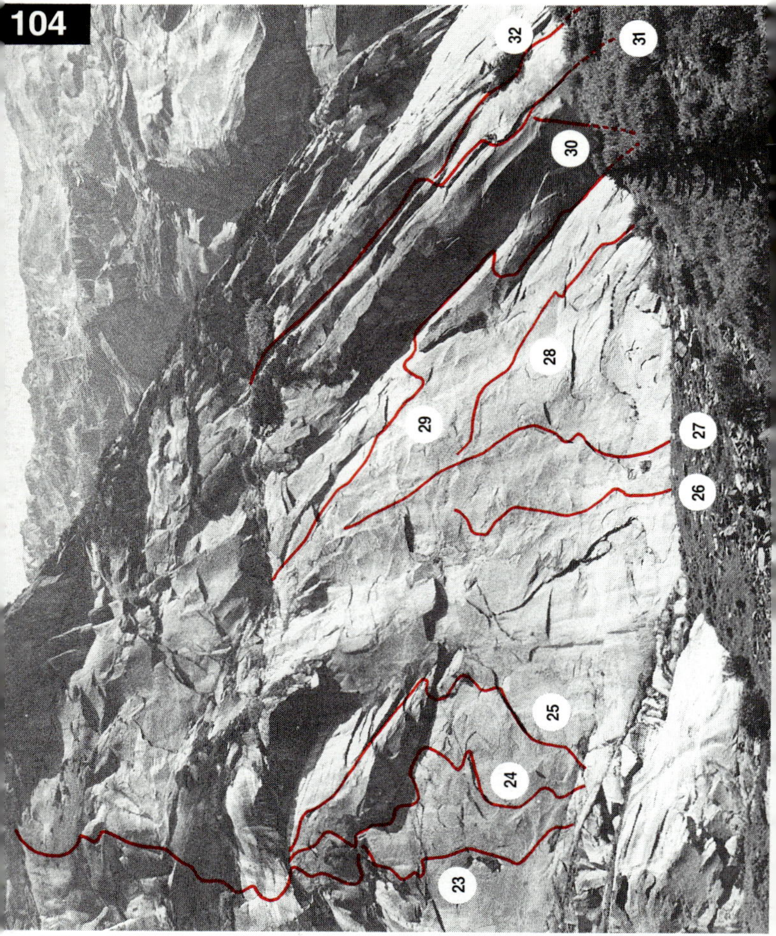

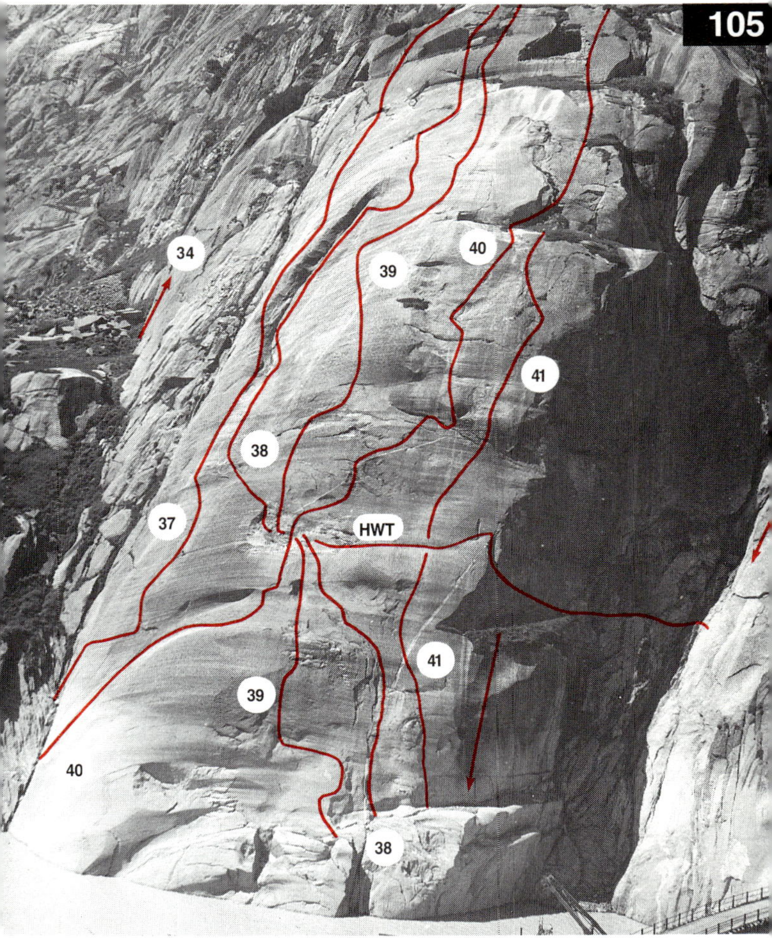
34
40
39
41
38
37
HWT
41
39
40
38

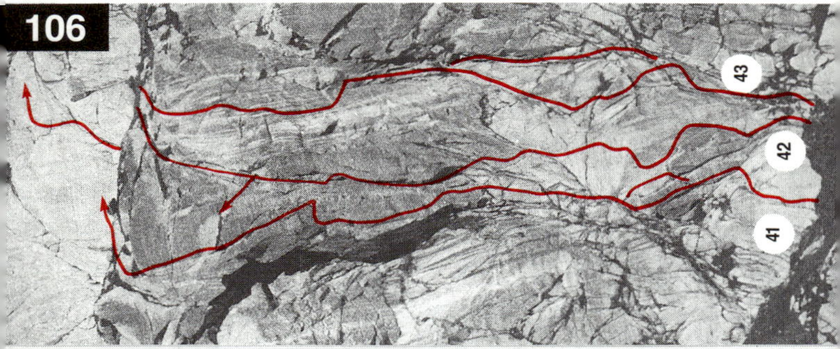
106
43
42
41

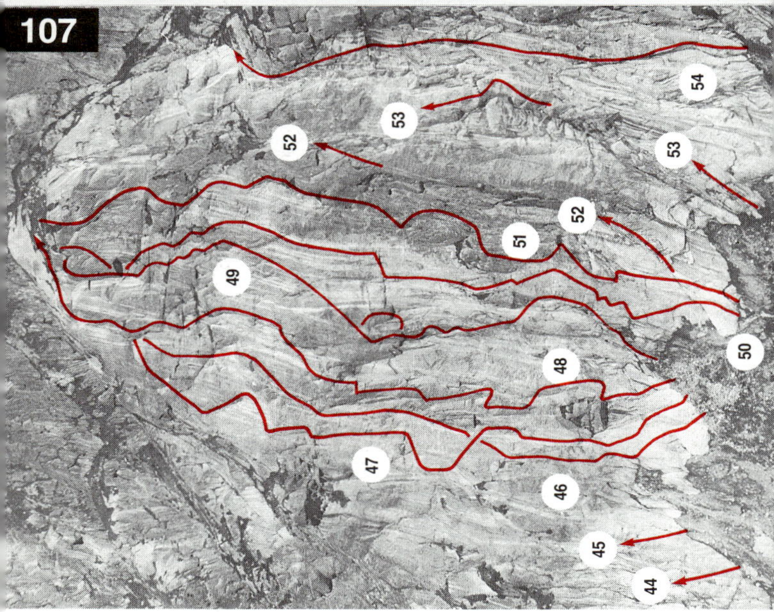
107
54
53
52
53
52
51
49
50
48
47
46
45
44

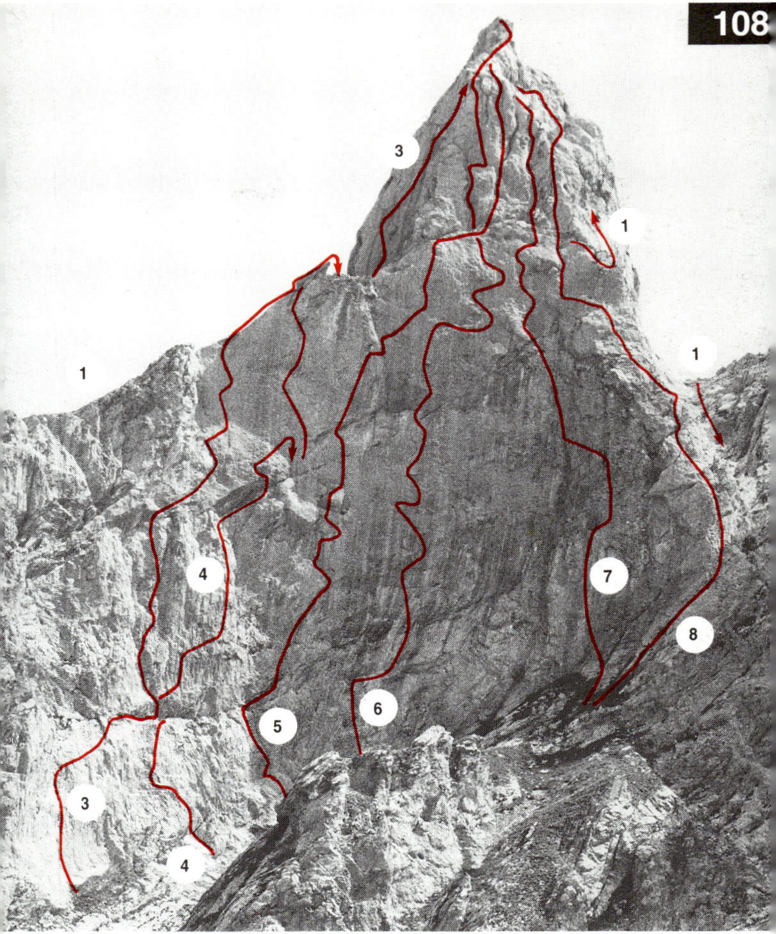
3
1
1
1
4
7
8
6
5
3
4

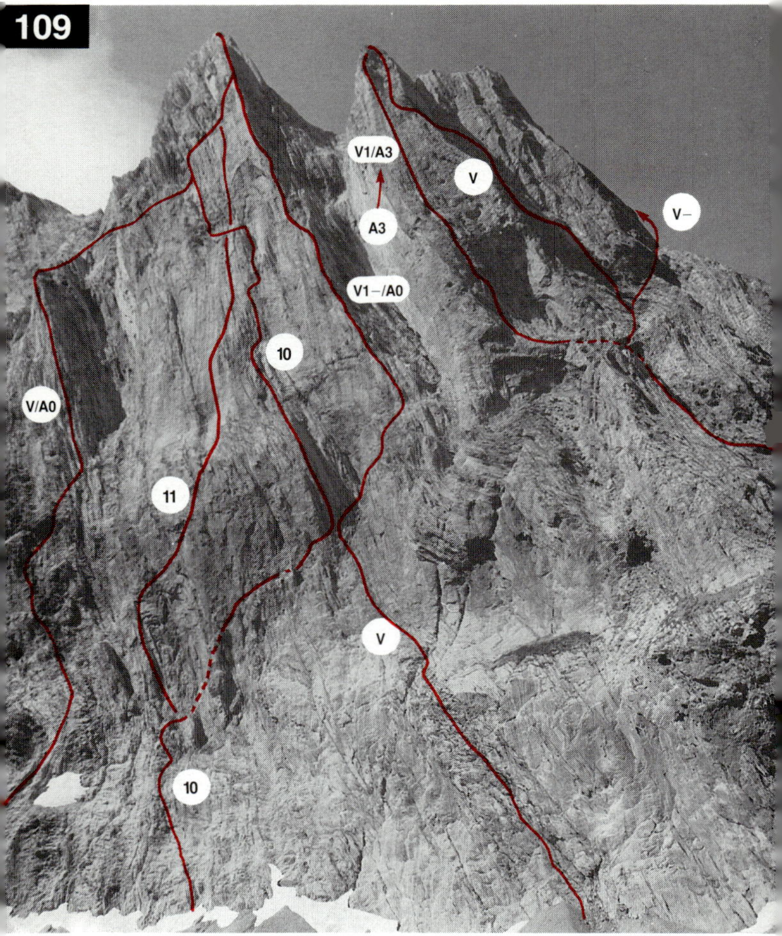
109
V1/A3
V
A3
V–
V1–/A0
10
V/A0
11
V
10

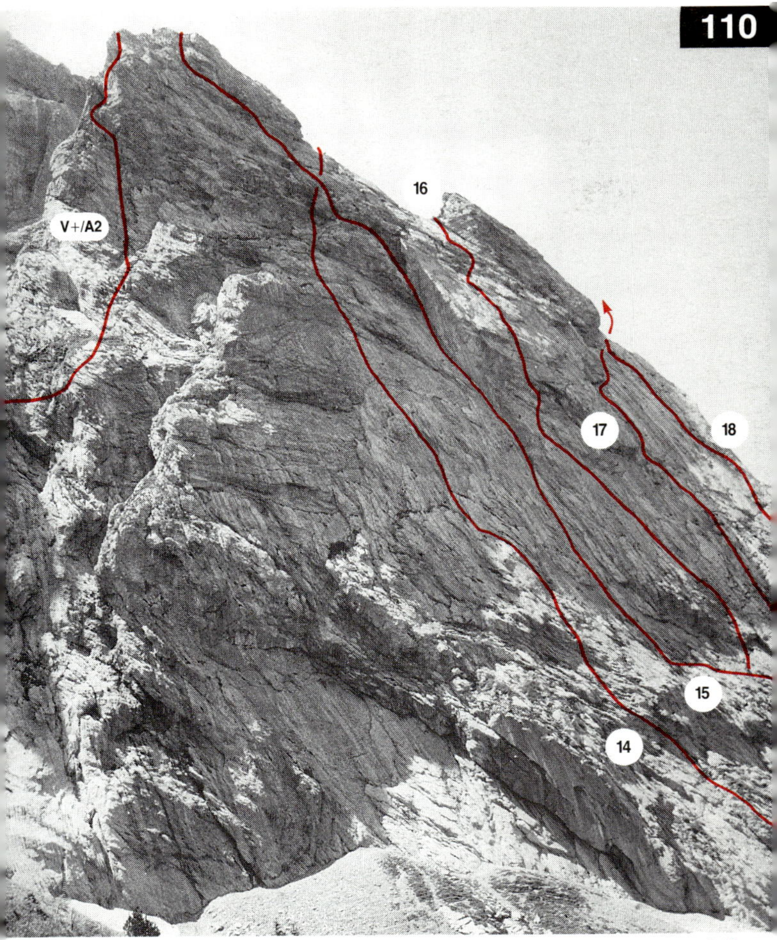
16
V+/A2
17
18
15
14

Rothorn S Flank

111

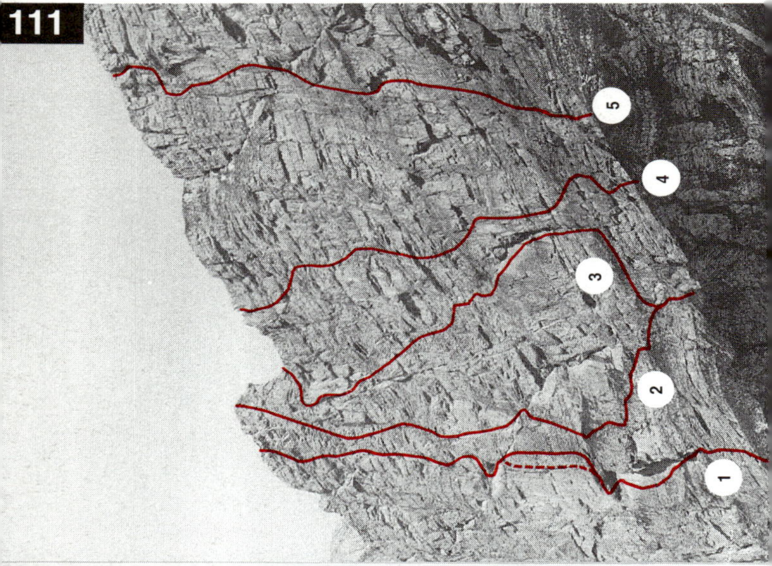

112

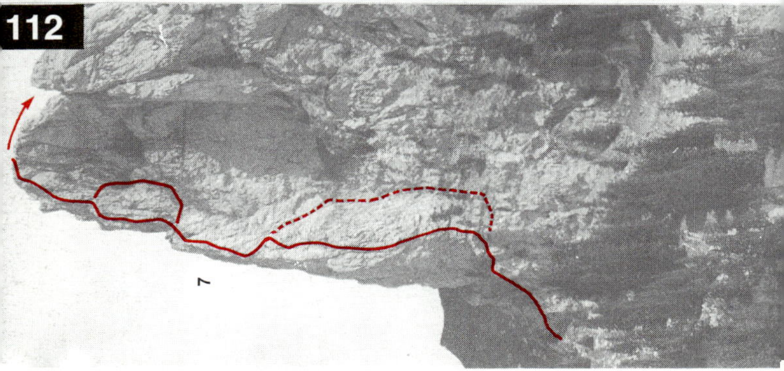

Trümelhorn

NOTE
6

114

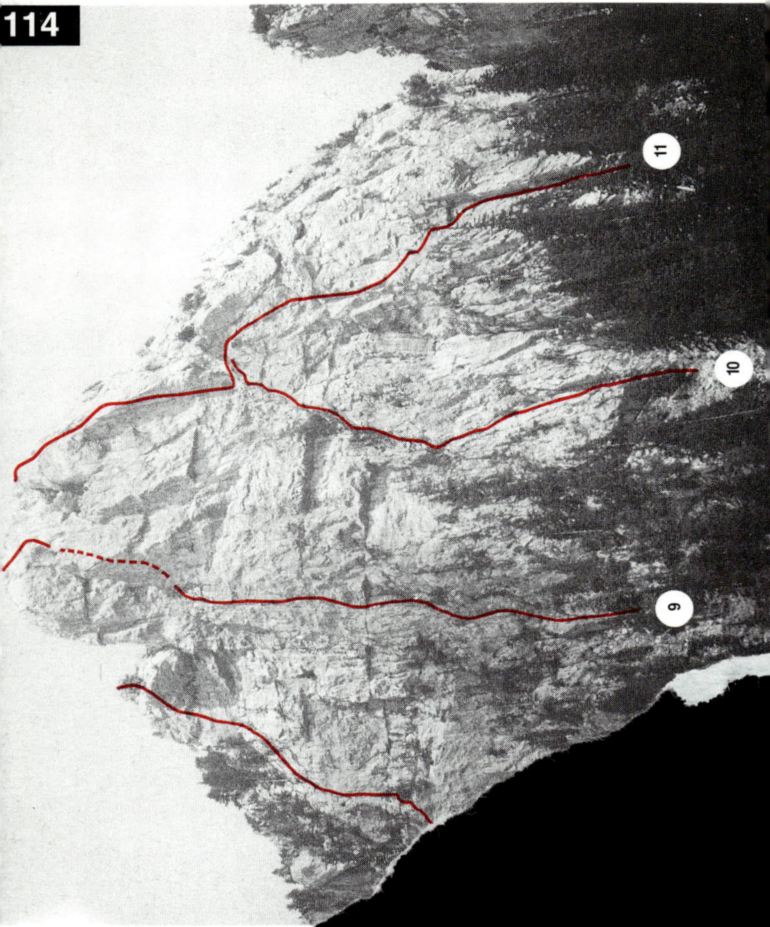

13
14
16
17
13
15
18
19

116

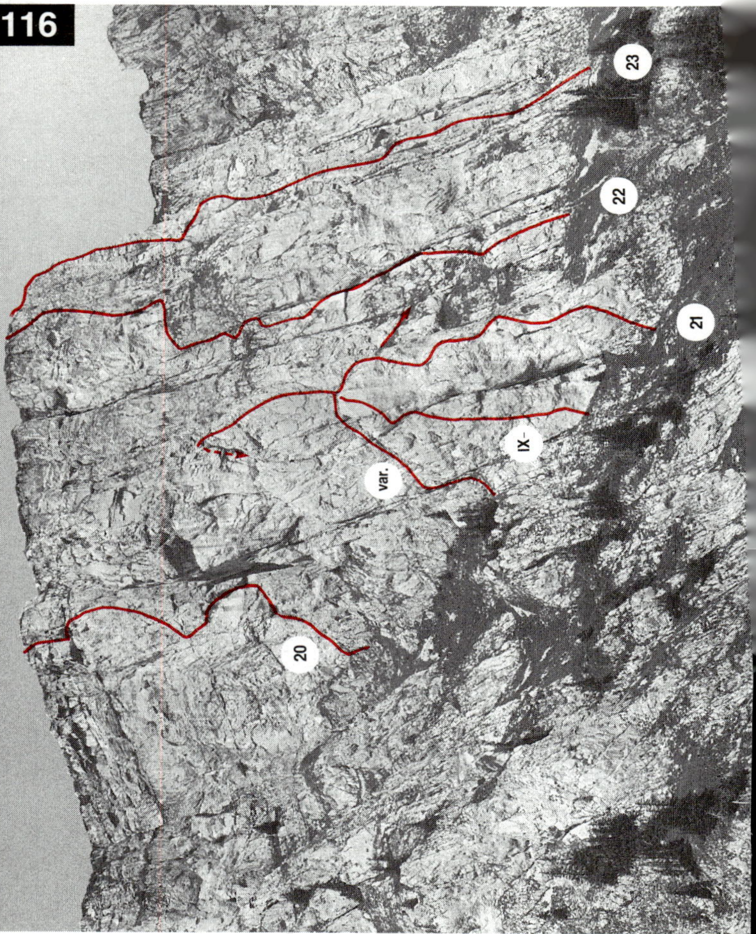

29
28
27
26
25
24

118

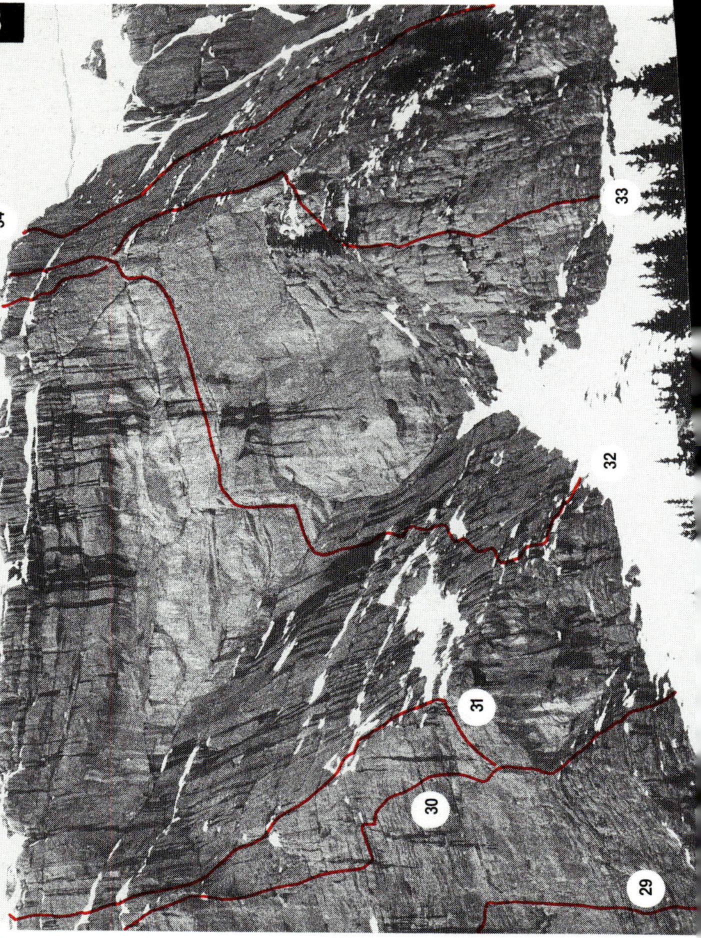

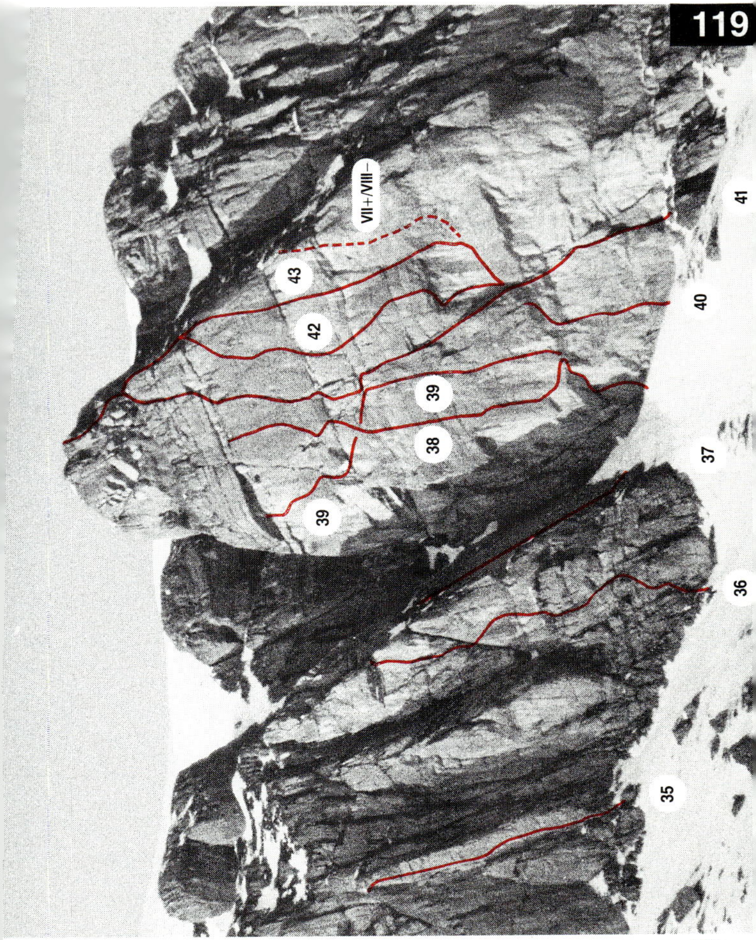
VII+/VIII–
43
42
39
38
39
41
40
37
36
35

120

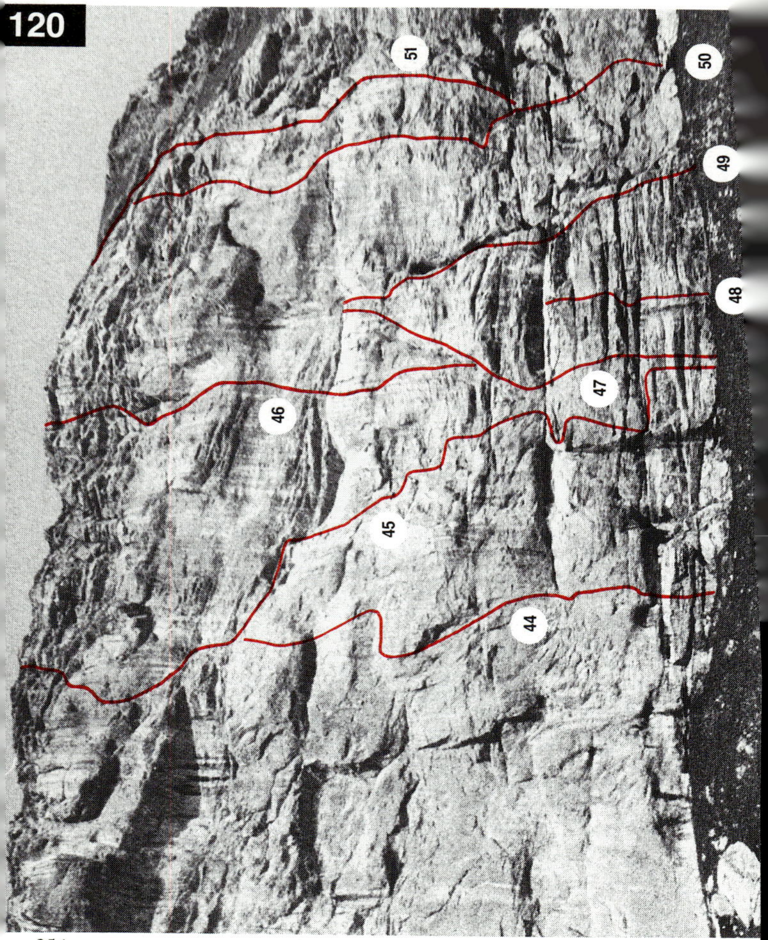

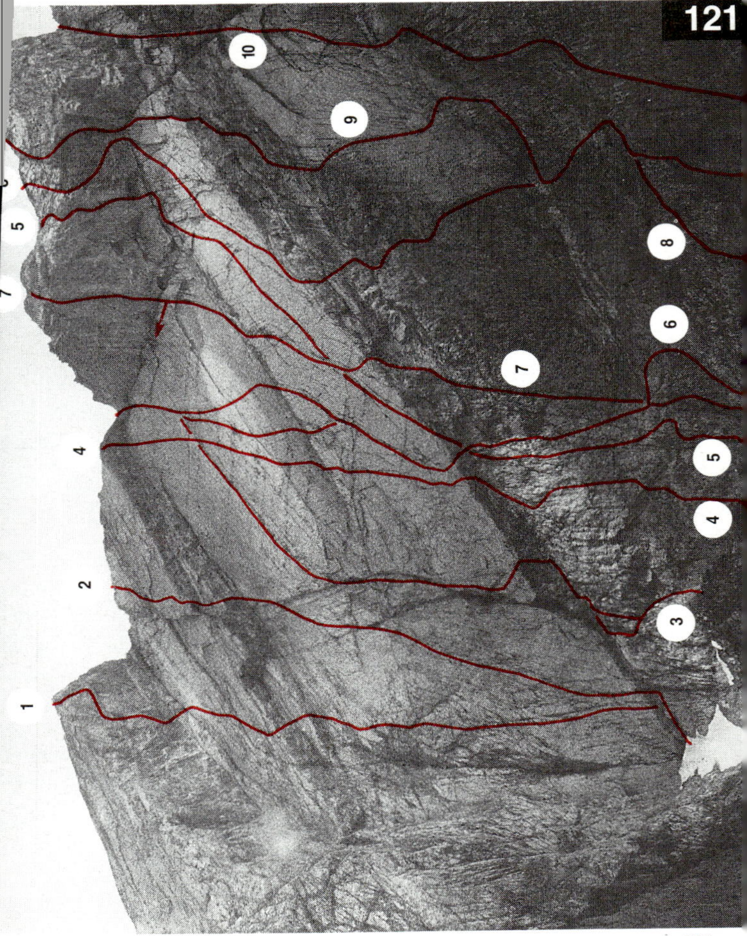

Lobhorner S Side

122

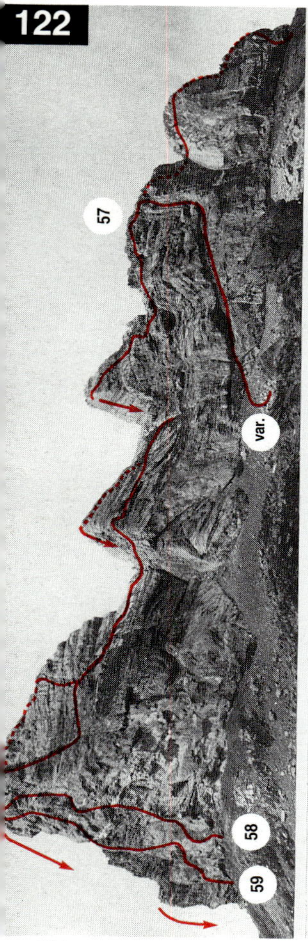

Tour d'Ai – WSW Face

123

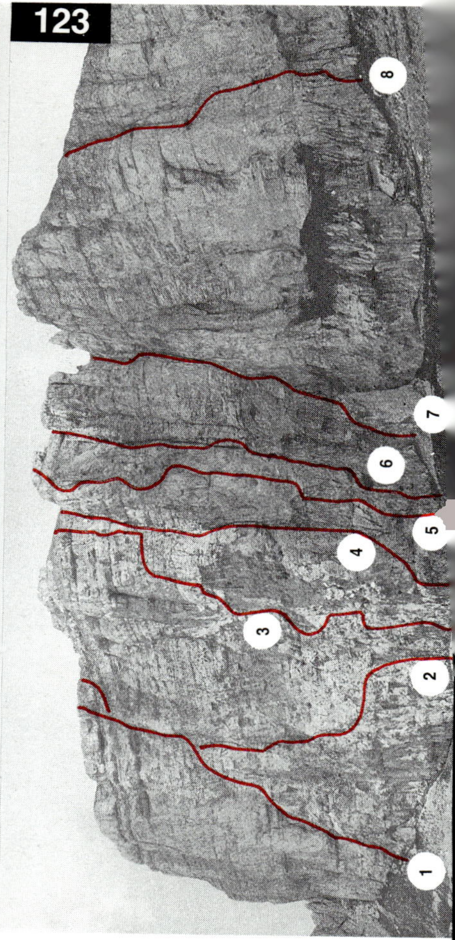

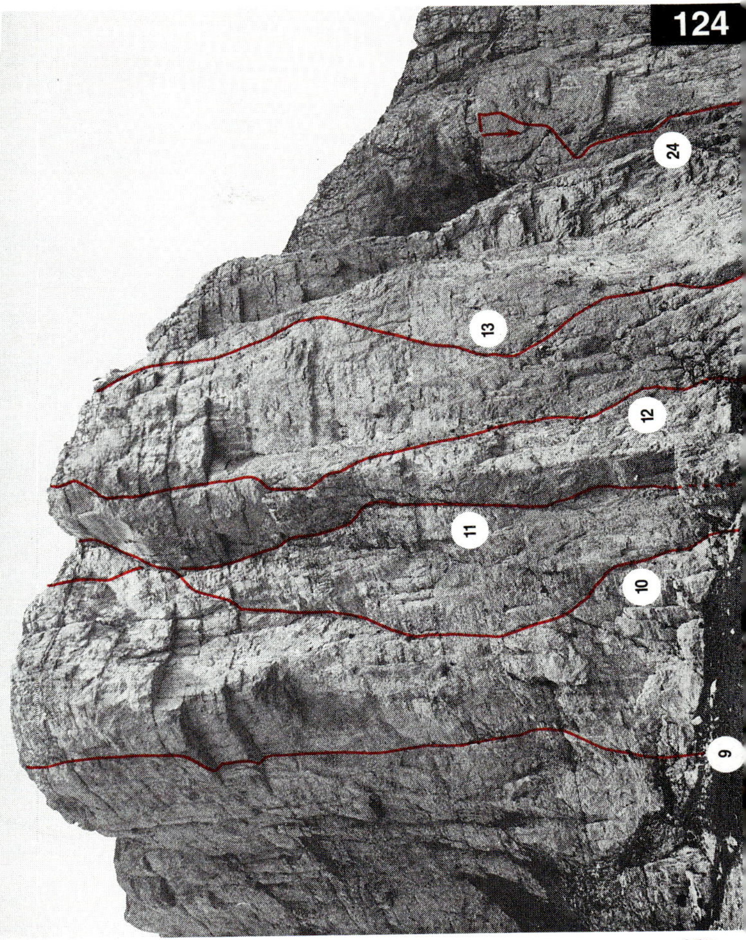
124
24
13
12
11
10
9

125

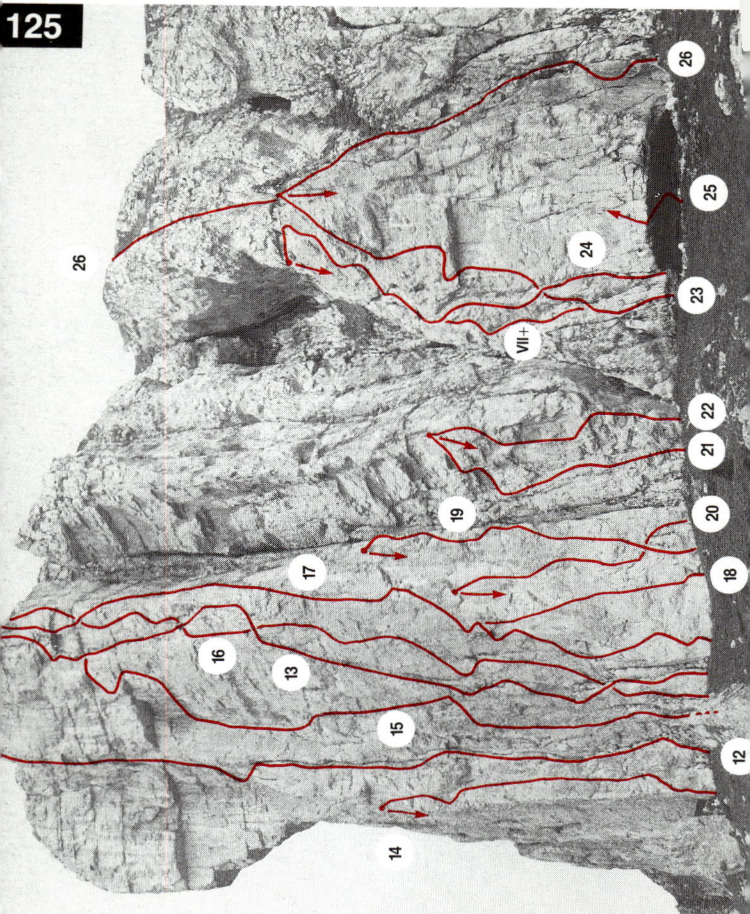

126

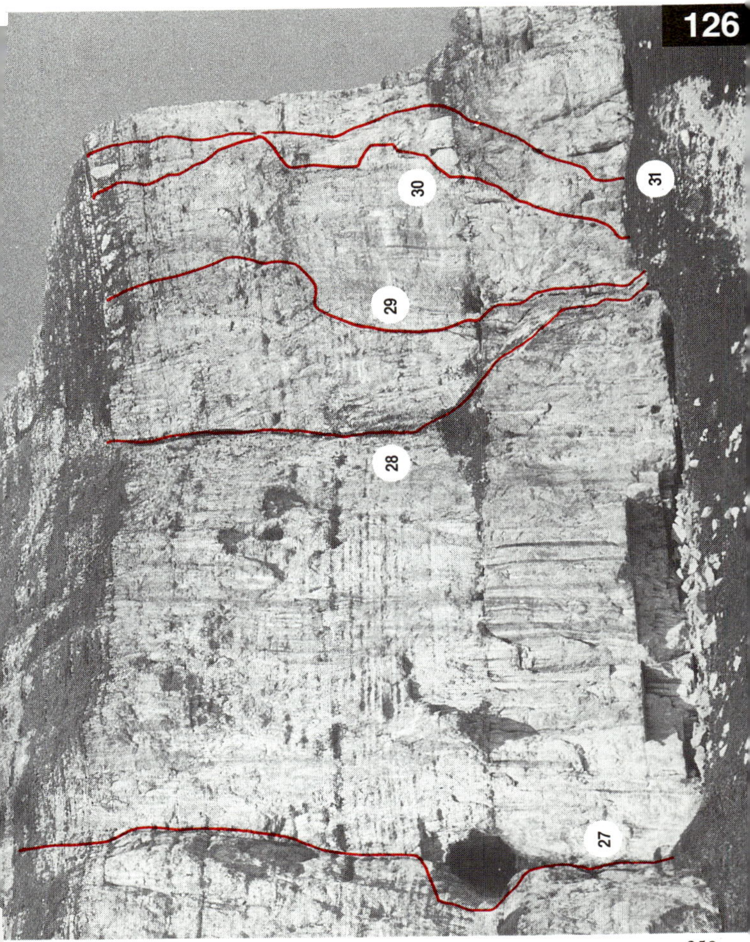

127

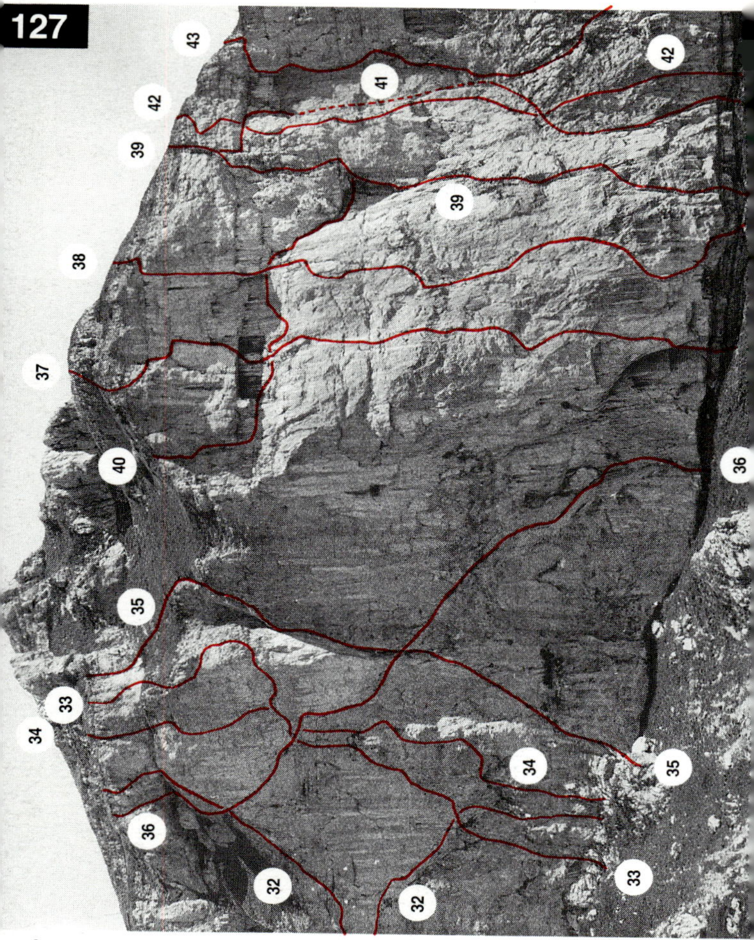

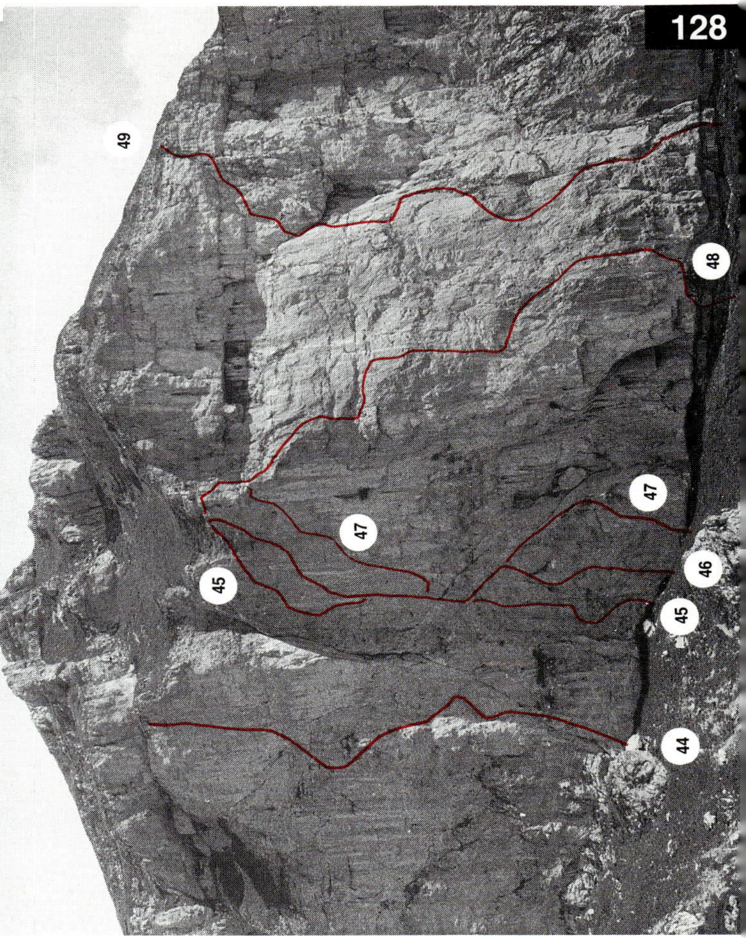
49
48
47
47
46
45
45
44

Ärmighorn SW Summit

129

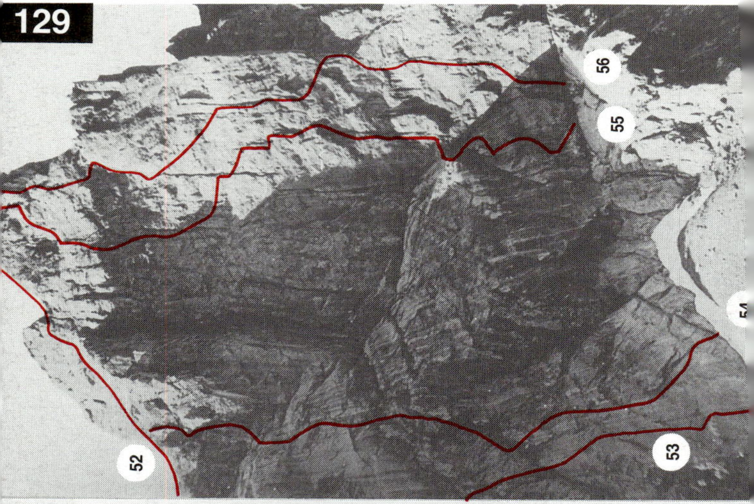

130

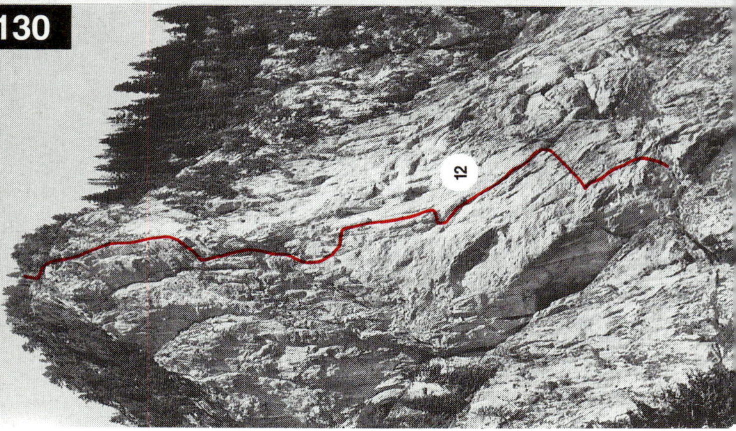

 Buufal – Meniggrund Pillar

Sanetsch – Les Montons
Far L Hand Section

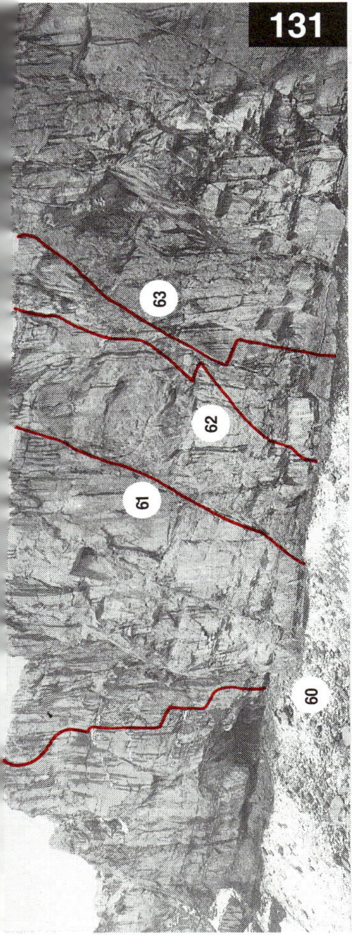

Sanetsch – Les Montons
L. Hand Section

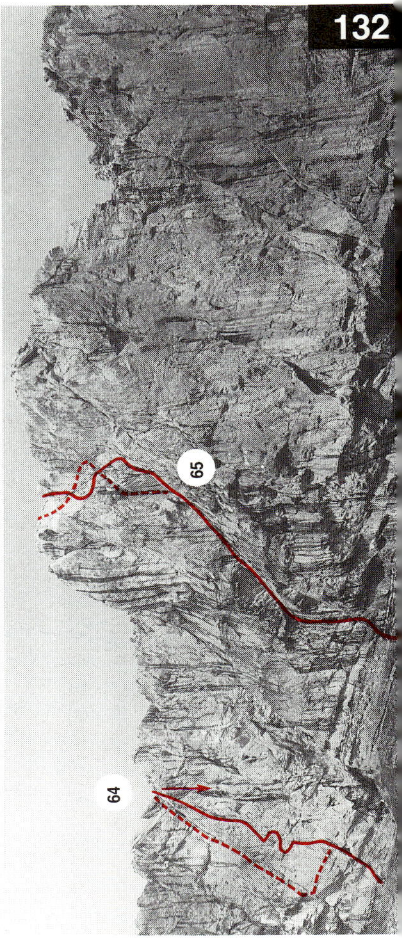

133

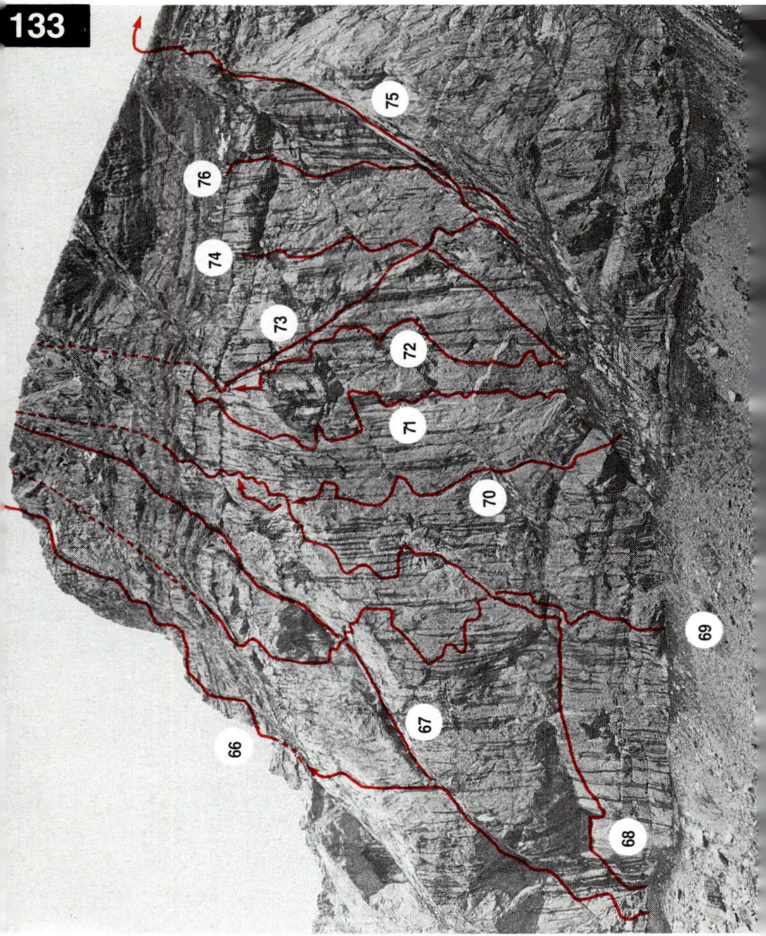

Sanetsch – Orphée L Side

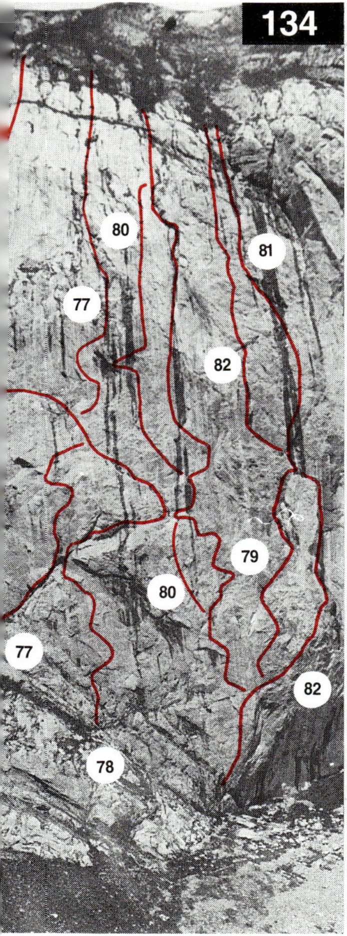

Sanetsch – Orphée R Side

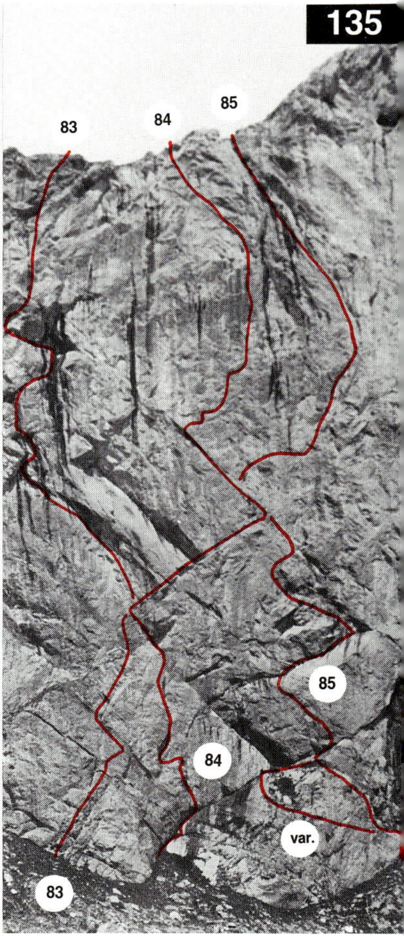

MEMBERSHIP

The Alpine Club – which includes the Alpine Climbing Group – has among its members the best of today's active mountaineers. This unique group of men and women is responsible for much of mountaineering's development and they are still exploring the untrodden corners of the greater ranges. The Alpine Club Library is one of the largest collections of mountaineering literature in the world. It is a working library, open regularly for reference and research. If you are climbing regularly in the Alps or the greater ranges, why not join? Full Membership is open to competent mountaineers over the age of 21 and Aspirant Membership is available from age 18 or for those who do not yet qualify for full membership. Benefits of membership include:

- free Alpine Journal and quarterly newsletters
- free access to the Alpine Club Library
- monthly lectures from prominent mountaineers
- climbing meets in the UK, the Alps and the Greater Ranges
- reduced rates in many alpine huts
- discount on climbing equipment, journals and AC publications
- Full details can be obtained from the Alpine Club, 55/56 Charlotte Road, London EC2A 3QT. Telephone 071-613 0755